Communications in Canadian Society

second revised edition

Edited by Benjamin D. Singer

Department of Sociology
University of Western Ontario

Copp Clark Publishing
A division of Copp Clark Limited
Vancouver Calgary Toronto Montreal

Cover design by Hodges & Freeman Ltd.

ISBN 0 7730 3131 6

Copp Clark Publishing
517 Wellington Street West
Toronto, Ontario
M5V 1G1

Printed and bound in Canada

For Eleanore, Lisa and Heidi

Contents

Preface

The present volume was generated by a pressing need in communications courses in Canada for materials with a social science perspective that deal with the Canadian scene. It is hoped that the book will serve as a primary source or for collateral reading in social science and arts courses in communication and journalism, as well as in other areas where there is a wish to provide materials dealing with social issues in Canadian communication.

Because of the dearth of published material dealing with these issues, approximately two-thirds of the articles are new and have been commissioned for this book. The authors represent a wide spectrum of disciplines, professions and perspectives, including sociology, political science, economics, journalism and futuristics.

Since this is the first book to deal with this area and these concerns in Canada, there are bound to be omissions which succeeding efforts will no doubt rectify, and in this sense it is hoped a stimulus has been provided to more work within the field. Because of the limitations of space, we have restricted ourselves to those issues considered most important at this time: the broad sociological forces conditioning communications institutions; the problem of control and how it is asserted; the issue of Canadian identity as it is affected by mass communication; and a number of critical areas subsumed under the broad rubric of social problems. In this last section, a new field of study has been highlighted that examines the issue of social coping and communication channels, an issue that will receive more and more attention in North America during the next decade.

I wish to express here my indebtedness to co-workers who have provided me with invaluable aid in the production of this volume. John Hannigan, Andrew Cameron, Ted Seacrest and Lyndsay Green have been perceptive critics, as well. Mrs. Nina Allinson's secretarial skills often saved the day. Paul Audley, formerly with Copp Clark, helped provide encouragement to me to undertake the preparation of this volume and Mrs. Ruth Russell's editorial competence clarified many a difficult passage.

London, Ontario
December 1971

Benjamin D. Singer

Preface to second, revised edition

The first edition of *Communications in Canadian Society,* having been exhausted within three years, now gives way to the second, revised, and expanded edition. The book has been used in undergraduate, professional, and graduate courses in sociology, communication, journalism, political science, and other disciplines in Canada and abroad.

The revised edition takes cognizance of suggestions and helpful criticisms of university teachers, students, and book reviewers; as editor I have retained the most useful material and deleted that which no longer fits into course requirements. The proportion of articles which are original has also increased, from approximately two-thirds to three-quarters.

Some of the new material reports on the original and imaginative research that has been generated in Ottawa during the past three years, particularly during the golden years of the social research arm of Communications Canada. Also added in response to suggestions is a bibliography of Canadian or Canadian-related material, along with a wide range of material on communication training and research activities in Canada. The first edition suffered from the lack of an index; that deficiency has now been corrected.

It is my hope that the added chapters — which address themselves to some of the main themes of recent research, such as crisis communication, citizen communication, and television in the classroom, as well as to areas normally associated with communication but not included in the first edition, such as public opinion and propaganda — will help to make this book a more comprehensive compendium of Canadian communications. It is also hoped that it will contribute in a generic sense to communications scholarship. I would like to acknowledge my debt to the well-organized planning efforts of the managing editor Charles Kahn and the perceptive editing talents of Pamela Erlichman.

London, Ontario
September 1975

Benjamin D. Singer

Social Forces and Communications Media

Traditionally, much analysis of the mass media has been focused upon the way in which media content reflects the events transpiring within a social system or, alternatively, upon the kinds of effects that media content produces. Media institutions, however, respond to a number of imperatives rooted in demographic forces, the economy, technological developments and in the policies adopted and put into effect by governments. Communication channels also have social effects apart from those generated by their content—a point McLuhan has made repeatedly. And thus, before concerning ourselves with the issue of media content *and its effects, we shall examine the social forces underlying and the social consequences resulting from the structure of media institutions.*

The first mass media were printed. Their relationships to population movements, commerce and governmental activities are traced and analyzed by Kesterton. A newspaper's circulation is a function not merely of content but of other forces in the social system; thus, the number of newspapers and the way in which they are represented in Canadian communities is not merely an effect of the kind of journalism provided but is a sociological consequence as well. Amalgamation and monopoly (treated further in Part Two, Control of Communications Media*) are further results of this chain of forces.*

Perhaps the most under-researched area of communication is that of the social forces linked to the pattern and growth of telephone usage. Latham indicates in "The Telephone and Social Change" the way in which one aspect of communications technology—the telephone—affects social patterns and events. The telephone encourages greater geographical dispersion of friendship networks, affects the economics of real estate, and makes possible the development of socially deviant enterprises, to mention just a few of the social consequences.

Stewart, in "The Canadian Social System and the Canadian Broadcasting Audience," alerts us to the effects of "the physical system, the source of the message, the message and the receiver" and within this model, specifies the problems of geography and population distribution, language groups, the economics of broadcasting, and the social classes of the audience, in order to more fully appreciate the effects of such phenomena on content and policy in broadcasting. Underlying his analysis is the question, who is speaking to whom? *He suggests that in the future, English Canadians may be "speaking" more with Americans than among themselves, and French Canadians may be "speaking" more among themselves than with anyone else.*

"Mass Communications in a Canadian City," by Cameron and Hannigan, is the first analysis in depth of the communications institutions in a Canadian city. In it they analyze the historical basis for present media structures, the problem of competition and monopoly, and the issue of U.S. influence near the border. They examine newspapers, magazines and broadcasting media; both policies and actual behavior are subjected to critical scrutiny.

Gotlieb and Gwyn, in "Social Planning of Communications," survey some of the social effects of the new communications technology—a precondition to social planning of communications systems. They alert us to three socially relevant problems that the burgeoning technology may obscure. First, technology is a socially created force that generates the potential for more people to communicate, but this does not mean that all will benefit since some people lack access to important parts of the communications system. Second, individual privacy may be in danger due to the awesome power of communications technology to record and make available for rapid retrieval vast amounts of information. Third, mere access to the information that communications systems can provide is not enough, for individuals must be equipped to use the systems, and thus training is an absolute necessity.

If Stewart asks who is speaking to whom in the larger societal communication system, Lee transforms the question into a discussion of what happens *when certain individuals speak to others in a circumscribed setting. In "Mentors and Monitors: Mass Media in the Canadian Classroom," he describes the complementary roles of professors and students when mass communication replaces the traditional interpersonal interaction of the classroom. His case history of a media defeat — of the surprising failure of television during a time when we came to believe it could accomplish anything — considers the social determinants, social relationships, technology, social change, alienation and needs of youth, and the psychology of perception. In arriving at an explanation, Professor Lee does not eschew a dash of McLuhanism to aid in understanding* why *what is a phenomenal success in the larger society may not work in all settings or systems.*

The Growth of the Newspaper in Canada

WILFRED H. KESTERTON

The basic preconditions of print journalism are human and physical. There must be enough people, a conducive social climate and the material ingredients which go into the making of a printed news organ: printing press, type, ink and paper. During the early years of British North American history—the first possible time for development of the English-language newspaper, the subject of this discussion—social conditions were not propitious for journalism. Long after New England had received its first newspaper, the colonies which were to become Canada were enduring conditions of war and near-war.

First Press Period: 1752-1807

The first serious attempt at colonization came in 1749 when the Honorable Edward Cornwallis brought 2,576 emigrants to the Nova Scotia coast. Many of the newcomers were so discouraged by hardships that they soon left for New York and Boston. The dreaded typhus killed many more. But immigrants from New England, lured by the government aid which the original settlers seemed only too ready to relinquish to their more enterprising replacements, were quick to replace those who moved away or died. As a result, conditions became suitable for the establishment of an English-language journal. When John Bushell founded the *Halifax Gazette* on March 23, 1752 he became the business colleague of the joiner, the linen draper, the distiller, the blacksmith, the attorney, the cabinet maker, the tallow candler and the soap maker.

Pioneer journalism was a tenacious growth, small but hardy. It was the revenue earned as King's Printer which nurtured the printer-editor's modest enterprise during its first years. The money received was not much, but when a "shirt-tail full of type" and a wooden, flat-bed handpress were sufficient to start a newspaper, it was enough. The pioneer printer-editor served as King's Printer, sometimes without carrying the title of his office. His was not always an exclusive contract, and often his newspaper contemporaries shared the governmental largesse. Often the King's Printer for a province was also its postmaster, making the financial position of his news organ more secure.

With its 72 subscribers, the fortnightly *Halifax Gazette* typified pioneer newspapers. Its main content was government matter, items from foreign papers and local advertisements. There was little local news in it. The editor usually did all the tasks connected with the news-sheet, either unaided or with the help of one apprentice, but he met the needs of his community in a day when populations were small and illiteracy high. Thus the *Royal American Gazette* of Charlottetown at first served about fifty subscribers, and the *Quebec Gazette* 143. Even in 1800, towards the end of the first pioneering press period, the three Halifax newspapers had a combined circulation of only two thousand.

After the Peace of Paris in 1763, English-speaking immigrants, notably those from the colonies to the south, brought journalism to Lower Canada. No religious or political authoritarianism discouraged their press ventures. Moreover, the appearance of the newspaper was hastened by the establishment of a government which needed a gazette to give currency to its records, enactments and pronouncements. The capital of the province of Quebec was a middle-class, stable community which provided a suitable climate and market for the *Quebec Gazette*, established by William Brown and Thomas Gilmore in 1764.

The County of Sunbury, later New Brunswick, was the next colony to acquire a newspaper. When the American Revolution caused Loyalists to stream northward, many came to a large, uninhabited area across the Bay of Fundy from peninsular Nova Scotia. On an apparently unpromising part of the St. John river they started the only important city owing its origin to United Empire Loyalists. It was first called Carleton, later Parrtown, and finally Saint John. A total of 3,000 refugees from New York came there on May 10, 1783; 2,000 more arrived in late June, and 3,000 in September.

However, after this initial unstable boom the population dropped to 2,000. With less fluctuating numbers, the centre began a sound development. The citizens were politically alert and proud of their country's progress; from Saint John's very beginning the *Royal Gazette and Nova Scotia Intelligencer*, issued first on December 18, 1783 by John Ryan and William Lewis, reflected the life of the energetic town.

Eight months later the County of Sunbury became New Brunswick when it was separated from the rest of Nova Scotia. This separation, made because England preferred small colonies and because the settlers disliked being so far from the capital at Halifax, meant more government patronage for New Brunswick journalists. Christopher Sower III became the first King's Printer for New Brunswick and began the *Royal Gazette and New Brunswick Advertiser.*

Prince Edward Island was called Saint Jean Island in 1713 when the Treaty of Utrecht left it in the possession of France. It came under British rule in 1763 and was granted to about a dozen proprietors at a *quit-rent*, a term dating from the feudal system whereby rent was paid in money rather than services rendered. After a series of corrupt land dealings, its economy was strangled and its cultural development stifled. Under such unfavorable conditions, the newspaper finally appeared only with the artificial stimulus of government commissions. Arriving in the colony of Prince Edward Island in 1787, Lt.-Gov. Edmund Fanning found that the settlement had no printed laws, no printed assembly records, and no newspaper to give notice of legal business. He saw the immediate need for a printer, and brought in James Robertson, who, before the year was out, began to print the laws and to edit the *Royal American Gazette and Weekly Intelligencer.*

Upper Canada was an untouched wilderness when the *Halifax Gazette* reached its thirtieth birthday. First appreciable development of the western area began when the United Empire Loyalists started to arrive in large numbers in 1783-4. At first the Loyalists were so busy overcoming hardships they had little time to think about newspapers; however, conditions improved by 1789, and transportation and communications developed quickly. The change brought the first urgent need for a newspaper, and the new lieutenant-governor, John Graves Simcoe, brought Louis Roy from Quebec City as his printer. It was in the new capital of Newark, today's Niagara-on-the-Lake, that Roy began to publish the *Upper Canada Gazette or American Oracle*, first issued April 18, 1793.

Although newspapers appeared in Upper Canada several years later than in three of today's Maritime Provinces, the *Upper Canada Gazette* predated any journalism in Newfoundland. There were many reasons why Newfoundland was slow to receive and develop its journalism transplant. For more than two centuries it was little more than a fishing station in the North Atlantic. Each year fishermen would come in the spring, set up temporary quarters on the coast, gather as large a catch as possible, then return to Europe for the winter. Geography and climate discouraged settlement, and the rockiness of the soil hampered agriculture.

In addition to these factors, the impermanence of the Newfoundland government discouraged such social institutions as newspapers. However, between 1764 and 1774 residents began to outnumber visitors to the island, and population rose to 12,000, helping to generate the preconditions necessary for a newspaper. Thereafter the population reached 17,000 in 1792, 20,000 in 1804, and 52,000 in 1822. Greatest concentration of people was in St. John's, and it was here that the first stirrings of civic growth took place. About 1800 the city's inhabitants established schools, a sanitation system, a fire-brigade, a post office, and a newspaper. St. John's was the most important settlement, the other coastline communities being mere outports of the government seat. The governor lived there, and the city was the logical site for a government printing business. Here the New Brunswick journalist, John Ryan, first published the *Royal Gazette and Newfoundland Advertiser* on August 27, 1807.

Second Press Period: 1807-1858

After the first transplant, British North American newspapers proliferated. As communities multiplied, so did the newspapers. The growth of population and wealth, along with healthy new industries, provided the economic basis for a non-government press financed by subscriptions and advertising.

The War of 1812 over,[1] a wave of immigration in the 1820s raised the population of Upper Canada from 213,000 to 430,000. In the decade of the forties, when the Canadas made a combined gain of 677,000, Canada West more than doubled its population. More significant than numerical increase as a factor in press growth, however, was the rise of towns. This development was aided by the specialization of primitive manufacturing. It was a modest change, merely involving a transfer of work from the home to the local shop, but it encouraged pioneer artisans to come together.

An April 1853 newspaper listing[2] records forty-four cities, towns and villages being served by newspapers. A November 1857 list[3] gives the names of seventy-six such centers. Because five communities on the first list had disappeared from the second, this meant that thirty-seven new regions gained a newspaper press during a four-and-a-half-year period. The rise in numbers of journals throughout the whole of this press period was rapid: in 1813 there had only been one newspaper in Upper Canada and five in Lower Canada.[4] In 1824 there were nineteen newspapers in the Canadas, twelve in the lower province. By 1827 the two-province total had dropped to seventeen, but in 1829 the number had risen to twenty-seven, in 1831 to thirty-seven, and in 1836 to fifty. In the latter year, thirty of the journals were in Upper and twenty in Lower Canada.[5] By 1853 there were 114 news organs in Canada West alone.[6] By November 1857 the figure for Canada West was 159,[7] and in the same year the provinces of Canada East and Canada West boasted a total of 213 journals.[8]

In Newfoundland there were 27 newspaper registrations between 1807 and 1860.[9] In 1855 there were twenty-two newspapers published in New Brunswick, twenty-one in Nova Scotia, and five in Prince Edward Island. It has been estimated that in 1857 a total of 291 papers were published in the provinces then constituting British North America.[10]

Third Press Period: 1858-1900

In 1858 the development of journalism entered a phase similar to the first press period. Similar social, political and economic factors were at work in both migrations. In the John Bushell tradition, the later pioneer editor followed the settler to the new Pacific settlements, the migrating farmer to the prairies, the prospector to the river valleys of interior British Columbia. Everywhere tiny villages and hamlets sprang up. And almost immediately newspapers appeared to serve these fledgling communities.

The discovery of gold attracted an influx of white immigrants and thus created conditions favorable to press development. In 1856 substantial gold discoveries were made on the Fraser and Thompson, and by 1858 migration was at the flood. In May of that year, 1,262 people set out from San Francisco for the Fraser; 7,149 departed in June, and 6,278 in July. Others came from Oregon, Washington, Minnesota, Utah, other western states, Hawaii, and Central and South America to an estimated total of 25,000. This number included merchants, traders and adventurers. The people were funnelled through Esquimalt, Victoria and Puget Sound, and many remained in Victoria. Victoria became the stopping place for ships and a supply point for prospectors, and the city boomed: population increased, stores, shops and houses sprang up and business flourished. On June 25, 1858 the *Victoria Gazette and Anglo American* became its first newspaper.

On the mainland, wherever settlement became permanent, the newspapers' hold became secure. Elsewhere, where towns mushroomed, flourished and died, the careers of both newspapers and towns were meteoric. Short-lived gold rushes meant short-lived mining centres and short-lived journals. As gold-seekers pushed upstream, the center of population moved deeper into the interior and the press followed.

The newspaper did not come to the Northwest Territories until two decades later. When Manitoba became a province and the rest of Rupert's Land was transferred to Dominion jurisdiction in 1870, the fur trader was unchallenged king in the non-provincial territories. Settlements were weak, isolated communities in the shadow of the fur-trading posts. However, in what was to become Saskatchewan, homesteaders and farmers, as well as shopkeepers and artisans, were beginning to flock to little towns where newspapers appeared. The first of these was the *Saskatchewan Herald*, established in Battleford in 1878. As territorial capital and North-West Mounted Police station, the center needed and gave highly prized governmental revenue to the press.

In what is today Alberta, railway and settlement also brought newspapers. However, in Edmonton, established early as a trading post, it was the extension of the telegraph which gave the needed impetus to journalism. To disseminate a weekly budget of news from the east through the Hay Lakes operator, the *Edmonton Bulletin* was first issued December 6, 1880. This service soon developed fuller coverage.

In Canada's north, press developments were similar to those in the interior of British Columbia forty years earlier. After gold discoveries in 1896, experienced prospectors and ill-prepared amateurs flocked into the Klondike from 1897 to 1905. During the eighteen months before 1900, some 40,000 persons entered the area. On January 10,

1899, the police estimated the population of the Klondike region to be 28,018.[11]

The largest center was Dawson City, the supply point and jumping-off place for every new find. Journalism was part of Dawson City life, with the *Yukon Sun* and *Klondike Nugget* established there as pioneer papers in June of 1898.

While the population of the territory making up modern-day Canada was rising from 3,300,000 in 1861 to 3,840,000 in 1871, 4,500,000 in 1881, 5,100,000 in 1891 and 5,592,299 in 1901, newspaper numbers were increasing as well. A tabulation[12] shows the increase:

Year	*Number of Newspapers and Periodicals in British North America*
1857	291
1864	298
1874	470
1881	579
1891	837
1895	919
1900	1227

Fourth Press Period: 1900 to Present

In the twentieth century Canadian journalism, originally a transplant, became firmly rooted and spread to the previously unoccupied interspaces of the country. The development resembled that of Canada's second press period but whereas the earlier change had been achieved by a proliferation of papers, twentieth-century growth was of a different nature. The greater prominence of the daily, which had become the most important kind of newspaper, came from soaring circulation and from the emergence of the newspaper as a giant business enterprise.

Modern journalism has become an industry requiring great resources of capital, equipment and personnel. To direct it the quasi civil-servant printer-editor of the eighteenth century and the "personal" editor of the nineteenth have given way to the publisher-capitalist of the twentieth. John Bushell would probably not recognize today's large metropolitan dailies with their thundering presses. One feature of the mutation of the basic methods used to produce printed media, has been a huge increase not only of total daily newspaper circulations, but of the circulations of individual dailies. The chief cause of the change was a sharp upward growth of Canada's twentieth-century population.

Changing economic conditions caused an irregular population growth. The first boom days lasted from 1901 to 1913, when, in percentage terms, the Dominion grew at its highest rate in history. Then, the Great War virtually cut off immigration and the population boom collapsed in 1914. However, immigration during the peaceful years and natural increase outweighed the wartime reduction in population growth.

A depression began and ended the 1921-31 period. After economic hardship lasting from late in 1920 until 1923, economic expansion was resumed, but when the stock market crashed in October 1929 the most serious depression in history began. Its full effect was not felt until the following decade.

Between 1931 and 1941 the government passed restrictive legislation to keep out immigrants so as to keep relief payments as low as possible. For similar reasons other countries made Canadians unwelcome and emigration dwindled. Most population gains came from natural increase, although the birth rate was low. World War II wiped out the dying depression but did not stimulate the growth of population.

When war ended in 1945, displaced persons and other immigrants flooded into a prosperous Canada. The development of Canada's largely untapped resources and an active armament industry fostered by cold war fears created a buoyant economy. The birth rate was high. As a result, Canada enjoyed the greatest absolute growth in population for any decade in its history in the years 1941-51.

The growth persisted during the first half of the 1950s. It was marked by a rising gross national product, high employment, extensive investment in Canada and vigorous industrial expansion. Postwar immigration held up. But a decline began in 1957. European prosperity, a damping down of the Canadian economy, government measures to discourage the entry of unskilled labour, and population losses to the United States made 1961 the year of smallest growth in more than a decade. Nevertheless, percentage growth for 1951-61 was second only to that of 1901-1911 and another record was set for absolute increase.

The 1971 decennial census disclosed a population picture for the 1961-71 period which was quite different. The percentage of increase was the second smallest for any twentieth-century decade. Although immigration maintained a fairly consistent rate, a steadily declining birth rate continued to check population growth. Special short-term factors adding to Canada's numbers were the Russian invasion of Czechoslovakia in 1968 and widespread desertions by American draftees opposed to service in Viet Nam. But at the end of the decade the Canadian economy lost strength and failed to create enough jobs to allow the labour force to expand at a healthy rate. The federal government introduced drastic anti-inflationary fiscal and monetary policies, and unemployment grew. The economic climate was not favourable to immigration and population increase.

The twentieth-century changes produced by the foregoing factors are indicated by the table on page 14. The table outlines the percentage of the total population which was urban at each chronological stage; the rise of urban population has been more important than total population increase to the development of daily newspapers, because it is in the cities and larger towns that dailies flourish.

A revolution in newspaper technology interacted with Canada's population increase to transform the Canadian daily. Electrically driven rotary presses, stereotyping, slug

CANADIAN POPULATION CHANGES DURING THE 20TH CENTURY*

Year	*Population*	*Increase over Previous Census*	*Urban or Non-Rural*	*% Urban*	*Newfoundland Population up to Confederation 1949*
1901	5,371,315	——	2,014,222	37.5%	220,984
1911	7,206,643	34.17%	3,272,947	45.42%	242,619
1921	8,787,949	21.96%	4,352,122	49.52%	263,033
1931	10,376,786	18.08%	5,572,058	53.7%	281,500 (estimated)
1941	11,506,655	10.9%	6,252,416	54.3%	303,300 (estimated)
1951	14,009,655	21.8%	8,628,253	61.6%[a]	361,416 (1949)[b]
1961	18,238,247	30.2%	12,700,390	67.9%	——
1971	21,568,315	18.26%	16,410,785	76.1%	——

*Compiled from *Canada Year Books* for appropriate years and from "Population: Urban and Rural Distribution," *1971 Census of Canada*, Catalogue 92-709, vol. 1, pt. 1 (Bulletin 1.1-9).

[a]It should be noted that in the 1951 and subsequent censuses a method of calculating urban-rural population was used which differed somewhat from the method used in previous censuses.

[b]The number added to the Canadian population when Newfoundland joined Canada in 1949.

casting of type and half-tone engraving, all pre-1900 inventions, were brought to full development in the twentieth century. Improved newsprint manufacture and better folder attachments increased efficiency. The teletype, teletypesetter, Scan-a-graver, Klischograph, photo-offset press, ROP colour, cathode ray editing terminals, and computerized typesetting of news and advertising material had far-reaching effects. With one modification, this statement made in 1960[13] accurately describes the 1971 situation:

> The hand-in-hand growth in circulation and technology has had a vicious circle quality. To serve vastly increased readership, newspapers require costly equipment; to pay for elaborate and costly equipment, publishers must secure vastly enlarged readership. Under such conditions, many an entrepreneur has found himself caught up in a situation in which he has had to gain all or nearly all the potential subscribers if his enterprise is to continue. Thus in many communities there has no longer been room for two newspapers as there had been in the days of Mackenzie and Howe and rival journals have given no quarter in publishing battles that have ended only when all but one contestant has been driven from the field. . . . This process has brought about what Oswald Garrison Villard has called, in reference to the United States, "the disappearing daily."

The necessary qualification to the foregoing statement derives from the recent rise of the "underground" newspaper, a phenomenon to be glanced at presently.

The change in the number of daily newspapers has been from 121 in 1900 to a high of 138 in 1913, to a low of 87 in 1953 to a total of 117 in 1974. Today, fewer dailies serve a population four times as great as it was in 1901. Total circulation has increased nearly eight times, from about 600,000 in 1901 to about 5 million in 1974. Average circulation per daily has risen from 5,000 in 1901 to 25,000 in 1940 to 40,000 in 1974.[14] In 1900, eighteen communities published two or more dailies, for a total of 66 daily newspapers in direct competition. In March 1974 nine cities (Victoria, Calgary, Winnipeg, Thunder Bay, Sherbrooke, Saint John, Halifax, Charlottetown, and St. John's) supported two dailies each.

In each of Victoria, Thunder Bay, Saint John, Halifax, and Charlottetown a single company owned the two papers. There were six dailies in Vancouver (including the four suburban journals of the *Columbian* group), seven in Montreal, four in Toronto (including one in Italian and excluding *The Daily Racing Form*), and three each in Ottawa, Quebec City, and Moncton.[15]

There has also been an increasing concentration of control in the hands of fewer and fewer publishers and owners. The trend is indicated by the fact that in 1930, 116 dailies were under the control of 99 publishers; in 1953, 89 were under the control of 57 publishers, with 11 publishers accounting for 42 dailies or about half the total.

In late 1973 the F. P., Southam, Thomson, Clifford Sifton, and K. C. Irving interests owned 61 dailies, with a combined circulation of more than 2,750,000 copies daily, about 70 per cent of the English-language total. Trans-Canada Ltée (Paul Desmarais, Jacques Francoeur, Jean Parisien, Pierre Dansereau principals) owned *La Voix de l'Est* of Granby, *La Tribune* of Sherbrooke, and *Le Nouvelliste* of Trois Rivières. Entreprises Gelco Ltée (Paul Desmarais, Jean Parisien principals) owned *La Presse* of Montreal, and Jacques Francoeur bought *Le Soleil* of Quebec City. Circulation of the five dailies was 427,329 at the end of 1973, or nearly 50 per cent of the 864,987 daily circulation of French-language newspapers.[16]

Confronted by such statistics, the critic might wonder whether the fate of all Canadian dailies is eventually to become group-owned. Yet during the 1960s there was evidence that the trend towards a monolithic press structure is not quite irresistible. The forces working against monopoly may derive their power from the very conditions whereby the conventional press has achieved its monopoly. During the twentieth century the characteristic daily has captured all or nearly all of its community's readership by trying to reflect majority opinion and refusing to offend minority opinion. As a result, some critics feel, dailies have tended to become bland, undoctrinaire, unlikely to disturb the status quo. This condition is coupled with the fact that the characteristic newspaper owner is a big business or a big businessman. Such journals, so say critics of the modern newspaper, reflect the views of the "Establishment." The claim has been made that such a press has failed to take account of the new mood of social revolution and activism which has become so much a part of the 1960s and 1970s.

It is to serve this unrepresented segment of society that the so-called "underground" press has appeared in Canada. The name is certainly a misnomer because the paper is not a newssheet furtively circulated as were the publications of the French underground during the Nazi occupation, although civic authorities have harassed some of its distributors and sometimes invoked the laws of libel and obscenity against its editors. A better designation for such publications might be "alternate" or "opposition" press. Canadian representatives of the genre, some of them short-lived, have been: *Georgia Straight*, Vancouver; *Omphalos*, Winnipeg; *Satyrday*, *Harbinger*, *Tribal Village*, Toronto; *Octopus*, *Free Press*, Ottawa; *Logos*, Montreal; *The 4th Estate*, Halifax; and *The Mysterious East*, Fredericton.

The appearance of such newspapers provides evidence that the print media still offer an opportunity for the expression of dissenting opinion in a manner impossible within the electronic media, where radio wave lengths and television channels are limited in number and where the approval of the Department of Transport and the Canadian Radio-Television Commission is required before a new broadcasting venture can begin. This is not to say that an entrepreneur can start from nothing and can successfully compete on equal terms with the Toronto *Star*, once valued at more than $25,000,000, or the *Globe and Mail*, once valued at more than $10,000,000. The fate of the *Winnipeg Citizen*, *Guelph Guardian*, *Vancouver Times*, and *Le Nouveau Journal* of Montreal gives sharp reminder of the foolhardiness of such ventures. But cheaper production processes such as photo-offset or the contracting out of newspaper printing and a willingness to work on a small expense-small profit basis have given another voice to journalists who strongly wish to say what they believe. Often that voice is a weak one, but where the newcomer forces the established press to take notice, its opinions gain a wider currency.

The future of such newspaper "alternates" is difficult to foresee. It may be that they will not survive and that similar papers will not replace them. Or it may be that they will gather enough readers to become a press supplemental to the conventional press. Together with tomorrow's facsimile newspaper they may help to prevent the ultimate achievement of the monopolistic mass media structure to which twentieth-century developments seem to point.

1. A. W. Currie, *Canadian Economic Development* (Toronto: T. Nelson and Sons, 1942), page 65.
2. Robert W. Stuart Mackay, *A Supplement to the Canada Directory . . . brought down to April, 1853* (Montreal: 1853), pages 360-1.
3. *The Canada Directory for 1857-8* (Montreal: 1857), pages 1140-5.
4. *The British Whig*, Special Number, May, 1895, Upon Opening of New Building, page 4.
5. *The Canadian Newspaper Directory, 1892* (Montreal: A. McKim and Company, 1892), page 58.
6. From a table in Mackay, *A Supplement to the Canada Directory . . . brought down to April, 1853*, pages 360-1.
7. From a table in *The Canada Directory for 1857-8*, pages 1140-5.
8. *Idem.*
9. *The Daily News*, St. John's, Newfoundland, 20 December, 1927.
10. *The Canadian Newspaper Directory, 1892* (Montreal: A. McKim and Company, 1892), page 58.
11. S. D. Clark, *The Social Development of Canada* (Toronto: University of Toronto Press, 1942), page 320.
12. W. H. Kesterton, *A History of Journalism in Canada* (Toronto: McClelland and Stewart, 1967), page 39.
13. W. H. Kesterton, "A History of Canadian Journalism, (Circa) 1900-1958," *Canada Year Book, 1959* (Ottawa: Queen's Printer, 1959), page 883.
14. Kesterton, *A History of Journalism in Canada*, page 71.
15. Computed from *Canadian Advertising*, February 1974, and contemporary newspaper accounts.
16. Computed from *Canadian Advertising* for appropriate months.

The Telephone and Social Change

ROBERT F. LATHAM

As society becomes more oriented to the manipulation and transfer of information, the communications media will achieve an even greater importance. Considerable research has been undertaken on communications in general and in particular on the impact of the mass media and literature on society, but very little interest has been shown in the impact of the telephone, despite the fact that it has often been used as a measure of the level of "modernization." Little effort has been spent on examining how this instrument has aided the modernization process. The addition of the visual mode (the picturephone) to the two-way communications process in the next few years will alter social patterns even further. This paper attempts to review some of the changes that have occurred as a result of the proliferation of the telephone throughout society.

Man throughout his history has strived for improved communications. Although writing enabled man to communicate through both space and time, for several centuries the speed of communication remained that of the swiftest runner or horse. Only when the laws of optics were understood, and the telescope developed, did communications over long distances increase in speed. Using the principle that the unaided eye can see further than the unaided ear can hear, Claude Chappe, a French engineer, developed a semaphore system in France during the period 1790-95. The largest and longest lasting semaphore system was developed by the railroads: this system required new control systems, and encompassed the later development of numerous forms of electronic telegraphic equipment.

In January 1845, Samuel Morse opened the first telegraph line in the United States. The telegraph had only limited use in the United States until 1850, when the New York newspapers developed a telegraphic news service. Three major customers, the state (to provide an efficient means of establishing central control), the railroads (to ensure safe and rapid function of their trains) and the commercial users (newspapers found that rapid news meant profit) brought about a continued and rapid growth of this new communications medium.

Although the telegraph technology represented a quantum jump in the speed of transaction, for the same expenditure of money and time a much greater amount of information could be exchanged using acoustical telephony. In March 1876, a new era was born when Alexander Graham Bell transmitted the first complete sentence over wires. Bell spent considerable time promoting his new invention and his efforts were rewarded in 1878 when the first telephone and switchboard were installed in New Haven, Connecticut. Two years later the first long-distance line was constructed between Boston and Providence. The introduction of new technologies and the rapid addition of new lines hastened the completion of a transcontinental linkage.

The growth in use of the telephone in Canada was brought about by the telegraph companies. In 1878, four months after the New Haven experiment, the first telephone exchange in Canada, and the first in the British Empire, was established in Hamilton. In 1879 the Dominion Telegraph Company opened the first exchange in Montreal, and the phenomenon of the telephone was well on its way in the Canadian market.

Misconceptions regarding the capabilities of the telephone and its lines were prevalent during the initial years. Some citizens were concerned about what could be transmitted through the telephone network and who could hear the transmissions. As a result, many people—including the leading lawyer of the telephone company—had their telephones installed in vaults. Some people considered that the wires strung between the poles made the poles sensitive to conversations held at or near the pole, causing a further reduction of privacy. In a smallpox epidemic in Montreal all telephone employees were inoculated; the public interpreted this to mean that the disease could be transferred through the telephone, and a riot broke out as citizens stormed the telephone company building.

The business community found the telephone to be a very useful tool for social interaction, but when it was necessary to "talk business" they were more comfortable in face-to-face interaction. This attitude changed somewhat during the great growth of business in the United States. The telephone proved to be superior to the telegraph in conducting dubious legal manipulations, for it was easier to speak and listen than to code and decode messages, and most important, telephone conversations left no written or printed record.[1]

Doctors were at first reluctant to use the service because it was not clear how to charge for medical advice provided by telephone. To overcome this problem, doctors were given a reduced rate on their service to encourage patients to obtain and make use of the telephone.

Present Canadian Systems

In Canada today there are 16 major companies that operate approximately 2000[2] intra-city telephone systems. These systems are managed and interconnected through two organizations that ensure continuity and operating efficiency in the Canadian telephone system. The Telephone Association of Canada was established in 1921 to provide a forum for the interchange of information to promote higher standards and cooperation. In 1931 the Trans-Canada Telephone System was established to coordinate long-distance service across the Dominion. In order to ensure that the Canadian systems can also interconnect with world systems, the industry is represented in the International Telecommunications Union (ITU), a specialized agency of the United Nations.

Regulation of the telephone company in any country is a very important factor in its development, since it has become such a large part of what economists call the "infra-structure." In a brief review of 231 countries of the world, 159 of the telephone networks were found to be completely controlled by the government, 26 were privately operated, and the remaining 46 were a mixture of the two. Both the United States and Canada fall into the last category.

Two of the Canadian systems—Bell Canada (Ontario and Quebec) and the British Columbia Telephone Company—are regulated by the Federal Government while the remaining organizations operate under provincial charters. In three of the provinces—Alberta, Saskatchewan, and Manitoba—the province owns and operates the telephone system. In the remainder the systems are generally privately owned. In several of the provinces there are a number of independent telephone companies that exist under provincial regulation. In Ontario, for example, there are fifty[3] independent telephone companies regulated through the Ontario Telephone Service Commission, a section of the Department of Agriculture. This system remains from the days when telephone companies were essentially small rural service units.

This brief review of the telephone industry defines the perspective for examining the growth of the telephone in Canadian society. However, before exploring the actual impact of the telephone on Canadian society, two fundamental operating principles of the industry should be reviewed.

Key Operating Principles

In evaluating the Canadian telephone systems the principles of "service on demand" and "flat rate calling" must be considered. The "service on demand" concept is one which telephone companies have tried to achieve at all times. As a result, except for the period after the war, unfilled orders or "held orders" have been limited. In many European countries this policy is not maintained, and people often must wait nine months or more to get service. This ability to obtain and use the telephone service "on demand" has led to a lack of concern or "take for granted" attitude towards the telephone system in North America. This represents a significant social difference from many other areas of the world.

The second key principle, that of flat rate calling, is a rating structure used in determining the rates of local (non-toll) telephone service. For a stated price, for a period of one month, a person can place an unlimited number of calls of any length within defined local calling areas. (For example, the local calling area in Toronto comprises 1.3 million telephones over an area of 650 square miles.) This policy has stimulated the use of the telephone, since the constraint of costs is overcome once the monthly charge has been paid. It has also had a significant impact on people's dependence on the telephone for communications. However, before examining in detail this dependence, it is important to consider the nature of communications by telephone.

Telephone Communications

In today's society people have many methods of communicating. Visual, oral and written messages are all part of our daily lives. The conventional telephone uses only one method of communication, the oral. The use of the telephone as the communications channel between the sender and receiver of information may be likened to communications between two individuals in a completely dark room. The individuals share a "common acoustical space"[4] in which they can interact. The difference between the radio and the telephone is primarily that the latter is dyadic (has two-way interaction) and the former is monadic (one-way interaction). This characteristic of the telephone is one of its major assets.

The elimination of the visual mode and the reliance solely on voice places some constraints on an individual's abilities to convey information. No longer is his appearance helpful; all that is available is his voice and some of its inflections. The loss of the visual element of interaction and presentation has an equalizing impact on society. Since all telephone calls originate in a ring which is common, "unequals may call but their calls are equal (at least until answered)."[5]

Pervasiveness

Perhaps the most significant sociological feature of the telephone is its massive pervasiveness. In 1970[6] there were 255.2 million telephones in the world. The growth of 7.3 per cent during 1969 represented the fourteenth consecutive year that the growth rate had exceeded six per cent, while the absolute increase of 17.3 million telephones was the highest in 13 years. The United States leads the world in the number of telephones with 115.2 million (45 per cent of the world total) followed by Japan and the United Kingdom with 23.1 and 13.9 million respectively.[7]

Table 1 TELEPHONE DEVELOPMENT IN CANADA

	Telephones in	*Number of Telephones per 100*	
Year	*Thousands*	*Population*	*Households*
1925	1,143	12.2	44.2
1930	1,103	13.6	54.5
1935	1,209	11.1	40.3
1940	1,461	12.8	44.4
1945	1,849	15.2	50.8
1950	2,917	21.0	70.1
1955	4,152	26.1	81.9
1960	5,728	37.5	93.0
1965	7,445	43.5	98.8
1970	9,751	45.2	NA

Source: Bell Canada Annual Charts, February 1971.

In Canada the growth of the telephone has been very rapid, particularly since the end of the war (see Table 1). In 1970 there were 9.8 million telephones in Canada. This figure represents 45.2 telephones per 100 population or 98.8 per 100 households,[8] and is evidence of considerable growth over the period 1945-1970 when telephones increased by 7.9 million or 30.0 telephones per 100 population. There are some regional differences in telephone development in Canada; the highest development in 1969 was in Ontario with 49.6 telephones per 100 population. British Columbia is next in proportion of telephones to population, and the lowest such development is in the Northwest Territories (see Table 2). These regional discrepancies are to some extent a direct result of a lack of business concentration, rather than of a low percentage of telephones in the home.

Table 2 TELEPHONE DEVELOPMENT IN CANADA BY PROVINCE (Jan. 1, 1970)

Province	*Telephone Development Per 100 Population*
Ontario	49.6
British Columbia	48.1
Alberta	46.0
Manitoba	44.4
Quebec	43.4
Saskatchewan	39.6
Yukon	39.4
Nova Scotia	37.1
New Brunswick	36.1
Prince Edward Island	31.0
Newfoundland	25.9
N.W. Territories	24.6

Source: Bell Canada Annual Charts, February 1971.

The pervasiveness and connecting power of the telephone system have steadily increased reliance on the telephone. In Canada there are some 35 million calls per day, while in the United States there are more than ten times this number. Table 3 gives some indication of the growth of calling in Canada over the period 1931-1969.

Canada was the most talkative nation in the world during the period 1951 to 1968, after which it relinquished this honour to the United States.[9] The high calling rate may be related to the flat rate billing (discussed earlier) and the small population spread over such a large area: both have increased the necessity or the desire for people to interact. The recent loss of the "most talkative" title may be attributed to the increased complexity of United States business and the greater necessity for "instant" communication.[10]

Table 3 TELEPHONE CALLING IN CANADA

Year	*Average Number of Calls per Year* *Per Telephone*	*Per Person*
1931	1799	236
1941	1928	262
1951	1694	376
1961	1720	561
1969	1617	710

Source: DBS Telephone Statistics.

The number of telephones in a system is an indication of growth, and interconnection of these telephones increases their value. Today throughout the North American continent (excluding Mexico and Greenland) an individual can "direct dial"—that is, make a connection without the use of an operator—to approximately 125 million telephones. For residents of New York City, direct international calling to Great Britain was introduced in March of 1970. France and Germany were added later in 1970; direct dialling to Italy and Japan was set up in 1971.[11] Eventually it is expected that there will be direct distance dialing throughout the world. In preparation for this global system, the members of the ITU have already segmented the world into nine regions to be used as the codes for direct dialing.

Today a person in North America can interconnect by telephone with some 209 countries or 97.2 per cent of the world's telephones; international telecommunications is one of the fastest-growing segments of North American industry, with a growth rate of 25% per annum. Overseas traffic from Canada in 1969 was 689,000 calls via Montreal and 53,000 via Vancouver. This ability to interconnect and call on a world scale has certainly assisted in creating what McLuhan calls the Global Village and what Drucker refers to as the Global Shopping Centre,[12] and this global aspect of communication has had a critical impact on both an individual's perspective of the world and our concern for the flow of information through society.

Society as an Information System

Richard Meier has indicated[13] that an increase in the rate of communication is a prerequisite to socio-economic growth. He has developed an analogy between today's society and an energy system. The system generates and destroys energy within it and transmits energy through it; if society is to remain viable as an open system its essential function is to conserve negative entropy. Energy to Meier is the flow of information through the system, and the rate of energy flow through the system (the metabolic rate) varies with the level of activity. The rate of flow is much faster in the urban than in the rural areas. The rate at which information moves from the originator to the receiver (the transaction rate) is integral to the growth of the city since cities evolved mainly to facilitate human communications and access to service. Their existence permits a large number of people to have efficient access to one another's ideas and expertise.

In 1966, 73.6 per cent of the Canadian population was classified as urban[14] and this proportion is expected to rise to 94 per cent by 2001. Canadian society at this time will be overwhelmingly urban and even more dependent than now on a high transaction rate. Meier believes that the city has no option on whether it should constantly improve communication and information systems, but rather must do so in order to survive.

Today's society is based on an efficient communication

system. The modern assembly plant could not exist without the telecommunication which permits all the parts to arrive at the required place at the appropriate time. Similarly, the evolution of the corporate headquarters is a function of the ability of the communication system to keep people informed. Other communications media like the newspaper, radio and television rely to a major degree on the availability of instant communications, in particular the telephone.

In the past the prevailing method of communicating was the transportation of the individual himself or of the written message. The revolutionary aspect of electronic environments is not that they reduce the friction of moving people or messages, but that they move the experience itself to the human nervous system. Traditionally we have moved the person to the experience; in the future we will more and more be moving the experience to the person. The essence of this change is that we are moving into an age of telemobility. In this age, the mechanism is replaced by electronic media. The impact on society, although gradual, is profound. In essence the time spent moving can now be used in other activities, thus altering the time-activity budget of the individual.

Space-Time Relationship

The telephone, through its improved technology, has had a considerable impact on the space-time relationship of people. For example, the first North American trans-continental telephone link was made in 1915 between New York and San Francisco. It required eight operators and fourteen minutes to make the connection. Since the first trans-Canada call in 1916[15] the calling time has decreased to about 25 seconds. In local calling, the average time required to make a connection with one's neighbour is about 5 seconds after dialing. Thus, there is a difference in time-space of some twenty seconds between a friend in Vancouver and a neighbour in Montreal. To many people this time difference is insignif-icant, and the space difference does not represent a barrier to interaction. Cost, however, does present some constraints.

Today a call between Vancouver and Montreal costs $1.95,[16] a decrease of $13.10 from the first calls in 1920, or an annual decline of 26 cents per annum. To some members of society—for example, people who use credit cards or operate on business expense accounts—the cost of calling does not interfere with their use of the telephone. Those people who are accustomed to using the telephone in their work (white-collar workers, particularly executives) tend to use the telephone more at home because of its familiarity. This phenomenon has led many people to think of the world as aspatial—unrelated to the factor of distance—for purposes of voice interaction.

Changing Concept of Community

A sociological phenomenon of considerable interest has developed from the changing space-time relationship. In the past an individual's community usually consisted of a number of people who lived and/or worked in a small area. The telephone network reflected this interaction in that the first telephone networks were restricted to a radius of approximately one-quarter of a mile. With the sprawl of urban communities, the increasing trend to suburban living and the gradual merging of many small towns, there has been a growing demand for a widening of the calling area. The introduction and growth of "Extended Calling Areas" has led to an increased amount of calling between the centres from 6 to10 times the previous amount, indicating the previous latent demand for interaction.

With further improvements in communications and transportation, an individual's community of interest may become even more widespread in the future. In a study in Toronto, a sample of people were asked about the place of residence of the six people with whom they were closest.[17] More than one-quarter lived beyond Metro boundaries and some resided as far as 100 miles away.

Only about thirteen per cent lived within what was regarded as walking distance.

A businessman may have an even wider community of interest than the average individual. He may live in Toronto with his subordinates in Halifax, Montreal, Winnipeg and Vancouver and his boss in New York. As well as these primary business associates, he may visit regularly other colleagues outside Toronto. If his corporation is involved in other than North American business, his community may well be global in size.

This pattern is distinctly different from previous situations in which the individual was restricted to his community of place; today we are more closely tied to interest communities than place communities. Already we can see the proliferation of individuals clustering around a variety of subjects in informal associations which Boulding[18] has referred to as "Invisible Colleges." These colleges are very common among academics and the development of common-interest groups has already spread to the publication industry, which has introduced numerous special-interest magazines. Such informal groups may congregate by using modern transportation, but it is doubtful if they could maintain their existence without the unification made possible by the telephone. In the United States, a group is organizing individuals who have common interests on a variety of subjects. Using a conference telephone circuit, individuals are connected at a specific time to discuss the subject in question.[19] The interaction is the same as it would be if they all had travelled to a common meeting hall. The formation of these "communities without propinquity," as Webber[20] refers to them, will have an even greater impact on society as telecommunications continue to alter the spatial relationships.

Changing Urban Patterns

The improvement in transaction time is affecting the shape of cities. The city or population clustering is a direct result of the drive to reduce the cost of interaction among the inhabitants. Within cities themselves the activities have tended to become nucleated and the demand for centrality or accessibility has been the prime selector in the location of economic activity. There is today, however, considerable evidence that with improved transportation and communications it is not necessary to locate at the centre of the city. In cities like Toronto there are several nucleations of large office complexes outside the central city. The sprawl of suburbia is a partial function of improved communication patterns as well as of improvements in transportation, and is further reflected in the movement into the rural countryside. The provision of a good system of communications has been one of the forces which has permitted centrifugal forces from the central city to overcome some of the centripetal forces which tend to reinforce nucleation.

The telephone was a significant factor in the separation of the home and the work place. In the future it may have a reverse effect. As information jobs proliferate and communication facilities improve, the number of people who may work at home or at local work centres will also increase. This reallocation of resources would also reduce the visual and air pollution that the transportation arteries propagate.

Much discussion has been generated on the future "wired city" and its implications for the urban form. This new, integrated communications network will probably not alter substantially the physical shape of the city in the suburban region until the other utilities such as water and sewage undergo some drastic changes. The major change introduced by new systems of communication may be in the decision-making process. New technologies will provide data collection procedures and feedback mechanisms to input into this process, and the participation of the average citizen might alter a number of decisions. The recent protest over the Spadina Expressway in Toronto is an example of this new participation. With improved communications these interventions will increase.

One of the major phenomena of the central city is the vertical growth of office and apartment buildings. The high-rise today is the result of a number of inventions—structural steel, elevators, indoor plumbing, central heating, electrical lighting, the telephone. If the telephone did not exist, the number of elevators required to transport messages would eliminate approximately half of the existing floor space, thus rendering most buildings uneconomical to the developers. The telephone thus facilitated the distribution of people in not only a horizontal but also a vertical direction.

Mobility

The changing concept of community is partially a result of the increased mobility of our society, a mobility which telecommunications has done much to stimulate. This mobility has been fostered by the telephone industry via the provision of mobile telephones for cars and trucks and remote paging devices; the latter are particularly useful to doctors who must maintain close contact with an answering service. McLuhan uses the call girl as an illustration of how the telephone has increased the mobility of one segment of society: the telephone brought about the decline of the brothel and rise of the call girl who, by using an answering service, could function over large sections of a city.

Substitution

Much of the impact of the telephone on our lives has resulted from the substitution of telecommunications for other methods of communication. The most common substitution is of telecommunications for transportation. From its beginning the telephone was successful because it obtained the same end for certain needs as transportation but with a lower expenditure of energy and money. The susceptibility of transportation trips to substitution by telecommunications appears to be the function of at least two factors. The purpose of the trip appears to be the most critical factor, with those trips concerned with the transfer of information having the greatest potential for substitution. Secondly, substitution is dependent on economic considerations: the substitution will be most profitable for persons earning high incomes. For example, the use of conference rooms connected by telecommunication for meetings would save executives air fare, time and fatigue.

Telecommunications might also offer an alternative to increases in building and administrative costs. A particular company must decide whether it is cheaper to centralize only certain administrative activities in one spot, thus increasing overall building space and duplicating some services in both the central office and other locations, or to substitute communications to other points for buildings and services there. Not all activities are capable of substitution, but rather may in time become complementary. The complex telecommunications network, for example, is essential for the operation of the transportation system itself, rather than being just a substitute for it.

Although substitution appears to be beneficial from an economic point of view, the social implications are not as obvious. There is much debate, for example, on the importance of personal presence in communications.

Telephone Uses

The telephone has several uses in society. The first is a "utility use" which arises in time of crisis, such as household sickness or intrusion by undesirables. In New York, the Welfare Department recently ruled that recipients of welfare should all have a telephone since many of them were located in potentially dangerous neighbourhoods. Groups of elderly widows living alone have been known to maintain daily telephone contacts as a means of ensuring the safety, health and emotional security of the group members. Over the past few years many major cities have introduced "Distress Centres"[21] in which an individual can call at a time of stress to talk to a trained person concerning his or her problem.

One might also cite the necessity to communicate associated with much larger crises. For example, during the power blackout in November of 1965, when some 80,000 square miles of North America were paralyzed and in darkness, there was a 100 per cent increase in calling. More importantly, the availability of telephone communications permitted the power supplier to restore the vital service.[22]

The telephone is also used, of course, as a daily messenger and information source. People regularly make appointments or reservations for theatres, shows, hairdressers, and so on, by telephone. The telephone also provides a quick source of information and news from various sources. Many corporations today use telephone recordings as a way to keep employees informed of new procedures and policies.

When the telephone was first introduced, its role as an information centre was even more pronounced than today. Originally the telephone provided a wake-up service similar to that in hotels today. In addition the telephone served as a primary time-check until 1922, at which time the demand for time-checks became unmanageable.[23] The telephone operator has also for many years been a centre of information. In the old manual system she had a good knowledge of the community and its activities, but as dial telephones were introduced her role as a news source declined. On the other hand, the information or directory assistance operators have continued this function to some extent. They regularly answer questions on bus departures, cooking, spot removal, highway directions, and a variety of subjects; and at times their information has been extremely useful in the saving of lives by providing prompt advice or getting help quickly.

The telephone has become even more important through its use on "hot line" radio shows. These shows have answered a latent demand in society to register opinion publicly and directly. The call-in shows provide people with an additional channel through which they can express their views and receive a response without leaving their homes. This use is perhaps important in determining trends in public opinion, although it is doubtful at present that the callers have much political influence.

An additional major use of the telephone is for the purchase of goods and services. For many years one has been able to phone the corner grocery store and order the weekly groceries. The original mail-order system of many large firms has evolved from the original Catalogue Business to the "In-House Convenience Shopping Business," whereby customer orders are phoned rather than mailed to the firm. This transfer from the mails to the telephone is not complete, however; in the Maritimes 60 per cent of the business comes in by mail, while in the west the corresponding figure is 35 per cent. This is in drastic contrast to highly urbanized central Canada where 88 per cent of the business is carried on by telephone.

Some Characteristics of Telephones

The installation of a telephone and the publication of the number in a directory are cues for individual interaction. The ringing telephone to many people is an irresistible force which demands reaction. Many of us have experienced situations in which the telephone has interrupted an activity which we would normally not allow to be disrupted—for example, a mother sometimes leaves small children in the bath or kitchen while she runs to the telephone. In Chicago recently, a bank robber answered the telephone call of a local radio station; his dilemma and ultimate arrest were broadcast live through the Chicago area, using the telephone and radio. This necessity to answer the telephone arises, in part at least, from the absence of any clues to the identity of the caller; all calls are equal until answered.

In order to overcome the anonymity of the telephone, many people have set up filtering methods to monitor their calls. These methods may be people who question the caller and verify his credentials, machines which question the caller and request him to leave a message, or unlisted numbers by which the individual can control all but accidental access to his telephone.

The pervasiveness of the telephone system and the anonymity which it provides have also been of value to people who use the telephone for illegal purposes. Bookies, call girls, and boiler room operations could not exist at their present level of activity without the telephone.

Similarly, burglars make ingenious use of the telephone. They call a number selected from the telephone book; if no-one answers, they then proceed to what they expect is an empty apartment. In New York City people have responded to this new approach by leaving their telephones "off the hook" when they go away. This then generates complications in the switching equipment, for the design of this equipment is based on the probability that only a certain number of people will be using the service at any given point in time.

As in the case of any new or old invention, then, people have used the device of the telephone to meet their own needs; it is interesting to imagine possible uses for the picturephone of the future.

The Telephone and Rural Areas

The telephone has had a significant impact in rural areas as well, in reducing the isolation of the rural landowner. On the other hand the building of the telephone service often was a joint project participated in by local inhabitants and the multi-party service or party line with its ensuing lack of privacy often reinforced the ideas of the rural population. However, the telephone did help to broaden the world for people, especially farmers' wives who were susceptible to feelings of loneliness and isolation.[24] In general, the introduction of the telephone has done much to bring to rural areas an urban style of living and a level of services closer to that found in the city. For example, doctors in rural sections of Saskatchewan can dial a central information unit that has tapes on a variety of medical subjects, thus remaining up-to-date and having easy access to special consultative skills. This is further evidence of the potentially equalizing impact of the telephone on society.

Northern Service[25]

In discussing the impact of the telephone on changing societal patterns in Canada, it would be a gross oversight to omit reference to communications in the Canadian north. At present, the number of phones found in communities in the north varies from one to several hundred. The most northerly community with telephone service is Resolute, some 600 miles within the Arctic Circle. Most of the connections between the various communities are by radio telephone but within some of the communities conventional service exists.

One of the major problems, at least for people with urban values, is the lack of privacy in the northern telephone system. Since the conversations are by radio anyone in the north tuned in to the proper frequency can listen in. A few years ago a young man who was working for the summer in the far north was attempting to correspond with a girlfriend in Toronto, and since there was no mail to his location all correspondence was by radio from Frobisher Bay. All the couple's letters were read over the radio at regular intervals, and provided evening entertainment to a number of isolated operators.

Another difference between the standard telephone and the radio telephone is that the latter does not provide a "common acoustical space." An operator must listen to the conversation and switch the receiver on the radio for sending and receiving. This interaction is interrupted by pauses while the switching takes place. It also reduces the privacy since the operators usually have the telephone calls on a speaker so that they know when to switch, and thus anyone in the relay station can hear the conversation. The privacy problem becomes very important in police work and in mining operations where confidential information is the norm. However, like the party line in the rural areas the radio telephone does provide a good information source. Government officials have been known from time to time to drop choice morsels for all to hear in order to circulate certain ideas.

The Eskimos find telephone service strange because it lacks the visual mode. They usually introduce themselves on the telephone with "Who's there?" rather than "Hello." A result of telephone service in the north, according to a northern resident, is that people have become less friendly, by which he means that they have less face-to-face interaction. Northerners also are noted for the long periods that they speak on the telephone—conversations lasting for two to three hours are not uncommon. In some cases people have talked so long that relay switches have been stuck.

It becomes quite apparent that the introduction of the telephone in the north bears many similarities to the introduction of the telephone in rural areas. The lack of privacy, the opening of people's horizons in terms of the area they can contact, the dependence on the service for information, are just a few examples of the similarities. Generally, however, there has been very little research into the impact of this new technology on the citizens of the north, and in many areas this is an appropriate time to evaluate the *before* and *after* of telephone service in these northern communities.

Summary

This paper has covered in a very cursory manner a number of ways in which Canadian society has been affected by the introduction and growth of telephone service. The telephone has acted as a unifying element across the continent; it has permitted the expansion of industry and the evolution of the mass media—radio, television and newspapers. In the past we have considered the telecommunications network as an overlay of man's constructions; in the future, we will have to understand to a much greater degree its impact on our interaction patterns and on the organization of our institutions.

1. Sidney A. Aronson, "A Sociology of Telephone—Prospectus for the Study of the Social Consequences of Telephone Communications." Paper presented at American Telephone and Telegraph Workshop, 9 October 1970.
2. John de Mercado, "Switched Multiservice Cable Systems—The Wired City." Paper presented at Seminar on Telecommunications and Participation, Montreal, 4 April 1970, p. 4.
3. Bell Canada Statistic, January 1971.
4. Gordon B. Thompson, "Molloch on Aquarius." (*The*, IV, February 1970.)
5. Donald W. Ball, "Toward a Sociology of Telephoners," in Marcello Teuzzi, ed., *Sociology and Everyday Life* (New Jersey: Prentice-Hall, 1968), p. 65.
6. *The World's Telephones at January 1, 1969* (AT&T Long Lines, 1970.)
7. All data is for January 1 of the year in question.
8. This figure does not mean that all but 1.2 homes of every 100 homes have telephones. The number of telephones cited here includes business services and extensions as well as second telephones in a number of homes.
9. The United States had 745 calls per person in 1969.
10. Canada still has more calls per telephone: 1617 versus 1320 in the U.S.
11. Direct dialling from Montreal and Toronto to Europe is planned for the near future.
12. Peter Drucker, *Age of Discontinuity* (New York: Harper and Row, 1961), pp. 77-101.
13. Richard Meier, *Communication Theory of Urban Growth* (Boston: M.I.T. Press, 1962.)
14. The term "urban" refers to all centres with over 1,000 people.
15. The first trans-Canada call was made via San Francisco and Boston in 1916. The first all-Canadian route was completed in 1932.
16. The $1.95 figure is for three minutes after 6 p.m. or all day Sunday.
17. B. Weelman, M. Hewson and D. Coats, "Primary Relationships in the City." Paper presented at the annual meeting of the Canadian Sociology and Anthropology Association, Toronto, 6 June 1969.
18. Kenneth Boulding, *The Meaning of the Twentieth Century: The Great Transition* (New York: Harper and Row, 1964.)
19. *Time*, 23 January 1971.
20. M. M. Webber, "Order in Diversity: Community without Propinquity" in L. Wingo, ed., *Cities and Space* (Baltimore: Johns Hopkins, 1963), pp. 23-54.
21. In September 1970, there were 18 "Distress Centres" operating in Canada and 5 in the discussion stage.
22. The telephone has a complete battery-powered backup system.
23. Between 8 and 9 a.m. on a normal morning in Montreal in 1922, the operators were required to answer 8,000 time checks.
24. Aronson, op. cit., pp. 22-24.
25. The author wishes to express his thanks to P. Gardiner of Bell Northern Research for his ideas on this subject.

The Canadian Social System and the Canadian Broadcasting Audience

W. BRIAN STEWART

In the past forty years the Canadian broadcasting system has been consciously planned by four Acts of Parliament and constantly regulated by a series of government agencies. About thirty Royal Commissions, lesser commissions and parliamentary committees have analyzed it and made recommendations on it. The press and the public have watched it, praised it, and damned it for being too highbrow, too lowbrow, too commercial, too extravagant with public funds, too American in its content, too self-consciously and restrictively Canadian. Many of these criticisms were repeated in early 1974 when the Canadian Broadcasting Corporation (CBC) applied to the Canadian Radio-Television Commission (CRTC) for renewal of its radio and television network licences. The English-language television service in particular was vigorously attacked and vigorously defended in more than 300 written briefs to the Commission.

In the late 1960s, a new technology threatened to destroy parts of the system and to limit severely the production capability of the remainder. The new technology was the Community Antenna Television System; the threat came from the fact that CATV provided a means for distributing three American networks to most large communities in Canada which they could not previously reach by direct, through-the-air transmission. In the 1970s, Canadian programming could become secondary in its own country, and the loss of audiences felt by the Canadian programs, followed by loss of commercial revenue, could undermine the system's economic base. In 1969, the present regulating body, the CRTC, suggested slowing down the spread of American channels through regulation. The idea met great public resistance and in the mid-seventies the subject is still under debate, the problem still unsolved.

If the problem is now particularly acute, it is nevertheless as old as the system itself. Underlying it is the ill-defined but powerful concept of a "national consciousness."

> The first parliamentary committee on radio in 1932 spoke of broadcasting as a medium for "developing a greater National and Empire consciousness within the Dominion and the British Commonwealth of Nations". Prime Minister Bennett, introducing the legislation of 1932, said, "This country must be assured of complete Canadian control of broadcasting from Canadian sources, free from foreign interference or influence". Broadcasting must become an agency by which "national consciousness must be fostered and sustained, and national unity still further strengthened".[1]

The reference to an "Empire consciousness" has now gone, but the rest is enshrined in the 1968 Broadcasting Act: "the Canadian broadcasting system should be effectively owned and controlled by Canadians so as to safeguard, enrich and strengthen the cultural, political and economic fabric of Canada."[2]

The concept of a "national consciousness" has been used in many ways in studies of nationalism in Canada and elsewhere. A nation consists of: a group of people (usually defined geographically) sharing a common culture (obviously difficult to apply in bilingual Canada); or of a group of people sharing memories of common victories and defeats (historians have claimed that Canada became a nation during the World Wars[3]); or of a group of people conducting a greater volume of transactions among themselves than they conduct with others outside of the group.[4] This last definition provides a useful framework within which to study broadcasting in Canada. We can measure to some extent how much Canadians "transact" with one another and "talk" with one another, through radio and television, and how much they listen to and watch American radio and television stations. With less precision, we can find out what they "talk" about among themselves and with outsiders.

To do this, we set up a simple model of the broadcasting system with four variables: the physical system, the source of the message (more directly, who is doing the talking), the message itself (what is being said), and the receiver (who is listening and watching, and how he is affected by the message).

The Physical System

Generally, six factors have conditioned the nature of the physical system: the geographic distribution of the population; the presence of two official language groups and of other language groups without official status; the existence of geographic regions and subregions where residents have a strong sense of regional identity; the economic resources of Canada; the proximity of the United States and the availability in many areas of American radio and television signals; and finally, the fact that the system has been consciously planned to cope with these other factors.

Geographic Distribution

About 11.9 million Canadians live in 22 metropolitan areas; 4.7 million live in smaller cities and towns; and 5.2 million or 23.9 per cent live in rural areas.[5] The heaviest concentrations of population—in southern Quebec, southern Ontario, and southern British Columbia—are wholly or in large part directly accessible to American radio and television signals. The main characteristic of this population distribution is the great distances between the major cities, and the number of small, isolated communities between major cities and in the north, all of which require a broadcast service.

A near-axiom of Canadian politics demands that all taxpayers should, as far as possible, be treated equally, and not in accordance with what they contribute in taxes. For broadcasting, this has meant a heavy expenditure in public funds by the CBC—the publicly-owned segment of the system—in taking its television services, both English and

French to some 21.8 million people, or 98.7 per cent of the population. To achieve this coverage, the CBC needs 192 of its own television transmitters and another 214 transmitters of privately-owned affiliated stations, a total of 406 stations.

The problems and costs imposed by Canadian geography are in sharp contrast to those in Britain where the British Broadcasting Corporation can distribute its primary services (BBC 1 and BBC Wales) through 113 transmitters covering about 55.5 million people. While a Canadian television transmitter covers an average of 60,000 people, its British equivalent covers an average of nearly half a million. Canadian geography makes for expensive broadcast distribution.

Costs for distributing these programs between stations reinforce the comparison. In 1973, the CBC required 9,826 miles of microwave network for the English TV service to hook up its stations, and about 2,900 miles for the French network, all of this supplemented by satellite distribution over three channels. The main east-west trunk of the English network extends more than 4,000 miles and, if built from Victoria out over the Pacific, would fall just short of Yokohama, Japan. The cost of lines, microwave, and satellite, for all CBC domestic services amounted to about 7 per cent of its 1972-73 budget. The comparable BBC figure is about 2.3 per cent of its total domestic budget. Comparable station transmission charges would probably be in much the same proportion.

In addition to the CBC French and English services, an independent English-language television network, independent French and English television stations, and about 177 independent radio stations also cover a high percentage of the population of Canada.

One result of these figures has been a great concentration of resources and attention on the distribution of programs, which necessarily means a corresponding diversion from program production. Nor are the coverage problems completely finished with. Early in 1974, the Secretary of State, Mr. Hugh Faulkner, announced an accelerated coverage plan to provide radio and/or TV service to some 300 additional communities across the country, at a capital cost over the next 5 years of $50 million and an estimated annual operating cost of $12 million. Radio and television will then be available to 99 per cent of all Canadians. At the same time, he announced plans to improve service to isolated communities in the Canadian North, and the CBC has declared that over the next 5 years it will build 21 transmitters to replace privately-owned affiliates to its English and French primary services (AM Radio) and 15 new stations to its alternative service (FM Radio). This is in addition to major new TV stations, the next of which will be in Calgary.

Language Groups

In the early days of radio, adverse public reaction made it impossible to carry both English and French programs on the same networks and stations. Early experience with bilingual television stations in Montreal and Ottawa confirmed this conclusion. The principle of separate services for the two language groups is now fully established and the CBC spends about 61 per cent of its television program budget on its English service and 39 per cent on its French, although the population is approximately 30 per cent French speaking. The 1972-73 CBC Annual Report does not break down the budget into English and French service costs, but the lower distribution and station costs on the French side (because of the concentration of the French population in Quebec) probably corresponds to the population breakdown.

The 1968 Act officially accepted the division of service between English and French and even extended the policy that "all Canadians are entitled to broadcasting services in English and French as public funds become available" regardless of mother tongue. Ultimately, then, the aim is not just to deliver English programming to English Canadians and French to French Canadians but, as funds become available, to distribute both services throughout the country.

The Corporation also broadcasts on its Northern Radio Service in the languages of indigenous groups—over fifty hours a week in Eskimo, Dogrib, Chipewyan, Loucheux, Slave, and Cree languages. The Corporation does not provide programs in languages of other groups, though a few private radio stations do so in German and Italian, and there is considerable pressure that broadcasters should do more.

Regional Identity

The literature of Canadian history, politics, and sociology is strewn with references to the importance of regionalism in Canadian life: "the Canadian mosaic," "unity in diversity," and "the tension between the political sense of unity and the imaginative sense of locality." Repetition has perhaps made clichés of these references, but for broadcasting, they are expensive facts. Of the Corporation's total assets in 1972—$237.4 million (with another $28.5 million under construction)—just over $84 million was in provinces other than Quebec and Ontario, centres of the network production headquarters. A large proportion of this regional capital was invested in production facilities at 27 radio and 13 television production centres in cities outside of central Canada.

These stations, together with the private stations, exert a powerful influence in defining and reinforcing local and regional identity. The 1968 Act, however, instructs the system as a whole to strengthen the fabric of Canada, and specifically instructs the CBC radio and television networks to "actively contribute to the flow and exchange of cultural and regional information and entertainment" and to "contribute to the development of national unity and provide for a continuing expression of Canadian identity." The Corporation tries to do this by feeding regional as well as Toronto- and Montreal-produced programs into the national network. In short, the broadcasting system defines and strengthens regional identities and at the same time tries to strengthen the national identity, in part by enabling regional expression at the national level. Northrop Frye's "tension between the political sense of unity and the imaginative sense of locality" applies acutely to Canadian broadcasting.

The Economics of the System

Private capital alone could not have financed the existing system, much less carried out the obligations imposed by the 1968 Act. Yet successive governments have found a wholly public system politically unacceptable and the result is a typically Canadian compromise. The publicly-owned Corporation was licensed to operate television stations in the very largest cities and also in the smallest communities where private enterprise could not afford to go. The intermediate-sized cities were opened to private enterprise with the stations affiliated to the CBC networks. In the early 1960s, a second network independent of the CBC, financed solely by advertising, was licensed and now has affiliates in eighteen major cities with rebroadcasting stations in many surrounding communities.

In 1972 the total revenue of public and private broadcasting in Canada came to about $498.0 million, 64 per cent of which was generated by advertising while the great bulk of the remainder was in the form of government grants (operating) to the CBC. (This public funding constituted about 77 per cent of the CBC's income.) Advertising on the CBC gives its television service a marked structural resemblance to American television, and it may also withdraw some advertising monies from the private stations—"may," because it is a debated question how much of the CBC advertising revenue would go to American border stations were CBC to give it up, how much would go to other mass media, and how much would go to other Canadian television stations.

These factors received considerable publicity in the first few months of 1974 following two important events. First, it became apparent that the new Global Television Network, with outlets in the major Ontario cities, was in financial trouble due in part to its first, very low, ratings. Then in March, the CRTC issued its report on the CBC network licence hearings. In *Radio Frequencies Are Public Property,* the Commission strongly criticized the Corporation for the alleged ill effects of seeking advertising on its programming and scheduling practices, and suggested that the Corporation should be "counteracting mass concepts" by which it meant both counteracting the role of advertising in North American life generally and specifically the use of "violence, cheap sensation, and facile treatment of serious human questions that so easily attract audiences."[6]

At the hearings, the CBC president, Mr. Laurent Picard, stated that although it would be simpler if the public system were independent of commercials, the $80 million he estimated as necessary to eliminate this source of revenue was probably too great a cost for the public treasury. Given that sort of money, he would prefer to use it to improve programming, especially since a survey commissioned by the CBC showed that only 10 per cent of the English sample and 27 per cent of the French sample favoured wholly public financial support for the Corporation. The Commission apparently rejected the CBC's argument and in its decision proposed as a condition of licence that within five years, the Corporation should reduce its advertising by half, although ideally it should be out of advertising altogether. This proposed condition of licence was still (mid-1974) under CBC-CRTC discussion and the result of that discussion will probably affect the nature of CBC television programs for many years.

In *Radio Frequencies,* the Commission based its case almost exclusively on aesthetic and ethical grounds, and that case deserves to be argued on its merits. But another argument was brought out at a press conference following the CRTC's report and decision, when the chairman of the Commission was asked if he thought the outlook for Global Television was brighter that morning than it had been the morning before. The implication, of course, was that the diminution of CBC advertising would leave more room for Global. The important, long-range problem underlying the differences is how to finance an increased volume of Canadian programming available to viewers in the face of increasing American programming from American border stations and on CATV. That is the problem for which the Commission is seeking an answer.

The American Presence and CATV

American radio stations have always reached far into Canada, but the shorter range of American television signals has restricted them to border areas, including the heavily populated areas of southern Ontario and southern British Columbia.

In the 1960s, Community Antenna systems (powerful receiving antennas that pick up distant signals and retransmit them by cable to paying subscribers) rapidly expanded in near-border areas. In the 1970s microwave carried from one to three American channels to more and more of the larger cities. By 1971, about one-quarter of all television viewing was on cable. Where cable was available in 1971, just over 30 per cent of all viewing was via cable. In Vancouver, for instance, nearly 70 per cent of all viewing was on cable.

The strong selling point of almost all CATV systems is their ability to provide from one to eight American stations which cannot be received by the standard home antenna. By 1969, entrepreneurs in cities where even CATV antennas could not pick up American signals were applying to the CRTC for licences to bring these stations in by microwave. The CRTC suggested limiting the number which could be carried, but it appears that public opinion will allow no such limitations.

The core of the problem can be simply stated. The number of stations traditionally licensed to a given community depended on that community's ability to support them commercially. Many of these stations are now suddenly faced by one or more additional stations, usually American, but sometimes distant Canadian. The new stations take a large share of the audience. The existing stations become less attractive to advertisers; their ability to produce Canadian programs is lessened; their commercial viability is threatened. Probably no other country in the world faces the dilemma of its own programming being outnumbered by foreign signals in the same language.

Were Canadian broadcasting conditioned solely by economic forces, a genuinely Canadian system could not have emerged; having emerged, it could not survive the conditions of the 1970s. It seems, therefore, that some sort of planning by legislation and by governmental regulation will continue. Much of this paper is a discussion of why this will be so.

The Source

Although millions of people listen to radio and watch television, relatively few have access to the microphones and cameras and studios. In 1969, for instance, about 30,000 Canadian artists, musicians, actors, commentators, and other performers appeared on CBC radio and television networks and stations. By 1972-73 the artists' payroll totalled $24.86 million with another $1.18 million in royalty payments. (Payments by the private sector would be considerably smaller than this.) A breakdown of this figure by province suggests the degree to which the Corporation meets the demands of various social groups for broadcast expression.

French-Language Users

Payments to French-language performers cannot be directly equated with talent payments in Quebec, since there is some English-language production in Quebec and a still smaller amount of French-language production outside of Quebec. Nevertheless, the $8.96 million talent payments in Quebec, or 34 per cent of the total suggest the scale of the French-language payments.

Regional Users

Ontario talent payments were $11.0 million or 42 per cent of the total. The remaining $6.1 million or 23 per cent went to talent in production centres outside of central Canada, with the Atlantic provinces getting about 6 per cent, the

Prairies 8 per cent, British Columbia 7 per cent, and a small amount going to the Northern Service. In addition to these talent expenditures are all the production costs of studio facilities, technicians and engineers, of staff groups, such as announcers and cameramen, who are not included in the talent figure, and administrative costs. Whether all this gives a sufficient voice to groups outside of central Canada was again debated at the 1974 CBC Network Licence Hearings, with a number of briefs arguing that the network headquarters, especially in Toronto, dominated the English service. The CBC argued that, though increased regional contributions to the network were a high priority, the Corporation was already doing better than comparable foreign systems, with 67 per cent of its television service produced outside of the network headquarters, compared with 33 per cent for the BBC, 20 per cent for Sweden, and 10 per cent for Japan. The problem here, as with many CBC objectives, is to establish reasonable and precise targets so that performance can be measured against them.

Socio-Economic Classes

Besides regional and language classifications, there is very little statistical data as to just what socio-economic groups the performers come from. However, one inference is possible; the majority of the performers have broadcasting skills, or academic, journalistic or other qualifications which put them in the well-educated bracket. Many programs are about the under-educated, "the poor and the dispossessed," and there are many programs from newscasts to full-length documentaries which give these groups an opportunity for expression. But the people who produce the programs and who derive financial benefit from them do not usually belong to these social strata, though they may originally have come from them.

Given the nature of traditional broadcasting, its middle-class characteristics are inevitable, both in Canada and throughout the western world. Traditional television requires sophisticated techniques that must be learned. Furthermore, the middle-class dominance of television may be claimed as one of its great virtues: it not only requires education to produce, it also educates; it stimulates upward mobility; it helps create the much discussed "tide of rising expectations."

However, rising activism among previously quiescent social groups in Canada—from Indians to students—has found a possible new outlet for expression. For in its guidelines on cable television, the CRTC encouraged CATV systems to set aside one channel for community programs in which local groups can express themselves spontaneously, freely, inexpensively, and without all the "production values," the acquired techniques and skills that conventional broadcasters demand from their performers in order to gain large audiences. CATV community channels have varied widely in their success, partly because of the licensee's problems of legal responsibility, and partly because of the varying enthusiasm and skills of individuals and groups wishing to program the channel.

Meanwhile, the CBC, the Department of Communications, the CRTC, and other interested government agencies have been working with various isolated communities in providing community radio stations and programs. These programs are produced by local groups and played either on their own transmitter or on CBC Low Power Relay Transmitters that normally provide just the CBC network service. In Espanola, for instance, the CBC provided equipment and, in the early stages, technical advice to a legally constituted citizens' group which programmed the local LPRT for four hours a day for over two years. When a Sudbury radio station reached Espanola—just forty miles away—the initial enthusiasm for the local programming died down. But with the lessons learned in Espanola the CBC continues to be involved with stations in Rankin Inlet and Baker Lake in the Keewatin district and Big Trout Lake in Northwestern Ontario. Rankin Inlet, a community of 600 Innuit, is especially interesting—any member of the community can use the local telephone service to dial up the station, be "patched in" to the transmitter, and state his or her views on any subject while up to three other people at a time can join in. The future of community radio and television is in question, but undoubtedly they provide one of the most interesting developments in recent years.

Canadian-American Programs

When discussing the source of television programs available in Canada we must consider American programs, whether they come in by American stations (directly, or through cable) or are purchased and aired by Canadian stations. The reason for the presence of American programs on Canadian stations, both CBC and private, is again largely economic. American programs have a worldwide popularity for their technical excellence and entertainment value—"Bonanza" at one time had weekly audiences of 350 million people in 59 countries. The American industry has an enormous production capacity and spends millions of dollars on audience pre-tested pilot programs, many of which never reach the television screen, or if they do may last but a few weeks. The successful programs pay their way in the home market with audiences of tens of millions and can be bought for Canadian showing at probably less than 10 per cent of the original production costs. For these two reasons, they are most attractive to advertisers and provide much of the profit for private Canadian television. More than that, their commercial success helps subsidize the production of Canadian programs whose costs are high but which reach a maximum of three or possibly four million Canadian viewers weekly.

The great variation in the number of stations available in different areas of Canada, both off-air and on cable, makes it difficult to generalize as to the amount of Canadian versus foreign programming available to viewers. In late 1970, between 7:00 p.m. and 11:00 p.m.—or for fifty-six half-hour periods of programming per station per week— Charlottetown, with only one (CBC) station, had thirty-four Canadian-produced program half-hours or 60 per cent of the schedule. Halifax, with two Canadian stations (CBC and CTV), offered fifty Canadian-origin programs or 45 per cent of all half-hours between 7:00 and 11:00 p.m. during the week. In Toronto, with effectively three Canadian and three American stations, the number of Canadian-origin programs rose to sixty-seven or 20 per cent of all half-hour programs offered. Thus as the number of stations increased, the number of Canadian programs also increased, but the percentage of Canadian programs dropped dramatically. The implication was that as cable increased the number of stations available, the same movements would occur with obvious effects on audiences to Canadian versus American programming.

By January 1974, the situation had changed quite as predicted, at least in Charlottetown where now there is a strong CTV signal, and in Halifax where the two Canadian stations are joined (on cable only) by an American station. Although the amount of Canadian programming increased in Charlottetown, the percentage dropped to just over 45 per cent. In Halifax, the presence of the American station meant that while the number of Canadian programs remained relatively constant, their percentage of all programs offered dropped to less than a third. In Toronto, with the addition of the local CITY television station and of the third network (Global) station, both the number of Canadian programs increased, from 67 to 135, and the percentage of Canadian programs increased from 20 per cent to 30 per cent. (This does not take into account either those whose signal reached the fringe of the city, or the CBC French, the Canadian educational or the American educational stations available on UHF or on cable.) Developments since Global's financial crisis suggest that in the Fall of 1975, the station will cut back its Canadian content significantly, perhaps to the point where the Canadian content of the total system in Toronto shows little percentage increase. Furthermore, the audience gains of the two new stations appear to be mainly at the expense of audiences to the existing Canadian stations, rather than drawing audiences away from American stations. It remains to be seen whether third Canadian stations now licensed in Western Canada have the same results.

Are Canadians Talking to Canadians? Or Are Americans Talking to Canadians?

We are back to the question facing the CRTC: What is the best way of increasing the availability of Canadian programming? Is the answer to increase the Canadian content on existing stations or to increase the number of Canadian stations? The Commission has tried both solutions with limited success in terms of audience response.

Between 1969 and 1973, the CBC increased its Canadian content from about 55 per cent to almost 70 per cent (the CRTC required 60 per cent of the Corporation). At the same time, the CRTC attempted to increase private television's quota to the same 60 per cent target, but in public hearings the private stations argued that this would impose an intolerable burden on them. Therefore, a compromise was reached allowing private stations to carry no more than 40 per cent foreign-origin programming throughout the day and 50 per cent foreign-origin material during the prime-time hours, 6:00 p.m. to midnight; but in return they were expected to increase their coverage.

Other attacks came in Toronto, first regarding the licensing of CITY TV, a station broadcasting on UHF which has achieved critical success with its local public affairs programming and a great deal of publicity with its late night "blue movies," and secondly regarding the licensing of the Global Television network in Ontario, with plans to extend it to other provinces. The Global stations were also primarily on UHF.

The reasons for the near failure of Global are complex—partly the financing, partly the distribution system, partly the ambitious Canadian programming which sometimes fell short of its promise despite considerable originality. But the big question it raises is whether there is room, in terms of available advertising monies and audiences, for another TV network, despite the wealth in Southern Ontario with its heavy concentration of population. Even if Global Television succeeds, and it is important that it does, Canadian programming is still likely to remain in the minority throughout most of Canada as CATV spreads. Nor can the balance be redressed until wherever there are three American stations representing three distinct network services there are also three distinct Canadian stations, all programming 100 per cent Canadian. And that seems far beyond the economic resources of the country.

The discussion of available programming made no reference to programs on the CATV community channels, nor to educational stations of which Toronto now has the first in Canada. As yet, these have made no significant impact on the numbers of people viewing the commercial channels in Toronto, but they serve as a reminder that numbers are not the whole story. We must look also at the message and who receives it.

The Message

The 1968 Broadcasting Act requires the CBC to offer a "balanced service of information, enlightenment and entertainment for people of different ages, interests and tastes covering the whole range of programming in fair proportion."

Television

Defining and naming program categories, and allocating programs to them, is a slippery undertaking. Furthermore, the resulting figures do not come to life without a knowledge of the programs concerned; we discuss some programs later in more detail. Nevertheless, the following table does give an idea of the extent to which the CBC television schedules cater to all tastes in a balanced service, as required by the Act.

As we have noted, American programs attract large audiences which, in turn, attract advertising monies used to subsidize the more expensive Canadian programming.

The most significant figure in Table 1, perhaps, is the percentage of information programming on the network, just under 50 per cent, which is much more than any of the private American or Canadian commercial networks offer in peak viewing time. The Corporation has been criticized for the relatively low 6 per cent in arts, letters, and science programming, and the Commission, in *Radio Frequencies Are Public Property*, suggests that this type of programming should be substantially increased. However, the 6 per cent is almost double the figure of 1969-70. How far the CBC should go in this type of programming with minority appeal is again a matter of debate requiring justified and quantified targets against which the CBC performance can be measured.

As the French network has very limited capacity for the production of local programs outside Montreal, its national network service operates for 110 hours a week in contrast to the English network's 75 hours. Direct comparisons between Tables 1 and 2 cannot, therefore, be made. However, we can note again the high content of the information category and the relatively low percentage of arts, letters, and science. These program categories are, of course, very broad and not too much can be learned from them. We need a much closer analysis of the content of these programs, but very little systematic work has been done. Further comment is best tied in with a discussion of the receivers of the message.

Radio

In radio, the situation is very different. Although American signals penetrate most of the heavily populated parts of Canada, these signals, unlike those of television, have relatively small audiences. However, with the exception of the CBC, most Canadian stations rely heavily on recorded popular music, the great bulk of which is produced in the United States. The 1970 CRTC regulations require that of all music titles played, at least 30 per cent must be recorded in Canada, while 5 per cent must be written or composed by Canadians. The objective here is to stimulate a recording industry in Canada, and to provide an outlet for Canadian lyricists and composers.

Unlike private radio stations that rely mainly on recorded light music, interspersed with local news, sports, and talk

Table 1 ANALYSIS OF PROGRAM CONTENT OF THE CBC ENGLISH TV NETWORK IN A REPRESENTATIVE WINTER WEEK, 1973

Category	*Hours and Minutes* *Canadian*	*U.S.*	*Other Foreign*	*Total*	*%*
Information	31:40	5:00	0:30	37:10	49.3
Light Entertainment	10:45	14:00	3:00	27:45	37.0
Arts, Letters, and Science	3:15	—	1:00	4:15	5.7
Sports and Outdoors	6:00	—	—	6:00	8.0
Total Hours	51:40	19:00	4:30	75:10	100.0
%	68.7	25.3	6.0	100.0	

Source: CBC Annual Report, 1972-73.

Table 2 ANALYSIS OF PROGRAM CONTENT OF CBC FRENCH TELEVISION NETWORK IN A REPRESENTATIVE WINTER WEEK, 1973

Category	*Hours and Minutes* *Canadian*	*U.S.*	*French*	*Other Foreign*	*Total*	*%*
Information	31:10	1:30	1:00	—	33:40	30.6
Light Entertainment	20:45	23:00	7:45	9:00	60:30	54.7
Arts, Letters, and Science	3:00	—	—	1:30	4:30	4.1
Sports and Outdoors	11:40	—	—	—	11:40	10.6
Total Hours	66:35	24:30	8:45	10:30	110:20	100.0
%	60.3	22.2	7.9	9.5	100.0	

Source: CBC Annual Report, 1972-73.

shows, the CBC operates a radio network carrying 58 per cent information programming and another 20 per cent in the area of arts, letters, and science. This is supplemented by local programming. The FM network, available in only five main centres, but planned for further extension, has 68 per cent of its programming in the arts, letters, and science category; in fact, it is a gold mine of talks and documentaries, plus the best in music and radio drama. The French-language AM network carries about 57 per cent information programming and 30 per cent arts, letters, and science, while the one French FM station (located in Montreal) carries nearly 83 per cent arts, letters, and science.

The Receivers

All audience measurement techniques confirm the great attraction of U.S. stations to Canadians. Toronto has long exemplified this: for each half-hour between 7:00 p.m. and 11:00 p.m., the U.S. stations average more than a third of the half-hour viewing audience. We also saw that cable television is spreading one, two, three and more U.S. channels into areas where they were not previously available. The audience results are what we would expect from the Vancouver and Toronto experience.

The most dramatic case, perhaps, is London, Ontario. Without cable, U.S. signals in London are so weak they register hardly any off-air viewers at all. However, more than 80 per cent of all television viewing in London is on cable, with seven U.S. stations available to viewers. The result has been a loss of viewers to the local Canadian station from an 80 per cent weekly share of the audience throughout the day to about 45 per cent; the greatest gains go to the U.S. stations, which have a combined share of about 37 per cent.

Of the ten most popular programs in terms of audience size on the CBC national network, usually only two or three are Canadian and the rest are American. This is confirmed by a look at twenty programs and their audiences carried on the full CBC national network of 40 to 43

Table 3 SOME ENGLISH NATIONAL NETWORK PROGRAMS CARRIED BETWEEN 7:00 AND 11:00 P.M., MONDAY TO SUNDAY, IN THE 1972-73 WINTER SEASON

Program	*Type*	*Origin*	*Audience (in millions)*
Walt Disney	Children's	U.S.	4.4
All in the Family	Comedy	U.S.	3.5 to 3.9
M*A*S*H	Comedy	U.S.	3.0 to 3.4
The Waltons	Family drama	U.S.	"
Hockey Night	Sports	Canadian	"
The Beachcombers	Children's	Canadian	"
Partridge Family	Comedy	U.S.	"
National Dream	History	Canadian	2.5 to 2.9
Bugs Bunny	Children's	U.S.	"
Carol Burnett	Variety	U.S.	"
Cannon	Crime	U.S.	"
Tommy Hunter	Variety	Canadian	2.1 to 2.4
Mary Tyler Moore	Comedy	U.S.	"
Dick van Dyke	Comedy	U.S.	"
This Is the Law	Quiz	Canadian	"
Maude	Comedy	U.S.	"
The Collaborators	Crime	Canadian	2.0
The Irish Rovers	Variety	Canadian	"
Police Story	Crime	U.S.	"
CFL Football	Sports	Canadian	"

Source: CBC Annual Report, 1973-74.

stations in a week of the 1973-74 winter season. But at this point a qualitative factor, usually ignored, must be taken into account. All the American-produced programs in this list (and virtually all American produced programs carried on the CBC—see Table 1) are comedy, variety, or adventure programs—light entertainment programs designed to have as wide an audience appeal as possible. Further, just over 50 per cent of all light entertainment programs on the CBC national network (as we saw in Table 1) are American-produced. In contrast, nearly 43 per cent of the network schedule is made up of Canadian-produced information programming.

It is worth looking at some of the Canadian-produced information programming in more detail; following are ten programs selected from the 7:00 to 11:00 p.m. national network schedule for a typical week in January 1974. "Marketplace," a consumer program with an average audience of about 1.8 million, looked at fraudulent used car sales operations in Alberta, presented an economist's report on the 18 per cent Chargex interest rate, and discussed the function of egg marketing boards. Some 1.6 million people watched "The Nature of Things" which presented a half-hour of microscopic photography showing the world of bacteria, parasites, and predators living in the earth's "first inch." "Man Alive" presented to just over a million viewers the first of three programs subtitled "Life Before Birth," which interviewed pioneers in fetal research.

Other programs with audiences in excess of one million were "Up Canada," a satiric current affairs show featuring that week an interview with Malcolm Muggeridge; "This Land," with a profile of a 70-year-old film-maker who has been living and working in Canada's North; and the National Film Board series, "West," which profiled two women living in Alberta's Peace River district. Programs with smaller audiences on the national network were "In the Present Tense," which looked at "the fine art of government lying in a crisis"; "Some Honorable Members," a discussion with three Members of Parliament on the James Bay power project; and a documentary Profile of the retiring Governor General, Roland Michener. Two other information programs, "CBC Newsmagazine's" report on the crisis in Britain and "The World at War" were seen on a limited network of CBC stations.

All these programs except the last were Canadian-produced and all have a high information content. It is a sad fact that throughout the English-speaking world, such information programs tend to have significantly smaller audiences than do purely entertainment programs. (There are exceptions. The CBC's "The National Dream" about the building of the Canadian Pacific Railway attracted up to nearly 3 million viewers.) If, then, we wish to compare the audience sizes of Canadian and American programs, we must take this factor—the type of program—into account, remembering that such information programs constitute a high proportion of the CBC production. Not only do American programs outnumber Canadian programs, but also the great majority of the American programs are designed to have a mass appeal. If we take this into account, especially in the CBC schedules, then clearly in places such as Toronto and Vancouver, the total audiences attracted to American programs will tend to be larger than those attracted to Canadian programs. And this is in spite of the fact that many individual Canadian programs will compete successfully for audiences with individual American programs.

With the spread of cable television, audiences to Canadian English-language programs and the number of Canadian programs available may well diminish. Canadians will be "talking" more with outsiders than with other Canadians. Using our early definition of a nation, and applying it solely in terms of television viewing, the outlook for the "Canadian nation" appears to be bleak.

Nevertheless, there are brighter views for the future. First, television is only one of many types of communication involved in defining a nation, although private broadcasters, deploring the number of regulations imposed on them, have claimed that too often the whole burden seems to be placed on television. Secondly, the basic assumption in our analytical framework is at least debatable. All measurement techniques and all surveys show that American programs are very popular with Canadian viewers. Yet, though Toronto has been open to American signals for many years, there is no evidence that Torontonians are any the less Canadian for it. The point at issue is whether watching American television programs, which are mainly of the mass-appeal type, alters the value structures, the opinions, and the information of the viewers in a way that reduces their sense of possessing a "Canadian identity." To state the problem is to illustrate its difficulties. The nature of the values, opinions, and information that make up a "Canadian sense of identity" have never been isolated and stated precisely enough to make research possible. In fact, they probably cannot be stated, nor can the questions be treated analytically.

In addition, the assumption may also be debatable that if Canadian programs are written, acted, composed, and produced by Canadians, they will carry with them a distinctively Canadian sense of place, be concerned with distinctively Canadian institutions and symbols, which will lead, in some sense, to a "distinctively Canadian consciousness" in their audiences. A mountain of regulations, involving millions of dollars, rests in part on this assumption, though the hard evidence for it is very limited indeed, and even then of the common sense variety.

In 1962 the CBC made a study of attitudes of the Canadian public to television.[7] Many fundamental changes in broadcasting have occurred since then, but two points were confirmed in a 1972 unpublished study. First, the study showed that viewers could watch many American programs, including those on American stations, yet still prefer Canadian to American stations. The two things are not mutually exclusive. The attitude of many people to American stations may well be that, while pleasant to watch for entertainment, and while access to their signals is very desirable for that reason, they are not important as a source of information, and do not effectively alter the opinions and the value structures of their Canadian audiences.

Secondly, the study showed that while CBC programs found audiences in all major educational and occupational categories, and while those who preferred the CBC stations to American stations were certainly not limited to any educational élite, nevertheless, there was a tendency for those who preferred the CBC to have more education than those who preferred other stations; also they tended to be senior people in white-collar jobs and they tended to be somewhat older. As for program tastes, those who preferred CBC stations were less critical of CBC programs for being too heavy and serious; they felt their preferred station did a good job in drama; and they had a higher regard for discussions of current affairs than did those who preferred independent or American stations.

This in turn raises other questions: Are those who prefer CBC stations more socially aware, more politically active, more inclined to be active in clubs, unions, and associations, more apt to take their information and opinions from the mass media and spread them throughout the community? Do they have a greater impact on national and local affairs, and in the business of their primary groups? Unfortunately, there is virtually no hard data on this.

CBC research has done some work on program effects, including a study (through the national panel) of the effects of two CBC network television programs about pollution.[8] Prior to a program on pollution, "The Dying Waters," the study measured the extent of agreement or disagreement of half of the CBC national panel members (randomly selected) on three statements touching on public concern with pollution. For example, one of these statements was: "Towns and cities should be compelled to treat their sewage to prevent water pollution, even if it means higher taxes to pay for it." The other half of the panel was not pre-tested, but was sent questionnaires after the program. Both these groups were then subdivided into those who watched the program and those who did not. (Further details, and the reasons for selecting this out of various possible methods, are given in the study itself.) The responses of all four groups to the three questions were then collated.

The results showed that "the program quite obviously had a strong effect on its viewers," with those who viewed the program showing an increased concern with pollution problems, while non-viewers showed no significant before and after differences. Other questions were designed to measure increased awareness of, rather than concern with, pollution. As hypothesized, among those who viewed the program there was a significant reduction in the number of "no opinion/undecided" answers after the program, showing an increased awareness of the problem.

The effects measured were short-term. A similar test with another program on pollution, "The Deadly Mist," was designed to measure long-term effects. With qualifications, the second study suggests "a decay in concern about pesticides in the long term."

Clearly, we cannot generalize very far on the basis of one study. But, along with general comments by Panel members and their responses to specific questions in their regular diaries, the study indicates that public affairs and documentary programs do indeed alter the attitudes and the information of many viewers at least for a time. (About 1.75 million people watched "The Dying Waters.") Presumably these changes would be smaller, and in a different direction, were Canadians entirely dependent on American channels with their preponderance of entertainment programs. If that is not a very spectacular conclusion, it provides some objective justification for a belief in the importance of maintaining a Canadian broadcasting system.

French-Language Television

About 81 per cent of all French Canadians live in the province of Quebec; about 46 per cent of all French Canadians live within range of the Montreal French-language stations, with another substantial number capable of picking up the Montreal stations via CATV systems. Most French Canadians, then, share a common provincial political system, whereas English Canadians are divided among ten such provincial systems, plus that of the North. French Canadians share a common origin and over 400 years of history within French-speaking or bilingual institutions whereas English Canadians, originating from all over Europe and the world, have often had to subordinate their mother tongue within English-French language institutions. Most French Canadians live within one geographic region, while English Canadians live across the country in regions and cities with vastly differing social and economic problems. Above all, the possession of a minority language is a bulwark of the French Canadians against incursions of the majority culture, though by no means an impregnable one.

There are, of course, important divisions within French Canadian society. Nevertheless, in contrast to English Canada, French Canada can be described as a close-knit society. This is reflected in CBC French network programming and its audiences. Programs set in Montreal, such as the comedy show, "Moi et l'autre," and "Rue des Pignons," can appeal to the direct experience of most French Canadians in their characterization, their plots, their locale, and their symbols. Montreal personalities, *chansonniers* and actors are automatically "national" figures in a way that Toronto personalities may not be. Quebec political and social problems can be discussed on national French-language radio and television, as they directly affect the vast majority of the audience, whereas such problems in English Canada must be discussed primarily on local or regional network programs and have little national interest.

These factors of French Canadian programming attract much larger audiences than programming in English-speaking Canada. "Moi et l'autre," for example, consistently each week reached around 70 per cent of all French Canadians. *Feuilletons,* from "La Famille Plouffe" in the 1950s to "Rue des Pignons" today, have consistently captured more than half of their potential audiences. (*Feuilletons* are programs that are characterized by a plot carry-over from week to week and range from fairly light comedy to melodrama.)

It is worth speculating on the importance of Montreal in French Canadian broadcasting, since so much of both the programming and the total audience comes from this area. Commentators have often pointed out that urbanization (in the sense of a drift to the cities) and industrialization of the labour force (in the sense of a drift from primary to secondary industry) have been increasing in Quebec since the early 1900s. It has also been claimed that this physical movement of French Canadians to the cities and the secondary industries was for a long time not accompanied to a significant extent by a corresponding change in the dominant values of French Canadian society. The historian, Michel Brunet, in "Trois Dominantes de la Pensée," argues that the values of an agricultural society—not just love of rural life, but an active hostility to the contemporary industrial age—dominated the State, the Church, and the educational system in French Canada for a hundred years, with traces still apparent in the 1950s.[9] This philosophy of *agriculturalisme* did not prevent urbanization and industrialization, but it allegedly did retard French Canadians in acquiring the educational and occupational skills, even the motivation, to control and take full economic advantage of these changes.

Radio and then television have no doubt helped to sweep away these values, and to substitute new ones, especially the values centred around middle-class Montreal. This does not necessarily mean that separatist ideas are being expressed; it does mean that there is a stronger and more vigorous expression of French Canada not only in political terms, but also in drama such as the *téléromans,* music such as that of the *chansonniers,* and variety programs. French Canadians do talk a great deal with other French Canadians via radio and television.

English and French Radio

Radio listening is mainly functional in nature. For instance, radio is used most heavily around breakfast time when most people are on the move, with a daily half-hour average of 17 per cent of all people in Canada listening between 6:00 and 9:00 a.m. They listen to, particularly on private stations, daily news and weather with a heavy local emphasis, and light music. Audiences fall steadily throughout the day, with rises at noon and late afternoon, providing a background of music, news, and phone-in shows. Much radio programming is designed for young people, since many now have transistor radios and are independent of the family for their listening. By evening, when television viewing increases, radio audiences fall to an average half-hour audience of 4 per cent between 7:00 p.m. and 1:00 a.m.

As we saw earlier, CBC schedules are markedly different from those of the private stations, having a much more varied content. In addition, the programs of the CBC network, in particular the newscasts, have a national and international emphasis. In radio, Canadians do talk to Canadians, but apart from the CBC network programming which is listened to by a minority of total radio audiences, the talk is largely concerned with local matters or national and provincial matters as they affect the local scene.

The Two Cultures

We suggested that radio and television have probably played an important role in strengthening French Canadian nationalism. Those English Canadians who consider this nationalism a divisive force in Canadian society will deplore such an effect. But those who see French Canadian nationalism as being contained in, and sustained by, modified federalism may find a more constructive role for radio and television than the first view suggests.

The rapid extension of CBC French radio and television stations outside Quebec has a triple role here. It links the isolated pockets of French Canadians with the majority in Quebec as English Canadians in Quebec are linked with the rest of Canada. This means that the French/English cleavage does not totally coincide with the political cleavage of "Québec et les autres." Cross-cutting cleavages to modify the effects of cleavage is an old and plausible thesis.

Secondly, CBC French radio and television also provide evidence of the French fact in areas such as Toronto, Edmonton, and Vancouver where the French population constitutes a small percentage of the whole. The affair of CJBC, an English-language station in Toronto converted to French in 1964 with an ensuing large and vocal protest from English listeners and others, deserves study. CJBC audiences are today quite small, but there is evidence that many English-speaking Torontonians listen for the music, and consequently experience French-language elements. Response to a CBC Vancouver French-language station suggests that it may be playing a role in the extension of bilingualism.

Lastly, French-language radio stations outside Quebec already provide some input to the French network. The amount of this input should increase for both radio and television, as production facilities become available and as the reorganization now underway in the CBC gives Montreal network headquarters the responsibility for these "outlying" stations. Depending in part on the amount, this input may help provide Quebec audiences with a wider Canadian horizon than the Quebec borders.

On the programming side, the CBC was criticized at its 1974 network licence hearings before the CRTC for not "bridging the gap" sufficiently between the two cultures, although various techniques had been tried to accomplish this. Special bilingual programs have not been successful in attracting large or appreciative audiences. However, the exchange of dubbed programs between the two networks; the exchange of personalities; the use of French Canadian music on English stations; the co-production of programs—all these are techniques that the CBC television services have not used sufficiently in the past (though the radio networks' record is much better) and that they must use more in the future. In addition, programs about the two main language groups, about Canada as a whole and its regions and provinces, as well as about minority groups are basic to bridging the gap.

Conclusion

We defined a nation as a group of people who transact more with one another than they do with people outside the group. In simple quantitative broadcasting terms, the future may well show English Canadians communicating much more with Americans than among themselves, at least on television. French Canadians now talk much more among themselves than they talk with English Canadians. Only by increasing the number of stations and the Canadian content of those stations will the balance be redressed in English-speaking Canada, and as we have already seen, the extent to which either of these courses can be pursued is limited by economics. Only by increasing on both English and French stations the number of programs about the other cultural groups and about Canada as a whole, by increasing the interchange between the networks of programs, ideas, and personalities, and by the extension of the networks of both languages to cover all their peoples will the interchange between the two main language groups reach a satisfactory level. These objectives are shared by the CRTC, charged with supervising and regulating the broadcasting system, and by the CBC, charged with providing a comprehensive national service in both languages.

To be effective, analysis and prediction concerning the role of broadcasting in Canadian social and political life must go beyond counting how many people watch and listen to programs. There is much room for analysis of program content—for example, whether the program is purely entertainment or whether it contains information; for analysis of the characteristics of various audiences—for example, whether the audiences to minority appeal programs are more socially and politically active than the average audience; and for analysis of the effects of the programs on their audiences—whether they in fact alter information, opinions, and value structures, for how long, and in what directions.

In all these areas, the hard-core evidence is slight, but with the onrush of technology, especially with the growing incursion of cable television and the launching of a Canadian communications satellite, the Canadian broadcasting authorities cannot wait for exhaustive studies into their sociological effects. For the foreseeable future, we can expect more legislative and regulatory planning of the Canadian broadcasting system based on the assumption of the 1968 Act that the system can and should "safeguard, enrich and strengthen the cultural, political, social and economic fabric of Canada."

1. Frank W. Peers, *The Politics of Canadian Broadcasting, 1929-1951* (Toronto: University of Toronto Press, 1969).
2. Bill C-163, *Broadcasting Act*, House of Commons, March 7, 1968, Part 1, 2 (b).
3. For a short discussion of Canada and World War I see W.L. Morton, *The Canadian Identity* (Madison: Univeristy of Wisconsin Press, 1965).
4. See, for instance, Karl W. Deutsch in *The Integration of Political Communities,* edited by Philip E. Jacob and James V. Toscano (Philadelphia: P.J. Lippincott, 1964).
5. Rural areas are defined as communities of less than 1,000 people in *Canada Year Book,* 1969.
6. CRTC, *Radio Frequencies Are Public Property, Public Announcement and Decision on the Application for Renewal of the Canadian Broadcasting Corporation's Television and Radio Licence; CRTC Decision 74-70,* Ottawa, March 31, 1974, p. 39.
7. "What the Canadian Public Thinks of the CBC: An Empirical Study of the Public Attitudes towards the Canadian Broadcasting Corporation and to Certain Other Aspects of Broadcasting in Canada," CBC Research, February 1963.
8. "On Measuring the Effects of Television," CBC Research, May 1970, TV/70/4.
9. Michel Brunet, *La Présence anglaise et les Canadiens* (Montreal: Beauchemin, 1950).

Mass Communications in a Canadian City

ANDREW D. CAMERON and JOHN A. HANNIGAN

Introduction

The present article is an attempt to explore historical and present patterns of mass media institutions and their interrelationships in a typical Canadian city. Beginning with a socio-demographic portrait, we examine the histories of mass communications institutions, their present patterns and then suggest some of the resulting effects upon their audiences. Although we are examining in depth only one Canadian city, many of the elements shown at work in this microcosm may in fact reflect forces and processes operating within the larger system.

The Community of London

London, Ontario is a medium-sized city in the centre of southwestern Ontario. Its population of 216,000 makes it the twelfth largest city in Canada, and the fourth largest in Ontario.[1] From pioneer days, London has served as a regional centre for government, education, the courts, transportation and communications. The University of Western Ontario, a teacher's college, a college of education, and a community college are all situated in London, as are the seats of both Roman Catholic and Anglican dioceses.

The city has traditionally been a major connecting point on transportation routes: it is on the western section of the province-wide Highway 401; it is the mid-point on Air Canada flights between Cleveland and Toronto; and it is also a major stop on the Windsor-Detroit-Toronto railway routes. London is equidistant—approximately 120 miles—from both Toronto and Detroit and thus it might be instructive to consider it as a point at which Canadian and American communications systems have met.

London is often described as "conservative," and the city has continued to live under the shadow of its British heritage. Not surprisingly, streets, parks, bridges, the city market, and even a summer festival bear names borrowed from London, England. Demographically, the major portion of the population is of Anglo-Saxon stock. The next largest ethnic group is German, with pockets of Dutch, Italian, and French population.[2] Unlike Toronto or Windsor, the city has no Italian ward, or in fact any other significant ethnic population cluster. London's population is predominantly white collar, middle-income, and middle class, and most blue collar workers qualify as skilled labour.[3] The picture of London that arises then is that of a tranquil Canadian city with roots extending well back into Ontario's past. The description of its mass communications system should be considered in that context.

The Print Media in London: Newspapers

Historical Factors[4]

The first really successful newspaper in London was the *Canadian Free Press,* founded by William Sutherland in 1849.[5] In contrast to its political viewpoint today, the paper at that time was of a Reform or Liberal persuasion. Newspaper publishers in these early days had a much more direct audience "feedback" system than today; when the *Canadian Free Press* supported the Reformers in the 1849 Lord Elgin Rebellion Losses Bill, a mob burned its quarters to the ground.[6] A new building was erected in short order, and the paper remained successful in winning its circulation war with the conservative *London Times.* However, losses incurred in an expensive libel suit, combined with the mounting costs of a tri-weekly publication experiment in 1851, and a daily experiment in 1852, forced Sutherland to sell the *Free Press* to Josiah Blackburn, ancestor of the present owner.[7]

From the first, the purchase of the *Free Press* proved to be a financially astute move. In 1853, the Great Western Railroad reached London and brought a boom in land speculation, building, and population increases. The railroad and the adoption of the telegraph system enhanced London's communication links with the outside world. Blackburn was able to get important news from Europe by telegraph, as the ships docked in New York every day. Because of this, in 1855 the *Free Press* began daily publication as the *London Free Press and Daily Western Advertiser,* in addition to publishing the weekly *Canadian Free Press.* The *London Free Press* at this time was in competition with the *London Herald and Western Advertiser*, a daily launched by local Conservatives which replaced the ailing *London Times.* Curiously enough, London still had a town crier at this time, but his office was becoming increasingly superfluous.

Meanwhile, the Blackburn family were expanding their ownership of the communications media in Upper Canada. The family bought the *Chatham Chronicle*, and then, in 1871, Josiah Blackburn went into partnership with William Southam to form the London Free Press Printing Company. In 1871, Blackburn also founded the *Toronto Mail*, a staunchly conservative organ and his fifth newspaper, although its establishment did not at that time alter the editorial policy of the *Free Press.* In 1890, Josiah Blackburn died and Walter J. Blackburn, his eldest son, became owner. The *Free Press* at this time had a morning and evening circulation of 60 per cent of the city's population.[8] The *London Advertiser*, its only real competition, was a morning rural paper, while the *Free Press* was essentially an evening urban paper. This competition was destined to end. The downfall of the *Advertiser* came when it supported the Liberals in the 1917 election, a move interpreted as "treason" by conservative London. The paper was finally sold to the *London Free Press* and Blackburn ran it as a rival newspaper until its closing in 1936. The same year, upon the death of his father, the present owner, Walter Blackburn Jr., became the publisher and manager of the family media holdings.

Despite its early controversial years, the *Free Press* had by 1936 become strongly Conservative. This was mainly due to the political persuasion of editor Arthur

Ford, a leading Ontario Conservative, member of the Hunt Club and the Board of Governors of the University of Western Ontario, and confidant of Leslie Frost, at that time the Premier of Ontario. The *Free Press* remained closely associated with the Conservative party until 1962, when it refused to support Diefenbaker in the federal election of that year.

By 1971, the *Free Press* had become, editorially, a "middle-of-the-road" newspaper with a more evident concern for civil rights. For example, in February of 1971, the *Free Press* in an editorial defended the right of the American "yippie" Abbie Hoffman to enter Canada and appear on the television program "Under Attack," to be filmed at the University. This position was in opposition to that of Otto Lang, the Minister in charge of immigration, who twice barred Hoffman from entering Canada. Syndicated columnists carried by the *Free Press* in 1971 ranged from Conservative Dalton Camp to Quebec separatist journalist P. F. Michael King. However, the *Free Press* in 1971 had no columnists who regularly wrote on local political affairs. An important addition to the paper has been the thrice-weekly "Sound Off" column which has acted as an urban ombudsman, helping Londoners cope with problems ranging from defective merchandise to government inaction.

Newspaper Circulation In London

In the community of London, as elsewhere, the newspaper has traditionally been the most important information medium, with the largest news organization. Of all the local media, the newspaper alone provides both up-to-date daily information, and in-depth interpretation and background for these news stories.

The dominance of the *Free Press* in the London market area was nearly complete by 1970. In the county of Middlesex, of which London is the main centre, 65,741 people purchase the *Free Press* daily. Since there are approximately 76,500 households in the county, nearly six of every seven households receive the *London Free Press*.[9]

In addition, approximately 7,000 copies of out-of-town newspapers are sold daily in London. Approximately 6,500 of these are Toronto newspapers, with the *Globe and Mail* selling 5,436 copies.[10] The University of Western Ontario *Gazette,* a student-produced, free circulation publication, of particular interest to students and faculty, has a circulation of about 15,000 twice a week. Five times in the late 1960's, weeklies have been started, but none has lasted more than two years. Most of these were little more than advertising circulars distributed free of charge from house to house. Only the now defunct *London Weekly* took a strong editorial position, and this was most often as a voice of opposition to the Blackburn interests.

In the seven-county area around London there are 34 weekly newspapers. These do not penetrate the London metropolitan market and have a very small circulation.

Control of the London Free Press

The *London Free Press* is still a family business. Walter Blackburn, the publisher, holds 73.35 per cent of voting control in the London Free Press Printing Company Limited; the Southam Press, a newspaper chain which controls the *Ottawa Citizen, Calgary Herald, Hamilton Spectator, Vancouver Province, Winnipeg Tribune,* and *Edmonton Journal* among its many and varied holdings, has 24.75 per cent of voting control.[11] This association with the *Free Press* dates back to the previous century, when William Southam, founder of the Southam chain, rose from an apprentice at the *Free Press* to a minority stockholder in the company. Effective control of the daily press in London, then, rests with one man, Walter Blackburn. Blackburn has served in a wide number of executive posts and directorships, ranging from a directorship of the Canadian Daily Newspapers Publishers Association, to the University of Western Ontario Board of Governors. Socially, his background includes membership in the London Hunt Club, which his newspaper has criticized for discriminatory policies, the Masons, and the Delta Upsilon Fraternity. Blackburn admits that he keeps "daily editorial control" over the *Free Press,* leaving the radio and television stations more freedom of operation. He opposes government regulation and control of the media, while at the same time he acknowledges the need for "responsible media." For example, with Blackburn's support, the *London Free Press* is a participating newspaper in the self-regulating Ontario Press Council.

The Issue of Monopoly

There is a recognized pattern of newspaper ownership in the United States of only one publisher to a community in all except the larger cities. This situation is accepted by the American public.[12] To a large extent this is also true in Canada, but media owners argue that there are alternatives. Walter Blackburn and the *London Free Press* hold that any characterization of the *Free Press* as monopolistic is in fact only superficial. Their reasoning is based on four points: (1) Londoners have wide exposure to national news and commentaries and to the alternative newspapers from outside the city; (2) radio and television stations (there are eleven of the latter available on cable) give some coverage to community issues; (3) the *Free Press* itself takes great pains to ensure that its reporting is objective, and that Londoners are given a chance to be heard, even on matters in which they are in opposition to the editorial position of the paper. Parties criticized are consulted prior to publication and the editorial page is regulated only by the laws of libel and slander and by the contingencies of space; (4) as Blackburn has claimed before the Davey Committee, the University of Western Ontario *Gazette* represents a viable alternate to the *London Free Press.*

This optimistic view of the London situation might be challenged. One suspects that there is a major danger in any quasi-monopolistic situation in the mass media, for no matter what are the intentions and policies of the owners in question, the writers and editors of the newspaper may develop a fixed frame of reference, and this will be the only one available to newspaper readers.

The "John Dickins Affair" brought such a potential danger before the London public. John Dickins, Blackburn's CFPL "Open Line" host, terminated his association with the station in October 1969. Claiming that he was "fired," Dickins wrote a long letter to the *London Free Press* which was highly critical of the Blackburn interests. On October 20, 1969, this letter appeared in the *Free Press* in severely edited form. The letter was accompanied by an editor's note which read:

> As with all letters to the editor, this one has been edited to conform with this newspaper's standing policy requiring letters to be brief and to avoid possible libel.[13]

In this instance the only individuals who could have been "libeled" by the letter were Blackburn and his managers. A significant question arises out of this incident: In cases where criticism of personnel and policy of the media outlet itself is involved, can the station or publication rightly function in the roles of both plaintiff and judge?[14]

The Print Media in London: Magazines

According to the Davey Report, in 1969 Canadians bought nearly four times as many American magazines as Canadian ones. This trend was found to be especially typical of London where the ten top selling magazines on newsstands were: (1) *TV Guide* (2) *Woman's Day* (3) *Family Circle* (4) *Playboy* (5) *Redbook* (6) *National Enquirer* (7) *Reader's Digest* (8) *Better Homes and Gardens* (9) *Parents Magazine* (10) *McCalls.*[15] When respondents in a London survey conducted by Dr. B. D. Singer of the University of Western Ontario were asked which magazines they subscribed to, the top ten magazines were: (1) *Reader's Digest* (2) *Time* (3) *Chatelaine* (4) *Maclean's* (5) *National Geographic* (6) *Life* (7) *Playboy* (8) *Better Homes and Gardens* (9) *TV Guide* (10) *Parents Magazine.*[16] With American magazines occupying from 80 to 100 per cent of the ranks of the top ten magazines, it is clear how dominant American influence is in this critical sector of the mass media.

Radio

Historical Factors

Radio broadcasting began in London in 1922 when Arthur Blackburn, Walter Blackburn's father and an amateur radio buff, founded radio station CJGC. In the early 1920s, Hobbs Langford, a local merchant, operated a second and smaller radio station in London, but it closed in 1927. CJGC eventually became a 10,000 watt station and achieved a certain prominence in Canada. However, in a 1932 paper on radio broadcasting in London, W. R. Hickey confirmed that Londoners then listened to American stations more often than to the local radio station.[17] This factor, combined with losses in advertising revenues during the Depression, forced Blackburn to sell CJGC together with its new transmitter to a group of American investors. The call letters of the station were changed to CKLW (LW standing for London and Windsor), and most of the coverage the station provided was now directed away from London to the Windsor-Detroit area. In 1970 the Canadian Radio-Television Commission directed that CKLW be sold to predominantly Canadian buyers, a move intended to shift the focus of the station back to Canada. Subsequently, John Bassett, then publisher of the *Toronto Telegram*, and the CBC agreed to purchase the station, with Bassett interests holding 75 per cent control and the CBC 25 per cent.

In 1934, the Blackburn family started a new station, CFPL (the call letters FPL stood for Free Press London); this small 500 watt station became in 1936 a CBC affiliate. CFPL, at this time, was only the third most popular radio station in the city, with two American stations placed first and second.[18]

In 1947, the London Free Press Printing Company received a licence to broadcast on the FM band. For the first three years, it carried the programming of CFPL-AM, but by 1951, it had begun to devote several hours to separate programming.

Present Control of London Radio Stations

CJOE—Joe McManus CJOE is wholly owned by London millionaire Joe McManus. McManus is a Roman Catholic with high school education, who has been markedly successful in selling fuel oil, discount gasoline, and automobiles. In spite of his undeniable financial qualifications, McManus, unlike Jeffery and Blackburn, is outside the circle of London's social elite, and representative of a new force in the city. A number of media professionals predicted in 1966 when the station commenced operations that CJOE could not succeed since McManus seldom participates in the world of professional media operators. His operation of the station seems to be characterized by frequent resignations and changes of station managers and key personnel. The station format appears to be a repetition of that of other stations. Thus, there does not appear to be any new or unique function played by CJOE.[19]

CKSL—Joseph Jeffery CKSL is jointly owned by Vincent Regan, a Toronto barrister, and Joseph Jeffery, a London lawyer and financial executive. Jeffery's family has been established in London's business and social elite for most of this century. After studying law, Joseph Jeffery succeeded his father as president of London Life. In addition, he became a director of a number of "blue chip" firms ranging from the Toronto Dominion Bank to Hiram Walker. In 1970, he became Chairman of the Board of Governors of the University of Western Ontario. He is a member of the London Hunt Club and the prestigious Toronto Cricket Club.

Jeffery's interest in establishing a radio station had three bases: (1) like Walter Blackburn, he was an enthusiastic ham radio operator; (2) as a Liberal supporter, he wished to give the party a radio voice in Conservative London; (3) he professed a desire to provide an alternative to the Blackburn media monopoly. In 1956, with Regan backing 50 per cent of the venture, Jeffery established London Broadcasters Limited and was successful in obtaining a radio licence for station CKSL. His interest in broadcasting has not stopped at CKSL. For a time he owned a large portion of a London community antenna system but sold his interest in the firm prior to a CRTC decision which limited ownership of other media by cable operators within the area served by the cable system. In addition, he has long contemplated establishing a second newspaper in London but has realized that it would not be financially feasible.

CFPL CFPL AM and FM are owned and operated by the London Free Press Printing Company. This means that the dominant interest belongs to Walter Blackburn, who controls 74.02 per cent of the shares. Another 24.98 per cent is controlled by the Southam Press interests. This is essentially the same corporate arrangement as at the *London Free Press.*[20]

Programming

In general format, London radio stations are essentially uniform. The broadcasting day consists of a constant updating of news, weather, traffic reports, sports reports, and other such information. The time between these announcements is filled with recorded music, usually of a "contemporary" appeal; that is, the stations are engaged in selling the newest ephemeral record, which is the pattern of almost all North American radio music programming. The most striking area of difference between the London radio stations has been in the nature of their call-in shows, in great part the result of the "personalities" who moderate these shows.

The pioneer call-in program in London was CFPL's "Open Line" developed by John Dickins. Dickins projected an essentially accommodating image and the program was oriented towards solving such everyday problems as finding a lost dog or ridding a garage of a wasp's nest. In 1969, Dickins began to inject social criticism into the "Open Line" program and in October of 1969 his contract was not renewed. Dickins was replaced by Bill Brady, at that time one of the most popular of CFPL's broadcasters. With Brady, the old policy of "accommodate everyone" was again followed.

CKSL had operated a call-in show run by Ed Blake, a broadcaster whose tone was sometimes a little sharp and abrupt. In March of 1971, several days after CFPL announced that they would produce a new evening call-in program, in addition to the morning show, CKSL management withdrew the Ed Blake program.[21] This left CFPL as the lone station with call-in programming.

CJOE also produced a radio talk program, "Action Line," which was begun by John Dickins after his departure from CFPL. While Dickins was employed at CJOE, "Action Line" was generally controversial and marked by Dickins' frequent attacks on what he termed the "London establishment." Dickins was with CJOE only briefly, and after his departure the program became similar to CFPL's "Open Line." In December of 1970, CJOE dropped "Action Line" due to poor ratings, leaving CFPL alone with six hours of this programming.

Music

Music on all London radio stations is designed to have the widest appeal. CFPL broadcasts a combination of pop and rock music which it terms "adult-contemporary." CKSL has consistently appealed to the country music audience. However, station executives recognized that this was resulting in both continuing low ratings and a "hillbilly" image, and country music is now limited to evenings. CKSL had earlier launched a symphonic music format in the evenings called "Ventures in Music" but said that low ratings resulted in its demise.

CJOE has undergone as many changes in its music format as in its station personnel. McManus originally applied for a licence for a country music station but his application was not approved until the format was changed to a more conventional one. After the first months of operation, CJOE began to play pop music and with the coming of John Dickins shifted again to rock music. Upon the cancellation of "Action Line," this format was extended to 24 hours per day.

In London, there is a demand for classical music but none of the AM stations serves this need. CFPL-FM presents such music, but only in the late evening.[22] In addition, FM cable now provides access to two university stations from Michigan which broadcast classical music through some of the daytime hours.

The John Dickins Affair

The rift between Dickins and the CFPL management apparently had two causes, CFPL management claimed that Dickins was asking a salary which was far too ambitious. (Dickins said that CFPL had been underpaying him for years while it profited by his contribution.) Dickins claimed the other cause may have been his newly-found "liberal conscience" which led him to take stands on local issues which often ran counter to those of the station management and ownership he represented.[23]

There were a number of issues on which Dickins had disagreed with CFPL management. In Dickins' letter of October 20, 1969 to the *Free Press* he pointed out what he thought to be the two major instances in which his opinions were in opposition to those of management. "Mr. Brown's displeasure was aroused most by my stand on the police raid on 80 Maple St. last August, and by the jailing of 17 young people (many with money in their pockets) on vagrancy charges. He did not like my speaking of it as a travesty of justice."[24] And "Mr. Blackburn objected most to my outspoken support for the U.W.O. and Fanshawe students' anti-bomb demonstration at the Sarnia Bluewater bridge." In addition, Dickins claims to have disagreed with management on four other issues: (1) he strongly opposed the imposition of jail sentences on first-offence shoplifters, especially mothers on welfare; (2) he supported freer marijuana laws; (3) he took a "dovish" stand on the war in Viet Nam; (4) he criticized acceptance by the station of commercials from a "questionable" door-to-door carpet sales agency.[25]

In a letter to the *Free Press* Dickins described three instances in which he believed the Blackburn organization withheld facts: first, listeners to CFPL "Open Line" were given no indication that Dickins was no longer the "Open Line" moderator. According to Dickins: "On Thursday morning October 16, Bill Brady appeared on the 'Open Line' and did not mention my absence. In fact, he did not mention my name or even his own. Listeners who did phone the program to inquire about my absence were not permitted to go on the air."[26] Secondly, the initial CFPL handout to the *Free Press* on the matter mentioned only that Dickins had resigned in order to devote more time to the broadcasting school which he managed in his leisure time. Dickins claimed that he had asked that it be announced that he was fired. Thirdly, the letter which John Dickins wrote to the *Free Press* explaining his position was edited. However, these charges were in fact printed in an article on page three of the *London Free Press,* which does argue against Dickins' complaint of *Free Press* censorship.

Television

History

In 1952 the Canadian government announced that it had authorized receipt of applications for privately-owned television stations in the London area. The London Free Press Printing Company made the only application, and it was approved, despite the formal opposition before the licencing board of CHLO, a radio station situated in St. Thomas, a small city twenty miles from London. On November 28, 1953, CFPL commenced broadcasting as the second privately-owned television station in Canada. From this time, CFPL has been a CBC affiliate, and 53.8 per cent of prime time viewing is CBC.[27]

The CRTC has recently opened the way for the development of another television station in London by freeing channel 6 for licence application. Since CFCA in Kitchener, sixty miles from London, is a CTV affiliate it would be economically problematic to set up another CTV station in London. In addition, the heavy initial investment for equipment and program purchases makes an independent station unlikely. On the other hand, if the station were to be a CBC outlet, financing and programming would be aided by the larger network, and this seems the more logical choice. This situation might incidentally be of financial benefit to CFPL. With the establishment of a CBC station, CFPL could become an independent station with greater freedom. This might result in greater use of mass-appeal American productions or, alternatively, in more local productions. CFPL has generally engaged in an extensive amount of locally-produced programming, for example, a three-part series on the archaeological endeavours of Dr. Wilfred Jury in the Huronia district of Ontario, and a medical education series for doctors, both of which have been highly praised. CFPL has the technical equipment and the staff with which to become a successful independent station.[28]

Audiences

Without television cable, Londoners can receive clearly only one television station, CFPL. However, if one has cable, as over 80 per cent of London homes do, it is possible to receive ten other stations, eight of which are American (one educational) and two Canadian. With cable, one can also receive channel 13, the cablecast station. In terms of weekly circulation CFPL has a "weekly reach" of 91 per cent; CKCO has 71 per cent;[29] two Erie, Pennsylvania stations, WICU and WSEE, have 43 per cent and 42 per cent respectively, and CHCH in Hamilton has a "weekly reach" of 38 per cent.[30]

Cable

Television cable service has had a marked effect on the media consumption of the community. The city was one of the pioneers of cable T.V., with two systems dating from 1962. Cable television developed in London out of geographic necessity, as London is situated in a valley and consequently is unable to pick up American television stations from Erie, Pennsylvania, a city located across Lake Erie from London. To solve this problem, E. R. Jarmain, owner of a local city cleaning business, erected a large antenna and sold "hook-ups" to his neighbours. The cable business, now operated by Jarmain's son, who is also chairman of the Canadian Cable Television Association, has grown by leaps and bounds until today, London has the highest proportion of households subscribing to cable in the country. The Jarmain Company, London T.V. Cable Ltd., has 34,988 subscribers, while Maclean-Hunter T.V. Cable has 11,000.[31]

The charge for subscribing to cable television is five dollars per month, while the addition of FM radio cable costs an additional $1.25 per month. London has been one of the first communities to receive programs initiated by cable operators, called "cablecast." The community channel has broadcast a wide variety of shows ranging from figure skating championships to reading aloud for the blind, and among those who have produced shows are the Children's Psychiatric Research Institute and the Department of Labour.

One notable effect of cable television in London has been to reduce the audience for CFPL, according to a brief prepared by the station for the Davey Committee.[32] Those who are turning away from CFPL are turning to American channels. One study showed that in London, non-cable users viewed Canadian stations 97.7 per cent of the time and American stations 2.3 per cent of the time, whereas cable subscribers viewed Canadian stations only 47.3 per cent of the time and American stations 52.7 per cent of the time.[33]

Thus, the blessings of cable television in London seem somewhat mixed. On the one hand, services like local cablecasting promise a wider participation in the media for those in the community of London. On the other hand, cable portends a major threat to Canadian television as a whole.

The Problem of Canadian vs. American Content

One of the major considerations in the determination of Canadian broadcasting policy has been the question of the effect of American content in the media, and whether limitations should be imposed. The CRTC has taken bold steps to expand Canadian television content and to prevent the further spread of American programs via microwave, by establishing Canadian content quotas.

To pinpoint the effect of American programming on the attitudes, opinions, and behaviour of Londoners is difficult. However, if one looks at audience circulation figures and at available program content, it can clearly be seen that Londoners through American broadcasting probably are more closely tied to American culture than to that of Canada. In fact, when asked (in a communication survey in 1970) whether they would rather keep Canadian or American television, 55 per cent of the sample preferred to keep American programming as compared with 24.2 per cent who wished to keep Canadian.[34]

When circulation figures were first examined in this study, it appeared that Canadian television stations were dominant. CFPL has at least three times as many viewers in the course of a week as does any of its American competitors, and CKCO in Kitchener has nearly twice as many in the London area. However, if one totals the audiences for all American and for all Canadian stations, the picture changes greatly. In this case, more viewers will be found to be watching American stations in the course of a week (523,100) than Canadian stations (473,000).[35] Furthermore, approximately 45 per cent of Canadian television programming is of American origin. This leaves very little Canadian programming which is likely to be viewed by Londoners. Of 257 possible television shows which are available to Londoners on cable each day, only 39 are of Canadian origin. This means that Londoners who subscribe to T.V. cable (at least 80 per cent of London homes) have a choice of 84 per cent American programming and 16 per cent Canadian.[36] Is this adequate? Not only does this breed ignorance of Canadian writers, directors, and performers among London television viewers, but it also suggests greater exposure to American than to Canadian values and life styles.

Recently London merchants have begun to advertise on Erie television stations which are received via cable, largely because they are able to obtain much cheaper rates than CFPL TV offers. For example, on CFPL, the AA (prime time) rate is $165 for a thirty-second advertising spot, whereas on WJET, Erie, the station which carries most London advertising, the AA rate is $51 for a thirty-second spot.[37] In addition to this, while CFPL is tied to a number of national advertising packages, the American stations are freer to offer special cut-rate advertising. One result of this undoubtedly is to further confuse London viewers as to which channels are Canadian.

Conclusion

In any social system, the way in which its members view what is happening in the world is shaped by the image-making institutions of that society. It is in fact the communications institutions in modern societies which most powerfully and centrally affect the world views of most people.

In this paper, we have examined communications institutions in a Canadian city in order to better understand the historical and sociological forces conditioning their operation. The conditions which affect the image-making process in this city include: (1) a local "multi-media monopoly"; (2) a strong American presence, and (3) the national Canadian media. In the last decade, however, the third of these forces, the national Canadian media, has diminished in relative importance, resulting in a decreasing exposure to the Canadian national scene. In great part, television has accelerated this process.

In the future, the relative strengths of these three forces may well change. One possibility is that the local monopoly will escalate its battle with American television in an attempt to compete with the growing presence of American-based cable shows. Another possibility is that increasingly accentuated government moves to Canadianize the media will equalize the position of the Canadian national media in the battle for the London and for the Canadian audience.

The outcomes of these conflicts are of crucial importance. With American television and magazines promoting one set of identities and values while Canadian newspapers and radio promote another, Canadians are faced with the absence of a stable, uniform, continuous set of life definitions, especially in regard to world events.[38] This may make it increasingly difficult, as John Porter has suggested, for Canadian society to provide itself with a distinct structure of values, or with an image of itself as a distinct society.[39]

1. *London Free Press*, January 26, 1971, p. 21.
2. In 1968, those of British stock made up 73.12 per cent of the population of metropolitan London. Those of German background made up 5.75 per cent, and the Dutch comprised 3.90 per cent of the population. Those of French background made up 3.22 per cent of the London population, while the Italians made up 1.91 per cent.
   See Rudolf Helling and Edward Boyce, "A Demographic Survey of Metropolitan London and Middlesex County, Ontario." Mimeographed report, London, Ontario, May 7, 1968.
3. Of the total labour force of London, only 3.91 per cent can be classified as "labourers." Another 23.83 per cent are "craftsmen" (skilled labourers). On the other hand, 33.03 per cent are engaged in white collar occupations (8.86 per cent in managerial positions, 11.30 per cent in professional and technical occupations, and 13.54 per cent in clerical occupations). The remaining 29.93 per cent are engaged in sales and service occupations (8.81 per cent in sales occupations, 15.61 per cent in service and recreational occupations and 5.55 per cent in transportation and communication). Finally, 2.39 per cent are engaged in primary occupations. See Helling and Boyce, op. cit., pp. 82-102.
4. For an in-depth account of the development of the press in London and area, see Orlo Miller, *A Century of Western Ontario: The Story of The Free Press and Western Ontario: 1849-1949* (Toronto: Ryerson Press, 1949). Most of the historical data in the present account is derived from this source.
5. Miller, op. cit., p. 43.
6. Miller, op. cit., p. 46.
7. Miller, op. cit., pp. 74-75.
8. Miller, op. cit., p. 244.
9. Canadian Audit Bureau of Circulation, *Report*, July 18, 1969.
10. Ibid.

11. Walter J. Blackburn, "London Free Press Printing Company: Brief to the Special Senate Committee on Mass Media." Mimeographed brief, London, Ontario, December 1969, p. 9.
12. Raymond B. Ward and Jean Ward, "Trends in Newspaper Ownership," *Journalism Quarterly*, vol. 38 (1961), p. 3.
13. *London Free Press*, October 20, 1969, p. 3.
14. In a somewhat similar case in December 1972, the Ontario Press Council rejected a complaint from a West Montrose journalist who had come before it with the claim that the *Kitchener-Waterloo Record* had drastically altered the substance of a letter he wrote to the editor concerning the Kitchener-Waterloo Oktoberfest and violations of Ontario liquor laws, by shortening it for publication. In its decision, the Press Council stated that "an editor has the right to edit any letter, but not the right to alter one so as to change its meaning" (*Ottawa Citizen*, December 21, 1972, p. 35). The question remains, of course, as to whether selective shortening of a letter is justified in cases where the evidence supporting the "essential points" of the correspondent is necessary in order to validate the general points made in the letter.
15. Western Ontario Distributors, *Box Score*, September 1968.
16. B. D. Singer, "Communications in a Canadian City." Mimeographed report, University of Western Ontario, London, 1971. Table 3.1.
17. W. R. Hickey, "Radio Broadcasting: A Survey of Current Listening Habits and Program Popularity in London Ontario." Unpublished thesis, University of Western Ontario, 1932.
18. Kenneth S. Murray, "Ownership Statistics and Program Popularity: A Survey of Current Listening Habits and Program Popularity in London Ontario." Unpublished thesis, University of Western Ontario, 1937.
19. CJOE has since been sold by Mr. McManus and now bears the call letters CJBK.
20. Blackburn, "London Free Press Printing Company."
21. Ed Blake subsequently left CKSL and, after a short time as a broadcaster in Eastern Canada, returned to London to run for local municipal office. Blake was successful in his bid for a city controller's position and in his re-election attempt.
22. In 1973, after considering a privately commissioned listener survey, CFPL-FM adopted a new name — "Stereo 96" — and a new format that made more extensive use of local community figures in presenting a wider range of music and conversational subjects.
23. Personal interview with J. A. Hannigan, May 1970.
24. Murray Brown was the General Manager of CFPL Broadcasting.
25. *London Free Press*, October 20, 1969, p. 3.
26. Ibid.
27. Murray Brown, "CFPL Broadcasting Brief to the Special Senate Committee on Mass Media." Mimeographed brief, London, Ontario, Feburary 1970, pp. 30-32.
28. Channel 6 has subsequently been assigned by the CRTC to Canada's new third network, Global Television. London is thus likely to remain a one-television city for some time to come.
29. "Weekly reach" refers to the estimated number of different television households viewing a particular station at least once per week, Monday through Sunday, Sign-on to Sign-off. (*Television Factbook*,

No. 40, Television Digest Inc., Washington, 1970-71.)

30. Bureau of Broadcast Measurement, *Audience Survey*, March 1969.
31. *London Free Press*, September 12, 1970.
32. Brown, "CFPL Broadcasting," p. 41.
33. Ibid., p. 40
34. Singer, "Communications in a Canadian City." Table 4.17.
35. B.B.M., *Audience Survey*, March 1969.
36. These calculations are based upon an analysis of program listings for Western Ontario given in *TV Guide*, September 19-25, 1970.
37. *Television Factbook*, No. 40.
38. As an example of how Canadian and American media portray different values, see Benjamin D. Singer, "Violence, Protest, and War in Television News: The U.S. and Canada Compared," *Public Opinion Quarterly*, vol. 34 (Winter 1970-71), pp. 611-16. Reprinted in Section 4 of this book.
39. John Porter, *The Vertical Mosaic* (Toronto: University of Toronto Press, 1965), chapter 15.

Social Planning of Communications

ALLAN E. GOTLIEB and RICHARD J. GWYN

> The judicial regime is simply not adapted to technical civilization. It has not registered the essential transformation of our times.
>
> Jacques Ellul,
> *The Technological Society*

One need be neither lawyer nor technologist to recognize that the law almost always lags behind technology. To take one of the most obvious examples, the xerox machine has undermined, in little more than a decade, our legal concepts of copyright and these concepts could be entirely demolished by the new home video-recording machines, by direct broadcast satellites able to transmit programs beyond the boundaries of any single country, and by a new range of computerized information services. Another area where the law is laggard is in the lack of effective safeguards (and indeed of any safeguards) to protect individuals against the potential invasions of personal privacy made possible by our new and enormously efficient computerized information systems.

Ellul's comments about the frailty of the law in comparison with the power of technology can be applied with equal aptness to our existing social and political structures. Our institutions and ideologies are under intense critical attack as obsolescent, and, in some instances, as reactionary, largely because technology is transforming the social environment within which those institutions and ideologies evolved. Less and less does what we *have* correspond to what we *are*. Television, for instance, has extended the "democratization" of education and of politics far beyond even the most extravagant visions of nineteenth-century political egalitarians. The average western student is likely to have watched some 20,000 hours of television by the time he or she is 20: this incredible volume of virtually *identical* information will have been absorbed by (and in part been ignored by) each student regardless of his social, economic or educational background. Yet despite the dramatic impact of television our educational structure remains, with minor modifications, a mirror image of the elite educational systems of the pre-radio, let alone pre-television, days.

Ellul's comment is, of course, scarcely new. In the mid-nineteenth century Ralph Waldo Emerson wrote, more poetically, that "Stage-coach and Railroad are bursting through legislation like green withes." And it is easy also to fall into the trap of exaggerating the importance of technology. An electric lawn mower is a great improvement over a scythe, but it doesn't change the nature of the lawn, nor that of the man mowing it. Television, the telephone network and computer systems represent enormous improvements in information handling of multiple orders over smoke-signals or jungle drums or men travelling from village to village on horse or on foot; yet although electronic systems telescope time and space and permit almost limitless volumes of information to be moved over virtually limitless distances (including real-time television images from the moon), the messages themselves are constructed by men, received and interpreted by men and acted on by men.

One other cautionary note should be added: even when the environmental effects of technology are evident they are necessarily often ambivalent, and thus prediction can at times be erroneous and at other times sheer folly. A new road may bring fresh life to an isolated community or, as easily, it may drain life away. Similarly, computerized data banks could be used to make vast stores of information available to almost everyone and thus greatly enhance the public's ability to participate in the political decision-making process, or alternatively those same systems could be used to centralize the storage and processing of data and thus reinforce the power of central authorities at the expense of individual members of the public.

These conditions of imprecision about the relationship between technology and the social order, and of uncertainty about the specific as well as general effects brought about by particular technologies, clearly complicate the task of devising a sensitive and sane social planning structure for the development of communications systems. The very ambivalence of technology creates a danger that any socio-cultural analysis of communications will degenerate into a catalogue of on-the-one-hand-this, and on-the-other-hand-that.

In search of help both to understand the nature of the problem and to evolve basic principles which could provide a framework for planning, the Department of Communications, as part of its Telecommission inquiry into computers and telecommunications, organized a series of multi-disciplinary seminars participated in by some 400 Canadian authorities drawn from the widest possible variety of backgrounds, from electrical engineering and computer science to sociology and psychology, and from economics and urban planning to the arts, social work and education. The results of these seminars are summarized in the report, *Instant World*, of the Telecommission which was published in April, 1971. Individual reports on each of the meetings—"Computers and Privacy"; "Wired City"; "Telecommunications and Participation"; "Access to Information"—are also available. Those discussions and continuing studies have served to identify several concepts or broad principles which together form a foundation for the social planning of communications.

The Right to Communicate

While the nature of many of the environmental aspects of communications remains unclear, the central fact about the communications industry itself is obvious enough: a highly efficient network for the handling of information in all its forms—voice, audio, data and message—exists and this network is constantly expanding its capacity to handle, process and store information, and to distribute it at greater and greater speeds over longer and longer distances. Constant technological progress not only increases general operational efficiency, but it also reduces the cost of systems and components so that new communications services which have long been technically possible are carried over the threshold of reality. To take one example, local or community TV programming has been possible in theory at any time during the two decades that television has been generally available; however, the costs of making programs and of distributing them by means of a master antenna were so prohibitive that only the national networks could afford to originate programs. Today, though, the cable-television systems which connect more than 25% of all urban Canadian homes can provide additional distribution channels for community, or educational, programming at an insignificant cost; at the same time, the development of videotape technology and of half-inch VTR equipment has reduced the cost and eliminated most of the complexity of production to the point where almost anyone can produce his own programs. Thus a specific technological change—CATV systems and half-inch videotape—has made possible a major social change—the development of community-television programming. (It should be noted that the argument is not that CATV and videotape created local programming but that they made it possible, in technical and economic terms. That at the same time large numbers of citizens should want to produce local programs is a rare example of a convergence of supply and demand.)

The growth in the speed and volume of information distribution is following an exponential curve. Within a decade, communications satellites, such as the "Anik" model of Telesat, are likely to be succeeded by direct broadcast satellites which will be able to beam programs directly to homes and in the process leap across national boundaries. Today's technically crude cable-television systems will evolve into or be superseded by multipurpose broadband systems designed to provide a host of new services such as facsimile, high-speed data, television programs on demand, tele-mail. New patterns of social life may evolve, such as tele-shopping from the home, electronic banking in the "cashless" or at any rate "chequeless" society, and programmed education in which the principal instruments of instruction become computers and video-retrieval systems. Transportation flows may be significantly affected by tele-shopping, and by an increasing use of video-phones and two-way audio-video systems to conduct business and other affairs at a distance as an alternative to the time-consuming processing of travelling within and between cities. And finally, computerized information retrieval systems, which are still in their infancy, could make it possible for almost anyone to have instant access to vast stores of organized, codified data on everything from consumer prices to legal statutes and regulations, library services, stock market quotations, transportation schedules and reservations; the list can be extended almost as far as the imagination (and the pocketbook) allows. For various reasons, principally economic ones, at least some of these visionary systems will never be realized; at the same time there are no *technical* obstacles to the realization of any of these total information systems.

At various times in history man has been described as a social animal, a religious animal, a political animal and an economic animal. He may now be evolving towards becoming primarily a communicating animal. Less dramatically, it is quite clear that the production and distribution of information will become, within the next decade or so, at least as important as and most probably more important than the production and distribution of goods and materials upon which our existing industrial society is based.

In our present industrial society, we take for granted certain fundamental human freedoms or rights, among them the right of assembly and the right to freedom of expression. In a society of total communications these fundamental rights may no longer suffice. Many people are unable to communicate; they do not receive the messages distributed by communications systems; they lack the means or the knowledge to exploit the potential of those systems, and above all they are deprived of the opportunity to send their own messages through communications systems.

It may therefore be a necessary response to the communications explosion to develop the concept of a "right to communicate" as an essential human right, and to recognize that without such a right, individuals may no longer be able to exercise their full responsibilities and opportunities as members of society—just as today we cannot be full members of society without an unimpeded right to assemble.

Disconnection

The title for the Telecommission report, *Instant World*, was chosen from a short list compiled by officers of the Department of Communications. An alternative title, which was rejected by the narrowest of margins, was *Connect; Inter-Connect; Dis-connect.* "Connect" was intended here as a synonym for the right to communicate; "inter-connect" was used to express the principle that all users of communications systems should have the right, under equitable conditions, to connect their equipment to the basic national system; "dis-connect" was used to convey the obverse to the right to communicate, that is, the right *not* to communicate and not to be communicated to, when an individual so wishes.

Communications systems can expand man's horizons; they can also, if allowed to proliferate without any restraint, suffocate him by overloading him with messages or by intruding into his private space and personal life until he has nowhere left where he can be alone. An ability to disconnect, to switch off and out, at a chosen moment may be essential for psychic stability. At one of the Telecommission seminars a participant observed that: "Bombarded by ever-increasing rates of message transmission, man becomes fragmented and disoriented. Nothing seems real or permanent . . . . Images, character, styles, even his own identity are part of this sense of transience, breeding even more insecurity."

Perhaps even more important in an information-dominated society than the ability not to communicate at will may be the ability, also when willed, not to be communicated about. The sheer efficiency of information systems is making it harder and harder for anyone to remain anonymous, or to keep personal secrets to himself; in the future, and in the absence of any controls, such an exercise of freedom of choice could become impossible.

Privacy, or "the right to be alone" as Warren and Brandeis described it in their famous article for the Harvard Law Journal in 1890, is almost impossible to define because the perceived qualities of privacy change from one person to another, from one society to another and from one historical period to another. For example, a hundred years ago the architectural privacy which we take for granted was unknown except to the very rich. Yet privacy, the ability to be apart psychologically and physically, is clearly essential to individuality and to the development of personal character. People retreat into themselves to become themselves; they make contact with others to expose and test their developed personalities. If privacy becomes impossible individuals may be subjected to an irresistible pressure to conform. Instead of a democratic society we would degenerate into an atrophied society, barren of individuality, difference or distinction.

Computers have not of themselves created the threat to privacy; they have provided the means by which such a threat could be realized. The computer's storage capacity is vast, its memory infallible. The data processing capabilities of computers permit the integration of all types of personal files—medical, educational, career record, police record, financial statements—which until now have been maintained apart, not because of any rules preventing their merger, but because the costs of merging them were prohibitive.

The problem is that while information-handling techniques have been transformed beyond recognition, the state of the law concerning privacy is exactly where it was when Warren and Brandeis wrote their article 70 years ago. If the threat develops, the individual at present is virtually defenseless.

Because privacy is so pre-eminently an essential condition of our type of open society, the Department of Communications, together with the federal Department of Justice, has made the issue of computers and privacy a priority concern: a detailed study, including an analysis of possible legal and regulatory safeguards, is underway.

Access to Information

The promulgation of a "right to communicate" would be a passive act: it would simply be a declaration that individuals should be able to use communications systems with the same freedom that they can now assemble or speak in public. But for the ideal to have concrete meaning, positive steps will have to be taken to ensure that individuals are provided with the actual communications systems—without which any right to communicate becomes an empty slogan.

Canadians are blessed with one of the best communications systems in the world: 99% of Canadians have access to a telephone; 96% receive television and a higher proportion receive radio broadcasts; in terms of computers installed per head of population, Canada ranks second or third in the world, although a long way behind the United States. Yet with the conspicuous exception of broadcasting, this communications system has developed with few deliberate, or even conscious, attempts to make the system responsive to determined social goals. A specific exception is the "Anik" satellite which has been designed, among other objectives, to raise the standards of communications services in the north of our country to the levels that those living in the south take for granted.

The possible and as yet unrestrained impact of computers upon personal privacy illustrates how we have allowed communications systems to develop according to their own internal dynamics without first assessing their possible environmental effects, and then taking whatever steps are necessary to minimize any social disadvantages and, fully as important, to maximize their potential social benefits.

Telephone rates in Canada, when considered in relation to the earning power of the average Canadian, compare more than favorably with any in the world. Yet it can legitimately be asked whether the rate *structure,* including the division of costs between local and long-distance rates (which are approximately twice as high as those in the United States) is necessarily the best that could be devised, considering the urgent national need to develop east-west links and the peculiar geographic shape of Canada which places underdeveloped regions under a double handicap of poverty and distance. The point here is not that the present rate structure is inadequate; upon investigation it may prove to be the best possible from both the commercial and the political point of view. The point is rather that no attempt yet has been made to examine communications rates in the light of such social and political objectives.

"As a function of its complexity and cost, information technology tends to reinforce the powerful," Professor Alan Westin has said. Just as only the powerful television networks have been able to afford to produce programs and so have dominated television, so also only large and powerful institutions have been able to exploit the potential of expensive computer systems. Any policy of ensuring access to information requires that deliberate efforts be made to ensure that the benefits of computer power are made widely accessible to as many citizens as possible; particular attention will have to be paid to fields such as education and citizens' information services even when such systems are unlikely to be profitable as such, and so will never become accessible to ordinary citizens. The issue at stake is a political one: the balance of rights and powers between individuals and organizations and the extent to which the computer may tilt that balance irrevocably toward organizations, and by so doing "reinforce the powerful."

In order to promote the fullest possible access to information, proposals have been made that wherever possible a clear separation should be made between medium and message. In this system requirements for hardware systems are straightforward—they should be as efficient as possible and as widely available as possible; software messages and programs instead become the responsibility of anyone wishing to send them, as is the case now with the telephone system which subscribers can use to pass any information they wish with no restrictions on content, other than the general laws governing obscenity, slander and the like. Such "open access" systems, quite aside from their specific technical characteristics, become true two-way systems in the sense that they can be used to both send and receive messages. In contrast, television and radio (with the limited exception of Open Line shows) have been developed as one-way systems distributing prepackaged entertainment and information to a largely passive audience.

Last, any positive policy to promote access to information requires not only that systems should be physically available and at the lowest feasible price with access to them as unrestricted as possible, but that individuals should be equipped to use those systems, whether as receivers or contributors. A knowledge of film and videotape, of computer programming and of basic communications technology, requiring audio-visual and digital literacy, is likely to become as essential a part of our educational system as instruction in the reading and writing of print.

Multi-disciplinary Planning

At one of the Telecommission seminars, perhaps irritated by some of the implicit criticisms of existing communications systems made by other participants who claimed for themselves the title of "humanist," an engineer retorted: "Technology can give society just about anything it wants. But what does society want?"

His question was never answered, and indeed it is almost certainly unanswerable. No individual or group has the authority to decide all the social goals of society, and these social goals are themselves in constant change. Nevertheless, if the power of information technology is accepted then the need to plan its development toward broad social goals is evident. The method of doing so requires two simultaneous approaches: systematic attempts must be made to predict the probable environmental consequences of impending communication systems; at the same time, specific policies for the development of communications systems must take account of all environmental dimensions—the social, the cultural and the political as well as the technical and the economic.

Multi-disciplinary planning has become a fashionable expression more preached about than practised. Often the social dimensions of the multi-disciplinary approach are considered as an afterthought, and occasionally as a rationalization of technical and economic decisions already taken. Further, while the theoretical benefits of multi-disciplinary planning are self-evident, in practice multi-disciplinary teams, composed of members each talking a different language and interpreting identical facts by wholly different professional criteria, have often proved exercises in futility.

Nevertheless—and against a background of such errors of technological determinism as the SST and the Spadina Expressway—it is clear beyond any doubt that multi-disciplinary research and analysis is an essential foundation of policy planning.

Technology, whether of computers and communications, or of any other machines, can do a great deal for and to man. Yet it is worth remembering that technology can't do everything. As the poet e. e. cummings wrote:

> While you and i have lips and voices which
> are for kissing and to sing with
> who cares if some one-eyed son of a bitch
> invents an instrument to measure Spring with.

To measure Spring is not to understand it. Similarly, to create communications channels is not to create the messages or content sent through those channels, to whatever degree the medium may influence or modify the message. The communications explosion undoubtedly creates major new opportunities and dangers for man, and before this century is out man may have to contend with computing machines able to equal or exceed many of his intellectual powers. The right techniques and principles of social planning can do much to accentuate the good and diminish the bad. But like technology, they can't do everything. The ultimate decisions remain with individuals, and depend upon the consensus they arrive at about the kind of society they want, and therefore about the kind of messages they want to send to each other and only finally, and least important, about the kinds of communications systems they want.

Mentors and Monitors: Mass Media in the Canadian Classroom

JOHN ALAN LEE

The years immediately following World War II produced two phenomena destined for a remarkable conjunction: the baby boom and television. Canadian society produced its first TV generation, in which the most formative influences of childhood were not necessarily those of parents and peer group. The school system was recovering from the Depression years when plant and facilities had been cut to the bone, and from the war years when staffs had been thinned to meet the manpower needs of war. School planners foresaw a crisis of unprecedented proportions when the wave of postwar children began its irresistible sweep through kindergarten, grade school, high school, and college.

Educators enviously observed the power of the flickering blue light to spellbind children. They planned to enslave this living-room jester to a more useful role as classroom servant. It seemed reasonable at the time to teach with a device so effective in keeping children quiet and attentive. The extent of TV's magic is indicated by the fact that it bedazzled university educators too. One can hardly imagine, even in retrospect, how TV monitors were expected to replace the Socratic mentors of college students. Yet as early as 1957, D. C. Williams and other Canadian educators were experimenting with television teaching at the University of Toronto.[1]

By 1964, the results of more than 350 "scientific" experiments were on record in Canada and the United States, comparing the effectiveness of television teaching with classroom lectures, seminars, textbooks, and other teaching methods.[2] The general conclusion was that there was "no significant difference" in the performance of students on various tests conducted after televised classes, when compared with other teaching formats.[3]

University Television, a report by the Committee of Presidents of Ontario Universities, concluded in 1965 that the case for instructional television was proven.[4] But the planners had not waited for the final verdict to come in—Canada's first TV college was already under way.

Scarborough College, a suburban campus of the University of Toronto, was first conceived in 1962. It was part of a province-wide program to expand the postsecondary facilities of Ontario to meet the oncoming wave of postwar children who were now in their early teens.[5] But unlike the new universities and community colleges designed for the sudden expansion of postsecondary education, Scarborough College was a "first" for North America—a college designed, rather than converted, for the extensive use of television teaching in its classrooms and laboratories.[6]

The capital and operating budgets of the new college were heavily committed to television.[7] The teaching curriculum, especially in large introductory courses, depended on televised lectures. The number of teaching staff was predicated on monitors rather than mentors in many a classroom.[8] The size, shape, and number of classrooms and laboratories were designed for the effective use of television. The college was to have television studio facilities rivalling those of a broadcasting station and staffed by professional television producers.[9] The routing system for playback of videotaped lectures to classrooms permitted twelve different programs to be distributed simultaneously to forty-five different teaching areas.[10]

Although a new *medium* was to be employed for teaching university students, this did not imply a new method of teaching. As Marshall McLuhan had already noted, we had become accustomed to pouring the content of old media—novels, plays, radio, films—into the new medium of television, without realizing that the new medium itself conveyed a new "message."[11]

Scarborough leadership was aware that the use of the new medium of television would require eventual changes in the methods of teaching. Dean William Beckel argued,

"If we don't modify the message to suit the means, then we really aren't making use of the means."[12] But the majority of professors went on using their traditional teaching approach of lecture presentation with notes, blackboard, and classroom demonstration. The only difference was the delivery of this lecture before a TV camera, for videotape recording and later playback in the classroom.

Videotaped lectures offer several advantages. They can be replayed in the same course for several years, to successive cohorts of students. Only slight updating and revision may be necessary each year. For example, new discoveries in chemistry, biology, sociology, or English do not much affect the material taught in introductory courses. The same videotaped lecture can be shown to several classrooms simultaneously, even at remote distances, by flicking a switch in the master control room. The videotape can be replayed at different times of the week, increasing the number of students taught without requiring the professor to repeat his lecture.

It was not only argued that televised lectures would solve the problem of numbers of students flooding the universities. There would be a more important benefit. The best professors in each subject would be available to all of the students, since only one videotaped lecture series was necessary in each course.[13] Indeed, the choice was not limited to professors of the college or university—some of the lectures might be taped at the "great universities." No one explained what would happen to the college teachers who were less than "best," let alone anticipate the ways they might sabotage a system which threatened their livelihoods. Indeed, the college never bothered to determine the ability or willingness of many of its teachers to use instructional television.[14]

This failure was not due to administrative shortsightedness, for the problem was certainly considered. It was simply the path of least resistance in coping with faculty reaction against attempts to assess their teaching ability. Professors are not hired primarily for teaching, but for research and publication performance.[15] A very bad teaching record may go against a candidate in a staffing committee, but a good record will not compensate for a shortcoming in publication. Many professors reject outright or heavily discount the validity of anonymous student evaluation of their teaching performance.[16] At the same time, it is an understood norm of collegial relationship that no colleague or superior will enter a professor's everyday lectures without the instructor's advance knowledge and agreement.

Territorial imperatives are a real and potent factor in university teaching.[17] The Scarborough administration was unable or unwilling to challenge them directly by openly assessing the teaching ability of its newly hired staff. In the case of faculty transferred to the college from the downtown campus departments, there was even less possibility of subjecting them to a teaching assessment.[18] As a result, most of the professors hired to teach with television—in fact, all but two—had no previous experience with any electronic medium of communication in teaching.[19] The majority of them, when hired, did not even realize that they would be expected to teach by televised lectures.[20] When they arrived, persuasion and even coercion were used to get them into the TV studios.

> Programming starts with the teacher. First you have to convince him to use television. That's easy. The choice is between using television, or giving his lecture five times a week, or resigning.[21]

The optimists hoped that once a professor experienced the "advantages" of television, he would be converted to enthusiasm, or at least co-operation. Those who resisted, or only sullenly complied, were warned, "We can no longer afford this attitude in modern twentieth century technologically oriented society."[22] However, the oldest surviving guild in the world, the academic guild of professor-masters, proved able to resist and eventually overthrow this electronic invasion of their territory.

If the advocates of television innovation underestimated the resistance of the teachers, they overestimated the docility of the students. The economics of videotaped lectures makes sense only if there are large classes, year after year, studying the same subject matter. This is true even if the lecture-hall playback system is abandoned (which Scarborough did not do) and students have individual carrell access to videotaped material.[23]

The economic success of the Scarborough experiment was predicated on the continuation of the set province-wide curriculum and Departmental examination of high school students. That system has since been abandoned, the victim of a profound revolution in education highlighted by the "Living and Learning" report.[24] The Departmental system in the high schools was the logical base for the General and Honours programs in the university. Students were required to enter a defined stream. They were restricted in their subject choices and progressed by a series of measured sequential steps—semesters and years. The college planners felt they could safely assume substantial first-year enrolments when the college reached its full size—1,200 students in first-year English, 1,000 in biology, 500 in history, and so forth.[25]

These large captive audiences, repeated year after year, made the investment in television equipment and programming economically feasible. But this base was demolished in 1967 when the university adopted the New Program in arts and sciences. The predictable and measured cohorts of students passing through basic subjects year by year were replaced by fickle consumers of education choosing from a veritable smorgasbord of subject offerings. At first psychology was in fashion, and that department expanded. Then the demand swung to sociology. At the time of writing, biology is the popular choice. These fluctuations make all future planning difficult, and the large capital investments required by instruction television especially so.

Teachers and Television

When television was introduced to the lecture system, it was assumed that it would be used to deliver lectures. This was an inevitable consequence of the simple fact that many professors would scarcely know how to teach if they had to stop lecturing, and students would hardly know when to learn if they had no fixed schedule of lectures. For example, when students are allowed to study on their own without imposed schedules, many soon fall behind with their work, so individual study courses are restricted to the better (more self-motivated) students.

An interesting comparison of the impact of technology on the lecture system is provided by those colleges located on several campuses connected by bus. The college lecture system accommodates to the buses, for example, ending early so students won't miss a bus. But not so with television. Commercial television experience would have suggested that fifteen and thirty-minute lectures would be most effective, but colleges have continued to televise fifty-minute lectures rather than change overall timetables.

Scarborough teachers' inability to get away from the old methods was indicated by their early approach to televised lectures. Instead of rethinking the content of the course and converting it to television programs, most directly transferred their live lectures to videotape. A technician set up a voice recorder in the professor's class as he delivered his lectures live. Then a typist transcribed the audiotape to typescript, which the professor edited. If he wished, the main ideas were also printed on large cue cards. The professor went to the studio and spoke-read his lecture to the camera for videotaping, and it was ready for replay to next year's class as a canned lecture.

Some professors, realizing that the "head in a box" talking for fifty minutes was deadly dull, made an effort to add visual content such as a few slides or photographs to the televised lecture. But others, annoyed at having to use television, incorporated no more action in their videotaped program than an occasional turn to the blackboard or use of a graph or diagram.

A few professors broke out of the old system entirely. They set out to make good television programs. Not all were successful, and at least one lost his job by trying, while neglecting his regular research and publication work. If the test of time is a valid one, then only one professor succeeded in producing a series of lecture programs which remained popular with the student audience and respected for scholarly content. This teacher travelled far from the classroom, studio, and lab for his program material. He took the camera crew on field trips, into other institutions, back into history through slides and photographs, and indeed anywhere possible to avoid having his own face constantly appear on the screen. He supplemented his own voice with those of demonstrators and interviewed experts, thus adding auditory variety and easing the students' listening fatigue.

The inability of the majority of teachers using television in the college cannot be considered their fault. They had no role models in their experience on which to pattern themselves. None had experienced televised teaching himself as a student. Few considered the techniques of television in the commercial world relevant to their problems in teaching with the medium. Most important, they were not encouraged to produce good television programs by being assured of academic recognition equivalent to that of publishing a book or article. Nor were they given the large amounts of time necessary, as we shall see.

Even if the teachers had been effectively encouraged, it is possible that most would not have had the creative imagination to break into a new medium. Such an intellectual jump would have required a revision of their lifelong conception of the nature of academic production. Consider, for example, the process of producing a book, or even an article such as the present one. It begins by assembling the printed material expected to be relevant: documents, committee minutes, other studies of similar problems. Empirical investigation follows, and is immediately reduced to writing. A first draft is followed by several rewritings, until finally an edited and polished product is achieved.

A good television program—one that a contemporary audience will find interesting and absorbing—is the product of a quite different process. Television must begin with the visual, not with print. The producer-director must consider what will appear on the screen at any given time. Good television is effectively visual, not "radio with pictures."

Professors as teachers are meant to be heard more than seen. It is probably more accurate to say they prefer to be read than heard, since few professors would want their lectures published verbatim without careful editing. Indeed, any student who has voice-taped a professor's lectures is likely to have discovered that professors are rarely among the world's great public speakers. Even if all the "ahs" and "uhs" were deleted, there is still rather often an obvious shortage of challenging content in any randomly selected ten minutes of lecture verbiage. The delivery of subject matter in lectures is much "looser" (McLuhan would say "cooler") than in a tightly edited version suitable for publication.

When Scarborough professors entered the TV studios to deliver their lectures to a camera instead of a class, they found themselves robbed of some of the important elements of an effective lecture. Jokes go flat when no one laughs. Moments of pause seem calculated, and asides and anecdotes irrelevant. The studio situation itself creates a pressure to formalize and condense. When the time usually taken up by chatting with a student for a few moments before starting, or answering a few questions, is deleted from the presentation, the professor is faced with a full fifty minutes to fill with relevant content. The tape is rolling, and something must be recorded on it. The reader may have experienced the same pressure with a voice recorder, or even with a telephone. Long pauses and silences are much more uncomfortable when talking to someone on the phone than in person.

Thus the teachers very early in their taping experiences felt the urgent need for more material to fill out the videotapes. In addition, they became conscious of the need for visual variety. The search began for background illustrations, slides, graphics, film cuts, photographs from books, charts, anything with which to feed the voracious appetite of the electronic cyclops.

The capacity of television to absorb visual material is little appreciated by the ordinary viewer, but one can make oneself more aware of it by considering a typical home viewing of 35 mm coloured slides. Even though the photographic content of these slides may be of immediate and intimate personal interest, any slide becomes boring if on the screen more than about ten seconds. Using two or three cameras and the wizardry of master-control, a television producer can vary the visual content of a program to a surprising extent, but always within a narrow range of options if the object being screened remains the same.

If other visual material can be introduced, the possibilities increase geometrically. A shot of the professor close up can be followed by a slide from telecine, then back to the professor from a side angle, then a zoom on a chart or blackboard, and so forth. The camera eyes stay in action so the viewer's eyes remain active and interested.

But most professors don't think visually. They think in terms of ideas, abstractions, analysis, and words, not pictures. Even when an analysis can be summed up in a chart, they still want a verbal, linear-analytic explanation. In courses on fine art, more attention is often paid to talking about a painting or sculpture than actually looking at it. The eye is trained out of a scholar, for the eye is not trusted, and academics particularly distrust the television eye. None of Scarborough's television teachers began producing lecture programs—even when they were trying to make good programs, not merely televised lectures—by considering first what the visuals would be, and then adding the words. They started first with words. This is not a phenomenon new with television. Professors using films as audio-visual aids often feel compelled to introduce the films and analyse them afterward, even when the films are well made and could speak for themselves.

A classic case of distrust for the visual occurred in the college when a professor included the production of a certain TV lecture-program in a department report on his year's academic output. Sceptical about its scholastic merit, the department chairman asked for a description of the program's content—in words on paper, of course. It never occurred to him to look at the program itself. Although Scarborough professors are willing to read each other's written work, very few have been willing to attend prearranged showings of some of the better TV programs produced by a few of their colleagues.

University students, by contrast, are increasingly the products of an emerging visual culture.[26] They want illustrations, not analysis, much to the chagrin of university professors who can frequently be heard to complain these days about the inability of their students to analyse. It might well be a legitimate argument that visual illustration subverts careful analysis and rational argument, but if that were the case, then television should never have been introduced into academia in the first place.

If television is going to be used, its impact as a *visual* rather than auditory medium must be appreciated and understood. Otherwise, teachers are going to face the painful experience of students who pay more attention to what they see on the screen, than what they hear. In some cases, Scarborough students were amused for quite the wrong reasons from the teacher's point of view, for example, when the camera caught the teacher's face off guard in a "candid shot." In many cases, students were supremely bored by what they saw, therefore paid little attention to what they heard. They talked, ate lunch, read *The Varsity* in the dim light, or voted with their feet by absenting themselves. TV is essentially pictures. If the pictures aren't interesting, why watch?

Professors and Producers

Technically speaking, the college could have gone on the air as a broadcast station in black and white—its facilities were that good. Socially speaking, the college was no more prepared for television than Oxford in the fifteenth century. For many professors, troubles began when they arrived at the studio to televise their lectures. Up to this point, little that was unusual had occurred. They had prepared their notes and outlines, and perhaps gathered some illustrations and charts, or slides and films. This was no more than they might have done for a live lecture.

True, the professor had already experienced one potentially disturbing change. He had met a television director to discuss the proposed content of his videotaped lectures. No professor has to discuss what he is going to teach in his classroom with a professional in another (and to the professor, strange and unknown) field, before being able to deliver his lecture. Now the professor found himself forced to work with an interloper who often had his own ideas about how the show should go on.

The professor was always supposed to be in charge. The college administration repeatedly assured him of that.[27] But few professors knew enough about the technical problems of television to argue on a par with the television director. In addition, the television director had some concern for his own professional status. He did not want to be responsible for poor television programs. The directors usually came from the commercial television world, even if via another education television experience, and they had expectations based on successful commercial television.

When the professor arrived in the studio, there might almost have seemed a plot against him. Instead of a docile and respectful student audience, he found himself surrounded by a conspiring team of technicians, cameramen, sound men, light men, and floor men, in cahoots with others in a control room, and all masterminded by a TV director. These less malleable attendants were not there to audit his wisdom, or laugh at his jokes, or even to answer his questions. They were there to tell him—perhaps subtly and indirectly, but tell him none the less—how to teach his material to a television camera.

For his part, the television director had to learn that his ideas should be expressed in the manner of a court jester—casually, jokingly, lest the master take offence. Directors who did not adopt this role did not survive long at the college. This was a new experience for the directors, who generally came from a commercial world where actors and performers rarely questioned an instruction or expected an explanation for moving to a different position on stage, or retaking a scene with which the director was not satisfied.

The professor not only found himself working with a studio crew; he also found himself unable to control his own pacing or the total time of presentation. In the classroom the professor walks in at ten minutes after the hour, demands attention by his very presence, proceeds to deliver his material, allows only as much interruption from students as he cares to permit, and closes the delivery fifty minutes later to return to his office. Even the best organized studio television production cannot be accomplished in exactly the time of the finished program. At its worst, a studio production can take several times as long to complete as the length of the finished product.

Professors rarely treated the technical TV staff with the deference they might have shown to equally qualified professionals in other fields. They were especially determined to resist any apparent intrusion of the technical staff on their prerogative to teach. Even colleagues don't tell a professor how to teach.

A long-remembered incident illustrates the extent to which a professor could resist any effort by the TV staff to make the program more interesting. The subject matter was the phenomenon of action and reaction to physical force. The professor had developed various examples in his years of lecturing, one being the distortion of a golf ball when struck by a golf club. (The ball momentarily alters from a spherical to elliptoid shape, as demonstrated by slow-motion camera studies.) The professor customarily illustrated this effect with a simple sketch on the blackboard, and went on talking. In an attempt to liven up this teacher's wooden manner (complete with monotone voice) the desperate TV director suggested that an actual golf club and ball be used in the videotaping. As the professor was explaining his concept, he would casually pick up the club and take a swing at the ball. The outraged professor replied that this was a serious lecture, not a stage play. He was a teacher, not an actor, and learning was hard work, not entertainment.

When students began to make it obvious that they did not appreciate learning physics from a TV set, the TV staff was blamed, not the professor. After all, the teacher had gone on teaching the same concepts as ever in the same manner; how could he be at fault? The message had not changed, so it must be the medium, and its apprentice-sorcerers.

Instructors and Images

Most of the professors originally involved in televised lecturing at Scarborough were so distressed by the sight of their own image on the TV screen that they refused to watch more than the first few videotaped lectures they produced. For the first time, some professors saw themselves as others see them.

We become socially accustomed to the images of ourselves presented to us by communication media, especially if the socialization process begins in childhood. The simplest such medium is a mirror, reflecting back information about our exterior surface. Next time you look in your bathroom mirror, take a bar of soap and outline your head on the glass. You may be surprised to discover how much smaller than your real head the image is—yet you will not worry that your head has suddenly shrunk. From childhood, we learn to interpret the mirror's message. Primitive peoples with no mirrors understandably attribute magical qualities to the object, just as they often look behind a movie screen to see "where people go" after they "walk out of" the screen picture.

The contemporary young adult generation is probably the first to become accustomed to the sound of its own voices, since cassette tape recorders are now fairly common childhood toys. We are still a generation away from the toy videocassette, which will familarize children with their own visual image in a manner never possible with mirrors or even with home movies. That generation will learn to cope with the varied interpretations of the self provided by the TV screen in the same way we cope with different photographs of ourselves, considering one a truer likeness than another.

The experience of visual images of self on TV is not identical to that on film. Television is less defined and requires viewer completion. McLuhan uses the analogy of heat; film is hot and TV cool.[28] On film, for example, an exaggerated action or position *looks* exaggerated. But a commercial television actor selling a product in a TV advertisement must act more than naturally enthusiastic and lively, if on the screen he is to appear *normally* interested. If he talks and acts normally, he comes across as a bored, disinterested person.

This "cooling" quality of TV often gave Scarborough professors the appearance of being listless on screen. The students were less than kind in their anonymous evaluations. "The professor looks dead," some wrote. "Dull, boring, slow, drags."[29] On the other hand, the most popular professor in televised lectures was a dynamic, fast-talking person whose zeal and salesmanship often provoked distrust in real life, but who looked credible on the TV screen.[30]

Time and Television

Any Scarborough professor hoping to make effective televised lectures had to rethink his teaching methods, become accustomed to a new image of himself, work with a new breed of professionals, and think in an unfamiliar visual medium. This was a tall order, but with enough time and encouragement, it might have been achieved. There was never enough time.

Scarborough was a TV college to save money and teaching time, not to spend more. The vast expenditure on electronic hardware was justified on the basis of long-run economies in staff-student ratios. The administration realized that it would require more time to videotape a lecture than to present it live, but the most that could be afforded was a factor of three.[31] Each professor would be allowed to spend up to three times as much time preparing and producing a televised lecture, as would be required to prepare a live lecture. The resulting videotape would be replayed for three successive years, during which the professor would recoup his invested time, and devote it to the research on his own subject matter which had been neglected while making the tapes. At the end of the three years the tapes would be made over. (Even if the subject matter does not become dated, professors noticeably age in real life compared to the tape.)

Conscientious professors found that something more like ten times as much preparation was required for a TV lecture as for a live lecture. The professors who made this sacrifice rarely felt that they gained from it in any way.[32] They got no extra recognition from their colleagues. Well-made TV lectures produced no additions to citation indices or curricula vitae. They didn't get a notice in the journals, much less a review. There was no extra pay. Some professors felt they might be working themselves out of a job, since one good videotaped lecture on a subject might replace more than one professor. Since most found viewing their own programs unpleasant, they did not even gain the self-insight which might have made the experiment worthwhile.

An Audience Appraisal

The student audience was never consulted when the college undertook the TV experiment, and student reaction counted for little even in the final debacle. Ironically, however, television at Scarborough may have brought more reforms in faculty-student relations and teaching-learning practices than most observers realize. It is a common assumption in college teaching that students should be able to assimilate material whether or not it is effectively and attractively presented. It is the student's responsibility to face the hard work involved in learning. If there is a high failure rate, this redounds to the credit of the teacher and the shame of the students, not the reverse.[33] The professor will be respected by his colleagues for teaching a tough course, weeding out the slackers, maintaining high academic standards. It will rarely be suggested that perhaps the professor has failed as a teacher if his students have failed as learners.

When television intervened as a new variable in the teaching-learning milieu, the possibility arose that the students were not to blame for the high failure rates in televised courses. Of course, the professor wasn't to blame either—he taught the same material as ever. But television could be the culprit. Professors who disliked TV anyway were prepared to select a new scapegoat.

Willingness to blame TV for the high failure rates in televised courses served as something of an index of traditional versus innovative pedagogical attitudes among faculty.[34] At one extreme were those professors who disliked using TV, but declined to make it a new scapegoat. They saw no need for change in teaching methods, televised or live, because failure to learn was generally the stupid or lazy student's fault. At the other extreme were innovative professors who argued that problems with televised teaching were the symptoms of a need for profound changes in teaching methods, and not merely the product of a new medium.

At first no effort was made to consult the students themselves. In television situation a high audience rating was quite irrelevant. For example, no attempt was made to schedule the televised courses so as to avoid requiring students to sit through three or more televised lectures in succession—an experience which even the most TV-addicted home viewer would not relish. Audience opinion was finally voiced in a student council statement that the majority of students found the TV lectures "cold and impersonal." This verdict got newspaper headlines, and the college reacted swiftly. A survey of student opinion was commissioned and conveniently delivered the conclusion a few months later that most students were critical of TV lectures, but were still "willing to give TV a try."[35]

A later survey of undergraduates and graduates taught by televised courses at the college found that students appreciated the use of television in science laboratories and as a supplementary audio-visual aid in classrooms, but showed little enthusiasm for replacement of live lectures by videotape.[36] The more televised courses a student completed, the greater his distaste for them. The students generally avoided blaming their teachers for ineffective use of television, but rated their televised courses about one-third "good," one-third "fair," and one-third "poor." Obviously, Scarborough students did not give their televised courses rave reviews. But perhaps, as the "no-significant-difference" studies argued, they learned just as well with TV whether they liked it or not.

No Significant Difference (NSD)

As noted earlier, over 350 scientifically controlled experiments had demonstrated that there was no significant difference in learning by students when taught by television as compared with other forms of instruction.[37] The NSD findings were based on tests of performance, with little consideration of the way students felt about TV. Many researchers did not ask, any more than most professors ask, how students feel about a mathematical equation, a chemical formula, or a sociological definition. What counts is whether the student knows the data, not how he feels about it. Even in art and poetry courses, a professor is less likely to be interested in a student's essay on his *feelings about* the subject matter, than in his *knowledge about it.*

Yet it was clear from the Scarborough experience that professors could not teach on television independently of their feelings about it. Indeed, their feelings eventually got the better of them. Television was not scrapped at Scarborough because it was proven ineffective in teaching; *no controlled tests of that kind were ever attempted.* It was abandoned because the faculty didn't like it.

The problem of emotions in education is a philosophical question, and educators have a right to assume feelings are irrelevant so long as they are aware of the likely empirical consequences of that assumption. Apparently they were not. The educators also made a historical error. They assumed that results based on studies in the fifties would remain valid in the seventies. But the college students in the NSD experiments of the fifties were born in the thirties and did not grow up with television. College students of the late sixties were part of the TV generation. Television became almost universal in the early fifties, and most children born after 1950 experienced it as a familiar object of home furnishing.

Media as a Social Force

The media of communication in any society are a major social determinator. The Roman Empire for example, depended on its roads for administrative communication. The impact of communication media is everywhere evident but rarely obvious. It has been said that fish would be the last creatures to discover the existence of water, since they are totally immersed in it and take it for granted. The extent to which education fish can be unaware of the impact of their own milieu is indicated by one educator's statement:

> Television is neutral, it is neither educational nor instructive, it is a means and not an end. It is simply an instrument that can be used to do certain kinds of educational jobs.[38]

Television is by no means neutral but has its own impact or message in addition to the message it carries as a medium. The "TV is neutral" approach was rampant at Scarborough though very few professors behaved neutrally toward it. A former Dean of the college once likened college television to the college telephone system—an instrument to be used as people chose, but having no particular effects of its own. This is true neither of television nor telephones.

The milieu taken for granted by most professors is the medium of print culture. The professor who writes an article or book can draw on the accumulated experience and role models of twenty-five centuries. He can write in the style and form of Plato and Ovid and still be understood. Today's college student, by contrast, is the harbinger of a new culture of visual-tactile electronic media. He sees with different eyes. A simple example is the fact that frequently a student will title an essay on a topic with "A look at ..." It is hard to imagine a nineteenth-century student using such a title for an analytical paper.

Not only is television visual, but it is also, in McLuhan's term, tactile[39]. Like many of his analogies, this is perhaps more confusing than clarifying. McLuhan wants to point to the fact that TV is a powerful medium for evoking feeling and the desire to respond by feeling about the subject matter communicated.[40]The college student today is less interested in taking things apart than in relating to them whole, seeking their relevance, and having feelings about them.

Another social impact of television is the way its very presence affects social interaction. A familiar example is the effect of TV cameras at a riot to elicit more violent and dramatic crowd behaviour. Although TV as a teaching instrument has been scrapped in all but the science labs at Scarborough, the physical experience of television in the college has tended to elicit greater willingness to experiment and innovate in teaching approaches. For example, Scarborough was the first college in the province to adopt an "at your own pace" system of accreditation for the arts and science degrees.[41]

Inconsistent though it seems, John Adams, who called TV neutral, also had this to say:

> Inexorably, televised instruction separates the roles of teachers and students in the interacting process of education. It becomes clear that the role of the teacher should be auxiliary to the learning of the students and that the primary responsibility for academic achievement rests squarely with the students. . . . In this connection it seems possible that

> television might be used as an instrument to wean students away from immature dependency upon their instructors and to encourage their initiative, self-discipline, individual effort and unique personal development.[42]

Adams' conclusion is correct, but for the wrong reasons. It was the failure of the televised lecture at Scarborough which brought reforms in pedagogy and curriculum there. If the TV College had succeeded as planned, the students could have been reduced to docile blotters, soaking up canned knowledge. If the professors and directors had succeeded in producing absorbing, attractive TV programs, the students might have watched them happily. Televised lectures if effective can do none of the things John Adams argues. They merely seduce the student into a greater acceptance of the look-at perspective. At some point in his or her growth, the student must come to grips with the dialectical conflict between the older, analytical approach to knowledge represented by the professor's perspective, and his or her own new visual perspective.

In this connection it is interesting to note that the only place where television was absorbed into the college without contest and criticism was in the science labs. There, television was easily assimilated as an advanced audio-visual aid. Its facility for immediate multiplication of images and its relative ease of handling made it perfect for showing whole classrooms what was going on beneath a microscope or throughout a dissection. No other medium can provide infinite expansion of its images to any number of viewers simultaneous with the very action being viewed. Of course, this is a non-programmatic application of television, and merely served to improve the existing approach to the subject matter. Paradoxically, the extent to which television was absorbed into these uses without confrontation with the teaching process itself is a measure of the failure of television to produce the effects which Adams argues it would achieve.

An essay on the social impact of television at Scarborough would not be complete without reference to the wider impact of the experiment throughout the Ontario educational system. Bad news travels faster than good. The failure of the TV college experiment is wider known than are the benefits. The angry revolt of Scarborough teachers against television sent repercussions throughout the social network of professors in the province, and was certainly a contributing factor to the policy position taken by the Ontario Confederation of University Faculty Associations (OCUFA). In 1970, OCUFA recommended guidelines for any of its members who might become enmeshed in any attempted replication of the Scarborough experiment. A schedule of fees for services was also drawn up as a guideline for faculty making television teaching programs. The alarm was unwarranted, and the guidelines are already obsolete. No one seems to be planning a repeat of the Scarborough experiment.

What is most interesting about the OCUFA position was its assumption about the nature of University teaching. The statement argued:

> Since it is the transmission of knowledge that is the source of the faculty member's income, any use of his knowledge which *replaces* him should result in adequate compensation to the faculty member so that he does not find himself without a source of income. In these cases, the faculty member should be compensated each time the program is shown. *The compensation should reflect what he would have earned had he given the lecture.*[43] (Emphasis in original.)

It is hard to imagine a statement more explicitly descriptive of the fifteenth-century concept of the professor's role in the university. "His knowledge" is an incredible and presumptuous phrase in an age of knowledge expansion and availability. Sadder still is the idea that the professor's role is to be a transmission belt which can be *replaced* by a TV program. As for the proposal that compensation be in accordance with salaries for lecturing, how would the same principle apply if demanded whenever a professor published an article or book containing "his knowledge"?

The Road Back

Though the impacts of television at Scarborough have been many, the actual employment of TV in the college has been badly set back by the agonies of the videotaped lecture experiment. The splendid studios and control rooms have been stripped bare and their equipment sold off or transferred to the downtown campus. The spacious Studio One for large productions, is now a theatre workshop. Audio-visual storerooms and workshops have replaced all but one of the other TV studios. Not a single course is even partly taught by televised material (except in lab experiments). The one successful series of lecture programs referred to earlier in this paper is dated and its producing professor is near retirement. The series may not even be saved for posterity, but simply erased. Most of the TV staff have long since departed. Those remaining are servicing audio and film equipment more than television.

By the time Scarborough forgets and recovers from its unhappy experience with teacher-replacement television, a new generation of students will be enrolled, with a new and more developed visual perception of reality. At about the same time a new generation of television equipment will be within economic reach of the college. Pocket-size cameras, cassette videorecorders, and cheap videotape will make possible the kind of revolution in education which TV originally promised, but was unable to deliver, in the form of massive studio cameras and room-size master control equipment. The media advantages of TV will then come into their own. Videorecorders are capable of instant playback and viewing simultaneous with recording (compared to the delay in developing film). They use a recording material which can be wiped and recorded again and again. Tomorrow's videorecorders will become as common and easily operated as today's audiocassettes. Just as students today conduct interviews for various research projects using audiocassettes, or occasionally Super-8 cameras, students a decade hence will be able to use several cheap TV cameras simultaneously, employing an advantage film does not offer: on-location mixing and instant editing from several inputs to a single combined product. Videotape also has advantages in its ease of incorporation of other media—sound, film, slides, and special effects.

Whether these advantages of a new generation of television technology will be incorporated into the teaching program of Scarborough College is still uncertain. They may be resisted there long after they are an accomplished fact in other colleges and universities, simply because the faculty of Scarborough has not yet fully assimilated the lessons of their own experiment. It is ironic that all the engineering magic came to naught, despite elaborate planning and generous financing, while the social repercussions of television, given so little attention at the beginning, will go on reverberating through the college for years to come. The studios are bare and the monitors hang silent from the classroom ceilings, but the medium of television still has not exhausted its impact on the mentors of Scarborough College.

1. D. C. Williams et al., "Mass Media, Learning and Retention," *Canadian Journal of Pyschology*, vol. 11 (1957), pp. 157-63.
2. D. W. MacLennan and J. C. Reid, *Abstracts on Research on Instructional Television and Film, an Annotated Bibliography* (Stanford: Institute for Communication Research, Stanford University, 1964).
3. *University Television*, Supplementary Report of the Committee of Presidents of Provincially-Assisted Universities of Ontario (Toronto: University of Toronto Bookstores, 1965).
4. Ibid., p. 11.
5. *Post-Secondary Education in Ontario, 1962-70*, Report of the Committee of Presidents of Provincially-Assisted Universities of Ontario (Toronto: University of Toronto Bookstores, 1962, revised 1963).
6. D. C. Williams, "Progress Report," February 11, 1966.
7. "Budget for Scarborough College Special Teaching Facilities," September 1964.
8. W. E. Beckel, "An Economic Analysis of the Cost of Television Teaching," January 1968.
9. *Confidential Detailed Assessment of Scarborough College Instructional Television Facilities* (Toronto: Educational Television Authority of Ontario, 1969).
10. H. K. Davis, *Report of Inventory of Systems and Capabilities* (Toronto: University of Toronto Press, 1969), p. 28.
11. Marshall McLuhan, *Understanding Media* (Toronto: McGraw-Hill, 1964), p. 18.

12. Verbatim report of a college meeting to discuss the *Report of the Committee on Television Legal Questions*, April 21, 1966, p. 44.
13. *University Television*, p. 3; and W. E. Beckel, "The Fallacy of Hopkin's Effect." Mimeographed address, p. 5.
14. From personal interviews of Scarborough faculty.
15. At least, Scarborough faculty felt this way when interviewed.
16. For example, recent attempts to introduce college-wide anonymous student evaluation of courses met considerable resistance at College Council meetings.
17. See Richard Evans, *Resistance to Innovation in Higher Education* (San Francisco: Jossey-Bass, 1970), p. 55 ff.
18. Appointments to Scarborough College were made by downtown campus department chairmen and it was sometimes alleged that the College was used as a "dumping ground" for faculty who were *persona non grata* with the downtown chairman. Scarborough College had little more than veto power over many faculty appointments. These problems later led to the *Hare Report*, a special report on the status of the college.
19. From personal interviews of Scarborough faculty.
20. From personal interviews of Scarborough faculty.
21. W. E. Beckel, address on educational television at University of Alberta, October 1966.
22. W. E. Beckel, "TV Teaching at Scarborough College." To Acting President of University of Toronto, May 1968.
23. Beckel, "An Economic Analysis of the Cost of Television Teaching."
24. *The Hall-Dennis Report of the Provincial Committee on Aims and Objectives of Education in the Schools of Ontario* (Toronto: Ministry of Education, 1968).
25. W. E. Beckel, "TV at Scarborough." To the President of University of Toronto, 1966, p. 3.
26. See Caleb Gattegno, *Towards a Visual Culture* (New York: Outerbridge, 1969).
27. W. E. Beckel, "The Fallacy of Hopkin's Effect." Mimeographed address, p. 7: "The professor is boss right from the beginning."
28. McLuhan,*Understanding Media*, p. 22 ff.
29. From anonymous student evaluations conducted by the author.
30. This professor was "popular" according to student evaluations.
31. Beckel, "TV at Scarborough," p. 2.
32. From personal interviews of Scarborough faculty.
33. For a discussion, see Neil Postman and Charles Weingartner, *Teaching as a Subversive Activity* (New York: Delacorte, 1969). It is interesting to note that the college administration has recently shifted to a greater criticism of faculty for high failure rates in certain courses.
34. See Evans, *Resistance to Innovation in Higher Education*, for a comparison of innovative and non-innovative professors, p. 78 ff.
35. D. S. Abbey, "Staff and Student Attitudes to ITV at Scarborough College." Mimeographed, June 1967.
36. From an anonymous random questionnaire of graduate and undergraduate students conducted by the author.
37. MacLennan and Reid, *Abstracts on Research on Instructional Television and Film*.
38. J. C. Adams, *College Teaching by Television* (Washington: American Council on Education, 1958), p. 14.

39. Marshall McLuhan, *The Medium is the Massage* (New York: Bantam, 1972).
40. McLuhan, *Understanding Media*, p. 144.
41. In this system students may enrol in one to eight courses per session, and the "year" system is abolished. Five courses used to equal one "year."
42. Adams, *College Teaching by Television*
43. Ontario Confederation of University Faculty Associations Newsletter, Special Issue 1, November 1970, Item 3.

Control of Communications Media

Porter's article, "The Ideological System: The Mass Media," has been very influential in providing a sociological perspective from which to examine ownership of media. Porter traces the control of newspapers and broadcasting properties in Canada through networks of elite ownership associated with big business in general and maintained through family relationships — "generational continuity," in Porter's words. Although direction of these institutions is in Canadian hands, the control of this ideological tool is in the hands, as well, of men who think alike. Even the "professionals" who work for them, like the professionals or managers of Mills' Power Elite, *share the ideological commitments of the owners. Thus, the product, conditioned by this pattern, unconsciously shapes itself to the ideological requirements of one sector of the social system.*

The Davey Report's emphasis is first on the growth of the now familiar multi-media ownership pattern in Canada. One of the most central points deals with the contention that the growth of this kind of control has an effect on the quality of the medium, in contrast with Porter's emphasis on the common ideological perspectives developed by employees of media owners.

With the advent of broadcasting, a new social invention which involved formal control came into being. Harry Boyle, in "The Media Control Institution in Society: Canada and the U.S. Compared" examines the Canadian and American institutions whose function is to regulate the operations of broadcasters, and indicates how the differences in the rules and regulations reflect the particular problems of the two social systems.

The Ideological System: The Mass Media

JOHN PORTER

Individual human beings are linked together in social groups and in societies by ideas. Social cohesion depends to a great extent on the intensity with which people accept collective sentiments and values as their own. Thus societies must make provision for the articulation and reinforcing of social values. Because values tend to be conservative and traditional, the reinforcement of old values is more general than the articulation of new ones. The reinforcement of social values is one of the important social functions of ritualistic ceremonies. Moreover, because all social groups are subject to internal strains, ceremonies in which symbols and emotionally charged words are used serve to reduce tensions by appealing to values which are "above" a society's internal divisions.

Social Structure and Value Systems

In very small groups the sociological need to articulate and reinforce values is satisfied unconsciously and informally through the interactions of members.[1] In very large groups, such as modern nation states, the problems of internal cohesion, and the maintenance of social values and of the institutional forms that the values support, are so great that informal processes are not enough. Specialized social roles are also required. Those activities concerned with providing social cohesion and the maintenance of the value system we shall here call the ideological function. In earlier historical periods this function was performed by religion. In modern times, although religion is still an important ingredient of ideology it has often been replaced by a quasi-religious nationalism. Religion and secular ideology can become interwoven as, for example, when claims are made that a society is a "Christian" one, or that a particular type of economic system is in accord with a divine plan. National and secular ideology always take precedence over religion if the two value systems conflict.[2]

An essential characteristic of ideology is that it is otherworldly. If values are not heaven-oriented they are oriented to the future, or to a non-existent state of worldly perfection. Many societies have a millennial myth, the implementation of which is the purpose of their existence. Modern ideologies, with their secular flavour, are no more subjected to empirical checks than religion has been. Consequently, value systems, particularly at the level of popular consumption, appear always to be dominated by super-empirical, religious modes of thought, even in societies with a rational science and an industrial economy.

There are differing views about the origins of beliefs and values. The sociological view is that they arise from the processes of social life, from the multiplicity of social interactions that take place among a group of humans who share a given territory. Beliefs and values are social products. Those who live in different societies believe different things, both about themselves and about the world around them. Societies have different values and goals which are both a reflection of, and support for, a different set of social institutions and a different kind of social structure. Modern anthropology has shown us the tremendous variations in social structures and the values which support them. This relativity of values can be taken as evidence that values can be reduced to social phenomena.

Although value systems and belief systems are social rather than supernatural in their origins it would be wrong to suppose that all members of a society are equal in their contribution to the social psychology of value formation. Societies have histories, and hence they have traditional values which are ready made for all new members, be they the younger generation or adult immigrants. The process of socialization is concerned with the transmission of values to newcomers. Values and beliefs in already structured societies, therefore, are acquired through indoctrination, and so any argument about their origins is irrelevant. It is an empirical fact that social institutions exist—the churches for example—to indoctrinate the members of the society in certain beliefs. It is unlikely that members would hold those beliefs if they were not indoctrinated.

Besides providing cohesion and unity, value systems give a sense of rightness to the social order and legitimacy for particular practices and usages, including class and power structures, within a given society. For individuals, the value system with which they have been indoctrinated provides a view of the world and an explanation of life in society. Thus the beliefs and values of the society are used for individual, private needs. In the private assimilation of social beliefs subtle transformations take place, but at the same time a sufficient consistency remains to ensure that the social function of the value system is not impaired. The very fact that the vocabulary of a belief system ("freedom," "equality," and so forth) is used so frequently results in the loss of any precise meaning of the words used to describe the values. The loss of meaning makes it easier for individuals to feel that their private interpretations conform to a general social consensus.

To ensure that a value system does not become so vague that it ceases to perform its social function of providing cohesion, it is necessary to build into certain social roles the task of restating and generalizing values. Individuals who have a particular facility with the written and spoken word and who can manipulate symbols assume these ideological roles. At the lower levels of social development such are the roles of the medicine man, magician, shaman, soothsayer, myth-maker, and story-teller. In the modern complex society the roles are found in the operation of the mass media, the educational system, and the churches, that is, the roles of writer, publisher, editor, teacher, clergyman, professor, and lawyer. To assume these roles may require specialized training. Although the restatement of values may be undertaken in institutional systems other than the ideological, and will run the gamut from the efforts of the courts to find precise legal definitions of values to Chamber of Commerce and trade union convention rhetoric, it is the incumbents of ideological roles who are the real custodians of values and interpreters of social experience.

The ideological system functions at different intellectual levels. The clientele of the evangelical preacher is not the same as that of the Anglican priest. The masses who read the tabloid press and consume the output of the mass media do not generally read the specialized "learned" publications or intellectual journals of opinion. Despite these different levels within the ideological system there must be a unity of themes running through them. A social structure would fall apart without this unity of values. Sometimes social structures do fall apart in revolutionary or separatist movements. One of the problems of unity in highly differentiated social structures is that groups which are placed differently in the social structure do not experience the same social life because they are cut off from one another by class, religion, ethnicity, language, or some other barrier. But somehow, if a complex structure is to survive, the over-all value system for the society must have some meaning for all groups, and at the same time consistency for the total society.

The consensus which is necessary for the maintenance of social structure does not come about through some metaphysical entity of a group or social mind, or a general will. Rather, the unifying of value themes is achieved through the control of media of communication, and therefore the structure of the ideological system becomes articulated with other systems of power. The ideological system must provide the justification for the economic system, the political system, and so forth, and this it does by attempting to show that the existing arrangements conform with the traditional value system. But the ideological system in highly developed societies has become specialized in terms of both content and technology so that like other institutional systems it acquires some degree of autonomy from which it acquires a power of its own.

Thus we can designate as an ideological elite those at the top of ideological institutions, specifically in the modern period, the mass media, the educational system, and the churches. Although the ideological elite does not have the control over human and non-human resources that the economic elite for example has, it does have some power over men's minds. Thus the ideological elite may at times be in coalition with, and at other times in conflict with, other elite groups.

Church hierarchies have always had power based on their monopolies of esoteric theologies and complicated rituals. In the light of their specialized "knowledge" religious bodies make pronouncements about the rightness or wrongness of economic, political, or military policy. They can if they wish condemn decisions made by other elites. Because of this power of withholding their legitimatizing approval, church leaders may be consulted before decisions are made, or they may be brought into the decision-making processes of other elites. Church hierarchies also appropriate for themselves the right to speak on behalf of the community on a whole range of social life and, in doing so, have consolidated their power. Education, marriage and divorce, liquor legislation, birth control, and so forth, are aspects of social life about which church hierarchies are presumed to have not only special insights, but, as well, some right of decision-making.

The power of the modern mass media also stems from specialization. Not only is there the "art" of presenting entertainment and news, but there is also the skill of mobilizing modern technological resources of the press, radio, and television. Owners, publishers, and editors who control large metropolitan dailies and broadcasting outlets will be approached for their support of particular economic and political undertakings. There is now a great deal of evidence accumulated on the effects of the mass media on behaviour. Although this evidence suggests that there should be caution in making statements about specific content and specific effects, the fact remains that the mass media make "sense" of and give structure to a wide range of national and international life. The mass media, from news coverage to comic strips, are the shared experience of millions of people. The structure and control of the mass media could scarcely be left out of a study of power.

Power is also found in educational institutions. A society's most highly trained experts are usually found in the professional ranks of the universities, although in Canada, as we have seen, a large number are concentrated in the federal bureaucracy. These experts have a very important role within the ideological system. In many ways they define the potential of the society by their studies of the economical and political systems. From their writings the society gets some indication of the best way of doing things—best, that is, in terms either of efficiency, or of conforming to values of the society itself and of a wider cultural group such as "western civilization." The learned men, the wise men, the sages are the humanists, historians, economists, and other social scientists articulating the values of tradition or rational expediency, and thus producing for every society its conventional wisdom, a catalogue of the correct things to do.

Although the learned men are not widely read, and only occasionally are found on the mass media, they are read often by those who occupy important positions in the mass media so that the conventional wisdom percolates downwards in a process of popularization. It also percolates downwards through the lower educational system by way of university trained teachers. The very position of the sages as the most learned men of the society gives what they have to say an extraordinary air of authenticity. These men frequently have a direct influence on policy because they are used as consultants by business and military, and for governments they draw up plans and sit on boards and commissions. At times they work for political parties.

Therefore, the mass media, the institutions of higher learning, and the churches are the main loci of power within the ideological system. We shall study the first of these here.

Structure and Control of the Mass Media

Canada's mass media are operated as big business. Many of them, particularly in the large cities, are closely linked with corporate enterprise. Concentration of the control of the mass media is to be found in all industrialized and urbanized societies. There seems to be a contradiction in the process by which as cities increase in population the number of newspapers which they support decreases. In Canada in 1913 there were 138 daily newspapers, but by 1958 there were ninety-nine.[3] Along with the actual decrease in the number of dailies there was an increase in the number of single newspaper cities. In 1958 there were sixty-seven cities served by a single newspaper. Many small cities, like Brockville, Ontario, had two newspapers at the turn of the century. In thirty-four urban centres of over 30,000 there were only eight in 1957 in which there was more than one independently owned daily newspaper.

The main reason for the rise of the single newspaper city is economic. The investment in plant required to print 5,000 copies during a day was very small compared to that required to produce several hundred thousand. In addition technological changes to produce better looking newspapers have added greatly to the capital investment required. Thus modern newspaper production has experienced the rationalizing touch of the modern corporation. So great are the amounts of capital required to own, control, and operate metropolitan dailies that new newspapers no longer appear. It was reported that George McCullagh, who already owned the Toronto *Globe and Mail,* paid $3.6 million for the Toronto *Telegram* in 1948. After he died the *Globe and Mail* was sold to Howard Webster, a Montreal financier, for a reported $10 million. The *Telegram* was sold for an undisclosed sum to John Bassett Jr. with some of the money put up by John Bassett Sr., publisher of the Montreal *Gazette,* and John David Eaton, the president of the T. Eaton Company.[4] The value of the *Toronto Star,* when it was sold in the late 1950's, exceeded $25 million. In western Canada the growth of the Sifton-Bell--F.P. Publications Ltd. into a combination of six daily newspapers was undertaken by a member of the wealthy Sifton family which has been in the newspaper business for three generations, and Max Bell, the son of a Calgary newspaper proprietor. Thus only the very wealthy, or those successful in the corporate world, can buy and sell large daily newspapers which become, in effect, the instruments of an established upper class.

The controlling interest in the major newspaper complexes, in all of which the stock is closely held, is in the hands of families or individuals with two or three generations of wealth behind them. Any new daily newspapers that appear are in small urban centres where population has grown to the point where a weekly or semi-weekly can develop into a daily. In time such a daily may be bought up by a chain like Thomson Newspapers Ltd.

In 1958 three groups, the Southam Publishing Company, the Sifton, and the Thomson chains accounted for about 25 per cent of all daily newspaper circulation in Canada.[5] There are other ways in which the concentration of newspaper circulation can be measured. In 1960 the Southam chain, the Sifton-Bell and Sifton papers, the Thomson chain, the *Toronto Star,* the *Globe and Mail,* the *Telegram,* the Montreal *Gazette,* the *Montreal Star,* and the Halifax *Chronicle-Herald* accounted for all the newspapers circulating in census metropolitan areas (excluding Newfoundland), and they accounted for almost 80 per cent of all English language daily newspaper circulation. If we add to this the proportion of the Thomson newspapers produced in middle sized cities, but not metropolitan areas, the proportion of English language daily newspaper circulation accounted for by these ten units came to about 87 per cent.[6] About 12 per cent of all English and French daily newspapers accounted for more than half the total circulation. In 1953, fifty-seven publishers controlled the eighty-nine dailies in operation, but eleven publishers controlled nearly half of them.[7] The facts of newspaper concentration can, therefore, be shown in a variety of ways.

A similar pattern of concentration can be found in periodical publishing. Periodicals can be divided into two groups, the trade periodicals and the slick "consumer" magazines like *Maclean's* and *Liberty.* Trade periodicals are heavily concentrated in Maclean-Hunter Publishing Company Ltd. or in Hugh C. MacLean Publications Ltd., which is controlled by Southam Publishing Company Ltd., the owners of the Southam newspaper chain. The Hugh C. MacLean company publishes twenty-one trade periodicals, and Maclean-Hunter publishes fifty-four. Most of the trade periodicals are published monthly but a few are annual publications. Maclean-Hunter is the dominant publisher of consumer magazines. In 1961 its three main consumer publications, *Maclean's, Chatelaine,* and *Canadian Homes,* accounted for two-thirds of the circulation of all Canadian consumer magazines with a circulation over 20,000.[8] Almost all the rest of the circulation was accounted for by *Liberty* (591,000) and *Saturday Night* (77,000) which have had over the last few years a peculiar ownership history, but one which has not been connected with the major units of mass media publication. There is one other English language Canadian periodical which just comes into the 20,000 circulation category, and that is the *Atlantic Advocate*, owned by the Fredericton *Gleaner* and circulating mainly in the Atlantic provinces. For present purposes we shall leave it aside. We shall also omit the many periodicals appealing to more specialized tastes, which come and go, and which have circulations of less than 20,000.

The trade journals and consumer magazines already mentioned do not exhaust the publications of Maclean-Hunter. It also publishes the *Financial Post,* the leading newspaper of business and industry. More important, however, is the recent move of this company into French language publication. Historically French and English language newspaper and periodical publication has been separated, no doubt because the ideological function of the French language publications has been to articulate French-Canadian values, and this could only be achieved by French ownership. By 1960, however, Maclean-Hunter was publishing French counterparts of *Chatelaine (La Revue Moderne)* and of *Maclean's (Le Magazine Maclean),* which came close to rivalling in circulation the two main French periodicals, *La Revue Populaire* and *Le Samedi,* both owned by the same French company.

In the 1950's there appeared another type of consumer periodical which has become an important rival, particularly for advertising revenue, to Maclean-Hunter. These are the week-end magazines distributed on Saturdays with daily newspapers. The largest of these, *Weekend Magazine,* is owned by the Montreal Standard Publishing Company, and is distributed by arrangements with several newspapers across the country, including Southam papers. With 1.8 million in 1961 it had the largest circulation of any Canadian publication. Its closest rival, the *Star Weekly,* published by the Toronto Star Ltd., had a circulation of just over one million. The *Star Weekly* has been in existence for a much longer period. Another newcomer is the *Globe Magazine,* published by the Globe and Mail Ltd., and circulated with that paper. Thus if we add Maclean-Hunter Publishing Company and the smaller Fengate Publishing Company Ltd. *(Liberty* and *Saturday Night)* to the ten major metropolitan newspaper publishing companies previously mentioned we account for all significant English language Canadian periodical publication.

Anyone familiar with the reading habits of Canadians knows that the handful of magazines and periodicals published in Canada does not represent the ideological exposure of the general population. Publications from the United States circulate far more widely than do those of Canadian origin. The consumption of American periodicals in Canada is an ideological counterpart of the external control of the economic system. There can be little doubt that these foreign publications contribute substantially to "Canadian" values and to the view of the world held by Canadians. Although, as we shall see, the daily press is wholly Canadian owned, the periodicals in circulation are overwhelmingly American. There were in 1959 only five Canadian English language consumer magazines with more than 20,000 circulation. Of these *Maclean's* had a circulation of 494,000 every two weeks, *Liberty* 593,000 every month, and *Chatelaine* 738,000 every month. In the same year *Time* had a weekly circulation of 210,000, *Life* 282,000, and *Saturday Evening Post* 231,000. Of the monthly publications *Reader's Digest* had a combined English and French circulation of almost one million. Other high circulation American monthlies were *Everywoman's Family Circle* 281,000, *Ladies Home Journal* 236,000, *McCalls* 233,000, and *Woman's Day* 198,000. There were in 1959 at least fifty United States publications with a circulation over 20,000. These included seven weeklies, thirty-six monthlies, three twice monthlies, and four every two months, but excluded pulp magazines ranging from children's comics to romance stories. In 1959 there were twenty such groups of pulp magazines with more than 20,000 circulation and they had a combined annual circulation of more than 30 million.[9]

If the reading of periodicals contributes to the structure of ideology in any modern society, Canadians expose themselves far more to external influences than to internal ones. Similarly Canadians expose themselves far more to radio and television programmes from the United States than to Canadian ones. It is difficult under these conditions for a society to provide itself with a distinct structure of values or with an image of itself as a distinct society. Many societies have similar values, and therefore ideological exposure across national boundaries can help to reinforce values held in common. At the same time it is doubtful that there can be a distinctive social structure without distinctive values. Many Canadian intellectuals recognize this particular problem, and continue a seemingly endless search for national identity. Royal commissions examine what might be done to correct exposure to external ideologies.[10]

Centralized control of the mass media extends beyond newspapers and periodicals to radio and television, although broadcasting has been subject to government regulation in ways in which the press never has been. In Canada, as in many other countries, there has been not only government regulation of broadcasting, but also government participation in broadcasting through the publicly owned Canadian Broadcasting Corporation. There has always been in Canada bitter conflict between the proponents of "private enterprise" control and ownership of broadcasting, and those supporting publicly owned and controlled broadcasting. In this prolonged dispute two contradictory principles have been articulated, as has a confused analogy that broadcasting is a form of publishing, and, therefore, can claim a status similar to that which "freedom of the press" gives to newspapers and periodicals.[11]

The first principle is that broadcasting is a commercial activity, and, therefore, a legitimate area of profit-making. The second is that broadcasting is a public service which provides information, shapes the value structure of the society, and fosters cultural development. If the second principle is to prevail broadcasting is unlikely to be profitable, and must, therefore, be subsidized and undertaken by some government agency. Although this debate is not exclusive to Canada it has been given added intensity in Canada because of the exposure of a large majority of the population to media from the United States. Thus the preservation of a national identity has become a further argument of those who favour the dominance of the Canadian Broadcasting Corporation and governmental control through the Board of Broadcast Governors, established in 1958 to replace the C.B.C. as the regulatory agency. This important ideological function of the mass media has been clearly stated by the spokesmen for public ownership and control of broadcasting. The theme of a national identity recurs in the unending discussions in parliamentary committees and in briefs to and reports of various royal commissions concerned with the mass media.[12]

That broadcasting is publishing and therefore should be free of government participation, and with only a minimum of regulation required by the technical nature of the medium, has been most forcibly argued by the publishers who also own or seek to own broadcasting outlets. The analogy is based mainly on the view that broadcasting is a source of information and opinion which in a free society everyone should be free to dispense or consume. Thus government ownership and regulation of the broadcasting medium is a violation of a basic principle of freedom for which the press has fought for centuries.[13] In a society such as Canada, where elites are devoted to the norms of corporate enterprise and profit-making and where the freedom of the press from government interference has been established, the arguments for the private ownership of broadcasting have appeared formidable. However, in the discussion it is not clear if it is the public's freedom or the publisher's freedom which is being sought. The publishing media are private domains run, as are corporations, by private governments. Any danger arising from the private government of the press, it is argued, is offset by the "responsibility" of the press. However, the criteria of responsibility are not easy to establish. Nor can a very convincing case be made that responsibility is more likely to be present with private rather than public government. Both can be subject to abuse because both give power to individuals to make important decisions about the content of the media.

The argument that broadcasting is publishing breaks down on technical grounds. Although it is almost impossible to compete with established publications without great financial resources, some cheap forms of printing are available for the dissemination of ideas. Broadcasting, however, is limited by the number of frequencies and channels, and there must, therefore, be an orderly allocation of a scarce and valuable resource.

Although broadcasting has always been profitable, it became, with the higher population densities in metropolitan areas after World War II, a much more attractive commercial venture and, with the advent of television, one which required larger amounts of capital. It is not surprising that after the war private commercial interests intensified their efforts to secure greater exploitation of broadcasting. In a carefully documented study[14] Gladys Mussen has shown how a heavy propaganda campaign was mounted by the Canadian Association of Broadcasters, the trade association of the privately owned stations, and the Canadian Daily Newspapers Association, the trade association of newspaper publishers. The aim of the campaign was to persuade the public in general, and legislators in particular, that privately owned broadcasting was best for the country. Many of the newspaper publishers who also controlled broadcasting outlets used both media to solicit public support for private broadcasting. Ownership links between radio and television stations further facilitated the campaign. Thus although stations variously described as "community" stations, "independent" stations, or "private" stations may appear to be discrete units they are more likely to be, particularly in the larger cities, a part of a wider economic organization. In their trade association, the Canadian Association of Broadcasters, the owners of broadcasting outlets have acted with a uniformity that could scarcely be more complete if all the outlets were owned by the same person.[15]

Where there are no direct ownership links between broadcasting outlets there are managerial devices which in effect make them a "network" of privately owned stations. For example, the Sifton and Southam newspaper groups have been two major shareholders in All-Canada

Radio Facilities Ltd., a management company for advertising sales and the supplying of transcriptions to twenty-nine stations across the country. A further important shareholder in All-Canada Radio Facilities, at least until the late 1950's, was Taylor, Pearson and Carson, the owners of other radio stations. There has been a further ownership and management link between All-Canada Radio Facilities and All-Canada Mutually Operated Stations, an organization which operates stations under contractual arrangements. Individuals in All-Canada Radio Facilities and All-Canada Mutually Operated Stations have been active in the Canadian Association of Broadcasters. This last organization has since 1944 operated the Radio Bureau in Ottawa, a newsgathering office which distributes public service broadcasts to member stations of the Canadian Association of Broadcasters. The Radio Bureau has also provided members of Parliament with free radio time to report to their constituents through the local privately owned stations, and has supplied member stations with news reports of the activities of the House of Commons. According to evidence submitted to the Massey Commission there were sixty-seven stations affiliated with the Radio Bureau and 180 members of the Canadian Association of Broadcasters used it.[16]

If broadcasting outlets are not owned by publishing interests there may be links with large corporations, particularly in large cities. These links vary from direct ownership to common directors. Canadian Marconi Company, which in 1919 started the first radio station, XWA, in Canada, owns CFCF and CFCF-TV in Montreal. Standard Radio Broadcasting, a subsidiary of Argus Corporation, owns CFRB in Toronto and CJAD in Montreal. Canadian Westinghouse has an interest in CKEY, Toronto. In Vancouver, Van Tel Broadcasting Ltd. owns CHAN-TV. It was financed by various Vancouver businessmen, and there are directorship links through N. R. Whittall, investment dealers, with Westcoast Transmission and Pacific Petroleums. As we shall see, both newspaper publishing and broadcasting are closely linked to the corporate world.

As far as broadcasting is concerned, no combination of private ownership links or managerial devices exceeds the Canadian Broadcasting Corporation in concentration of control over outlets. In 1961, the C.B.C. owned thirty-eight radio stations and fourteen television stations across the country. At the same time there were 201 privately owned radio stations and forty-six privately owned television stations.[17] Until the Broadcasting Act of 1958, which established the Board of Broadcast Governors, the C.B.C. was both the regulator of all broadcasting as well as the largest operator. When the B.B.G. became the supreme regulator of broadcasting, the C.B.C. was relegated to the position of operator only and forced to compete much more than formerly on a commercial basis with private broadcasters. There is a further concentration of broadcasting within the C.B.C. because many of the privately owned television and radio stations have been affiliated with the C.B.C. networks, carrying varying amounts of national radio and television services. Of the 201 privately owned radio stations in 1961, thirty were in some way associated with the Trans-Canada Network, forty-nine with the Dominion Network (which was to disappear as a separate network in 1962), and twenty-three with the French Network. All but eight of the privately owned television stations in 1961 had some affiliation with the C.B.C. Thus there is a substantial element of concentration of broadcasting through the complicated interlocking of private stations and the publicly owned C.B.C. By the 1960's this peculiar structure of public and private enterprise was subject to many internal strains which raised the question of how long the structure could continue.[18]

After World War II it was, apparently, government policy that the C.B.C. should get the "cream" of the commercial television market in the large metropolitan areas, and that private stations would be left the smaller urban centres.[19] Pressure gradually mounted to open up the lucrative commercial markets to private broadcasting, and after it was formed in 1958 the B.B.G., which had now assumed the regulatory powers, began to hear applications from commercial companies for second television stations in most metropolitan areas. By 1961 the C.B.C. had, in many metropolitan areas, television competitors which themselves became linked in the first privately owned commercial broadcasting network, C.T.V.

The power of the privately owned stations in their struggle against the C.B.C. does not arise from concentration within the broadcasting industry, but rather it arises from the close links between private broadcasters, publishers, and large corporations. When the B.B.G. held its hearings in the metropolitan areas where there were to be second television stations, the corporate world descended in a great array. Most of the applicants either were the owners of newspapers and newspaper chains, or were syndicates of individuals closely associated with the corporate world. In Toronto each of the daily newspapers as well as Maclean-Hunter and Southam Publishing made applications for the licence. So did Argus Corporation through its subsidiary, Rogers Radio Broadcasting.[20] The licence was eventually awarded to CFTO owned by John Bassett (in association with John David Eaton) who also owned the Toronto *Telegram.* In Winnipeg the elite appeared as a cohesive group. In the words of one journalist observer:

> Never had Winnipeg seen such a spectacle. . . . Before them on their left was assembled most of the wealth of Winnipeg. The Richardson family was there and both branches of the Sifton family. Joseph Harris of meat-packing and life insurance fame was there. So was the chairman of the Canadian Committee of the Hudson's Bay Co.
>
> All of them were there to announce that they had $1,800,000 cash on the line to start another television station in Winnipeg under the title of the Red River Television Association.[21]

This group, however, failed to get the television station. Instead it was awarded to Channel Seven Television Ltd., whose president is Ralph S. Misener, also president and general manager of Consolidated Shippers Ltd., and whose other directors have connections with other broadcasting media in the west. In Montreal the licence went to CFCF-TV, owned by the Marconi Company. Although most of the applicants were connected either with newspaper chains, single newspapers, or the corporate world, they also were associated, through small stockholdings, with people from the various fields of the arts, letters, and drama; no doubt these applicants wanted to give the impression that they intended to provide television programmes that in the words of the Broadcasting Act would be "of a high standard . . . [and would be] basically Canadian in content and character."[22]

The C.B.C. with the loss of its regulatory powers and with the growth of commercialized broadcasting has had an increasingly difficult role within the ideological system. Canadian elites, political and corporate, felt apparently that national identity and national consciousness could be equally well, if not better, served through the principle of profit-making as through public ownership. Increasingly the C.B.C. was forced to work on commercial criteria and thus become more like those who were in broadcasting for profit-making.

Our task now is to provide a picture of the structure of control of the mass media, that is, newspapers, periodicals, and privately owned broadcasting outlets. This structure can be seen from the following pages where the major newspaper and periodical complexes are listed with the metropolitan newspapers they control, and as well, their periodicals and their owned or affiliated broadcasting outlets. Attention has been paid mainly to the metropolitan areas, although ownership of the various media will extend from metropolitan areas to smaller cities. Ownership data have been collected to provide the picture of concentration that existed in 1961. Like all commercial undertakings ownership participation is subject to change. Moreover, many of the companies involved are private so that there is a limited amount of information available. Every effort has been made to present an accurate picture of the networks of ownership.

The Major Mass Media Complexes, 1961

1. The Southam Company Ltd. (including Pacific Press Ltd.)

Total Assets: $27 million

Daily newspapers wholly owned	*Circulation metropolitan dailies*
Ottawa Citizen	70,000
Hamilton Spectator	104,000
North Bay Nugget	
Winnipeg Tribune	74,000
Medicine Hat News	
Calgary Herald	72,000
Edmonton Journal	109,000
Daily newspapers partially owned	
Vancouver *Province* (50%)	106,000
Vancouver *Sun* (50%)	216,000
London Free Press (25%)	105,000
Kitchener-Waterloo Record (47%)	
Total circulation metropolitan dailies	856,000

Periodicals controlled

Southam had 79 per cent interest in Hugh C. MacLean Publications Ltd. which published twenty-one Canadian business and professional magazines ranging from *Industrial Digest* (21,000 circulation) to *Retro Process Engineering* (2,600), and also the *Financial Times.*

Other interests in radio and television

CHCH-TV, Hamilton (through Niagara Television, 25%)
CFAC, Calgary (Calgary Broadcasting Ltd., 40%)
CHCT-TV, Calgary (Calgary Broadcasting Ltd., 20%)
CJCA, Edmonton (40%)
CFPL, CFPL-TV (London Free Press, 25%)
All-Canada Radio and Television Ltd. (25%)

The Southam Company was founded in 1877 when William Southam acquired a half interest in the *Hamilton Spectator.* The various holdings of the company have been built up since that time. Although it is a public company, with 1,954 shareholders in 1960,[23] there is little doubt that control still rests with members of the Southam family. There are three Southams on the board of directors of the company. In addition, the President, St. Clair Balfour, is a member of the family through his mother, Ethel May Southam. Phillip S. Fisher, chairman of the board, married the daughter of Frederick Neil Southam. D. K. MacTavish married the daughter of H. S. Southam. Another director, T. E. Nichols, is the son of M. E. Nichols who was associated with the Southam newspapers almost from the turn of the century. Other directors of Southam, such as W. C. Riley, B. B. Osler, and J. G. Glassco, link the company closely with the corporate world. D. K. MacTavish was also a bank director. These four directors held three bank directorships, three directorships in insurance companies, and four other directorships in the dominant corporations dealt with in an earlier chapter. Most of the directors come from prominent upper class families and attended private schools such as Trinity College School and Ridley College.

In 1957 the Southam Company which owned the Vancouver *Province* joined with the Sun Publishing Company which owned the Vancouver *Sun* to form Pacific Press Ltd. in which both companies would have 50 per cent interest. After the merger the *Province* became a morning paper and the *Sun* an evening paper both owned by Pacific Press. This merger became the subject of an investigation by the Restrictive Trade Practices Commission. Although the commission appeared to be satisfied with the argument of Pacific Press, made principally by Mr. St. Clair Balfour and Mr. D. C. Cromie, president of the Sun Publishing Company, that the two papers were competing with each other, and that the publishers of both papers controlled their own editorial, advertising, and circulation policies, it none the less felt that the public required a further safeguard in the form of a court order which would restrain the parties from making any alteration in their agreements without the approval of the court. In its report the commission concluded:

> Changes in personnel of a newspaper may occur within a relatively short time and it is evident that there can be no assurance that the successors will continue to engage in the same healthy rivalry. It is evident that there would have to be a constant striving for independence in editorial direction to offset the effect of unified ownership which would tend to erode the sense of separate identity in the two newspapers. The end result might be an appearance of rivalry without serious conviction, such as the rivalry of two articles under different brands produced by the same manufacturer.[24]

The ownership of the Sun Publishing Company remained primarily in the hands of five Cromie families who between them owned about 60 per cent of the stock. According to Mr. Donald Cromie, whose father, Robert Cromie, acquired the paper early in the present century, this family ownership was independent, "without any formal grouping beyond the ties of mutual interest and friendship."[25] The rest of the stock, some of it non-voting, was divided among 500 shareholders.[26] The directors of Pacific Press are drawn from both Sun and from Southam. In 1963 the ownership of Sun Publishing passed to F.P. Publications, linking the two largest newspaper chains in Canada in joint ownership of Vancouver's two newspapers.[27]

The generational continuity which can be seen in the control of both the Southam and Cromie publications can be seen also in the two other groups in which the Southam Company has some interest. The Southam subsidiary, Hugh C. MacLean Publications Ltd. was founded by Hugh C. MacLean, brother of John Bayne Maclean who founded the Maclean-Hunter publications.[28] At present the Chairman of the board of Hugh C. MacLean is Andrew D. MacLean, son of the founder. Andrew D. MacLean was educated at Upper Canada College and Royal Naval College, Greenwich. At one time he was secretary to former Prime Minister R. B. Bennett.

The majority ownership of the *London Free Press* has been in the Blackburn family since 1853 when Josiah

Blackburn acquired it. He was succeeded by his two sons, W. J. and A. S. Blackburn. The latter died in 1935, and he was succeeded as owner and publisher by his son, W. J. Blackburn Jr.

2. Sifton-Bell (F.P. Publications Ltd.) and Sifton Group
   Total Assets: Unknown

Daily newspapers owned	*Circulation metropolitan dailies*
Winnipeg Free Press	121,000
Ottawa Journal	68,000
Calgary *Albertan*	39,000
Lethbridge Herald	
Victoria *Daily Colonist*	33,000
Victoria Daily Times	24,000
Total circulation metropolitan dailies	285,000
Periodical owned	
Free Press Weekly Prairie Farmer	
Daily newspapers with ownership retained by members of the Sifton family	
Regina *Leader-Post*	51,000
Saskatoon Star-Phoenix	40,000
Total circulation	91,000

Radio and Television stations affiliated with F.P. Publications Ltd. or with Sifton Papers
- CJLH-TV (*Lethbridge Herald*)
- CKCK, CKCK-TV (Regina *Leader-Post*)
- CKRC, Winnipeg (Trans-Canada Communications Ltd. (Sifton))
- CKOC, Hamilton (Wentworth Radio Broadcasting Co. Ltd. (Sifton))
- Some interest in All-Canada Radio and Television Ltd.

In terms of corporate ownership these two groups of newspapers are separated. F.P. Publications Ltd. was formed jointly by Victor Sifton and G. Max Bell. The latter owned the *Calgary Albertan* which previously had been owned by his father. He acquired the *Victoria Times* and the Victoria *Colonist* in 1943. Victor Sifton and his brother Clifford divided their properties in 1953, with the ownership of the Saskatchewan papers acquired by the Sifton family in 1928 being retained by Clifford Sifton. The two brothers were sons of Sir Clifford Sifton who acquired the *Winnipeg Free Press* in 1889. Sir Clifford, who had extensive investments in the west, was a member of Laurier's cabinet. The Sifton family has long been prominent in Canadian life and has links with the corporate world. (Both Sifton and Southam groups of papers have a directorship link with Great West Life.) The sons of both Victor and Clifford Sifton are in executive positions in the family's mass media holdings. As already noted F.P. Publications in 1963 bought controlling interest in the Sun Publishing Company and hence an equal share with the Southam Company in Pacific Press Ltd.

3. Thomson Newspapers Ltd.
   Total Assets: $20 million

Daily newspapers owned	*Circulation metropolitan dailies*
Charlottetown *Guardian*	19,000
Quebec Chronicle-Telegraph	6,000
Total circulation metropolitan dailies	25,000

In addition Thomson Newspapers owned nineteen dailies and two weeklies in smaller cities.

Radio and Television stations owned or affiliated

CKOB (Timmins Press)

Other interests (through Thomson Subsidiaries or Members of Thomson Family)

Brookland Co. Ltd., of which R. H. Thomson was vice-president, owned radio and television stations at Kingston and Peterborough, Ontario.
CKGN-TV, North Bay
Northern Broadcasting Ltd.
Frontenac Broadcasting Ltd.
Kawartha Broadcasting Ltd.

Thomson Newspapers Ltd. was founded by Roy H. Thomson, a self-made man who has acquired the most extensive newspaper holdings in the United Kingdom and probably the world. In 1964 he acquired a peerage as well. The president of the company which controls the Canadian business is the son of Roy Thomson, K. R. Thomson, who is also a director of his father's United Kingdom companies. K. R. Thomson was educated at Upper Canada College and Cambridge University. Among the directors of Thomson Newspapers is J. D. S. Tory, a director of the Royal Bank of Canada and of Argus Corporation. Roy Thomson is also a director of the Royal Bank of Canada. There are other links between Thomson newspapers and the corporate world.

Mrs. C. E. Campbell, Roy Thomson's daughter, has 90 per cent interest in Northern Broadcasting Ltd., as well as minority interest in her father's other companies. In 1960 she was given permission by the Board of Broadcast Governors to purchase CKGN-TV in North Bay. The Thomson plan has been to acquire over the years daily newspapers and broadcasting outlets in smaller Canadian cities.

4. Toronto Star Ltd.
   Total Assets: $22 million

	Circulation metropolitan daily
Daily newspaper owned	
Toronto Star	330,000
Weekly owned	
Star Weekly (one million circulation)	

The *Toronto Star* was built up and placed in its present leading position among Canadian newspapers by Joseph Atkinson, a man who began his career in a woollen mill when he was fifteen.[29] In 1899 Atkinson, who was at that time thirty-four and had had considerable experience as a reporter, was offered the editorship of the *Star* by a group of prominent Toronto Liberals who were seeking support for Laurier. Atkinson agreed providing he would be paid partly in stock and could eventually acquire control. When Atkinson took over the *Star* it was in very poor condition. In the process of building it into the metropolitan daily with the largest circulation in Canada he was assisted by Harry C. Hindmarsh who became city editor in 1911, and subsequently managing editor. In 1915 Hindmarsh married Ruth Atkinson, the daughter of the Publisher, and he became president of the Star company after the death of Atkinson in 1948. The present president of the controlling company is Joseph S. Atkinson, the son of Joseph E. Atkinson. The secretary is H. A. Hindmarsh, the son of Harry C. Hindmarsh. Mrs. (Ruth Atkinson) Hindmarsh is also a director. In addition to the three members of the Atkinson and Hindmarsh families there are three technical directors representing the editorial, advertising, and production departments. Control appears to lie with the second generation of the Atkinson and Hindmarsh families. Under the will of Joseph E. Atkinson the ownership of the *Star* was held in trust for the Atkinson Charitable Foundation, of which the Atkinsons and the Hindmarshes were trustees. However, because the Ontario Charitable Gifts Act forbade any charitable foundation from holding more than 10 per cent of the capital of any one company, the foundation was forced to dispose of its holdings in the *Star.* Apparently a variety of people including E. P. Taylor, Cyrus Eaton, Roy Thomson, and the Southam Company all sought at various times to buy the *Star*, but it was eventually purchased by Hawthorn Publishing Company which was formed for the purpose by the present directors. Thus in a complicated series of moves control was retained by the families of the two men who built it up, an arrangement which the court ruled conformed with the provision of the Charitable Gifts Act and the Atkinson will.

5. The Globe and Mail Ltd.
   Total Assets: Unknown

	Circulation
Daily newspaper owned	*metropolitan daily*
Globe and Mail	226,000

Weekly owned
Weekly Globe and Mail (239,000 circulation)
Interest in radio station
CKEY, Toronto
(through Shoreacres Broadcasting Co.)

The *Globe and Mail* is owned by Newsco Investments, a company formed for the purpose in 1955 by R. Howard Webster of Montreal who appears to be the sole owner. He is a director of Imperial Trust Company and various industrial corporations. His father was Senator Lorne Webster whose wealth was founded on the St. Lawrence coal business in the early part of the present century. R. H. Webster was educated at Lower Canada College and McGill University. He purchased the *Globe and Mail* from the estate of George McCullagh, who had merged the old Toronto *Globe* and the *Mail and Empire* in the 1930's. The *Globe*, a famous Toronto paper in the latter part of the nineteenth century under its founder George Brown, was bought by McCullagh from the Jaffray family. Senator Jaffray had acquired control in the 1880's. William Gladstone Jaffray, son of Senator Jaffray, was president from 1915 to 1936 when McCullagh purchased it. McCullagh bought the *Mail and Empire* from Isaac Walton Killam, whose fortune was based on stock promotion and whose estate duties, along with those of Sir James Dunn, founded the Canada Council. Although McCullagh made a considerable fortune himself in stock promotion he seems to have been assisted in the buying of these two papers by W. H. Wright, a promoter in the mining industry. The purchase price of the *Globe and Mail* to R. H. Webster was said to be in excess of $10 million.

6. Telegram Publishing Company
   Total Assets: Unknown

Daily newspapers owned	*Circulation metropolitan daily*
Toronto *Telegram*	235,000
Sherbrooke Daily Record	

Television station controlled

CFTO-TV, Toronto (through Baton Aldred Rogers, 51%)

Other links

Foster Hewitt of Foster Hewitt Broadcasting Ltd. (CKFH, Toronto) was a shareholder in Baton Aldred Rogers.

The Toronto *Telegram* was another asset purchased from the McCullagh estate. It was acquired by John Bassett, Jr., educated at Ashbury College and Bishops College School, and son of John Bassett, president and publisher of the Montreal *Gazette*. In 1937 the father had purchased the Sherbrooke *Daily Record*, which he sold to his son in 1946. At some time John David Eaton, president of the T. Eaton Company, was involved in the financing of the *Telegram*. Ownership of the paper rests in 23,999 common shares held by trusts, the beneficiaries of which are the children of John Bassett Jr. and John David Eaton. It is interesting that the founder of the Eaton dynasty, Timothy Eaton, was among the Liberal businessmen who offered the editorship of the *Toronto Star* to Joseph Atkinson. Control of the *Telegram*, like the other newspapers so far examined, rests with members of upper class families with similar backgrounds. John Bassett Jr. is also a director of the Argonaut Football Club and of Maple Leaf Gardens Ltd.

The *Telegram* was founded in 1876 by John Ross Robertson, son of a wealthy dry-goods merchant and former city editor of the *Globe*. When Robertson died in 1918 he left the paper to a trust with all the profits to go to the Hospital for Sick Children. He stipulated that, on the death of his wife and children, the paper was to be sold with the profits going to the hospital. His widow died in 1947 and the paper was sold to George McCullagh for over three million dollars.

7. The Montreal Star Co. Ltd.
   Total Assets: Unknown

	Circulation metropolitan daily
Daily newspaper owned	
Montreal Star	191,000

Weekly owned (through Montreal Standard Publishing Co. Ltd.)
- *Weekend Magazine* (circulation 1,837,000)
- *Perspectives* (French language weekend magazine)

The *Montreal Star* has seen an inter-generational continuity of control. Its ownership lies with the McConnell family. Its former president was John Wilson McConnell, who began working in business at an early age before moving to the Montreal financial world in 1906. He subsequently took over the management of St. Lawrence Sugar Refineries and became an investment broker and a director of several large corporations. He acquired control of the *Star* in 1938 after the death of Lord Atholstan who, as Hugh Graham, built it up from the feeble four-page daily that it was in 1869. John Griffith McConnell, son of the former President, later became president of the company. He was educated at Lower Canada College, McGill University, and Cambridge, joining the Montreal Star Company in 1938. He also had directorships in other corporations.

8. Gazette Printing Co. Ltd.
   Total Assets: Unknown

Daily newspaper owned	*Circulation metropolitan daily*
Montreal *Gazette*	123,000

The Montreal *Gazette* was founded in 1778. Control of the paper was acquired by two brothers, Richard and Thomas White, in 1870. They had previously owned the *Hamilton Spectator.* Thomas White entered the House of Commons in 1878 and eventually Sir John A. Macdonald's government, and Richard became president and managing director of the *Gazette* until his death in 1910. Robert Smeaton White, son of Thomas White, was also associated, as editor-in-chief, with the *Gazette*, until he succeeded his father as Conservative M. P. for Cardwell, Ontario. He eventually became a senator. At present the president of the Gazette Company is C. H. Peters, nephew of Senator Robert Smeaton White. Peters was educated at Lower Canada College and McGill University and has been with the *Gazette* since he was twenty-two. For nineteen years the president and publisher was John Bassett who came to Canada in 1909 at the age of twenty-three and in 1913 became a director of the paper. Owing to his position of prominence in Canadian life, it was with his name that the *Gazette* was usually associated. Because he was involved with his son in the purchase of the *Daily Record* and the *Telegram,* it is reasonable to assume that there was a minimum ownership participation by Bassett in the *Gazette*, or, if there was more, it reverted to the White family, maintaining their continuity of ownership.

9. The Halifax Herald Ltd.
   Total Assets: Unknown

Daily newspaper owned	*Circulation metropolitan daily*
Halifax *Chronicle-Herald* / *Halifax Mail-Star* (evening)	110,000

Interest in radio station
CHNS, Halifax (through Maritime Broadcasting Co. Ltd.)

There has been a similar continuity of family ownership with the Halifax *Chronicle-Herald.* It was acquired in the 1870's by William Dennis who became a senator in 1912. When he died in 1921, his nephew, W. H. Dennis, also a senator, became the publisher. W. H. Dennis was succeeded in 1952 by his son, Graham W. Dennis.

10. Maclean-Hunter Publishing Co. Ltd.
    Total Assets: Unknown

Maclean's (524,000 circulation)
Chatelaine (775,000 circulation)
Canadian Homes (135,000 circulation)
La Revue Moderne (106,000 circulation)
In addition Maclean-Hunter published the *Financial Post* (86,000), two weeklies, four bi-monthlies, thirty-eight monthlies, and eleven other publications either semi-annually or annually.

Until his death Horace T. Hunter held the controlling interest in this company. When Colonel John Bayne Maclean died in 1948, Hunter acquired control by an agreement which had been made eleven years earlier. Hunter began working as an advertising salesman for J. B. Maclean Publishing Company in 1903, after graduating from the University of Toronto when he was twenty-two. The present president of the company is Donald F. Hunter, son of Horace T., and educated at Upper Canada College and the University of Toronto. Controlling interests rest with various members of the Hunter family.

11. Fengate Publishing Co. Ltd.
    Total Assets: Unknown

Liberty (591,000 circulation)
Saturday Night (77,000 circulation)

Until 1961 *Liberty* and *Saturday Night* were owned by Consolidated Press Ltd., which was controlled by Jack Kent Cooke, then of Toronto. In 1961 it was sold to Percy W. Bishop of Toronto, a financier with interests in natural oil and gas, who formed the Fengate Publishing Company. In 1961 a new publication, *The Canadian*, was begun by Fengate, and in the following year the seventy-five year old *Saturday Night*, which had had a distinguished place in Canada in magazine literature, was merged with *The Canadian* to form the *Canadian Saturday Night*. In 1963 *Saturday Night* became independent again with its former editor, Arnold Edinborough, as publisher and president of the company formed to buy it from Fengate Publishing.

Social Structure and Mass Media Control

Several observations may be made about the ownership and control of the mass media of English Canada. Ownership, with the exception of some foreign capital in private broadcasting, is exclusively Canadian, a fact which is in sharp contrast to the high degree of foreign ownership of Canadian industry. The absence of foreign control of the metropolitan daily newspapers would suggest that they are not sufficiently profitable to be taken over by foreign investors. It might also suggest a reluctance on the part of Canadian owners to sell these properties because they are viewed, not primarily as economic instruments, but as institutions which have a public responsibility. Because newspapers get involved in the political process by being associated with political parties, politicians would probably not want newspapers to become foreign owned for fear of being accused of getting their support from outside the country. Furthermore it is likely that high prestige attaches to the ownership of newspapers, and that ownership is retained for that purpose.

Not only does the ownership of the mass media lie within Canada, but also it is closely held within families, even where there is, as in the case of the Southam Company, some public participation in ownership. Moreover, as we have seen, in most instances control has remained within families for more than one generation, and in some cases for several generations. This generational continuity in ownership would suggest that the newspaper families see their newspapers as performing important public functions and are reluctant to let them pass out of family control. In a last letter to his sons Sir Clifford Sifton is reported to have said about the *Winnipeg Free Press*: "When I pass on it will be the thing that I am most proud of, that [*sic*] I can rely on you to be workers throughout life and to train your children in the same tradition."[30] Both E. H. Macklin, general manager, and John W. Dafoe, editor-in-chief of the *Winnipeg Free Press*, acquired stock in the newspaper as some form of payment during their early years with the paper. In the 1930's the Sifton family purchased back the holdings of both Dafoe and Macklin for sums reportedly as high as $500,000 each.[31]

Of the entire group that now controls the major mass media in English Canada, Roy Thomson seems to be the only self-made man, but as far as his Canadian holdings are concerned they are now operated by Thomsons of the second generation. Even the *Globe and Mail*, which has not been a family property as have so many of the other newspapers, was bought by an individual belonging to an established upper class family. The pattern of generational continuity in the ownership of newspapers seems to be established in all major cities from the Dennis family's ownership of the *Chronicle-Herald* in Halifax to the Cromie family's ownership until 1963 of the *Sun* in Vancouver.

The Southams, the Bassetts, the Whites, the McConnells, the Atkinsons and Hindmarshes, the Siftons, the Bells, the Cromies, the Hunters are all newspaper and publishing families well established in the Canadian upper class. A large proportion of the men who control the major newspapers belong to upper class institutions. They are graduates of private schools and belong to the same exclusive metropolitan clubs as do members of the economic elite. Almost all of them have been to university. They all belong to the British charter group of Canadian society.

Carlton McNaught, whose book *Canada Gets the News* is the only one to make an over-all survey of newspapers in Canada, has said of the class position of newspaper publishers:

> Since newspaper publishing has become such a complex business, it is natural that a publisher should be first and foremost a business man. There has come about a separation of the business and professional elements in newspaper production, with both business and editorial functions largely delegated by the publisher but with the latter giving his principal attention to the business side. One result is that the publisher often acquires a point of view which is that of the business groups in a community rather than of other and perhaps opposed groups; and this point of view is more likely than not to be reflected in his paper's treatment of news. The publisher usually belongs to the same clubs, moves in the same social circles, and breathes the same atmosphere as other business men.[32]

McNaught made no distinction between publishers who are owners or part-owners, and publishers who are employees and have arrived at their positions after journalistic careers. It is the former group in particular who have social backgrounds very comparable to that of the economic elite. It is not so much that owner-publishers inhabit a rarefied upper class world along with top business leaders, but rather that they have a class background from their early years which is identical to a very large group of business leaders. Publishers who have experienced upward social mobility through a journalistic career constitute a different group, and we shall return to them a little later.

Thus inheritance through kinship, rather than upward social mobility, is now the principal means of recruitment to that group which owns the major mass media instruments. Men such as Hugh Graham and Joseph Atkinson, who started from nothing and made great newspapers, and created legends while doing it, are now a social type lost in history as are the individual entrepreneurs, their counterparts in industry.

No major newspaper is owned and controlled by its employees or working journalists, although there may be a few instances where employees own a small proportion of the stock. The *Ottawa Journal,* for example, until it came under the control of F.P. Publications was owned in part by its senior editors. Nor is there any segment of the mass media owned by the trade union movement or by a political party. The ideological orientation that results from the existing pattern of ownership is conservative, supporting the *status quo* over a wide range of social and economic policy. Newspapers support Liberals or Conservatives, although they do not hesitate to switch their support when publishers consider it in their interests. But, in Canada, to support the two major political parties is to support the brokerage politics analyzed earlier. No newspaper has ever supported the social democratic C.C.F. nor its successor, the N.D.P. Nor do newspapers do very much to bring about the progressive-conservative dialogue of creative politics.

Owners of newspapers, it is sometimes said, regard

their publications purely as financial assets, and, providing these assets make a reasonable profit, owners do little to establish the ideological tone of editorials or to interfere with the presentation of news. This argument overlooks the fact that, in a large number of cases, owners are also publishers and so retain the chief executive positions for themselves, or if the paper is family-owned some member of the family may have the position of publisher or managing editor or editor-in-chief. One can scarcely imagine that the owners of newspapers were not parties to the decisions of almost all the metropolitan dailies to support the Liberal party in the 1963 general election. It is clear, too, that some of the dynamic owners of newspapers, men such as Joseph Atkinson and George McCullagh, for example, have had a very direct influence on the ideological complexion of their newspapers. No one would seriously hold that owners make decisions all along the hard pressed and carefully timed schedule of newspaper production, but it can be said that they set down general boundary lines which will become known to the editorial staffs. It would be naive to exclude, for example, John Bassett Jr. from a power of position in the ideological context with which we are dealing here, in regard to the Toronto *Telegram,* or Joseph S. Atkinson in regard to the *Toronto Star.*

The structure of the ownership and control of the mass media is not so simple that there is one well-defined group of owners and another well-defined group of "professional" operators called publishers and editors. If there are two well-defined groups, and frequently newspaper men themselves imagine that there are, the relations between the two are discussed in terms of the freedom of the press. The notion that "independent" publishers and editors should have more power to determine the ideological direction of the press than owners is an element in the doctrine of the freedom of the press. Although the main element in this doctrine is the proposition that the press should be free from government censorship and regulation, there is, as well, the idea that newspapers should be free from the interests and pressures of those who happen to own them. For some the press is ideally free when some public spirited man of wealth or a corporation buys or builds a newspaper and hands over its operation to a "professional" group of journalists who run the paper in the public interest, or at least their interpretation of the public interest. Owners supposedly do not interfere with the "professional" role of publisher and editor. Built into this "professional" role is the technical competence required to produce a newspaper, as well as great wisdom to make profound judgments in editorials and in the presentation of news about the state of the nation and the world. Perhaps no other occupational group in modern society appropriates to itself a role which requires all-seeing wisdom in so many spheres. This technical competence and this insight into all human and social problems is supposed to be acquired through a career as a newspaper reporter. Mr. Stuart Keate, publisher of the *Victoria Daily Times,* in a brief discussion of the problem of pressures arising from ownership relations has said, no doubt with pride, that "four out of the five most recent appointments as publisher in the Southam newspaper group have been ex-reporters. . . . Precisely the same ratio applies in our own Sifton-Bell operation."[33]

There is, of course, nothing professional about the role of newspaper reporting. As a group reporters have no disciplined academic training in any particular sphere, although they seem prepared to write about almost anything. They do not as an occupational group license themselves, govern their own affairs, or establish their own norms of performance. As Bernard Shaw pointed out so long ago they have no public register.[34] As an occupational group they are not highly paid, nor do they seem to have high prestige.[35] Hence it is unlikely that, as a profession, journalists would have the social standing or professional expertise or group solidarity to offset ownership pressure, although occasionally, as individuals, editors can rise to great prominence.

Some of the Canadian publications we have just examined are operated by employed publishers and editors some of whom may acquire nominal stockholdings. Although the data about this group of employee editors and publishers, as distinct from the ownership group, are rather fragmentary they do indicate that the group collectively is quite a different social type to the upper class owners. For the major newspapers and magazines we have examined there are a group of thirty-five publishers and editors who appear not to have significant ownership rights. Social background data are available for about one-half of this group only. Of this one-half the great majority are university graduates and three have graduate degrees. In social origins they are mainly middle class so that their present positions within the controlling group of the mass media may represent some upward social mobility. But they are, in the main, on the periphery of the elite. Only occasionally, for example, do they belong to the highest status clubs in the large cities. But, like the ownership group which has hired them, they are exclusively British in origin. No doubt they have been assessed by the ownership group as safe as far as ideas and values are concerned. It is unlikely that very many members of this group have had experience of lower class life, and none have experienced life as one of Canada's many minority groups.

The ownership group in their selection of personnel to run their newspapers and periodicals have to concern themselves not only with technical competence, but also with ideological acceptability which means sharing the attitudes and values of the owner. Thus the image of Canada, inasmuch as the mass media contribute to that image, is created by the British charter group as represented by the upper class owning group or the successful middle class journalists. Minority groups participate scarcely at all in the creation of this image. Even in the west, where minority groups are more concentrated than elsewhere, there is no representation at the top of the mass media operations. Immigrants, if they are

British, can reach top positions of newspapers and periodicals. Tom Kent, Basil Dean, Arnold Edinborough, all made relatively quick jumps into top editorial positions, after immigrating from the United Kingdom. In 1963 James L. Cooper was appointed vice-president and editor-in-chief of the *Globe and Mail,* the only Canadian daily with any claims to being a national newspaper. He was an English journalist whose career had been mostly with the English press, some eight years of which was as a correspondent in Canada.[36] He began to work for the *Globe and Mail* in 1958. Mr. Cooper replaced Oakley Dalgleish who, before his death in 1963, was an interesting example of a middle class, university trained journalist who reached the top as an extremely influential publisher. When this external recruitment to ideological roles takes place on a sizable scale it makes for the curious situation where a society's definition of itself is provided by those who have come to it as adults.

Although we have here tended to downgrade the employed publisher and editor to a much less significant power position than the ownership group, there are always exceptions. Some editors, such as John W. Dafoe in his time, have become powerful in their own right and have made their way into the most elite circles of clubs, honorific status posts, and philanthropic activities. However, the number who achieve complete upward mobility in this way are few.

The French Mass Media

In the structure and control of the French language mass media there are both similarities and differences to the English language media just examined. French language newspapers, which have played an important role in articulating a French-Canadian viewpoint and providing a self-image for French-Canadian society, are owned and edited by French Canadians. There are no chains, except that which has linked *Le Soleil—L'Evénement-Journal* of Quebec, *La Tribune* of Sherbrooke, and *Le Nouvelliste* of

Three Rivers, established by Senator Jacob Nicol.[37] One-half of all French language dailies account for about 90 per cent of all French language daily circulation.[38] These dailies include *La Presse* of Montreal, with a circulation in 1961 of 273,000. Others in order of circulation size were *Le Soleil—L'Evénement-Journal,* Quebec, 136,000; *Montreal Matin,* 109,000; *L'Action Catholique,* Quebec, 52,000; *Le Devoir,* Montreal, 36,000; and *Le Droit,* Ottawa, 34,000. As with English Canada there are links between newspapers and radio stations. *La Presse* owns CKAC in Montreal, and *Le Droit*'s parent company, Syndicat d'Oeuvres Sociales Ltée, owns CKCH, Hull and Ottawa. Outside of the metropolitan areas, notably in Sherbrooke and Three Rivers, there are ownership links between newspapers and radio broadcasting. There appear to be no substantial interlocking interests between newspapers and television broadcasting. There is, in both television and radio, the French language network of the C.B.C. The privately owned French television station in Montreal, CFTM-TV, owned by Tele-Metropole, does not appear to be connected with newspaper interests. Some of Tele-Metropole's directors have links with the corporate world, although the majority of them have had careers in radio, television, and motion picture production rather than in business. In Quebec City the English television station, CKMI-TV, and the French station, CFCM-TV, are both owned by Television de Quebec (Canada) Ltée which has directorship links with radio station CKCV in Quebec, but not with the local newspapers.

La Presse, the largest circulating French newspaper has a generational continuity similar to many English language newspapers. It was acquired and built up late in the last century by Trefflé Berthiaume. After his death his son-in-law, Pamphile DuTremblay, appointed to the Senate in 1942, became president of the company. When Senator DuTremblay died in 1955 his wife, Mme Angeline DuTremblay, Berthiaume's daughter, became the president. Four grandchildren of Trefflé Berthiaume continued to have a direct financial interest in the paper and two of them were on the board of directors when in 1961 the four had a falling out with their aunt. Mme DuTremblay sought to have the paper owned and operated by a charitable trust. According to her own statement[39] she guaranteed the Berthiaume grandchildren between fifty and sixty thousand dollars a year income. The Quebec government, however, refused to pass the necessary legislation, and Mme DuTremblay resigned along with other directors and the paper's Managing Editor, Jean-Louis Gagnon. The group who resigned from *La Presse* set about founding a new paper, *Le Nouveau Journal.* The failure of the latter within a few months indicates what an impossible task it is to establish a new metropolitan daily, even under the direction of such experienced people. In the meantime Gérard Pelletier, closely connected with the national syndicates of the Quebec trade union movement, became editor-in-chief of *La Presse.*

Although its circulation of 36,000 is small *Le Devoir* is credited with being the most influential paper in French Canada. There is little doubt that it is very influential within the narrow educated middle and upper classes of French Canada. Because of its high standard of journalism, much like the *New York Times,* the Manchester *Guardian,* or *Temps,* it does not have a mass appeal. It has no counterpart in English Canada. Founded in 1910 by Henri Bourassa the paper has always been the most eloquent voice of French-Canadian nationalism. After the death of Bourassa the paper was placed under the control of a trust. For many years the publisher and editorial director was Gérard Filion who, after the victory of the Lesage Liberals, became an official of the Quebec government. Another distinguished editor has been André Laurendeau. Intellectual journalists such as Gérard Filion, Jean-Louis Gagnon, André Laurendeau, and Gérard Pelletier have played a crucial role in the articulation of values for the "social revolution" in contemporary French Canada. As a group they have no counterpart among English-Canadian editors who do not seem to have the skills, or who are not in a position, to articulate for English Canada, or the whole of Canada, a national and indigenous ideology.

Le Droit in Ottawa and *L'Action Catholique* in Quebec represent an attempt to link two separate elements within the ideological system, the mass media and the Catholic philosophy. The fact that the circulation of both is low may well be an indication that the mixture of religion and daily news is not a very popular one. For example, the *United Church Observer,* a widely circulating Protestant paper, does not attempt to combine both functions.

Although there are no ownership links between the newspapers of English and French Canada two of the largest circulating magazines, *Le Magazine Maclean,* 95,000, and *Châtelaine--La Revue Moderne,* 106,000, are both owned by Maclean-Hunter. The editors of both magazines are French. The French edition of *Reader's Digest, Selection du Reader's Digest,* with 200,000 circulation, seems to be the most widely read periodical in French Canada. Two French periodicals both owned by Poirier, Bessette et Cie, are the weekly, *Le Samedi,* 80,000, and the monthly, *La Revue Populaire,* 104,000. The extent of French-Canadian readership of English language periodicals which are external to their own culture is difficult to establish. But we have already seen how United States periodicals exceed in their Canadian circulation that of many Canadian publications, and it seems reasonable to conclude that through the mass media French Canadians are exposed to external values.

It is against this external threat to French culture that the intellectuals of French-Canadian journalism seem to be seeking a counter-ideology. Yet the very values appealed to in the new reform movement in Quebec are contrary to the traditional French-Canadian values which have been authoritarian, within the church and within politics.[40] Extended social welfare, public ownership within the economy, a free educational system, upward social mobility, are values brought to French Canada, despite its traditions rather than because of them. Much of the French protest of the 1960's is a protest based on generalized egalitarian values of North America which have seeped into French-Canadian thought from the outside. The French intellectuals have expressed these values within the framework of ethnic protest rather than class protest, the latter being the original source of egalitarianism. Earlier we noted the high proportion of middle class intellectuals within the trade union movement in Quebec, and it was suggested that these leaders were far ahead of the proletariat they were leading.

In many respects French-Canadian intellectuals of the mass media and the trade unions are alike. Uniformly middle class, educated in the classical colleges and French Canadian universities, and retaining their Catholic religious affiliation, they are unlikely to see as useful to their purposes a protest within a class rather than an ethnic framework. Those who own and edit the French media we have just been examining are middle class, and because there has been little upward mobility in French society it is unlikely that class perspectives would appeal to these intellectuals. Moreover, the ownership of the media through which values are articulated and protests made has in most cases directorship links with the petty capitalism of French Canada. Speculatively it might be said that the dilemma posed for French-Canadian intellectuals is that, by articulating economic deprivation in ethnic rather than class terms, they will succeed only in strengthening the divided character of Canadian society. They seem to be fully supported by their English speaking counterparts who place such a high evaluation on ethnic differentiation. In time such an ideological position can only perpetuate the fragmentation of political structure and the consolidation of power within provincial structures.

1. The best discussions of values in small groups are in the works of George Homans, *The Human Group* (New York, 1950) and *Social Behavior: Its Elementary Forms* (New York, 1961).
2. This is very clearly demonstrated during wars when religions uphold behaviour such as killing, which they would normally condemn. On the division of the churches in the north and south

of the United States see Richard Niebuht, *The Social Sources of Denominationalism* (Hamden, Conn., 1954).

3. W. H. Kesterton, "A History of Canadian Journalism, 1752-1958," in *Canada Year Book, 1959* (D.B.S., Ottawa). I am most grateful to Professor Kesterton for helpful discussions on the history of the press in Canada. His articles in the *Canadian Annual Review* (ed. J. T. Saywell) have also been helpful.
4. Kesterton, "History of Canadian Journalism." The Eaton interest in the *Telegram* is apparent from the evidence in the application of John Bassett Jr. for the second television outlet in Toronto. See the later discussion on the ownership and control of the mass media.
5. Kesterton, *ibid.*
6. These proportions were arrived at by taking circulation figures from *Canadian Advertising,* March-April 1961, and *Canada Year Book, 1961,* 881ff.
7. Kesterton, "History of Canadian Journalism."
8. Computed from circulation figures in *Canadian Advertising,* March-April 1961.
9. The preceding circulation figures were taken from the appendix to the submission of the Periodical Press Association to the Royal Commission on Publications, *Proceedings of the Royal Commission on Publications* (Ottawa, 1961).
10. Notably the Royal Commission on National Development in the Arts, Letters and Sciences, The Royal Commission on Publications, and in 1963 the Royal Commission on Bilingualism and Biculturalism.
11. For a detailed discussion of the analogy that broadcasting is publishing see Gladys Coke Mussen, "The Use of Propaganda in the Battle over Broadcasting in Canada" (unpublished Ph.D. thesis, Columbia University, 1960).
12. See the review of these in Mussen, *ibid.*
13. See *ibid.* for a full account of the methods used by private broadcasters in making these arguments.
14. Mussen, "The Use of Propaganda in the Battle over Broadcasting."
15. *Ibid.*
16. *Ibid.*, 29, 127. The Massey Commission referred to was the Royal Commission on National Development in the Arts, Letters and Sciences.
17. *Canada Year Book, 1961,* 869ff.
18. This problem was the subject of an important policy speech by Mr. J. Alphonse Ouimet, the president of the C.B.C., in December 1962. He called for the completion of the C.B.C.'s national broadcasting coverage and the freeing of the C.B.C. from regulation by the B.B.G. See report in *Ottawa Journal,* Dec. 8, 1962.
19. See W. H. N. Hull, "The Public Control of Broadcasting: The Canadian and Australian Experiences," *C.J.E.P.S.,* XXVIII, no. 1 (Feb. 1962).
20. See report in *Globe and Mail* through the third week of March 1960.
21. Ted Byfield, "Winnipeg's Wealth Adds Glitter to Broadcast Board Hearings," *Globe and Mail,* Jan. 16, 1960.
22. Canada, *Statutes,* 1958, c. 22, s. 10.

23. *Financial Post Corporation Service* from which most of the preceding data on the Southam Company were taken.
24. Restrictive Trade Practices Commission, *Report,* no. 9 (Ottawa, 1960), 176-77.
25. *Ibid.,* 107.
26. *Ibid.*
27. *Ottawa Journal,* July 8, 1963.
28. The Maclean brothers did not agree about capitalizing the "L" in their surname.
29. Most of the data concerning Atkinson and the *Toronto Star* were taken from various biographical sketches of Atkinson. There is now available the full biography by Ross Harkness, *J. E. Atkinson of the Star* (Toronto, 1963). I am grateful to Professor Kesterton and his files on Canadian journalism for many aspects of this account of the *Star* and other metropolitan newspapers. Much of the ownership structure of the mass media became revealed in the Toronto hearings of the B.B.G. in March 1960. Most of the applicants for the second television station had interests in newspapers, periodicals, or other radio and television stations.
30. See sketch of Victor Sifton in Carolyn Cox, *Canadian Strength* (Toronto, 1946), 169ff.
31. M. E. Nichols, *CP: The Story of the Canadian Press* (Toronto, 1948), 290.
32. Carlton McNaught, *Canada Gets the News* (Toronto, 1940), 20.
33. Stuart Keate, "Pressures On the Press," *Globe and Mail,* Feb. 19, 1962.
34. See the preface to *The Doctor's Dilemma* (Penguin Books, London, 1946).
35. See Keate, "Pressures on the Press."
36. *Globe and Mail,* Aug. 30, 1963.
37. See Donatien Fremont, "La Presse de langue Française au Canada," *Royal Commission Studies: A Selection of Essays Prepared for the Royal Commission on National Development in the Arts, Letters and Sciences* (Queen's Printer, Ottawa, 1951).
38. Circulation figures are taken from *Canadian Advertising,* March-April 1961, and *Canada Year Book, 1961,* 881ff.
39. Montreal *Gazette,* April 20, 1961.
40. See the discussions by P.-E. Trudeau in *La Grève de l'amiante* (Montreal, 1956). See also his "Some Obstacles to Democracy in Quebec," *C.J.E.P.S.,* XXIV, no. 3 (Aug. 1958.).

The Davey Report: Main Findings and Recommendations

T. C. SEACREST

Introduction

On March 18, 1969, the Senate of Canada created the Special Senate Committee on Mass Media, headed by Senator Keith Davey, to study two separate aspects of mass communication in Canada. First, this Committee was to study the ownership and control patterns of the printing and broadcasting industries in Canada. Secondly, it was to report on the impact of the mass media on the Canadian public.

Originally, the Davey Committee had intended to investigate only the print media in Canada. However, the Committee soon discovered that the multi-media ownership patterns were so pervasive and the interrelationship between the printing industry and the broadcasting industry was so great that it was necessary to expand the study to encompass all forms of mass media. Senator Davey explained the rationale for this new comprehensive study of Canadian media in the following manner:

> It occurred to me that there had never been a national accounting for the media. Most people agreed that freedom of the press presumes responsibility, but few had really stopped to assess that responsibility. It also occurred to me that Parliament might be the ideal instrument through which the people of Canada could determine whether they have the press they need or simply the press they deserve.[1]

From the outset the Special Committee on Mass Media had three prime concerns: (1) the increasing concentration of mass media ownership; (2) the poor quality of a great deal of Canada's media; and (3) the Americanization of the mass media in Canada. Thus, the main recommendations of the Davey Report stressed ways of achieving a multiplication of different media voices, of improving the quality and professionalism of Canadian media, and of ensuring the survival of a distinctive Canadian mass media system, as well as a distinctive Canadian culture.

The interrelated nature of these three concerns of the Committee should be noted. For example, the increasing concentration of mass media ownership in fewer and fewer hands has a decided effect on the quality of the mass media, if the owners are more interested in profits than editorial excellence. Similarly, the growing domination and influence of lowest-common-denominator programming from the United States on Canadian broadcasting has had a noticeable effect in lowering the quality of the electronic media in Canada.

The Davey Committee used three basic sources of data and research in compiling its findings. First, briefs were submitted by the owners and representatives of various mass media enterprises concerning their particular operations and their general opinions on mass communication in Canada. Secondly, the Committee made extensive use of the existing records and collected data of the Canadian Radio-Television Commission, the Dominion Bureau of Statistics, and other public and private organizations. Finally, the Committee commissioned research and surveys to investigate the opinions and usage patterns of the Canadian public with regard to the mass media, and to study the present economic state of the Canadian mass media system.

Mass Media Ownership

It is the contention of the Special Senate Committee on Mass Media that the effectiveness of our democratic government depends to a great extent on how well the mass media system keeps the public informed about what is going on in our society. The more divergent the views and interests represented within the media (i.e., the more numerous the sources of information), the better the media is able to perform this essential function.

> The more separate voices we have telling us what's going on, telling us how we're doing, telling us how we *should* be doing, the more effectively we can govern ourselves. In this sense, the mass media are society's suggestion box. The more suggestions there are from below, the better will be the decisions made at the top. . . . And in a technological society, the media are one of the chief instruments by which this need is met.[2]

But although numerous sources of information may be beneficial to our democratic society, fewer sources are more economical. There is a natural tendency, called the process of "natural monopoly," for the print and broadcasting media to merge into bigger and bigger production units. This multi-media ownership pattern is encouraged not only by the "economics of scale," but also by the Canadian tax structure.

In the 103 Canadian cities that have daily newspapers, for instance, out of the 485 possible single units of mass communication in these cities (newspapers, radio stations, television stations, cable television enterprises, and magazine publishing firms), over half of these operations are owned or partially controlled by groups with multimedia holdings. The breakdown of specific mass media forms reveals that 66.4% of Canada's daily newspapers are owned or partially controlled by groups; that 48.5% of Canada's television stations are managed by multimedia interests; and that groups run 47.4% of our radio stations.

But the above figures present only a partial picture of the concentration of ownership of the mass media in Canada. For example, newspaper circulation figures reveal more about the trend toward monopoly and multimedia ownership. The Davey Report notes that:

> There are only five cities in the country where genuine competition between newspapers exists; and in all five cities some or all of these competing dailies are owned by chains. . . . Of Canada's eleven largest cities, chains enjoy monopolies in seven. The three biggest newspaper chains—Thomson, Southam, and F. P.—today control

> 44.7% of the circulation of all Canadian daily newspapers; a dozen years ago the total was only 25%. . . . Fully 77% of the circulation of all Canadian newspapers is now controlled by . . . chains.[3]

The ownership of radio and television media is much more diversified (owing probably to the relative youth of these industries and the tighter regulatory controls by the Canadian Radio-Television Commission), but the same trend towards increasing concentration of ownership is present and, as with newspapers, this trend is accelerating.

The Davey Report points out that one of the attractions of mass media ownership for large-scale corporations is the extremely profitable nature of most forms of mass media. For example, in 1965, owning a newspaper was almost twice as profitable a business venture as most manufacturing and retail enterprises. Also, although 1967 was economically a bad year for Canada's biggest television stations because their ratio of pre-tax profits to investment declined to 40% (from a high of 98.5% in 1964), both these figures would be regarded as astronomically high in any other industry. And there are indications of an even more profitable future for Canadian media owners, since revenues seem to be currently growing at a much faster rate than production costs.

The Report does not simply focus on the negative side of chain or multi-media ownership; it also shows the beneficial aspects of such ownership. For example, chain newspaper ownership has saved several daily newspapers from becoming weeklies or going out of business; it has served to financially strengthen several "shaky" newspapers; and it has often resulted in improving the editorial quality of papers.

But the good points about chain or multi-media ownership, do not overshadow the fact that the control of Canada's mass media is becoming increasingly concentrated in the hands of a smaller and smaller privileged group of businessmen.

> What matters is the fact that control of the media is passing into fewer and fewer hands, and that the experts agree this trend is likely to continue and perhaps accelerate. . . . If the trend towards ownership concentration is allowed to continue unabated, sooner or later it must reach the point where it collides with the public interest. The Committee believes it to be in the national interest to ensure that that point is not reached.[4]

Recommendations on Mass Media Ownership

In the area of media ownership, the Special Senate Committee on Mass Media had two basic recommendations. First, the Committee recommended the establishment of a Press Ownership Review Board patterned after the British Monopolies Commission. The philosophy and function of this Board are outlined in the following passage from the Davey Report:

> . . . *we urge the government to establish a Press Ownership Review Board with powers to approve or disapprove mergers between, or acquisitions of, newspapers and periodicals.* The Board should have one basic guideline, spelled out in its enabling legislation: *all* transactions that increase concentration of ownership in the mass media are undesirable and contrary to the public interest—unless shown to be otherwise.[5]

The Committee did not recommend the establishment of a similar regulatory body to oversee broadcasting mergers and acquisitions, since the Canadian Radio-Television Commission already has such authority.

Secondly, the Report recommended the creation by the government of a Publications Development Loan Fund to provide financial help to new Canadian publishing concerns in getting started. It was felt by the Committee that this Fund would help to combat the increasing concentration of media ownership by encouraging, through a "matching" funds financing arrangement, the emergence of more new and diverse media voices.

Quality of the Mass Media

In addition to its concern with the ownership of Canadian media, the Special Senate Committee on Mass Media was interested in the quality and professionalism of mass communication in Canada. The Committee's principal standard for judging the quality of media is seen in the following sentence:

> The standard we choose to employ is pretty straightforward: *how successful is that newspaper, or broadcasting station, in preparing its audience for social change?*[6]

The mass media today must not only give the Who, What, When, and Where of daily news in its coverage and programming, but also the more difficult and ambiguous Why behind the news. It is in performing this last function that the mass media is clearly falling down in its job. The Committee points out the lack of editorial excellence and of high-quality programming in most Canadian media —a particularly disturbing fact given the high profits of the industry.

> But the general pattern, we regret to say, is of newspapers and broadcasting stations that are pulling the maximum out of their communities, and giving back a minimum in return. . . . Too many newspapers and broadcasting stations, in other words, are delivering a product that is not as good as they could afford to make it. They don't try hard enough to improve their product because there is no economic incentive to do so—quite the reverse, in fact.[7]

This "give-'em-as-little-as-possible" attitude of the mass media management, according to the Report, has had a definite detrimental effect on the maintenance of high journalistic standards, ethics, professionalism, and quality. And the mass media owners equate any government suggestions for ensuring a more "diverse and antagonistic" press, for improving the quality of the information service provided by the industry, and for raising professional standards of working journalists, with government interference with the freedom of the press.

The Committee maintained that freedom of the press must be accompanied by responsibility of the press for maintaining high professional standards, quality information services, and numerous divergent viewpoints. All too often the owners of Canadian media have forgotten that they are involved in a public service and are not simply another commercial industry.

Recommendations for Improving the Quality of Mass Media

The Davey Report recommended the establishment of national and regional press councils, as well as local community press committees, to monitor the activities of the press in Canada. These press councils and press committees would be modeled after the British Press Council, and they would discuss the issues of professional standards, ethics, and quality within the mass media. They would be concerned only with printed media, since the Canadian Radio-Television Commission already serves a similar function for the broadcasting industry.

The membership of the national and regional press councils and local community press committees should consist of representatives of the media owners, working journalists, and consumers. The Davey Committee thought the surest way to avoid direct government interference in the printed media is to establish a rigorous system of self-regulation within the journalism profession, similar to that which now exists in such public-service professions as law and medicine. But the Davey Report, in addition, seemed to reflect the opinion that the mass-media consumers should also have some voice in determining how the media operate for their supposed benefit. For just as war is too important a thing to be left solely to the control of generals, the mass media are much too important to our society to be left simply to the control of their owners.

In addition, the Committee thought that the quality of the media could be improved by checking the monopolistic tendencies of media control and by encouraging the multiplication of diverse media voices.

Americanization of Mass Media

The Davey Report presented a number of alarming findings about American domination in Canadian media. For example, two American magazines, *Time* and *Reader's Digest*, with special Canadian sections in them, together share 56% of the total advertising revenue spent in Canada on major consumer magazines. This situation is due to the fact that, although the Canadian Income Tax Act prohibits Canadian businesses from deducting expenses for advertising in foreign magazines, *Time* and *Reader's Digest* are exempted from this legislation. This means that these two magazines are in a preferred economic position to compete with Canadian magazines and with other American magazines. Also, although Canadians said they preferred Canadian magazines to American magazines by a margin of 56% to 37%, in 1969 Canadians bought American magazines in nearly a four to one ratio to Canadian magazines (130.5 million American magazines to 33.8 million Canadian magazines).

The significant portion of Canada's population which lives in areas bordering the United States, is within direct range of American television station broadcasts. The influence of American television in Canada has been further increased by the appearance of cable television, which 15.3% of the total Canadian population over two years old watched in 1969. In addition, 36.5% of the weekly programming on the CBC English television network was American.[8]

The dominance of American television is clearly seen in such border areas as the Toronto-Hamilton area. In this area Canadians watched 34 million hours a month of American programming on American stations and 43 million hours of Canadian television. But when the American programs carried by Canadian television stations are taken into account, it becomes clear that American programming predominates. Another disturbing fact reported by the Davey Commission was that Canadians preferred American television programming to their own television programming at a rate of 54% to 43%.

Recommendations for Curbing Americanization of Mass Media

The Special Senate Committee on Mass Media made one principal recommendation in the area of the Americanization of Canadian media. The Committee recommended that the tax exemptions now granted to *Time* and *Reader's Digest* magazines be removed, and if future events warrant it, that these magazines be required to sell 75% of their Canadian subsidiaries to Canadians.

The Davey Committee did not have to make any recommendations to curb American influence in Canadian television and radio, since the Canadian Radio-Television Commission had already ruled that by 1972 all Canadian stations must carry 60% Canadian programming, and of the 40% foreign content, no more than 30% could come from any one foreign country, such as the United States.

1. Senator Keith Davey, Chairman, *Report of the Special Senate Committee on Mass Media* (Ottawa: Queen's Printer, 1970), vol. 1, *The Uncertain Mirror*, p. vii. Findings and recommendations included in vol. 2, *Words, Music and Dollars* and vol. 3, *Good, Bad or Simply Inevitable* are also referred to in the article.
2. *The Uncertain Mirror*, p. 3.
3. *The Uncertain Mirror*, p. 5.
4. *The Uncertain Mirror*, p. 6.
5. *The Uncertain Mirror*, p. 71.
6. *The Uncertain Mirror*, p. 84.
7. *The Uncertain Mirror*, pp. 63-64.
8. Canadian Broadcasting Corporation, *Annual Report, 1969-70.*

The Davey Report: In Retrospect

KEITH DAVEY

The Uncertain Mirror, the first volume of the *Report of the Special Senate Committee on Mass Media*, has been selling extremely well across the country; this is especially gratifying in view of the significance the Report attaches to public involvement in the media.

The Committee really had three concerns: the first of these was to achieve, and find ways and means of encouraging, a multiplication of media voices. We were concerned that our research confirmed that 66 per cent of the daily newspapers in Canada and almost 50 per cent of the television and broadcasting stations are involved in some form or other of common or concentrated ownership. More voices may be healthier, but fewer voices are cheaper. The Report explains the irresistible tendency, which economists describe as the process of "natural monopoly," of the print and electronic media to merge into larger and larger economic units. With that background, we then proceeded to a series of recommendations which included a publications loan development fund and a press ownership review board.

Secondly, we wanted to bring forward ideas which would result in an improvement in the quality of all the media voices and all the messages of those voices. Inevitably this brought to us a number of very significant value-loaded questions concerning the quality of media voices: what in fact is a good newspaper? what is a good radio station? what is a good television station? We decided that good media are those that prepare their audiences for the onslaught of social change. Senator Richard Stanbury effectively summed up the entire argument in the following statement:

> Change need not be feared if it is understood, but if day after day we are assaulted with the news of violent events

> which we have not anticipated, or whose causative factors have not been explained, we can hardly expect to avoid the feeling that events chase each other across our lives without rhythm or reason and are so far beyond our ability to affect or control that we might just as well lapse into apathy or seek change or authority through violence.

The media act as a check upon institutional power centres in our society; there is, however, no check upon the media. Freedom of the press must be accompanied by responsibility of the press. Our research showed very clearly that the media collectively possess the resources to do much better. The problem is not that the media enterprises are charging too much but that they are spending too little.

The third concern of the Committee, and a very vital concern, was not for economic nationalism but for economic nationalism's twin brother—cultural survival. The Report effectively puts the problem into perspective in this passage:

> We all know the obstacles involved in this task. Geography, language, and perhaps a failure of confidence and imagination have made us into a cultural as well as an economic satellite of the United States. And nowhere is this trend more pronounced than in the media.
>
> We are not suggesting that these influences are undesirable, nor that they can or should be restricted. The United States happens to be the most important, most interesting country on earth. The vigour and diversity of its popular culture—which is close to becoming a world culture—obsesses, alarms, and amuses not just Canadians, but half the people of the world.
>
> What we are suggesting is that the Canadian media—especially broadcasting—have an interest in and an obligation to promote our apartness from the American reality. For all our similarities, for all our sharing, for all our friendships, we are somebody else.

These, then, were the objectives: more voices, better voices and our cultural survival. Out of these objectives flowed the series of recommendations to government, to media owners, to the working press and to the people of Canada. Perhaps "recommendations" overstates the case; the Report itself refers to them as "exhortations, wistful wishes and expressions of earnest hope."

In considering the question of concentration of ownership, we asked almost every media owner who appeared before the Committee, "How much is too much?" At the hearings, of course, there was no clear agreement as to the amount. No one advanced even a tentative formula. However, practically all the media owners conceded that there was a point beyond which common ownership was no longer in the public interest and most were prepared to concede that the ongoing trend towards concentrated ownership was in fact a problem.

Our Committee made a recommendation which did not involve a pat mathematical formula, for we rejected such a formula as incompatible with the reality of Canadian economics and geography. We proposed a press ownership review board, whose criterion should be that all transactions to increase common ownership in the mass media are undesirable and contrary to the public interest unless shown to be otherwise.

The debate in the Senate which followed the tabling of the Report was begun by Senator Grattan O'Leary. While taking eloquent issue with several of our positions, he nonetheless began his remarks by underlining the usefulness of such an exercise because "on the whole it rescued the press from a state of complacency and euphoria in which it had dwelt too long."

Senator O'Leary, after commenting that "I do not think that a lot of amalgamations are a good thing," went on to reject our proposal for a press ownership review board in these words: "Surely the anti-combines legislation should cover that." His comment pretty well sums up the position of publishers on this question.

It seems to me that one thing is wrong with the existing combines legislation as it relates to newspapers. Simply stated, this is the fact that it has not worked. That is apparent from the very extent of the concentration of press control in this country. The review board might be an ideal solution. I am not married to that concept, nor are the other members of the Committee. However, I am vitally concerned with solving the problem by means which are preventive before the fact rather than—as is the case with the existing legislation which does not work anyway—punitive after the fact. Perhaps the existing legislation could be amended to produce a solution.

The working press, in particular, responded enthusiastically to our recommendation for a publications loan development fund. Most daily newspaper publishers rejected this proposal on the grounds that such "subsidization" might be the thin edge of the wedge where press freedom was concerned. In fact, of course, our proposal was for a form of high risk loans, which for the life of me I cannot see as a subsidy in any sense of the word. It would help, however, to maintain and extend our developing alternate press.

The Committee enthusiastically endorsed some form of press council for Canada. Such a council would have two great virtues. It would serve as a watchdog to monitor the press in much the same way as the press now monitors society. An incidental value would be that for the first time journalists and publishers would meet on a more or less regular basis to discuss something other than monetary matters: something other than salaries, as is the case with the working press; something other than advertising revenues, as is the case with the publishers. They would discuss standards, ethics, professionalism, and quality. The press council would consist of publishers, journalists and media consumers. There would, of course, be no government involvement.

Unfortunately, however, many publishers, though by no means all, continue to reject even this degree of reader involvement in their activities. A great part of this resistance comes from one city where publishers should know that if a newspaper treats its readers badly there is practically nothing the readers can do about it.

One of the more familiar arguments advanced by

publishers before the Committee in opposing the press council was the contention, which is at variance with the facts, that the press council in the United Kingdom has not been very effective. Several of us visited there; we spoke to publishers, journalists, politicians, and other people, and it seemed to be generally agreed that the Press Council had significantly improved the quality of British journalism.

Some people express concern about the Committee's standard for judging performance. That concern was expressed in the Senate debate by Senator Paul Desruisseaux, who stated his position thus:

> It is the function of the press and the function of broadcasting to assure freedom of the views of its public in the light of faithful, truthful, and completely reported events from everywhere in the world.

No one could disagree with that, but surely there is something more. Surely these are rock-bottom requirements, and surely such obvious and minimal standards are not those against which we should measure performance and quality. Change is ubiquitous; its high-velocity movement engulfs us every day. The media have an obligation to explore the causes and the nature of such change.

Magazines are a special case, for they constitute the only national press we have in Canada. Magazines also add journalistic dimensions which no other medium can provide: depth, wholeness, and texture. Because of their freedom from daily deadlines magazines can aspire to a level of excellence that is seldom attained in any other medium. Magazines, in a different way from any other medium, can help to foster in Canadians a sense of themselves. There are, however, very few Canadian home consumer magazines that can claim with any degree of assurance that their survival is certain.

Time and *Reader's Digest* together account for more than half of the advertising revenue that all major consumer magazines receive in Canada, and it is reasonable to anticipate that they will continue to grab off larger and larger portions of the available revenue. I should stress my continuing conviction that the special privileges granted to *Time* and *Reader's Digest* should be removed. We recommend that the exemptions now granted to both magazines under section 12(a) of the Income Tax Act be repealed, and the sooner the better. Even if *Time* and *Reader's Digest* did find it possible to continue to publish their Canadian editions despite the removal of the exemptions, they would at least be competing on a more equitable basis than before. If this did not improve the health of the Canadian magazine industry, the Committee suggests that the two magazines could be required to sell 75 per cent of the stock of their Canadian subsidiaries to Canadian residents, after the example of the C.R.T.C. which requires 80 per cent Canadian control of broadcasting corporations.

The *Time* and *Reader's Digest* lobbies on Parliament Hill have been predictably and understandably opposed to our recommendations. To protect their profits they have tended to concentrate on three themes: first, that what we are proposing is a form of retroactivity; second, that it would not work anyway but would make the climate for Canadian magazines less rather than more attractive; and third, that the Canadian industry itself did not favour the removal of these special privileges.

The "it-won't-help-anyway" argument actually goes much further. It says that if you take *Time* and *Reader's Digest* out of Canada you will not have any magazine budget at all. It will be the beginning of the end of magazine advertising in Canada. This position is buttressed by a study referred to in our Report, which stated that Canada's largest advertisers indicated that even if the two magazines in question folded up their Canadian editions, only 13 per cent of their advertising expenditure would be diverted to other Canadian magazines.

That private survey was made ten years ago, and ten years is a long time. The bloom is off the television rose. For the first time in a long while there are television availabilities in just about every major market in Canada. In addition, in our country now there is a very distinct and growing concern about the survival of Canadian culture. I also dare to assert that Canadian magazines themselves are better than ever and certainly better than they were ten years ago.

It is true that the corporate magazine establishment did not seek the removal of these special privileges; but the working press, as opposed to the corporate magazine press, was in agreement with our position. This was apparent from the petition we received from 364 working magazine people representing 186 publications. And, indeed, since the tabling of the Report I have continued to receive significant letters from members of the working press. One was from Doris Anderson, the remarkably successful editor of *Chatelaine*. She wrote:

> As long as *Time* and *Reader's Digest* are here enjoying a favourable and a competitive situation, I cannot see this situation changing. In fact, the situation will almost certainly deteriorate. I think if we care about Canada and a strong periodical press (and I don't think that the two can very well be separated) then action to end the special Canadian editions of *Time* and *Reader's Digest* must be taken.

I heard as well from Peter Newman, now the editor of *Maclean's*. His letter concluded:

> In my personal view, this will be achieved in the long run, only if *Time* and *Reader's Digest* revert to what they really are: American magazines which should be coming into this country on exactly the same basis as all the other U.S. publications.

As for the retroactivity argument, I cannot accept the principle that the government ever grants special privileges in perpetuity.

I am optimistic that the government will do something about this particular set of recommendations. The government has before it the nearly unanimous recommendation of the Special Senate Committee on Mass Media. It is similar to the unanimous recommendation of the all-party committee of the House of Commons. It has also before it the opinion of the delegates to last fall's policy convention of the Liberal party: these delegates voted 817 for ending the concession, 57 against, and 78 unsure. The Prime Minister, in a letter to a young lady who attended the convention, wrote that "the views of the delegates to the 1970 Liberal Policy Convention will not be shelved somewhere to gather dust for years."

The Mass Media Committee endorsed the national broadcasting system with its twin dimensions—public and private—as not only desirable but essential in the Canadian situation. It probably made Senate history by endorsing, although not without reservation, the whole concept of public broadcasting. We hope that one positive result of our report will be the decision to grant the CBC the five-year financing which it so obviously requires. I have been constantly amazed at private broadcasters who seem to think that the CBC is supposed to make a profit. The Canadian Broadcasting Corporation is a public service and performs functions well beyond the scope of the private sector.

The Report was extremely critical of private broadcasters. Until these people realize that they are involved in a service as well as an industry they will, I am afraid, continue to leave their mandate unfulfilled.

How did the newspapers, radio stations, and television stations across the country respond to the Report? I think it is fair to say that the coverage was extensive and that most of it was favourable. Each medium tended, of course, to be rather parochial; that is, the daily newspapers focused on the comments we had made about newspapers, the radio stations concerned themselves with our comments about radio stations, the weeklies worried about what we said about weeklies—each medium tending, with the possible exception of the daily newspapers, to ignore the comments we had made about the other media.

Has anything really happened as a result of this

considerable activity? Yes, I honestly think so. First of all, the response from the academic community has been overwhelming. I have received many letters from members of this community, and a number of the universities and community colleges intend to use the Report as a basic text in their various courses of instruction. There is even some evidence of possible use of the Report at the high school level.

Our Report stated that "Quebec is already close to the formation of a press council for that province." Since the tabling of the Report, the Quebec press council has become a reality. Our Report had stated that we thought it desirable and inevitable that Quebec have its own regional organization. We think it equally desirable that a counterpart organization be formed for English-speaking Canada and that the two bodies be affiliated to form a national body.

I was extremely encouraged by a Gallup poll report which appeared in many newspapers across Canada. The question asked was:

> The Senate Committee on Mass Media—that is newspapers, TV, and radio—has suggested that a voluntary press council should be established to examine complaints from the public about them. Do you think that this would be a good idea, or don't you think it necessary?

In spite of the rather limited amount of publicity the press council had received, only 26 per cent of Canadians thought it was not necessary, 14 per cent were undecided, and 60 per cent supported the creation of a voluntary press council.

The 1971 meeting of the Canadian Daily Newspapers Publishers Association had a useful discussion of press councils—useful because some publishers, although not a majority, clearly favoured the idea. Too many publishers continue to soft-pedal their responsibility, to cloak their activity behind the venerable cliché of press freedom. But just as clearly, there are some who want to move Canadian media into the second half of the twentieth century. It is apparent that the working press will get there first but not before at least some of the more progressive publishers and broadcasters.

The Committee lamented the absence of professionalism in Canadian journalism:

> The basis of professionalism, surely, is that there are certain things a professional will not do, and other things he must do. The recognition and definition of these standards, and the definition of the practitioners to whom they apply, is what separates accountants, teachers, physicians, and lawyers from steamfitters, plumbers, garage mechanics, TV repairmen—and journalists. As a matter of fact, steamfitters, plumbers et al. have taken a more professional approach to their trade than journalists have; they at least insist on certain minimum standards of training. We don't think the journalistic environment is going to change very much unless and until journalists start assuming—or demanding—such responsibility.

Happily, this kind of change is now evident. Early in May, a conference of nearly 400 journalists from every corner of Canada met in Ottawa and took the first steps toward ultimate professional status.

Any real improvement in the media is not in the hands of the Committee; nor is there very much the government can do. This is why I honestly believe that our recommendations really represent only the tertiary value of the Report. The Report's fundamental significance is that it has provided the people of Canada—including viewers, readers, owners, and members of the working press—with one considered assessment of their performance, one set of insights into their activities. A free press presumes responsibility. While urging the preservation of press freedom, we have tried to remind owners that it is not only governments that can curtail press freedom.

We have also tried to alert the people of Canada to their responsibility as consumers of the mass media. Unhappily, too many of us spend too much time watching rather than reading, listening rather than participating. Too many of us are appealed to by lowest-common-denominator programming. Too many Canadians—a majority, according to our research—find out what is happening in the world by watching television news. These people cannot possibly constitute a well-informed citizenry.

On the other hand, more people are becoming involved in the working of political and other processes in Canada. I think that publishers, broadcasters, and others who really care about the quality of the media—and I do not for a moment quarrel with the sincerity of most of these people—should accept the new politics of involvement, for we hope it will accentuate and renew public interest in the media.

The Media Control Institution in Society: Canada and the U.S. Compared

HARRY J. BOYLE

Because of the unique characteristic of broadcasting—the technical limitations imposed on it by the finite number of waveband frequencies—control institutions have come into being in democratic societies. Technical limitations thus make it necessary to consider the issue of priorities in broadcasting, and this consideration inevitably results in broadcasting control institutions becoming involved to some degree in policies concerning programming content.

These technical limitations also give rise to problems that are external to the social system. Sovereign states must agree on frequencies on an international basis, as well as allocate frequencies within their own systems. Once a control institution exists, it must concern itself with broadcasting content from without the system as well as with technical issues that relate to frequency agreements.

The development of control institutions in both Canada and the United States has been influenced by the proximity of the two countries. Without doubt, though, the development and policies of the Canadian institution, the Canadian Radio-Television Commission, have been conditioned by the proximity of the United States more than the reverse.

As early as 1919, the Canadian Government established control of the licensing of both radio stations and receiving sets, while conditions in the United States were still chaotic. In 1921, when commercial broadcasting began, only six clear channels were available to Canadian stations. One year later, the United States appropriated every channel, including those being used by Canada, although in 1924 the American government agreed to vacate six clear channels and restrict the power of a few others. They maintained that the allocation of channels should be on the basis of population irrespective of geography. In 1925, Canada complained that six channels were inadequate, but at that time American efforts to bring about effective controlling legislation broke down, and American operators again appropriated all the channels. The resulting chaos led Canada, in 1926, to notify its neighbour that a treaty should be concluded that would be respected by both countries. In 1927, a delegation was appointed to negotiate such a treaty. The United States demanded seventy-seven exclusive channels, leaving only six to Canada. Negotiations were broken off, both countries asserting their rights to any and all channels. It was not until 1937 that frequency allocations were finally settled for North America in a treaty signed at Havana.

Broadcasting and Cultural Dominance

Weir has noted a number of important early historical factors that caused Canadian concern over the issue of U.S. cultural dominance. First, the aggregate power of Canadian stations, by 1932, was well under ten per cent of the combined American wattage and the U.S. stations could be heard in many parts of Canada. In addition, much of Canada's power was concentrated in its two largest cities, Toronto and Montreal, leaving Canada's isolated areas even more vulnerable. In addition, Weir points out that by this time, two Toronto stations and two in Montreal were also serving as "part time outlets"[1] for American networks, and that nearly 40 per cent of the time of the three English language stations that were American affiliates was taken up with American programming. By that time, many Canadians were becoming alarmed that "Canada was fast becoming a mere satellite of American broadcasting."[2]

It is in such situations as these that control institutions can play a role in helping maintain Canada's cultural autonomy. One method is by restricting content from other countries, and another is through government-financed broadcasting. In 1932, the Chairman of the Royal Commission on Broadcasting (the Aird Commission) said:

> It seemed plain in 1929, it is plainer still in 1932, that an adequate broadcasting service in this country will need more revenue than private enterprise can earn from operating broadcasting stations for gain.[3]

Our system, then, evolved into one of private broadcasting stations and public ones—the public stations financed at first by license fees. For a time the public corporation also served as the regulatory body for all broadcasting in Canada. The license fees were abolished in lieu of state subsidy and a limited amount of advertising revenue. By 1958, a separate regulatory body, called the Board of Broadcast Governors, was set up.

Each part of the Canadian broadcasting system—the private and the public—has had its exponents. It hasn't been easy for many of the pioneers and entrepreneurs who regarded broadcasting as essentially a "business" in the accepted North American sense of private enterprise, to accept regulation. Most have agreed that the allocation of channels and frequencies is necessary to prevent chaos, but it is difficult for many to accept that broadcasting has a number of purposes—from education to information, from relaxation to merchandising. These private broadcasters regard the industry more simply as a service industry with a fairly high degree of profitability—a degree of profitability which is generally increased by the protection of regulation, although this point is seldom conceded in tones above a whisper.

Comparing Control Institutions

Canada's control institution shares some of the concerns of the British and American institutions, but obviously has concerns of its own that go beyond either. Most national statutes governing broadcasting do not define the obligations of a broadcaster or the purpose of broadcasting, or at least do not do so in terms which give substance and clarity to the real function of broadcasting, which is the production and transmission of programs. The American statute does not go beyond the terms "public interest, convenience and necessity".[4] The Royal Charter governing the British Broadcasting Corporation, financed by the listeners and viewers without advertising or yearly revenue from the taxpayer, provides for the production and dissemination of programs which offer "information, education and entertainment . . . in the interest of our Peoples in Our United Kingdom and elsewhere within the British Commonwealth of Nations."[5] The Television Act of 1964 which governs the commercial sector of British broadcasting requires the Independent Television Authority to disseminate programs which provide "information, education and entertainment,"[6] but requires as well that its programs, produced by commercial program contractors, maintain a high general standard in all respects, and in particular in respect of their content and quality, and a proper balance and wide range in their subject matter. Wisely, these admirable—even pious—aspirations are not rigidly defined; every broadcaster knows only too well that terms like "balance" and "quality" cannot be so clearly spelled out. Good broadcasting is a practice, not a prescription; an art, not an education. Finally, in the commercial sector of British broadcasting, the transmitting stations are wholly owned by the State, while the program contractors, unlike the British Broadcasting Corporation, derive their revenues from advertising.

The Canadian Statute of 1968 added to comparable obligations of broadcasters, the provision that Canadian broadcasting should promote national unity. The Act also set up a regulatory body, the Canadian Radio-Television Commission, to which both the publicly-owned Canadian Broadcasting Corporation and the more numerous privately-owned stations are responsible; similarly, both public and private stations are subject to control by the Canadian Radio-Television Commission. This Commission, in addition to licensing new stations, has a regulatory authority over programming, advertising and other uses of the channel or wavelength which the licensee for periods of up to five years may use. In all these statutes, it is stated specifically or by implication that broadcasters must obey the laws respecting libel, obscenity, and so on, as must any publisher or any private citizen orating on the street corner, and in some statutes due attention is required to good taste and decency in programs and care in the presentation of violence.

The obligations of the broadcaster in programming are not, then, easily explicable in statutory terms. It will also be observed that the statutes do not themselves through regulations limit profits or, on the other hand, require the broadcasters to operate profitably. That is left to the broadcaster's wisdom and, where there are market considerations, as distinct from license fees or statutory grants as sources of revenue, to the forces of the market.

The Broadcasting Act of 1968 in Canada was a follow-up to a committee on Broadcasting of 1965, chaired by a distinguished Canadian, R.M. Fowler. Here are some conclusions of the 1965 report upon which, it may be assumed, the present Broadcasting Act was largely based:

> The Canadian broadcasting system has many tasks to perform. It should, as one of its central purposes, bring news and information to as many Canadians as it can physically reach, and the news it provides should be immediate, accurate and dispassionate. Important news from both local and foreign sources should be seen through Canadian eyes to reflect Canadian values and judgments.
>
> Radio and television must also enlighten and entertain their listeners and viewers. In Canada, specifically, broadcasting services have a vitally important role in interpreting the views and differences and achievements of widely scattered regions and groups in the country to each other.[7]

The Fowler report went on to say that:

> One of the essential tasks of a broadcasting system is to stir up the minds and emotions of the people, and occasionally to make large numbers of them acutely uncomfortable.
>
> In a vital broadcasting system, there must be room for the thinker, the disturber, and the creator of new forms and ideas.
>
> The reverse side of the coin of freedom is responsibility and discipline. No broadcasting agency can validly claim to be independent of detailed political interference and control unless it is prepared to be responsible and realistic in the use it makes of its freedom. All broadcasting agencies—both public and private—are recipients of public support in the right to use scarce public assets. They must pay for these valuable rights by giving a responsible performance, and the State is fully entitled to ensure that the trust is honoured.[8]

For 52 years Canada has been evolving—or trying to evolve—a sense of what the responsibility of broadcasters is in scrambling to keep up with technology and social change, and it is still not by any means certain what effect communications has had on the nation or its people.

Under the Broadcasting Act the Canadian Radio-Television Commission is bound by strict procedures, including publication in the *Canada Gazette* of any application received by it for the issue, amendment or renewal of a broadcasting license, and publication in the local newspaper of the area affected—and it is strictly bound in terms of public hearings.

The Broadcasting Act states, in summary, that:

1. Licensing and technical matters are separate.
2. Licensing authority exercises certain limited controls over programming in general.
3. The CRTC can obtain information from wherever it pleases in addition to public hearings.
4. The Canadian broadcasting system consists of public and private broadcasting stations.

5. The public body, that is, the Canadian Broadcasting Corporation, owns and operates educational stations with programming being supplied by the provincial educational authority.
6. CATV is part of broadcasting and licensed by the same authority under the same procedure, but again a technical certificate must be issued by the Department of Communications before we issue a license.
7. Broadcasting service is provided in two languages.
8. The Act provides for direction by the Government to the licensing authority on specific issues. An example occurred when the C.R.T.C. specified that broadcasting must be 80 per cent owned by Canadians.
9. A directive of the federal government provides that an educational institution may not own a broadcasting station. In the province of Ontario, for instance, the facility is licensed to the CBC while the programming is provided by the provincial educational authority.
10. All public hearings are headed by Commissioners—staff does not hold examination hearings.[9]

Canada has had a publicly-owned body since 1932 for the purpose of operating a national broadcasting network. It became the CBC in 1936.

The CBC operates under a Board of Directors appointed by the Governor-in-Council. The Corporation is independent of the Government, reports to Parliament but is responsible to the licensing authority.

Approximately four-fifths of CBC revenue is obtained from the public Treasury and the balance is from commercial revenue.

The Corporation operates networks for:

1. English language television;
2. French language television;
3. French language radio AM;
4. English language radio AM;
5. English language radio FM;
6. Educational television to carry programs of the provincial educational authority.

The CBC network consists of owned and operated stations and affiliated privately-owned stations.

In most cases, TV service is provided in the language of the majority, but it has stations for each language in Moncton, New Brunswick, Quebec and Montreal, P.Q., Ottawa, Ontario and Winnipeg, Manitoba.

In radio, dual language is more widespread. There are several low-power stations operating as network repeaters which service pockets of population in seven of the ten provinces (not in Newfoundland, Prince Edward Island, or British Columbia.) Radio stations provide service in two languages at Moncton, Sherbrooke, Quebec, Montreal, Ottawa, Timmins, Windsor, Cornwall, Winnipeg, Saskatoon, Gravelbourg and Edmonton.

The privately-owned network, CTV, operates on commercial revenue only. There is no privately-owned national radio network.

The Canadian political and social system is a complicated one. The Canadian broadcasting system is an exercise in delicate balances—between local and national considerations, between isolated areas and highly developed areas, between public and private interests—which provides all but about one million Canadians with television service, and all the rest, hopefully, with at least radio service. These necessary balances have been recognized by every official body from the Aird Commission in 1929 to the Parliament of Canada which passed the Broadcasting Act of 1968.

In the United States, the Federal Communications Commission issued a programming policy statement in 1960, which is still the basic guideline for broadcast programming in the United States. In this policy statement, the F.C.C. suggested to applicants and licensees the prime considerations to be taken into account in devising programme structures. Briefly, the broadcaster is directed to consider "the tastes, needs and desires of the public he is licensed to serve" and to attempt "to meet all such needs and interests on an equitable basis" and recognize at the same time that the tastes, needs and desires and interests "may of course differ from community to community, and from time to time."[10] The major programming areas reflecting the "needs and interests" were listed thus:

1. the opportunity for local self-expression;
2. the development and use of local talent;
3. programmes for children;
4. religious programmes;
5. educational programmes;
6. public affairs programmes;
7. editorialization by licensees;
8. political broadcasts;
9. agricultural broadcasts;
10. news programmes;
11. weather and market reports;
12. sport programmes;
13. service to minority groups;
14. entertainment programming.[11]

The category system established in Canada by the Board of Broadcast Governors reflects in many respects the elements outlined in this policy statement of the F.C.C., although the emphasis is sometimes different. A formal category system like that of the B.B.G./C.R.T.C. may be of value in spelling out clearly the individual conditions of license to be attached when licensing broadcast undertakings. However, conditions of license in this sense, spelling out programming obligations in terms of the proportion of time which may be devoted to particular categories of programming or qualitative considerations, have always been considered by the F.C.C. as beyond its authority. The Supreme Court's decision in 1968 that the F.C.C., although it does not license CATV undertakings, has the responsibility to regulate them, and the F.C.C.'s own suggestion that it may require PAY-TV systems to devote no more than 45% of their daily programming time to sports and movies, suggest that the F.C.C. may be abandoning its earlier reluctance to issue directives in the programming field. The purpose of the draft bill containing this proposal is primarily to maintain a competitive position among the various broadcast media.[12] It offers another example of the fact that "the growth of communications law generally parallels the startling evolution of communications technology. Since technology usually precedes the regulation of its economic and social effects, radio regulation has never quite kept pace with technical developments in the field."[13]

Primarily because of the wide range of technical factors it is obliged to deal with, the Federal Communications Commission's rule-making is vastly more extensive than that of the Canadian Radio-Television Commission, and it is essentially legalistic in tone. Redress of grievances against the F.C.C. is more commonly sought in the courts than is the case with grievances brought before the C.R.T.C., where political methods are more commonly used. Public hearings in Canada, involving the full Commission, constitute a public forum rather than a legal examination. Maintenance of adequate records, log reporting systems for programming and technical operations, careful examination of applicants in terms of citizenship, character, and financial, technical and other qualifications are common to both systems. Preponderance of domestic ownership in all broadcast systems, in more or less similar terms, is characteristic of both F.F.C. and C.R.T.C. operations, but ownership limitations, to ensure competition and to conform to anti-trust legislation, are more clearly defined by the F.C.C. than by the C.R.T.C. Substantial penalties for breaches of the regulations, and the use of the licensing authority for disciplinary purposes, are common to both systems, and in both the statutory and regulatory authorities are supported in certain ways by provisions in the Criminal Code, for example against fraud, obscenity, lotteries (where applicable) and misleading advertising. In questions of misleading advertising, the F.C.C. co-operates closely with the primary authority, the Federal Trade Commission. The parallel Canadian agency is now the Department of Consumer and Corporate Affairs.

A comparison of the two systems of rules and regulations reveals something of the larger systems in which they operate. The American institution traditionally has concerned itself less with content and, in laissez-faire fashion, seems dedicated more to preventing conflicts and misuse. The Canadian institution, on the other hand, is oriented to the ideal of serving widely separated communities and diverse interests, and at the same time of functioning as a technologically-based force to bring unity out of diversity. Both the Canadian and American institutions for broadcasting control thus reflect some of the problems and objectives of the social systems in which they were generated.

1. E.A. Weir, *The Struggle for National Broadcasting in Canada* (Toronto: McClelland and Stewart, 1965), p. 98.
2. *Ibid.*
3. *Ibid.*, p. 107 et seq. for summary.
4. "Communications Act 1934," in Frank J. Kahn, ed., *Documents of American Broadcasting* (New York: Appleton-Century-Crofts, 1968), pp. 54 et seq.
5. British Broadcasting Corporation Royal Charters 1927-1969 (*BBC Handbook 1971,* pp. 236-250). For a description of the steps leading to the grant of the original Royal Charter, see Asa Briggs, *The History of Broadcasting in the United Kingdom* (Oxford University Press, 1961), vol. 1, pp. 325 et seq.
6. *ITV 1970—A Guide to Independent Television* (London: Independent Television Authority, 1970), p. 19.
7. Robert M. Fowler, Chairman, *Report of the Committee on Broadcasting, 1965* (Ottawa: Queen's Printer, 1965), pp. 4 et seq.
8. *Ibid.*
9. *Broadcasting Act 1968,* 16-17 Elizabeth II Chap. 25 (Ottawa: Queen's Printer, 1968).
10. *Documents of American Broadcasting,* p. 219.
11. *Ibid.*
12. (United States) House Communications Subcommittee, *Draft Bill on Development of Pay TV.* For comments on the bill see *Weekly Television Digest,* June-December 1969.
13. *Documents of American Broadcasting,* p. 3.

Identity, Unity and Mass Communication

Cultural autonomy and national identity are intertwined; in the days before international mass media, cultural autonomy was more easily preserved against incursions from without. In Part II Boyle has highlighted the functions performed to this end by internal institutions of control such as the Canadian Radio-Television Commission. In this section, we look at some of the factors that relate the issue of national unity and identity to the mass media.

Toffler, in "Mass Media: A Force in Identity Change," helps us to understand the power of the mass media to generate change in character styles and ultimately in individual identity. If modern media have the force that Toffler asserts, then we must be more concerned with the power of American media to impose such identities on individuals in other countries as well.

Peers provides us with an historical analysis of the forces behind public and private broadcasting in Canada and of the attempt to mould the public sector of broadcasting into a force for national unity and identity. Broadcasting, as he points out, can promote Canadian identity and a national system is necessary in order to achieve national goals; the private sector, however, has been most likely not only to adopt the American model in which broadcasting is seen as light entertainment tied to the primacy of advertising, but to encourage the diffusion of American content.

Elkin defines the concept of identity and then asks about the role of mass media in creating and reinforcing a sense of Canadian *identity: mass media may either strengthen or weaken identity. In Canada there are two types of threats, internal and external, and it can be said that Canada's ideology regarding mass media in certain respects works against Canadian identity. But the mass media, in addition to operating in a causal fashion, must be understood to reflect the underlying problems and dilemmas of Canada.*

A comparative assessment of the changing roles of the different mass media is necessary if we are to understand the function of mass media in shaping beliefs, values, and behaviour. Jowett and Hemmings, by providing this kind of data and analysis of the relative positions of the different media, point to their relationship to social change and investigate the role of mass communication in creating a national social bond. Thus, mass communication should be seen as a means for reinforcing national unity in spite of the mosiac quality of our country.

In "Propaganda in Canadian Society," Professor Qualter aids us in understanding the function of propaganda at the psychological level; its use is to affect attitudes and through them to influence actual behaviour. After defining and limiting the concept so that it becomes less value-laden, Qualter examines the use of Canadian propaganda in the sense that it is used to heighten national awareness and hence identity, and sets the stage for further consideration of the concept of Canadian identity.

From different perspectives, the authors in this part have addressed themselves to the problem of national identity, but what constitutes Canadian identity still is unclear. The authors assert, in any case, that the communication system is a major force in building unity and identity. Other studies have pointed out that communication systems help define "community boundaries." This notion of community, then, becomes linked to communication through the phenomenon we call cohesiveness in the work of one of the leading students of Canadian public opinion, Mildred Schwartz. Using public opinion data, Professor Schwartz demonstrates the kind of social cohesiveness that must lie behind unity and that is one of the stanchions upon which identity is supported.

Mass Media: A Force in Identity Change

ALVIN TOFFLER

In a society in which instant food, instant education and even instant cities are everyday phenomena, no product is more swiftly fabricated or more ruthlessly destroyed than the instant celebrity. Nations advancing toward super-industrialism sharply step up their output of these "psycho-economic" products. Instant celebrities burst upon the consciousness of millions like an image-bomb —which is exactly what they are.

Within less than one year from the time a Cockney girl-child nicknamed "Twiggy" took her first modelling job, millions of human beings around the globe stored mental images of her in their brain. A dewy-eyed blonde with minimal mammaries and pipestem legs, Twiggy exploded into celebrityhood in 1967. Her winsome face and malnourished figure suddenly appeared on the covers of magazines in Britain, America, France, Italy and other countries. Overnight, Twiggy eyelashes, mannikins, perfumes and clothes began to gush from the fad mills. Critics pontificated about her social significance. Newsmen accorded her the kind of coverage normally reserved for a peace treaty or a papal election.

By now, however, our stored mental images of Twiggy have been largely erased. She has all but vanished from public view. Reality has confirmed her own shrewd estimate that "I may not be around here for another six months." For images, too, have become increasingly transient—and not only the images of models, athletes or entertainers. Not long ago I asked a highly intelligent teenager whether she and her classmates had any heroes. I said, "Do you regard John Glenn, for example, as a hero?" (Glenn being, lest the reader has forgotten, the first American astronaut to orbit in space.) The child's response was revealing. "No," she said, "he's too old."

At first I thought she regarded a man in his forties as being too old to be a hero. Soon I realized this was mistaken. What she meant was that Glenn's exploits had taken place too long ago to be of interest. (John H. Glenn's history-making flight occurred in February, 1962.) Today Glenn has receded from the foreground of public attention. In effect, his image has decayed.

Twiggy, the Beatles, John Glenn, Billie Sol Estes, Bob Dylan, Jack Ruby, Norman Mailer, Eichmann, Jean-Paul Sartre, Georgi Malenkov, Jacqueline Kennedy—thousands of "personalities" parade across the stage of contemporary history. Real people, magnified and projected by the mass media, they are stored as images in the minds of millions of people who have never met them, never spoken to them, never seen them "in person." They take on a reality almost as (and sometimes even more) intense than that of many people with whom we do have "in-person" relationships.

We form relationships with these "vicarious people," just as we do with friends, neighbors and colleagues. And just as the through-put of real, in-person people in our lives is increasing, and the duration of our average relationships with them decreasing, the same is true of our ties with the vicarious people who populate our minds.

Their rate of flow-through is influenced by the real rate of change in the world. Thus, in politics, for example, we find that the British prime ministership has been turning over since 1922 at a rate some 13 percent faster than in the base period 1721-1922. In sports, the heavyweight boxing championship now changes hands twice as fast as it did during our fathers' youth.[1] Events, moving faster, constantly throw new personalities into the charmed circle of celebrityhood, and old images in the mind decay to make way for the new.

The same might be said for the fictional characters

spewed out from the pages of books, from television screens, theaters, movies and magazines. No previous generation in history has had so many fictional characters flung at it. Commenting on the mass media, historian Marshall Fishwick wryly declares: "We may not even get used to Super-Hero, Captain Nice and Mr. Terrific before they fly off our television screens forever."

These vicarious people, both live and fictional, play a significant role in our lives, providing models for behavior, acting out for us various roles and situations from which we draw conclusions about our own lives. We deduce lessons from their activities, consciously or not. We learn from their triumphs and tribulations. They make it possible for us to "try on" various roles or life styles without suffering the consequences that might attend such experiments in real life. The accelerated flow-through of vicarious people cannot but contribute to the instability of personality patterns among many real people who have difficulty in finding a suitable life style.

These vicarious people, however, are not independent of one another. They perform their roles in a vast, complexly organized "public drama" which is, in the words of sociologist Orrin Klapp, author of a fascinating book called *Symbolic Leaders,* largely a product of the new communications technology. This public drama, in which celebrities upstage and replace celebrities at an accelerating rate, has the effect, according to Klapp, of making leadership "more unstable than it would be otherwise. Contretemps, upsets, follies, contests, scandals, make a feast of entertainment or a spinning political roulette wheel. Fads come and go at a dizzying pace. . . . A country like the United States has an open public drama, in which new faces appear daily, there is always a contest to steal the show, and almost anything can happen and often does." What we are observing, says Klapp, is a "rapid turnover of symbolic leaders."

This can be extended, however, into a far more powerful statement: what is happening is not merely a turnover of real people or even fictional characters, but a more rapid turnover of the images and image-structures in our brains. Our relationships with these images of reality, upon which we base our behavior, are growing, on average, more and more transient. The entire knowledge system in society is undergoing violent upheaval. The very concepts and codes in terms of which we think are turning over at a furious and accelerating pace. We are increasing the rate at which we must form and forget our images of reality.

Twiggy and the K-Mesons

Every person carries within his head a mental model of the world—a subjective representation of external reality. This model consists of tens upon tens of thousands of images. These may be as simple as a mental picture of clouds scudding across the sky. Or they may be abstract inferences about the way things are organized in society. We may think of this mental model as a fantastic internal warehouse, an image emporium in which we store our inner portraits of Twiggy, Charles De Gaulle or Cassius Clay, along with such sweeping propositions as "Man is basically good" or "God is dead."

Any person's mental model will contain some images that approximate reality closely, along with others that are distorted or inaccurate. But for the person to function, even to survive, the model must bear some overall resemblance to reality. As V. Gordon Childe has written in *Society and Knowledge,* "Every reproduction of the external world, constructed and used as a guide to action by an historical society, must in some degree correspond to that reality. Otherwise the society could not have maintained itself; its members, if acting in accordance with totally untrue propositions, would not have succeeded in making even the simplest tools and in securing therewith food and shelter from the external world."

No man's model of reality is a purely personal product. While some of his images are based on first-hand observation, an increasing proportion of them today are based on messages beamed to us by the mass media and the people around us. Thus the degree of accuracy in his model to some extent reflects the general level of knowledge in society. And as experience and scientific research pump more refined and accurate knowledge into society, new concepts, new ways of thinking, supersede, contradict, and render obsolete older ideas and world views.

The Engineered Message

If our inner images of reality appear to be turning over more and more rapidly, one reason may well be an increase in the rate at which image-laden messages are being hurled at our senses. Little effort has been made to investigate this scientifically, but there is evidence that we are increasing the exposure of the individual to image-bearing stimuli.

To understand why, we need first to examine the basic sources of imagery. Where do the thousands of images filed in our mental model come from? The external environment showers stimuli upon us. Signals originating outside ourselves—sound waves, light, etc.—strike our sensory organs. Once perceived, these signals are converted, through a still mysterious process, into symbols of reality, into images.

These incoming signals are of several types. Some might be called *uncoded.* Thus, for example, a man walks along a street and notices a leaf whipped along the sidewalk by the wind. He perceives this event through his sensory apparatus. He hears a rustling sound. He sees movement and greenness. He feels the wind. From these sensory perceptions he somehow forms a mental image. We can refer to these sensory signals as a message. But the message was not, in any ordinary sense of the term, man-made. It was not designed by anyone to communicate anything, and the man's understanding of it does not depend directly on a social code—a set of socially agreed-upon signs and definitions. We are all surrounded by and participate in such events. When they occur within range of our senses, we may pick up uncoded messages from them and convert these messages into mental images. In fact, some proportion of the images in every individual's mental model are derived from such uncoded messages.

But we also receive *coded* messages from outside ourselves. Coded messages are any which depend upon social convention for their meaning. All languages, whether based on words or gestures, drumbeats or dance-steps, hieroglyphs, pictographs or the arrangement of knots in a string, are codes. All messages conveyed by means of such languages are coded.

We may speculate with some safety that as societies have grown larger and more complex, proliferating codes for the transmission of images from person to person, the ratio of uncoded messages received by the ordinary person has declined in favor of coded messages. We may guess, in other words, that today more of our imagery derives from man-made messages than from personal observation of raw, "uncoded" events.

Furthermore, we can discern a subtle but significant shift in the type of coded messages as well. For the illiterate villager in an agricultural society of the past, most of the incoming messages were what might be called casual or "do-it-yourself" communications. The peasant might engage in ordinary household conversation, banter, cracker-barrel or tavern talk, griping, complaining, boasting, baby talk, (and, in the same sense, animal talk), etc. This determined the nature of most of the coded messages he received, and one characteristic of this sort of communication is its loose, unstructured, garrulous or unedited quality.

Compare this message input with the kind of coded messages received by the ordinary citizen of the present-day industrial society. In addition to all of the above, he also receives messages—mainly from the mass media—that have been artfully fashioned by communications experts. He listens to the news; he watches carefully scripted plays, telecasts, movies; he hears much more music (a highly disciplined form of communication); he hears frequent speeches. Above all, he does something his peasant ancestor could not do: he reads—thousands of words every day, all of them carefully edited in advance.

The industrial revolution, bringing with it the enormous elaboration of the mass media, thus alters radically the nature of the messages received by the ordinary individual. In addition to receiving uncoded messages from the environment, and coded but casual messages from the people around him, the individual now begins to receive a growing number of coded but pre-engineered messages as well.

These engineered messages differ from the casual or do-it-yourself product in one crucial respect: instead of being loose or carelessly framed, the engineered product tends to be tighter, more condensed, less redundant. It is highly purposive, preprocessed to eliminate unnecessary repetition, consciously designed to maximize informational content. It is, as communications theorists say, "information-rich."

This highly significant but often overlooked fact can be observed by anyone who takes the trouble to compare a tape recorded sample of 500 words of ordinary household conversation (i.e., coded, but casual) with 500 words of newspaper text or movie dialogue (also coded, but engineered). Casual conversation tends to be filled with repetition and pauses. Ideas are repeated several times, often in identical words, but if not, then varied only slightly.

In contrast, the 500 words of newspaper copy or movie dialogue are carefully pre-edited, streamlined. They convey relatively nonrepetitive ideas. They tend to be more grammatically accurate than ordinary conversation and, if presented orally, they tend to be enunciated more clearly. Waste material has been trimmed away. Editor, writer, director—everyone involved in the production of the engineered message—fights to "keep the story moving" or to produce "fast-paced action." It is no accident that books, movies, television plays, are so frequently advertised as "high-speed adventure," "fast-reading," or "breathless." No publisher or movie producer would dare advertise his work as "repetitive" or "redundant."

Thus, as radio, television, newspapers, magazines and novels sweep through society, as the proportion of engineered messages received by the individual rises (and the proportion of uncoded and coded casual messages correspondingly declines), we witness a profound change: a steady speed-up in the average pace at which image-producing messages are presented to the individual. The sea of coded information that surrounds him begins to beat at his senses with new urgency.

This helps account for the sense of hurry in everyday affairs. But if industrialism is marked by a communications speed-up, the transition to super-industrialism is marked by intense efforts to accelerate the process even further. The waves of coded information turn into violent breakers and come at a faster and faster clip, pounding at us, seeking entry, as it were, to our nervous system.

1. Between 1882 and 1932, there were ten new world heavyweight boxing champions, each holding the crown an average of 5 years. Between 1932 and 1951, there were 7 champions, each with an average tenure of 3.2 years. From 1951 to 1967, when the World Boxing Association declared the title vacant, 7 men held the championship for an average of 2.3 years each.

Broadcasting and National Unity

FRANK W. PEERS

There had been thirty years of radio broadcasting in Canada, and now there was television. For the Canadian system, the most significant fact was that Parliament had decided to continue the mixture of public and private ownership as before, reaffirming the clear pre-eminence of the public sector. As another government explained it fifteen years later, "The determination to develop and maintain a national system of radio and television is an essential part of the continuing resolve for Canadian identity and Canadian unity."[1] The compulsion to have a broadcasting system to serve national needs was just as strong in 1951 as it had been in 1929, when the Aird Commission found unanimity in Canada on one fundamental question—Canadian radio listeners wanted *Canadian* broadcasting.

Nationalist sentiment had achieved Canadian ownership and control of stations and networks, full coverage for the scattered population of an immense territory, and the use of broadcasting to foster national objectives. The aims had been national survival, whether in English or in French Canada or in Canada as a whole; a Canadian sense of identity; national unity; increased understanding between regions and language groups; cultural development; and the serving of Canadian economic interests. Often the objective was described negatively as the development of an identity separate and distinguishable from that of the United States. Seldom was nationalist sentiment precisely articulated, but it was broader than patriotic jingoism and something more ambiguous than national self-interest. In particular, the differing assumptions in French- and English-speaking Canada were left almost unexplored. Yet, in the name of nationalism much had been done by 1951, in less than twenty years.

In the early 1920's only a few had thought of radio as an instrument for the clearer delineation of a Canadian identity—notably among these, Sir Henry Thornton. But as the decade wore on, others expressed concern that American commercial interests were about to gain control of Canadian broadcasting—J. S. Woodsworth in the House of Commons, Charles Bowman in the pages of the *Ottawa Citizen* and as a member of the Royal Commission established in 1929. The other two members of the Aird Commission had been predisposed to favour private ownership and development of radio broadcasting, but they came around to Bowman's point of view as they became convinced the prevailing system would deny Canadians Canadian programs. The Canadian nation, they said, could be adequately served only by some form of public ownership, operation, and control "behind which is the national power and prestige of the whole public of the Dominion of Canada."

It was the Canadian Radio League, under the leadership of Graham Spry, Alan Plaunt, and Brooke Claxton, who succeeded in forcing a decision. Their central concern was not "nationalism," but better broadcasting—broader in scope than the service provided by the commercial system, free of the limits of the popular success, of the "profit and loss" value system. But they discovered very early that the most powerful public appeal they could exercise was a national one. This was expressed in such tags as "Canadian radio for Canadians" and "The state or the United States." In 1935 Graham Spry explained that there were two motives that led to the broadcasting legislation of 1932. "The first of these driving motives was the national motive, and it was predominant. The second motive was the free use of broadcasting by all sections of opinion. The positive aspect of the national motive was the use of broadcasting for the development of Canadian national unity, and the negative aspect was the apprehension of American influences upon Canadian nationality, particularly as it concerned public opinion."[2]

The first parliamentary committee on radio in 1932 spoke of broadcasting as a medium for "developing a greater National and Empire consciousness within the Dominion and the British Commonwealth of Nations." Prime Minister Bennett, introducing the legislation of 1932, said: "This country must be assured of complete Canadian control of broadcasting from Canadian sources, free from foreign interference or influence." Broadcasting must become an agency by which "national consciousness may be fostered and sustained and national unity still further strengthened."[3] And in 1936 Mackenzie King, impressed by the Radio League's presentation, was reported to have said, "We want the Aird Report, and this is the Aird Report brought up to date."

When it was time to select the man who would manage the CBC, Plaunt and Claxton, for specifically nationalist reasons, were determined that the man preferred by C. D. Howe would not be chosen. As Claxton wrote the Hon. Norman Rogers: "Brophy . . . has always opposed national radio in Canada, having worked tooth and nail against it at the time when Murray was out here before. . . . No one has suggested that he has any idea that it [the corporation] will be used for purposes of strengthening national unity and healing the rapidly widening gap between the races and sections of Canada. Murray, on the other hand, I believe sees this completely." And the Radio League's supporters in the press spoke of a lobby at Ottawa "designed to deliver the Canadian Radio field to American interests."[4]

In their radio broadcasts and public addresses, Brockington and Murray emphasized the national objectives of the CBC in promoting Canadian unity and in bringing about a better understanding between the two language groups and the different regions; and they insisted that the construction program advanced by the board of governors was necessary for "national policy." Howe's effort to slow down public ownership was in effect overruled by the prime minister, and the building of a nationally owned system of high-powered stations went ahead. The parliamentary committees of 1938 and 1939, in unanimous or nearly unanimous reports, supported the construction plans and the loans and increased licence fee necessary to put them into effect. Later committees, not so unanimously, reiterated that the CBC was to be the single body, responsible to Parliament, exercising control of the national broadcasting system.

But we cannot push this too far. Canadians have never made a clear choice between broadcasting as "public service" and broadcasting as a commercial medium and predominantly the purveyor of light entertainment. The earliest public opinion surveys on record indicate that most Canadians thought the CBC was doing a "good" job or a "fair" job: in 1949 the Canadian Gallup Poll reported that 69 per cent of a national sample replied in these terms, whereas only 16 per cent thought the CBC was doing a poor job. The Massey Commission found overwhelming support among leaders of organizations for the purposes of the national broadcasting system. Yet, Canadians were strongly attracted to the entertainment programs from the United States, and their derivative Canadian equivalents. Canadian governments, furthermore, had deliberately maintained the private ownership of local or community stations, alongside and within the CBC networks, encouraging the CBC to carry its own and imported commercial programs on those networks. The Canadian system therefore incorporated not only a national objective of public service broadcasting, but also the commercial principle that had determined the structure of broadcasting in the United States.

By 1951, in spite of the repeated statements of commissions and committees affirming the primacy of the public sector, the private broadcasters had made steady gains. By the time of the Massey Report, the balance had already shifted, and no one could predict whether the commercial rationale might not ultimately displace the national motive as the primary principle of the Canadian system. In the propaganda battles over broadcasting, the fully commercial system of the United States appeared to have several advantages. It seemed to offer freedom of speech, and freedom from government dictation or influence. It seemed "free" in another sense: for the listener, there was no tax or licence. Then, too, most of the programs had mass appeal, since otherwise they would not attract advertisers, and the stations would not make the greatest profits.

In respect to the first claim, experience showed that private networks and stations afforded opportunity for a rather limited range of expression. Controversial broadcasting was not a money-maker and probably did not help the ratings. On the other hand, fifteen years of experience had shown that freedom of speech could be maintained (on the whole) under the CBC set-up. The historian, Arthur Lower, wrote in 1953:

> I cannot see any turn towards true freedom coming out of private radio and television. On the other hand, ninety out of a hundred people who have had any experience in the matter will agree that under the CBC the essential conditions of true freedom *have* been preserved. . . .
>
> May I ask how much freer the American air is than our own? It is freer in the sense of there being more mutually interfering stations, as a casual turn of the dial indicates. The American radio has the traditional American form of freedom—anarchy. But is *opinion* there any freer? Is news any more accurately and impartially broadcast? Who dares to contend that such is the case?
>
> . . . So let us have no more talk of freedom! What is up is profits, *and* the Americanization of the new medium.[5]

Under the American system, because people were not aware of paying for the service provided, they did not think of holding the broadcaster accountable. Rather they assumed that if a person did not like a particular program or a particular station, he merely switched to another. Occasionally an educator or a professional critic would complain that the choice offered was not a real choice, since every commercial station or network, trying for a mass audience, offered much the same kind of thing. But in the main, American audiences seemed pleased with their lively and entertaining radio fare; and just when radio was coming under heavier critical fire, the appearance of television captured popular attention and enthusiasm.

But there was more to recommend the American system of private broadcasting than the painless way in which it was paid for, and the lively entertainment that it produced. It also seemed to be an important (some said indispensable) part of the capitalist system on the North American continent. Advertising agencies and sales representatives were sure that the benefits of mass production could never have been realized in such great measure if radio had not been used to disseminate information about goods and services, and so increase the market. If broadcasting was to be a means of advertising, it seemed natural that, like other forms of business, it should be privately owned, and respond to the same laws of supply and demand as other forms of business enterprise.

This accorded well with an attitude that most Canadians had in common with other liberal democracies of the twentieth century, and notably with the United States: a belief that, whenever possible, choices should be made by the processes of the free market; a feeling that individuals should be allowed to engage in economic enterprise without government interference; a feeling that "the government should stay out of it." Allied to this attitude is a belief that a close analogy exists between the competitive market system and the process of liberal-democratic government. The most "democratic" system of broadcasting, so this argument runs, allows individuals to enter the field, where physical and other conditions permit, with the least possible restraint from any centralized authority. The system is even more "democratic" if it gives all other individuals a chance to choose the programs they receive from a multiplicity of offerings; and it is more "democratic" still if such choices have a direct effect on the way in which entrepreneurs are rewarded or penalized: that is, through the sale of goods or the maximizing of profits. Here is the rationale for the United States broadcasting system as expressed by Professor Hettinger in 1935:

> The program service offered by American broadcasting is unusually complete. It is typically American, adapted to national conditions, the broadcaster giving the public those programs which constant research and direct expression of opinion indicate to be most popular. It is necessary that he do this if he is to build station and network circulation with which to attract advertisers.
>
> The democratic control of programs is by no means a perfect one, though there is probably no better method available. It possesses all the strengths and weaknesses of democracy operating in the social and political fields. Democratic control of programs implies control by the listening majority.[6]

This is usually called, "Giving the listener what he wants." As Hettinger adds, "It is only to be expected that the majority of listeners would rather be entertained than edified."

The concept of broadcasters being responsible to the general will of listeners, who are able to make their wishes known through means other than the political mechanism, is implicit in various statements by Canadian broadcasters. In 1934 Harry Sedgwick, president of CFRB, told a committee of the House of Commons: "The Parliamentary Committee, the Radio Commission, the Radio Advertiser, and the Station Operator are all before the bar of the listening audience, and subservient to its interest. . . . There will be a much happier listening audience if it is left largely to take care of itself and express its disapproval by refusing to listen rather than have a commission arbitrarily enact regulations as to what the public itself wants."[7] In 1949 the Canadian Association of Broadcasters, arguing for "free" radio before the Massey Commission, expressed confidence that "your review of the activities of the privately-owned broadcasting stations in Canada will reveal that they are being operated, in effect, by the listeners."[8]

But this is disingenuous, concealing some of the real differences between the philosophies of public and private ownership of broadcasting. It does not face up to the question of who controls program policy, network policy, and the extension of service throughout the country; of whose values the broadcasts will reflect. In the commercial system, these values will be of the private owners and the advertisers; or, if not the values that they hold as individuals, those of the market system, those that encourage the growth of profits. The tastes that are catered to are those of the passing moment; the system does not take into account the variety of tastes that audiences have, nor the long-term interests of society as a whole. In Canada, the philosophy of private broadcasting had another and special implication. In terms of marketing and industry, Canada was becoming more and more a branch plant of the U.S.A. If the usual market conditions determined program fare on Canadian stations and networks, there was no doubt that American broadcasting would overwhelm the domestic product. The economies in importing programs, the thrust of American publicity and promotion, the orientation of the big advertisers and agencies, would mean that the "Canadian" character of the broadcasting system would all but disappear. Legislation could ensure that the stations were still in the hands of Canadian owners. But the programming would be an extension or replica of that produced in New York and Hollywood. A regulatory board, as demonstrated in the United States, could provide only negative restrictions, or guideposts marking limits. It could hardly create what the system found antithetical.

Given the assumptions of the private owners, however, their protests against "state monopoly" and "unfair competition" seem to make perfect sense. It was their view, the Massey Report said, that radio was primarily a means of entertainment, a by-product of the advertising business. The United States, according to the Massey Commission, follows the view that radio broadcasting is primarily an industry; there radio has been treated primarily as a means of entertainment open to commercial exploitation, limited only by the public controls found necessary in all countries.[9]

Four of the five members of the Massey Commission concluded that such an outlook was a denial of the principle on which Canadian broadcasting had been based and of the assumption that there should be one national system, controlled in the public interest by a body responsible to Parliament. The concept of a single system was related to the idea, accepted for twenty years, that broadcasting was a public trust. Stations were expected to help distribute the important national programs, and most private stations were still affiliated with one of the CBC networks. The commissioners with the exception of Mr. Surveyer considered that national control could most effectively be provided by the CBC, and not by a separate regulatory board. They added that the complaints of the private stations, that the CBC Board of Governors was at once their judge and their business rival, implied a view of the national system that had no foundation in law, and which had never been accepted by parliamentary committees or by the general public. (The conclusions of the Royal Commission headed by Robert Fowler in 1957, and of the Fowler Advisory Committee in 1965, were substantially similar.)

The commissioners must have been aware, however, that there were powerful influences at work to change the system, and that there was at least an even chance that in a few years' time the priorities would be reversed. We have noted the popular preference for American programs and acceptance of the advertising rationale which accompanies them—a preference which was even then spreading throughout the English-speaking world, and which gained impetus with the arrival of television. These programs were often produced, distributed, or promoted by American corporations with business interests extending into Canada, either directly or through Canadian subsidiaries. At the very least, Canadian companies on the receiving end were eager to fit into the American pattern of radio stations, station representatives, advertising agencies, and potential sponsors. As the vested interests were drifting more and more into the United States orbit, Canadian private radio found itself becoming increasingly dependent on the American recording industry. To hold the line on the "public" or "national" principle would be harder and harder.

Public broadcasting had begun with inter-party agreement in 1932 and again in 1936, but by the mid-forties, this agreement had crumbled. Partly this was due to the circumstances of the war, and the use made of the facilities of the CBC by government leaders in broadcasting "non-partisan" messages to the Canadian people. Even more, it was due to the unwillingness of the Liberal party to extend political time to the opposition, weak and divided though it was after the election of 1940. This would not have mattered if the CBC had been under strong leadership, determined to put into effect the provisions of the White Paper that had been approved in 1939. But the hegemony of the Liberal party coincided with dissension within the CBC board and administration, and the CBC did not recover its determination to be independent of the minister until after its board and general manager had been partially discredited by the investigation of 1942. Even then, the board was short-sighted in refusing requests to broadcast from the leaders of the Conservative party, Mr. Meighen and Mr. Bracken. The commercial interests were able to persuade first some of the members from Toronto, and then other leading Conservatives, that their cause was just, that the CBC was a menace to free speech, and that the private stations suffered under a system in which the regulating authority was "cop and competitor." By the mid-forties, the Social Credit and Progressive-Conservative parties had changed their position, now favouring not only abolition of the licence fee, but a separate regulatory board. Whenever there was a dispute between private stations and the CBC, as in the shifting of wavelengths for CFRB and CFCN, the private stations could count on support from the Conservative and Social Credit members in the House of Commons. Even some Liberals would on occasion stray from party discipline to flay the CBC. We find, then, the reports of the parliamentary committees in 1946 and 1947 becoming more tentative in their rejection of the private broadcasters' demands for a separate regulatory board and a down-grading of the CBC.

Throughout this period, the CBC kept the support of most of the voluntary associations that had wanted a national broadcasting system: the Canadian Federation of Agriculture, the labour unions and the labour congresses, the women's organizations, the adult education movement, and other groups concerned with education and citizenship. But none of them could match the persistence of the private broadcasters' lobby. They were, after all, concerned with many other things; none of them had a substantial economic interest in the outcome of the struggle; and it was hard for them to organize their support year after year, as committee succeeded committee. The appointment of the Massey Commission, some of them hoped, would settle the matter for a good long period ahead.

The private stations necessarily led the battle against the existing system, at least in public. And they were much richer and more powerful than they had been a decade earlier. During one span of three years, according to the Massey Report (p. 281), the total operating revenues of the private stations increased from nearly ten to over fourteen million dollars. During the same period CBC operating revenues rose from nearly six millions to seven and a half millions, little more than half the revenue of the private broadcasters. The total assets of the private stations at the end of 1948 were twenty-seven millions, three times as great as the assets of the CBC.

Moreover, the private broadcasters had fashioned their association into an increasingly effective pressure group, profiting from the skilled and experienced leadership of such men as Harry and Joseph Sedgwick of Toronto. The CAB encouraged its members to take an active part in local boards of trade and various charitable drives; not unnaturally, private stations gained the full support of the Canadian Chamber of Commerce and its local or provincial counterparts. In many constituencies station owners had easy access to members of parliament of whatever party, since such an advantageous channel of communication with constituents as radio was not likely to go unappreciated by the parliamentarian.

And they had public support from a powerful group that had nearly completely changed sides: the country's newspapers. At the time of the Aird Report, and later during the campaign of the Radio League, the newspapers had predominantly supported the principle of a national broadcasting system. A few large papers with radio stations of their own, or papers which hoped to get stations, opposed the creation of the CRBC or the CBC: *La Presse*, the *Globe* (later the *Globe and Mail*), the *Telegram*. But these were exceptions. Most of the newspapers in the 1930's regarded private stations as their competitors for advertising revenue, and thought that a national, largely noncommercial system was in every way superior to that which had been in existence. Newspaper editors such as Charles Bowman and J. W. Dafoe had taken the lead in rallying support for the efforts of the Radio League; and these two men never wavered in their support of the system created in 1936, even when their publishers did.

Some of the Southam papers were the first to change their editorial position, starting with the *Edmonton Journal*, followed by the *Calgary Herald*—both of them owning stations. After the death of Dafoe, the Sifton chain followed suit—the *Winnipeg Free Press*, the *Saskatoon Star-Phoenix*, and the Regina *Leader-Post*. The Siftons also had become owners of several stations. When the CBC did not reduce its commercial activities as much as had been hoped, several other newspapers became strongly critical of it: the Montreal *Gazette* and the *Vancouver Sun,* for example. By 1950, 41 of the 119 private radio stations were owned in whole or in part by newspaper interests. Many publishers therefore thought of the public broadcasting system as their business rival.

Beyond these questions of how the forces on each side were mobilized, and what tactics they used to make the system more amenable to their interests, is the question of how Canadian society itself was being shaped and transformed. Two decades earlier, it had not been difficult to enlist the country's elite to support the idea of a national system, publicly controlled. There was Sir John Aird himself, direct from the boardroom of the Canadian Bank of Commerce; Sir Robert Borden, Newton Rowell, Arthur Meighen, John Dafoe, two members of the Southam family, Louis St. Laurent, Vincent Massey, George Wrong. In 1951 it would have been much harder to enlist so representative a group from the "establishment," certainly from the business establishment.

And then, if after the Massey Report a group had been formed comparable to that which backed the Radio League, how many of the Canadian people in 1951 would take their lead from those who stood for traditional values? Commercial values—in an affluent Canada—seemed to have taken over. Broadcasting as it had developed no doubt contributed to that phenomenon. There was money for mass consumption of consumer goods (U.S. style), and a ready market for the mass programming it paid for. Commercial broadcasting fitted the postwar escapist mood, and even now it continues propagating the notion that there are no serious problems, or that if problems exist, they are all approximately equal—the kind that can be wrapped up in a thirty-minute package. Consumer-oriented public opinion is encouraged in the attitude, "You've never had it so good," or "If you have problems, change yourself, not society."

In its fear of "Americanization" the Massey Report may have reflected an elitist distrust of mass culture and new technologies; if so, it was wielding a broom to hold back the tide. But Massey and his fellow commissioners spoke for a large segment of the Canadian public, and not just those who bewailed the decline of aristocratic values, when they advocated maintaining a broadcasting system that operated in the long-term interests of Canadian listeners and the Canadian nation. Like Spry and Plaunt, they too were concerned not just with Canadian identity, but with "better broadcasting." The commission realized that nationalism is not a sufficient justification for a broadcasting system, but that broadcasting had to be under national control if it is to develop broadly and flexibly as a medium of communication. Their recommendations showed faith that broadcasting can serve changing Canadian needs, and that while continuing to be entertaining, it should provide more than passing fun.

Broadcasting which operates as an auxiliary to advertising must treat man as essentially a consumer, a buyer of goods; and the programs are subservient to that end. A full broadcasting service operates on quite another principle, appealing to man as an active and creative person, Aristotle's "political being," with a potential for growth. National control, then, is not an end in itself, and never has been in Canada. It is the necessary condition for a system designed, in the North American context, to assist Canadians to know the changing society around them, and to adapt successfully to it. The framework for such broadcasting was established in Canada forty years ago. The struggle to improve, even to maintain it, is greater today than ever before, and more crucial still to our survival as a nation.

1. Secretary of State, *White Paper On Broadcasting* (Ottawa, 1966), p. 5.
2. G. Spry, "Radio Broadcasting and Aspects of Canadian-American Relations," in Carnegie Endowment for International Peace, Conference on Canadian-American Affairs, *Proceedings*, edited by McLaren, Corey, and Trotter, p. 107.
3. *Debates*, May 18, 1932, p. 3035.
4. Plaunt Papers, box 6. The second quotation is from a letter to Plaunt from M. E. Nichols of the *Vancouver Daily Province*, July 14, 1936.
5. A. R. M. Lower, "The Question of Private Television," *Queen's Quarterly* LX (Summer 1953), p. 175.
6. H. S. Hettinger, "Broadcasting in the United States," *The Annals of the American Academy of Political and Social Science,* CLXXVII (Jan. 1935), p. 11.
7. *1934 Proceedings*, p. 335.
8. *Canadian Broadcaster*, Sept. 21, 1949, p. 13.
9. *Massey Report*, pp. 276-9.

Communications Media and Identity Formation in Canada

FREDERICK ELKIN

In recent years, probably no psychological concept has become so widely adopted in the analysis of other topics as that of *identity.* It has become a central idea in discussions of young people who have difficulty in crystallizing their life choices, women who are ambivalent about their status, occupations seeking to gain more professional images, children whose family life is unstable, primitive societies in the throes of modernization, ethnic and racial groups seeking to strengthen internal bonds, and nations in danger of division and dissolution. Three elements are common in all these concerns: (1) there is some problem which demands attention, (2) a positive identity, for whatever reasons, will presumably help resolve the problem, and (3) one crucial component is a sense of self-awareness.

The primary social relevance of the concept "identity" derives from its application to significant collectivities or reference groups. Its dimensions are many. The scope may be broad or narrow—from Christian to Protestant to Baptist; from student, to student of a particular university, to student in a department. The salience may vary—to be a first-generation Italian in Canada is a more meaningful and encompassing identity than to be of the third generation. The content may change—the implications of being French Canadian in Quebec in 1972 are different from the implications of being French Canadian in Quebec a decade ago. Usually identities concern different compartments of life and do not conflict with one another, but sometimes one identity is reinforced through being set against other groups—the identity of blacks against whites, college students against faculty or administration, women against men, one generation against another, French Canadian against English Canadian, Canadian against American. And sometimes ambivalences are built into particular positions such as the woman as engineer, clergyman as husband, son as employee, and Canadian as executive in an American-owned corporation.

Our concern here is with the Canadian identity and the role of Canadian communications in its development, its clarification or obfuscation, and its strengthening or weakening. Just by virtue of being a nation, with its own citizenship, territory, government, flag and other symbols, we inevitably have some national identity as Canadians. Yet, in Canada, we do not take a strong sense of national identity for granted. Historically, Canadian identity was not forged in revolution and has never been held up as an overriding ideal.[1] Some forces opposing a strong national identity are essentially internal, stemming from other structures and ideals within the country; some are external, stemming from structures and ideals without. In the context of the communications media, we shall consider first those major forces working against a Canadian identity and second, those working for it. In each instance we shall consider ideological factors, relevant aspects of social organization and media content.

We assume a close link between culture and identity. An identity which stems from any collectivity implies some distinctive cultural elements. To experience the Canadian identity implies at least a concern with some things considered Canadian, and may imply a complete absorption in Canadian institutions and Canadian problems. For most Canadians, it probably includes a concern with Canada vis-à-vis other countries on the international scene; an interest in federal government policies, political parties and leading political figures; an awareness of problems associated with the Arctic, Quebec, Indians and Eskimos; a familiarity with a distinctive geography and history; and perhaps an enjoyment of the popular culture associated with Canada's holidays, popular entertainment stars, hockey, and Canadian professional football and the Grey Cup—all of which are given considerable attention in the mass media.

We assume too a close link between the collective identity applied to a nation, large group or institution and the individual identity, experienced by those who make up the collectivity. For the individual, the image of the group is internalized and is part of the psychological world which enters into his sentiments, thought and behaviour.

The Media Against Canadian Identity

In many respects our media ideology operates against the development of a distinctive Canadian culture and identity. In principle, in the tradition of the classic liberal writings of John Milton and John Stuart Mill, we extol the virtues of a free press and a free flow of information.[2] Citizens should be free to express their opinions and publishers should be free to publish and a government should not restrict the flow of ideas. The prevalence of such beliefs in Canada is shown in the remarks of the President of the Canadian Daily Newspaper Publishers Association to the Special Senate Committee on Mass Media in 1969:

> A free press is one of our most cherished freedoms . . . a great disservice can be performed, can be perpetrated if there is any infringement on press freedoms . . . the press should be able to publish . . . without interference. In my own view [it should publish] without the worse type of interference; that would be the interference of government.[3]

By extension of this principle, our borders should be equally open to any communications media, be they British, American or Chinese, and we the people should have the right to read, hear and see what we choose from that which is available. Neither we nor the publishers should be restricted. In theory, we trust ourselves in a democracy to weigh the information we receive and to make the sensible and proper decisions.

This broad ideology was developed primarily in the context of political activities. It is in some respects akin, however, to an ideology affirmed in dramatic and "human interest" spheres. The producers of popular, non-intellectual films and television shows and the publishers of similarly oriented tabloids and magazines—as well, of course, as the purveyors in various media of crude melodrama and sex—argue that they are merely "giving the people what they want" and if the mass of people choose the sensational and uncritical, that is their right.

Among those who generally uphold the ideology of free choice are those who are likely to profit thereby—the private radio and T.V. broadcasters and certain multinational corporations which sell directly to a consuming public. Private broadcasters have often balked at regulations which limit their right to choose popular foreign programmes; similarly, the makers of such products as cars, soft drinks, beauty products and major appliances, who consider their market to be North American, wish to feel free to use the same commercials and programmes in Canada that they use in the United States and to buy space or time in whatever medium will be most effective in selling their products.

In fact, the present situation in Canada in which we follow a classical liberal ideology and let the media directors, advertisers and people choose the media and media content they wish, reinforces U.S. influence and presumably weakens Canadian identity as such. When the choice is free, Canadians are likely to choose American movies, magazines and television shows. For the popular movies, Canadians offer little competition. For magazines, Canadians buy almost four times as many American as Canadian magazines, including *Playboy, Life, True Story, National Geographic, Time* and *Reader's Digest* and others.[4] Although *Time* and *Reader's Digest* are printed in Canada and include Canadian advertising and some other Canadian material, the greater part of the content is American in origin.

On television, American programmes are much more popular than Canadian. A comparison of Canadians with and without cable television may serve as one index, since the former can more easily receive U.S. channels. In 1969, viewers in British Columbia without cable watched

American channels 26% of the time, while viewers with cable watched American channels 57% of the time; in Saskatchewan the proportions were 14% and 41% respectively, in New Brunswick 3% and 33% and even in Quebec the proportions were 2% and 13%.[5]

It is of course not surprising that Canadians, unprotected by the shield of a different language, choose American-made mass media. As a market, the United States is ten times the size of Canada, and American media can produce a quantity and certain quality that Canadians cannot match. Canada cannot very well support a *New York Times,* or the range of magazines or films found in the United States, and such expensive or elaborate television shows and commercials.

Other ideologies and interests which extend beyond our borders also run counter to the formation and maintenance of Canadian culture and identity. Sometimes, for example in music, we value certain universal qualities. Few would ask that we require FM radio stations, which play a high proportion of classical music, to limit themselves to Canadian material. We maintain many international links, for example with UNESCO, UNICEF, the Commonwealth, or even the International Rotary and Boy Scout groups, which move us to other than Canadian identities. Limited groups of Canadians also may have distinctive and strong international ties. Some ethnic groups are deeply concerned with events in the European countries from which their families have come; management, labour and professional groups may have ties with their counterparts elsewhere; and we are all likely to have some interest in international events. In that these and various other concerns are given attention in the mass media, they point out some of our broader-than-Canadian identities which may or may not be very significant, depending on the circumstances.

Equally as important as the external ideologies and organizations operating against a Canadian identity are those that are internal, especially those which derive from our dual English and French heritage. The dual heritage ideology is affirmed in numerous documents from the Quebec Act of 1774 to the British North America Act of 1867 to the establishment of the Royal Commission on Bilingualism and Biculturalism in 1963 to the Official Languages Act of 1969. Theoretically this dual character might be experienced as an equality of heritages; in reality, however—except for the rather rare instance—the identity is experienced as either English Canadian or French Canadian; the place of Canada in the identity set of the English Canadian is ordinarily very different from the place of Canada in the identity set of the French Canadian.

The dual language and culture is manifested in both the public and private sectors of the mass media. In the public sector, the Canadian Broadcasting Corporation from its very beginnings in radio was charged with the establishment of English and French networks and the pattern was continued in television. Thus we have CBC in English and *Radio Canada* in French, each with its own organization, language and programming. Rarely, except for certain sports and major political events, do we find the two networks showing the same programme. Likewise, in the private sector we find separate English and French language newspapers, magazines and radio and television stations. Few English-speaking Canadians see French language media; more French Canadians see English language films, newspapers, commercials, and T.V. programmes, but in general the two groups live in separate media compartments.

In recent years the French media have seen a further development. The Canadian Press, a cooperative news gathering and distributing agency, has improved its French language translation service and established a link with the leading news agency in France, Agence France-Presse. In advertising, French Canadians find their advice accepted more than ever before and often write original ads in French. The government of Quebec has its own film board, takes an active hand in educational television, and argues with the federal government over the right to control radio and television broadcasting in the province.

The content of the English and French media, although basically following similar styles, often reflect different cultures. Different stories are given headlines in the English and French language press and sometimes the same events are treated very differently.[6] The French know little of English commentators and radio and T.V. celebrities, and the English know even less of the French. With the language barrier dividing the two groups, each inhabits its own media world.

A second ideology which may run counter to Canadian identity derives from the value we place on the Canadian mosaic. In Canada, we have never preached the value of the melting pot—each ethnic group, we affirm, should be permitted to maintain its language and express its distinctive culture; as a result Canada presumably is a richer and more worthwhile society. Some thirty per cent of Canadians are descended from people who are neither English nor French, and this proportion increases each year. For some Canadians, little has remained over the generations of their traditional language and ethnic heritage, but for others, the culture and identity are still important.

In contemporary society, the mass media serve as one device for expressing the culture and identity of these groups. All told, some 150 publications along with dozens of radio programmes serve Canada's ethnic groups. Two radio stations—one in Montreal and one in Toronto—are licensed to broadcast up to 40% of their total programmes in languages other than English or French. In television, the cable companies especially are expanding their services to ethnic groups. These media are served by two national organizations, the Canadian Ethnic Press Federation and The Canadian Scene, a news and feature service.[7] The audience of these ethnic publications and programmes, it is estimated, runs into the millions. We do not know, however, what percentage of the total ethnic group population makes up this audience, what generations this audience comes from, and the proportion of time devoted to particular ethnic compared to non-ethnic media; but surely for those who choose to read, watch and listen—and perhaps even for those who don't—the media reinforce distinctive ethnic cultures and identities. We also know, from the briefs of the ethnic groups to the Royal Commission on Bilingualism and Biculturalism and from issues raised in many parts of the country, that conflicts may develop between the defenders of multiculturalism and the defenders of bilingualism and biculturalism.

Other values and structures within the country also encourage non-Canadian identities. One of these is provincialism. Is it of greater psychological significance to someone from Newfoundland that he is a Canadian or a Newfoundlander? This question could also be asked of the native of Quebec, or of British Columbia, or perhaps of other provinces. Regionalism is a closely related value. We label the person from the Maritimes—and he may so think of himself—as a Maritimer. The regionalism sometimes, as with natives from Windsor or the wheat farmers of the Canadian west, may even cross borders. Local community identity may at times also be important, especially for the major centres in the less populated areas. The specific topics of concern may be political or economic, or may focus on particular commentators or entertainers, but whatever the topic, local newspapers and radio stations give them wide expression. In and of themselves, such concerns and their associated identities and self-images do not necessarily mean a downgrading of the Canadian identity, but for some issues, they send Canadians off into different directions and for others, they pit one Canadian against another.

The Media for Canadian Identity

Speaking abstractly, historians have suggested that the theme of national consciousness, along with associated questions of national unity and identity, has long been a concern for Canada. A Canadian identity—at least for the English-speaking—was strengthened by the collective spirit of World War I and World War II, and by the postwar withdrawal of British authority on constitutional matters and the dropping of Dominion status. Since then, the question of Canadian identity has most often been considered in the context of economic and cultural domination by the United States.

Over the years, in discussing the role of the mass media in Canada, numerous Royal Commissions and Parliamentary Committees have affirmed the value of Canadian unity and identity. Speaking of the broadcasting system in 1929, the Aird Commission Report said:

> We believe that broadcasting should be considered of such importance in promoting the unity of the nation that a subsidy by the Dominion Government should be regarded as an essential aid . . . .[8]

The Massey Commission Report of the Royal Commission on the National Development in the Arts, Letters and Sciences in 1951 reported:

> The national system . . . has contributed powerfully . . . to a sense of Canadian unity . . . it does much to promote a knowledge and understanding of Canada as a whole and of every Canadian region and aids in the development of a truly Canadian cultural life.[9]

The Report of the Royal Commission on Broadcasting in 1957 said:

> . . . as a nation, we cannot accept in these powerful and persuasive media, the natural and complete flow of another nation's culture with danger to our national identity.[10]

And the Davey Committee Report of the Special Senate Committee on Mass Media in 1970 said:

> . . . what is at stake is not only the vigor of our democracy. It also involves the survival of our nationhood. A nation is a collection of people who share common images of themselves . . . it is the media—together with education and the arts—that can make it grow. Poets and teachers and artists, yes, but journalists too. It is their perceptions which help us to define who and what we are.[11]

That these values must be so often reaffirmed is a sign that the problem remains unresolved.

The value of a Canadian identity is reflected in the establishment of many organizations associated with the mass media which stress both the Canadian vis-à-vis the non-Canadian and the Canadian vis-à-vis smaller units within the country. The terms "Canada" or "Canadian" in their titles are both identifying and symbolic. Perhaps the most significant of these organizations is the Canadian Radio-Television Commission (CRTC) which has the authority to license and regulate all Canadian broadcasting, public and private. The CRTC's basic authority stems from the Broadcasting Act of 1968 according to which:

> The National Broadcasting service should contribute to the development of national unity and strive for a continuing expression of Canadian identity. . . .
> The Canadian Broadcasting system should be effectively owned and controlled by Canadians so as to safeguard, enrich and strengthen the cultural, political, social and economic fabric of Canada.

The communications media, like the banks, are considered so basic to the maintenance of Canadian independence and identity that they must not, the government has decreed, remain in the control of foreign hands.

Over the years radio and television have been regulated by several bodies, but none has more happily taken over the assignment that the national broadcasting system should serve the national purpose than the Canadian Radio-Television Commission. Following an Order-in-Council in 1969 that foreign ownership must be limited to a maximum of 20% and that control must be Canadian, the CRTC has moved to force foreign companies to divest themselves of ownership of radio, television and community cable operations.[12]

The CRTC has also acted to increase the Canadian content of our radio and T.V. programmes, operating against the counter-ideology of free choice. Since January 1971, 30% of all music on AM radio stations must be

"Canadian," that is, either the performer, the composer, the lyric writer or the recording studio must be Canadian. It has been proposed that in the near future at least two, rather than one, of these four conditions be met. Since 1970, at least 60% of the programming of the CBC has been Canadian, and the Canadian Television Network (CTV), a national network of 14 private stations, must have 50% Canadian programming in 1971 and 60% by October 1, 1972. Priorities also have been established for cable companies, requiring that they cover local Canadian channels before including any American. The stress of the CRTC is not quality programming as such, it is the opportunity for employment and development of Canadian talent and especially the furtherance of a Canadian culture and the associated awareness of a Canadian identity; at least, it is implied, let us not be submerged by the American culture and identity.

The CBC, once directly responsible to Parliament, is now responsible to the CRTC. Over the years the CBC has been a major national communications medium. In the words of the Special Senate Committee on the Mass Media:

> It is the only truly national broadcasting enterprise in Canada, offering service to all but a tiny minority of Canadians in both official languages. It has striven to develop Canadian talent, to reveal Canadians to one another, to strengthen the fabric of Canadian society. . . .[13]

The CBC's greatest success has been in the areas of news events and public affairs. It has been less successful in the realm of entertainment where, to maintain its sponsors and its audience, it has often shown popular American programmes. The CBC, as much as any communications medium in Canada, exhibits the basic dilemmas of the country—to stress a Canadian identity and, at the same time, to reflect the bilingualism and biculturalism, and the multicultural mosaic.

In the area of print, the most important mass media organization furthering a Canadian identity is the Canadian Press (CP), a cooperative of Canadian newspapers formed primarily for the purpose of gathering and distributing news in Canada. Through its links with Associated Press, Reuters and Agence France-Press, CP also serves as a channel for receiving foreign news. The president of CP has spoken proudly of a tribute to the association which reads:

> In pursuing its objective of independent, factual and unbiased information its contribution to informed citizenship has been of enormous importance. At the same time it has given Canadians everywhere a glowing feeling of what it means to be a part of Canada.[14]

The CP has had few regular foreign correspondents who write from a Canadian viewpoint, the French-language coverage is less than the English and several French-language newspapers are not members—yet the CP, through its reporting, distribution and selection of items, does focus on the culture of Canada, and does serve to interpret one part of the country to another.

Other organizations and trade associations, representing particular media interests such as CTV, the Institute of Canadian Advertising, the Magazine Advertising Bureau, the Canadian Public Relations Society, the Association of Canadian Advertisers, Broadcast News, the Canadian Daily Newspaper Publishers Association, the Canadian Cable Television Association, and the Canadian Advertising Advisory Board (CAAB) also have an all-Canada orientation although, in practice, many are representative only of English-speaking Canada.

In mass media content, there are occasionally conscious efforts to promote a Canadian national consciousness and identity. The CAAB and the Chambers of Commerce sponsored an advertising campaign in 1971 in both English and French media with the theme *Canada Stand Together—Understand Together* (in French, it was *Le Canada fait notre force—c'est l'unité dans la diversité*). Seagram sponsored a series of ads on *Our Country, Canada* and its whiskey is "Made in Canada . . . and proud of it." *Maclean's* in 1971, with a new editor, became a much more nationalist-oriented magazine. The major

Canadian effort in the media, however, does not derive from such self-conscious efforts. A considerable amount of material in the mass media implicitly emphasizes an identification with Canada. Most such content is political. An enormous amount of news emanates from Ottawa concerning government policies and committees, Parliament, and major political figures. We receive considerable news too on provincial and local matters, on such problems as education, finances, transportation and personalities. At election time, especially, the mass media are filled with reports of political parties, programmes and candidates. The "Trudeaumania" of 1968 was a phenomenon of the mass media. Occasionally Canadian issues on an international level—perhaps associated with visiting heads of state, Canadian reactions to U.S. economic or political moves, or voting at the United Nations—merit headlines and wide discussion. Many non-recurring major events—Expo 1967, the FLQ crisis of October 1970, the accident or hijacking of an Air Canada plane, the Olympics of 1976—have Canadian foci. Our advertisements often show Canadian scenes and demonstrate Canadian products; our voluntary associations, sports, and human interest stories are often Canadian; some of our well-known columnists and TV programmes are Canadian. We have our Canadian heroes and popular TV stars—Bobby Orr, Anne Murray, Nancy Greene, Jean Beliveau, Pierre Berton, Wayne and Shuster. Thus, although much of our mass media content is American—TV programmes, comic strips, guidance columns, popular music, ads—this should not blind us to the large and generally increasing Canadian share which contributes to a Canadian culture and Canadian awareness.

Not all of this Canadian content is integrating. Much, we have observed, is divisive in that it pits one group of Canadians against another and reinforces other than Canadian identities. Yet in that the base and the context of much of this material is a taken-for-granted Canada, we recognize the identity of the nation.

The problem of identity formation and maintenance in Canada will be a concern for many years to come. In general, the greater the threat to a Canadian identity, the greater the concern among the wholly committed Canadians. The major current threats derive from the economic and cultural influence of the United States and from those French Canadians who hold strongly to a Quebec and French-Canadian culture and identity. Secondary threats derive from all other identities which may become more salient and interfere with the Canadian identity. Whether a strong Canadian—or any other collective—identity is desirable is an entirely different question and not within our terms of reference.

The mass media are not alone in the formation or development of a Canadian identity. Identities are formed and maintained through interactions. Major events such as Expo and the FLQ crisis; contacts with government agencies; participation in activities and relationships with others, Canadian and non-Canadian—all play a part. Yet the mass media, as prime sources of our information, as gatekeepers for our news and human interest stories, as opinion leaders, as purveyors of culture identified as Canadian or non-Canadian, as the ground in which associated issues are fought, cannot help but loom large.

The problem of identity differs from other issues in the mass media in that it is so pervasive and cuts through so many topics. Discussions of media ownership and control, of selection and bias in news reporting, of national content quotas, of programme popularity, of the ethnic press and broadcasting, of advertising agency selection, of entertainment stars—all have facets associated with Canadian identity. The mass media reflect the problems and dilemmas of Canada and the tenor of the times; they serve, wittingly or unwittingly, as both mirrors of, and major contributors to, our problems of Canadian identity.

1. See Seymour Lipset, "Canada and the United States: A Comparative View," *Canadian Review of Sociology and Anthropology*, Vol. 1, No. 4 (Nov., 1964), 173-185; and George Heiman, "The 19th Century Legacy: Nationalism or Patriotism?" in Peter H. Russell, ed., *Nationalism in Canada* (Toronto: McGraw Hill, 1966), pp. 323-340.
2. John Milton, *Areopagitica*, 1644; John Stuart Mill, *On Liberty*, 1859.
3. Proceedings of the Special Senate Committee on Mass Media, 1969, No. 1, pp. 8-9.
4. Report of the Special Senate Committee on Mass Media, Vol. I: *The Uncertain Mirror* (Ottawa: Queen's Printer, 1970), p. 156.
5. Canadian Radio-Television Commission, *Annual Report '69-'70*, Appendix III.
6. For one example, note the different treatment of the shooting of three Du Pont executives by a discharged French-Canadian employee. The English language newspapers viewed the employee as a murderer and spoke sympathetically of the executives; the French language tabloid press, on the contrary, saw the employee as a victim of unemployment and discrimination and the executives as symbols of English big business. See Robert McKenzie, "Trouble in Quebec: A Killer is Popular with the People," *Toronto Daily Star*, Oct. 23, 1971, p. 20. Also see F. Elkin, "Mass Media, Advertising, and the Quiet Revolution," in R. J. Ossenberg, ed., *Canadian Society: Pluralism, Change, and Conflict* (Toronto: Prentice-Hall, 1971), pp. 184-209.
7. See Report of the Special Senate Committee on Mass Media, Vol. I: *The Uncertain Mirror*, "Ethnic Press: The Most Mixed Medium," pp. 179-183; and Report of the Royal Commission on Bilingualism and Biculturalism, Book IV: *The Cultural Contribution of the Other Ethnic Groups*, Chap. VII, "The Media of Communication," (Ottawa: Queen's Printer, 1969), pp. 171-196.
8. Cited in Appendix IV, Canadian Radio-Television Commission, *Annual Report '69-'70*, Appendix V.
9. *Ibid.*
10. *Ibid.*
11. Report of the Special Senate Committee on Mass Media, Vol. I, p. 11.
12. Canadian Radio-Television Commission, *Annual Report '69-'70* and *Annual Report '70-'71.*
13. Report of the Special Senate Committee on Mass Media, Vol. I, p. 195.
14. Proceedings of the Special Committee on Mass Media, 1969, No. 2, p. 8.

The Growth of the Mass Media in Canada

GARTH S. JOWETT AND BARRY R. HEMMINGS

The examination of the growth of mass communications within a society has attracted increasing attention from sociologists, as well as from other social scientists. There have been a number of reasons for this, not the least of which has been the controversy over the exact nature of the relationship between the extent of mass communication and the level of economic and social development within a country.[1] Although controversy continues over the direction of this relationship—whether mass media *cause* cultural, political, or economic changes, or whether such changes are normally accompanied by accelerated growth of the mass media—there is agreement that all developed societies have an extensive mass communication infrastructure.

The purpose of this study is to examine the growth trends of the various forms of mass communication in Canada during the last seventy-odd years. Such an examination will serve primarily to indicate the extent of the pervasiveness of Canadian mass media penetration, and in addition will provide the initial data and impetus for those wishing to explore further the role of mass communications as a possible agent for social change in Canadian society. However, before examining these trends, it would be useful to place them into a broader context, namely the development of the concept of "mass society" during the nineteenth and twentieth centuries.[2]

The Development of Mass Society

Although the terms "industrial revolution" and "mass society" are still debated, nevertheless, much of the world has experienced dramatic shifts in economic and social structures since the eighteenth century. These shifts have been marked by rapid and sustained rises in real output per capita, extensive increases in mechanization, high energy outputs and consumption, and a decline in the percentage of the labour force engaged in agriculture and other primary sectors of the economy. Correspondingly, there has been a rise in percentage of the population engaged in industrial, secondary, and tertiary sectors of the economy.[3] These economic changes have also been accompanied by an expansion in transportation and communications facilities. Literacy has increased greatly in most advanced societies because of improvements in the systems of formal education.

The mass media have also shown enormous growth and pervasiveness, while the decrease in the number of hours in the workweek has allowed more time for participation in all forms of recreation, of which the media are a large segment. Admittedly there are many theoretical difficulties to be reconciled regarding the role of mass communication in this "modernization" process, but it has generally been accepted by economists and others that, at the least, the level of mass communication sophistication in a country is a fairly reliable indicator of economic and social progress.[4]

Although these are all quantifiable changes, there have also been corresponding shifts in social structures, human beliefs, values, and expectations. The middle class has emerged into the central position of authority in most industrial countries, while the population as a whole is said to be afforded increasing opportunities to participate in the workings of all levels of government.[5] (There is, of course, some indication that as the nature of bureaucracies becomes more complex such participation will decrease.) Many social theorists have discussed the notion of the emergence of a mass society, although there is basic disagreement as to what mass society is, or whether or not it is a functional or dysfunctional phenomenon.[6] Nevertheless, the development of modern society has been greatly facilitated by the growth of the various forms of mass communication (normally seen as part and parcel of mass society) and their ability to reduce the perceived distance between individuals and groups. This has led to greater empathy amongst the population, as well as a wider recognition of common needs and values in the society as a whole. Thus, as the mass media become a more powerful social force, geographic separation appears to grow smaller; and the end results, some would argue, are a greater degree of internal unity, and a tendency toward centralization.[7] Some social critics have suggested that such centralizing tendencies are dangerous, and can lead to "rule by the mob," or even worse, totalitarian political states[8] Of course, the development of mass society may have some negative results, but it would be difficult to deny that on the whole societies have benefited from improved mass communication systems which are *national* in their coverage.

The Historical Examination of Mass Media Growth

An examination of the historical growth patterns of the mass media in a society can also be of benefit to an understanding of how these same media function in the present day[9] First, it allows us to infer what the impact of the society has been on the development of various forms of mass communication, and what political, economic, or cultural conditions have shaped the media into their present form. Second, it provides clues as to how the media function in that society: What is the process of mass communications, and how does it differ from the more direct (personal) forms of communication it often replaces? Third, and perhaps most important, it outlines the impact that mass communications have had on the society: How have they reshaped the beliefs, values, and behaviour of the population? In the past, historians have rarely examined the mass media as a major element in the processes of social change; but fortunately, in recent years the work of Harold Adams Innis, Lawrence W. Stone, Marshall McLuhan, Alvin Toffler, and others has created a greater awareness of the importance of communication systems as historical determinants.[10]

The Growth of the Mass Media in Canada

The growth and development of the mass media in Canada should be examined in the context of the shift in demographic patterns during the last seventy years. As Table 1 indicates, it was not until the late 1920s that Canada became a predominantly urban-based society, about twelve years later than the same development in the United States. This population shift to the cities had a profound effect on the development of the mass media since it provided the broad population base necessary for the successful introduction of commercially-based forms of communication, such as newspapers, motion pictures, radio, and television. Without a strong urban concentration of population, mass communication delivery costs would have become prohibitive; but with a guaranteed audience in close geographic proximity, delivery costs to a wider area could be subsidized.

As the Canadian population moved into cities they left behind the traditional, rural forms of recreation. In order to fill this cultural vacuum, new urban-based recreational pursuits were created, and foremost among these were various forms of mass communication. Also, with the shift

Table 1 POPULATION OF CANADA, RURAL vs. URBAN, 1901-1971

Year	*Total Population*	*Urban*	*Rural*
1901	5,371,315	37.0%	63.0%
1911	7,206,643	43.7%	56.3%
1921	8,787,949	48.4%	51.6%
1931	10,376,786	53.7%	46.3%
1941	11,506,655	56.9%	43.1%
1951	14,009,429	62.9%	37.1%
1956	16,080,791	66.6%	33.4%
1971	20,014,880	73.6%	26.4%

Sources: For 1901-1956, *1956 Census Bulletin;* for 1971, Statistics Canada.

from agriculture to manufacturing, most workers in the urban areas found more time available for recreational activity. Table 2 indicates that the average workweek for non-agricultural occupations declined nine hours between 1926 and 1955, while a slightly lower decline was experienced by agricultural workers.

Table 2 AVERAGE HOURS WORKED PER WEEK, 1926-1955

Year	*Non-agricultural workers*	*Agricultural workers*
1926	49.6	64.4
1931	44.9	61.9
1936	45.4	59.3
1941	48.4	61.9
1946	43.5	55.4
1951	41.6	52.7
1955	40.6	55.3

Source: M.C. Urquhart and K.A.H. Buckley, *Historical Statistics of Canada* Series D408, 410 (Toronto: Macmillan, 1965), p. 105.

The Growth of Newspapers

The first major form of mass communication in Canada was the daily newspaper.[11] Table 3 indicates the readership of daily newspapers in Canada per household from 1921 to 1971. Figure 1 shows the diffusion curve for daily newspapers in the same period. It can readily be seen that newspaper readership per household reached its peak in 1950, although the total daily circulation has continued to rise. The curve of diffusion indicates characteristics of the "S" shape, which is more or less typical of the acceptance pattern for innovations by a given population. [12]

It is interesting to compare the differences between the patterns of acceptance of the mass media in the United States and Canada, since it is generally assumed that the two countries constitute one giant "media monolith." This is not, in fact, an accurate assumption, as each society has been subjected to different pressures at different times

Table 3 GROWTH OF CANADIAN DAILY NEWSPAPERS (ENGLISH AND FRENCH), 1921-1971

Year	*Total circulation of dailies (000s)*	*Estimated households (000s)*	*Circulation per household*
1921	1,716	1,897	.905
1923	1,732	2,002	.865
1925	1,783	2,065	.863
1927	2,001	2,141	.935
1929	2,197	2,229	.986
1931	2,233	2,275	.982
1933	2,052	2,473	.830
1935	2,230	2,522	.884
1937	2,357	2,569	.918
1939	2,129	2,620	.813
1941	2,250	2,706	.832
1943	2,442	2,877	.849
1945	2,742	2,944	.931
1947	3,069	3,061	1.003
1949	3,453	3,280	1.053
1951	3,556	3,409	1.043
1953	3,656	3,641	1.004
1955	3,876	3,872	1.001
1957	4,003	4,053	.988
1959	3,867	4,303	.899
1961	4,064	4,509	.901
1963	4,213	4,671	.902
1965	4,272	4,853	.880
1967	n.a.	n.a.	n.a.
1969	4,549	5,514	.825
1971	4,692	5,779	.812

Sources: For newspaper circulation figures, *Canada Year Book,* all years; for households, estimated from Statistics Canada population figures.

in its history, and this is reflected in the differences in media growth patterns. For example, in the United States newspaper readership reached its peak in the 1920s, thirty years earlier than in Canada. Several factors account for this: first, the move to a predominantly urban-based society comes much later in Canada; second, there is a fairly

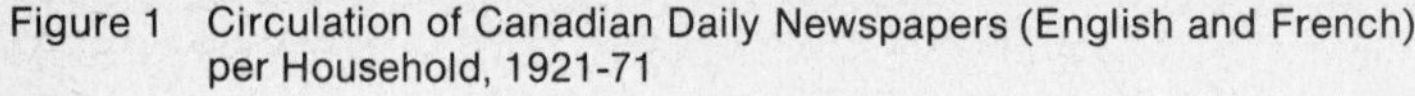

Figure 1 Circulation of Canadian Daily Newspapers (English and French) per Household, 1921-71

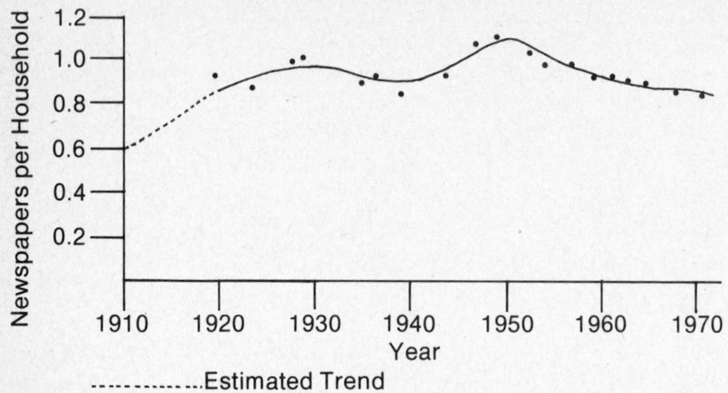

dramatic rise in the Canadian population after 1945, due mainly to immigration from Europe, and most of this additional population moved into urban areas; third, because of this new population, the other competing forms of mass communication, such as radio and newsmagazines, do not serve as *functional alternatives* in the same way as they did in the United States.[13] However, with the introduction of television into Canada in the early 1950s there has been a gradual shift away from newspapers as the primary source of news.

In spite of the decline in per household readership, newspapers continue to play an important part in the social fabric of Canada. However, Canada suffers from the same problem that has plagued all industrialized countries as the ownership of daily newspapers becomes concentrated in the hands of only a few major newspaper chains.[14] Before the First World War, there were 138 daily newspapers in Canada, but each of these had its own publisher. Today, only twelve publishing groups produce more than two-thirds of Canada's 116 dailies. As Professor Wilfred Kesterton has noted elsewhere in this volume, there are fewer daily newspapers today to serve a population approximately four times as great as it was in 1901.

The Rise of the Motion Picture

The motion picture became a major entertainment form in Canada just after the turn of the century. Originally shown as special features in vaudeville theatres, by 1903 motion pictures were seen in specialized "picture palaces" in all the major urban areas of Canada. The public immediately took this new entertainment to its heart, and in a very short time the movies were the largest paid amusement attraction Canada had ever known. The medium was readily accepted at this time of increasing immigration and urbanization, because it did not require a knowledge of the English language, it was easily accessible, especially for those living in cities, and it was cheap—an entire family could attend for less than fifty cents.[15]

Although we have no reliable statistics on movie attendance in Canada prior to 1934, the percentage of the population going to the movies was lower than that in the more urbanized United States. Thus in 1934, the Canadian population of 10.7 million averaged approximately 2 million admissions a week, while the American population of 126 million averaged over 70 million admissions per week. (In 1934, Canadian per household attendance at the movies was .83 a week compared to 2.24 in the U.S.)

Except for the wildly fluctuating attendances during the Depression years, Canadian movie audiences grew steadily, and peaked in 1952 when weekly attendance averaged over 4.76 million. Here again we have an interesting comparison with the United States, where peak attendance was achieved six years earlier in 1946, with a weekly average of over 90 million. The difference is largely attributable to the introduction of television in the U.S. in 1948, which attracted a large audience away from the movie theatres. Television only appeared in the major Canadian cities in 1952. It is significant to note, however, that in Canada the peak attendance per capita was also achieved in 1946 (Table 4).

Since 1953, the movie audience has shown a steady decline, with some indication of stabilization in the last four years. There has been much speculation concerning the reasons for the demise of the movies as the main form of entertainment, but the introduction of television must be considered the major factor. [16] However, in the period after 1945, Canadians were provided with a much wider choice of recreational opportunities from which to choose, and increasing interest in theatre, professional sports, and outdoor recreation have all diminished the audience for the movies. Nevertheless, the motion picture continues to attract a significant number of people, particularly those in the younger age groups.[17]

Table 4 MOTION PICTURE ATTENDANCE IN CANADA, 1934-1972

Year	*Movie houses*	*Paid admissions (000s)*	*Population (000s)*	*Attendance per capita*
1934	796	107,355	10,741	10
1936	956	126,914	10,950	12
1938	1,130	137,381	11,152	12
1940	1,229	151,591	11,381	13
1942	1,247	182,846	11,654	16
1944	1,298	208,167	11,946	17
1946	1,477	227,539	12,292	19
1948	1,604	219,289	12,823	17
1950[a]	1,801	231,747	13,712	17
1952	1,843	247,733	14,459	17
1954	1,938	218,509	15,287	14
1956	1,849	162,859	16,081	10
1958	1,622	136,335	17,080	8
1960	1,427	107,705	17,870	6
1962	1,278	91,258	18,583	5
1964	1,209	90,913	19,290	5
1966	1,149	87,694	20,015	4
1968	1,148	84,937	20,701	4
1970	1,157	78,918	21,001	4
1972	1,128	81,241	21,830	4

Sources: Motion Picture Attendance and establishments; Statistics Canada, Bulletin No. 63-207.

[a]Includes Newfoundland.

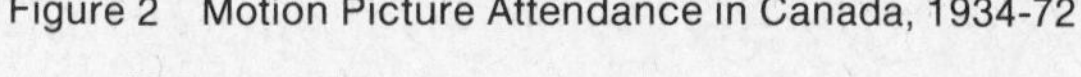

Figure 2 Motion Picture Attendance in Canada, 1934-72

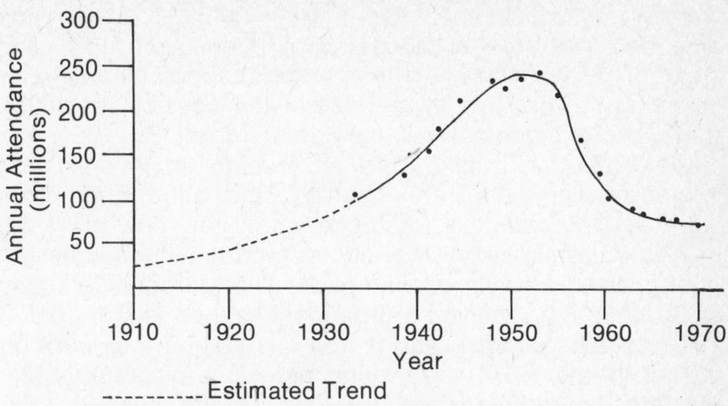

The Development of Radio

A means of instantaneous communication which could leap oceans and span continents had long been sought. Canada, with her immense geographic expanse and far-flung settlements, quickly realized the benefits to be derived from the development of wireless-telegraphy, and the subsequent refinement of radio-telephone technology. This dramatic innovation came as a result of the efforts of several inventors, such as Faraday, Maxwell, and Hertz, all of whom made important contributions to the apparatus eventually perfected by Guglielmo Marconi in the late nineteenth century.[18]

Canada and Canadians have played an important role in the development of radio. It was in Newfoundland in December 1901, where Marconi received his first trans-Atlantic radio-telegraph message; and later the Canadian government gave the Italian inventor an $80,000 subsidy to continue his experimental work. Further, the development of voice transmission was made possible by the work of two men—a Canadian, Reginald A. Fessenden, and an American, Dr. Lee de Forest.

Regular radio broadcasting began in Canada in December 1920, a month after similar broadcasts had been inaugurated by station KDKA in Pittsburgh in the U.S. The twenty-year period between Marconi's initial experience and the first public broadcasts had been taken up by the slow perfection of voice transmission technology and in increasing the public's awareness of the possibilities which the new communications medium offered. By 1920, the North American public were anxious to try this exciting new development for themselves, and once freed from wartime governmental restrictions on the use of radio, manufacturers quickly started to produce the necessary equipment for public consumption. The Marconi Company of Canada had received a broadcast licence in Montreal in 1919 for station XWA, and it was this station that went on the air in late 1920 with regular programs of gramophone records, news items, and weather reports. Station XWA later became CFCF, Montreal, and still broadcasts under these call letters.

It is significant to note that this station was established by a manufacturer of radio equipment as an inducement to potential buyers of domestic radio receivers. In fact, almost all the early radio stations in Canada, as in the U.S., were owned and operated either by a radio equipment manufacturer or a newspaper using the medium for self-promotional activities. By March 1923, the Canadian government had issued broadcasting licences to sixty-two private commercial broadcasting stations and to eight amateur groups. However, it is estimated that only about thirty-four of these stations were in actual operation. By comparison, in the U.S. there were 556 radio station licences issued by March 1923, although not all of these were operational either.[19]

Professor Frank W. Peers, in his admirable history of Canadian broadcasting, has shown that until 1928 public authorities paid very little attention to the state of radio, unlike the intense activity then taking place in both Great Britain and the United States.[20] However, the government had been involved in discussions with the United States regarding the problems of channel interference, and had imposed an annual licence fee on all owners of radio sets.

Even at this early stage there were numerous complaints that stations carried too many commercials and that station operators ignored Canadian talent in favour of recorded U.S. material. Another concern was the apparent reluctance of broadcasters to transmit to the less populated areas of the country because of their dependence upon the large audience base necessary to attract advertisers. Although there was a duplication of service in the urban areas, many rural parts of the country received no radio at all, or were forced to rely upon powerful U.S. stations.

After publication of the Aird Commission Report in 1929, the Canadian government was forced to agree with the Commission's observation that "public service" should be the basis of all broadcasting, and that it should be provided by one national system. At hearings conducted in 1932 to consider the Report, evidence was given that outside of Toronto and Montreal only about two-fifths of the population could regularly pick up Canadian programs, and even these consisted largely of imported recordings. Organizations such as the newly-formed Canadian Broadcast League argued vigorously in favour of public ownership of radio stations, contending that the radio spectrum was, in fact, part of the public domain. As a result of these hearings, proponents of public ownership won, and on May 26, 1932, Parliament, by a unanimous vote, passed the Canadian Radio Broadcasting Act providing for the creation of the Canadian Radio Broadcasting Commission (CRBC) which was the forerunner of the present CBC.

During its first year, the CRBC established stations in Vancouver, Montreal, Toronto, Ottawa, and Chicoutimi, and using these stations as a base, began a regular schedule of network programs in May 1933. By 1935, the network had expanded to include another forty-three private stations and by 1936 was broadcasting six hours of programs a day, though these were confined to the evening hours. There were still many serious deficiencies in this system of national broadcasting, and as a result a new committee recommended the complete recasting of the national radio organization. On November 2, 1936, Parliament passed a law establishing the Canadian Broadcasting Corporation. By 1941, there were nine CBC transmitters covering almost the entire country and a separate, more effective French language network had also been established.

After the War the CBC expanded its facilities, adding stations in the Prairie region, the Maritimes, and in 1958 even in the extreme northern part of the country. The CBC quite rightly has emphasized its role to provide an essential service to all Canadians and its function to maintain the vital links of communication in this vast country.

However, private radio stations have also been an important factor in Canadian broadcasting, and attract a much larger share of the radio audience than the CBC stations in the same markets. While most of these private stations do not have the same news facilities as the national network, they are relied upon by the vast majority of Canadians to provide for their entertainment needs. In the early years of radio in Canada, it was the private stations that provided broadcasting service for most of the country, and they have continued to do so.

Unfortunately, the statistics on the growth of radio listenership are not complete for the earliest period, but we do have rough measures by using the figures on the number of receiving licences issued in the period prior to 1940 (see Table 5); no valid data are available on the number of households with radios. We do know that while radio had a rapid diffusion in Canada, the problems of geography presented a formidable obstacle to complete coverage, and therefore such diffusion was not as complete as in the U.S. The period during the Second World War witnessed a rapid increase in the number of households with radios, no doubt spurred on by the desire to hear the latest war news (see Table 6). Since the 1950s, over 98 per cent of all Canadian households have had access to radio broadcasts; the remaining 2 per cent have either made a conscious decision not to own a radio, or live in a part of the country inaccessible to radio coverage.

Table 5 PRIVATE RADIO LICENCES ISSUED IN CANADA, 1923-1940

Year	*Licences*
1923	9,956
1925	91,996
1927	215,650
1929	297,398
1931	523,100
1933	761,288
1935	812,335
1937	1,038,500
1939	1,223,502

Source: *Canada Year Book.*

Table 6 ESTIMATED NUMBER OF CANADIAN HOUSEHOLDS WITH RADIOS, 1941-1973

Year	*Estimated Households (000s)*	*Households with Radios (000s)*	*Percentage with Radios*
1941	2,706	2,003	74%
1947	3,136	2,818	90
1949	3,504	3,247	93
1954	3,734	3,598	96
1956	3,974	3,817	96
1958	4,173	4,003	96
1960	4,404	4,236	96
1962	4,592	4,413	96
1964	4,757	4,565	96
1966	4,938	4,763	97
1968	5,394	5,222	97
1970	5,646	5,489	97
1972	6,108	5,961	98
1973	6,266	6,124	98

Source: Statistics Canada, *Household Facilities and Equipment Survey*, Bulletin No. 64-202.

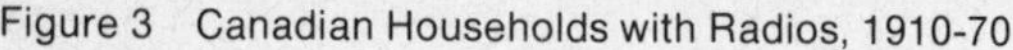

Figure 3 Canadian Households with Radios, 1910-70

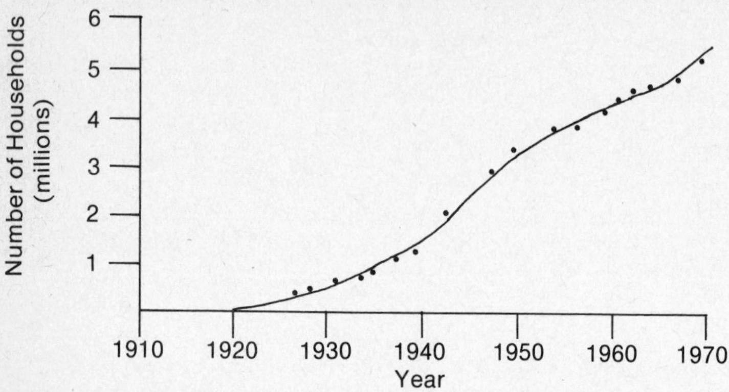

Radio has shown a remarkable resilience in the face of heavy competition from television. Ironically, when the introduction of television became obvious, it was radio which appeared to be doomed, and not the movies. However, radio was able to readjust its content sufficiently to provide a clear alternative to the newer medium, while the movies were not.[21] Now radio has secured a place for itself in the media mix of Canadian society by providing a wide variety of music, news, and sports. CBC radio continues to provide radio programming for minority interests, and the popularity of phone-in shows indicates the feedback potential inherent in this medium.[22] Further, since 1961 there has been a rapid increase in the number of households with FM radios, and in 1973, over 67 per cent could receive FM broadcasts. Although radio has reached a saturation point, it does not appear that listenership is being reduced; and unless there is a technological breakthrough to replace radio as we know it, there is little likelihood of any such decrease.

The Emergence of Television

Although Canadians began to experiment with television during the early thirties, it was not until after the Second

World War that government seriously considered the introduction of the visual medium. In 1951, the Royal Commission on National Development in the Arts, Letters, and Sciences proposed the development of a national system of television. In September 1952, the CBC started minor television operations in Toronto and Montreal, and by November 1955, new stations were on the air in Vancouver, Winnipeg, and Halifax. These stations formed the base of what was later to become the national CBC Television Network. In 1960, the Board of Broadcast Governors authorized the establishment of a privately-owned network—the Canadian Television Network (CTV)—and it began operation in October of that year. This new network provided an alternative service to the large majority of the Canadian audience.

Prior to the introduction of Canadian television programming, many viewers in Toronto, Vancouver, and Montreal had been watching television from U.S. border stations since the 1940s. Because of habit, and because of the greater diversity of programming available on American channels, Canadians continued to spend a significant portion of their viewing hours watching American channels. Only in recent years has the Canadian television audience begun to spend more time viewing Canadian programming.[23]

After the introduction of television in 1952-55, there was a rapid increase in the number of households with TV sets (see Table 7). By 1963, over 90 per cent of households were watching television, and by 1973, this had reached the saturation figure of 96 per cent. Recent advances in communications technology have allowed television transmission to remote areas in the north. As with radio, it is unlikely that there will be any immediate decline in television viewing in the near future. Television content provides a *functional alternative* to certain aspects of motion pictures and radio; however, while the latter was able to adapt and alter its content accordingly, and was therefore able to survive and even thrive, the movies are still attempting to counter the competition from television.

Table 7 ESTIMATED NUMBER OF CANADIAN HOUSEHOLDS WITH TELEVISION, 1953-1973

Year	*Estimated Households (000s)*	*Households with Television (000s)*	*Percentage with Television*
1953	3,641	373	10%
1955	3,872	1,496	39
1957	4,053	2,545	63
1959	4,303	3,206	75
1961	4,509	3,797	84
1963	4,671	4,195	90
1965	4,853	4,495	93
1967	5,262	4,977	95
1969	5,514	5,293	96
1971	5,779	5,554	96
1973	6,266	6,017	96

Source: Statistics Canada, *Household Facilities and Equipment Survey*, Bulletin No. 64-202.

Table 8 TELEVISION SETS IN USE PER CANADIAN HOUSEHOLD, 1953-1973

Year	*Estimated Households (000s)*	*Television Sets in Use (000s)*	*Television Sets per Household*
1953	3,641	373	0.10
1955	3,872	1,496	0.39
1957	4,053	2,545	0.63
1959	4,303	3,206	0.75
1961	4,509	3,977	0.88
1963	4,671	4,525	0.97
1965	4,853	5,022	1.04
1967	5,262	5,803	1.10
1969	5,514	6,396	1.16
1971	5,779	7,096	1.23
1973	6,266	7,923	1.26

Source: Statistics Canada, *Household Facilities and Equipment Survey*, Bulletin No. 64-202.

Figure 4 Canadian Households with Television, 1950-75

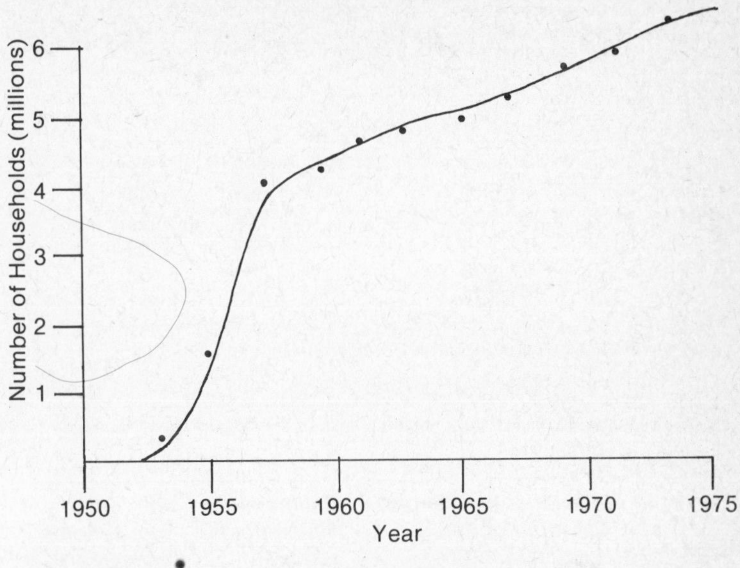

The Promise of Cable Television

Canada is currently the most "cablized" country in the world, with nearly 30 per cent of all households attached to a cable television system in 1972. In some cities, such as London, Ontario, and Vancouver, B.C., more than 75 per cent of all households receive cable television. The development of cable television has been rapid, but has also shown recent signs of slowing down, although the total number of subscribers has trebled since 1967 (see Table 9). More important, on a national basis only half of all the people who have access to a cable system actually accept the service and become subscribers. However, this acceptance rate is subject to wide regional variation depending on the number of channels available over the air. Cable television also provides a myriad of possibilities in the form of extra services which may serve to attract a greater proportion of subscribers in the future.[24]

Table 9 GROWTH OF CABLE TELEVISION IN CANADA, 1967-1972

Year	*Cable Systems*	*Individual Households and Multi-outlet Subscribers (000s)*	*Potential Subscribers (000s)*	*Percentage*
1967	314	517	1,225	42%
1968	377	710	1,607	44
1969	400	924	1,700	54
1970	314	1,164	2,392	49
1971	326	1,398	2,681	52
1972	344	1,689	3,313	51

Source: Statistics Canada, *Cable Television,* Bulletin No. 56-205.

Table 10 CANADIAN HOUSEHOLDS WITH CABLE TELEVISION, 1967-1972

Year	*Individual Households and Multi-outlet Subscribers (000s)*	*Estimated Households (000s)*	*Percentage of Households with Cable TV*
1967	517	5,262	9.8%
1968	710	5,394	13.2
1969	924	5,514	16.8
1970	1,164	5,646	20.6
1971	1,398	5,779	24.2
1972	1,689	6,108	27.6

Source: Statistics Canada, *Cable Television,* Bulletin No. 56-205.

Comparison of All Media

If the diffusion curves for all media are standardized, based upon the year of peak audience or participation, we readily see that newspapers and motion pictures are now in a decline, while radio and television have yet to reach their zenith.[25] It is particularly interesting to note the relationship between the growth of television and the decline of the movies.

Figure 5 Standardized Diffusion Curves for All Media

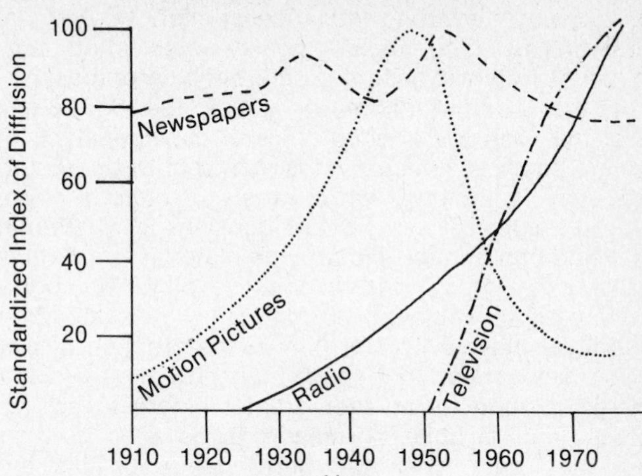

Future Mass Media Trends in Canada

It is fairly safe to predict that in Canada the broadcast media will continue to become more powerful at the expense of print media and the motion picture. There are, however, important developments currently taking place with respect to increasing the amount of indigenous content in all segments of the mass media, particularly broadcasting. Recent requirements of the Canadian Radio-Television Commission have served to force broadcast outlets to make more Canadian programming available, and public response has been generally favourable to this move. Because of its relatively small population base, Canada is still unable to produce a sufficient amount and variety of television programming to meet all the public's needs, and will have to rely upon U.S. and British productions for some time to come. The problem of "overflow" programming from U.S. border stations will remain, with very little hope of being resolved to everyone's satisfaction, as long as Canadians continue to exhibit a strong pull toward U.S. television content.

Canada's evolution towards a mass society will also continue, but with the strong influence of minority ethnic and cultural groups. The mosaic quality often attributed to Canadian society will ensure a different type of mass society from that found in the melting pot of the U.S. The existence of the French Canadian third of the population and enormous postwar immigration is sufficient to guarantee a heterogeneous society, with a variety of cultural expressions and values. The important question is whether the mass media can continue to provide material to satisfy this diversity of needs, while continuing to play an important role as a national *social bond.* Historically, mass communications have played a major part in the creation of a national consciousness in Canada, but now the media are being relied upon to an ever greater extent to act as a force for national unity. It remains to be seen how successful they can be in the performance of this most difficult task.

1. For a representative view of the various theories of the role of mass communication and development, see Lucien Pye (ed.), *Communications and Political Development* (Princeton: Princeton University Press, l963), and Frederick W. Frey, "Communications and Development," in Ithiel de Sola Pool et al. (eds.), *The Handbook of Communications* (Chicago: Rand McNally, l973), pp. 337-432.
2. For a detailed discussion of the concept of "mass society" see William Kornhauser, "Mass Society," in *The Encyclopedia of Social Sciences* (New York: Macmillan, 1968).
3. Frey, "Communications and Development," pp. 338-40.
4. UNESCO has published several studies examining the relative size of the communications infrastructure of countries and their socio-economic development. See *Mass Media in the Developing Countries*, Reports and Papers on Mass Communication No. 33 (Paris: UNESCO, 1961).
5. This theory of greater participation through centralization is clearly articulated in Edward Shils, "Mass Society and Its Culture," in Bernard Rosenberg and David Manning White (eds.), *Mass Culture Revisited* (New York: Van Nostrand Reinhold, 1971), pp. 61-84.
6. Kornhauser, "Mass Society."
7. The role of communications in the alteration of the spatial dimensions of society is discussed in Richard L. Meier, *A Communications Theory of Urban Growth* (Cambridge: M.I.T. Press, 1965); Allan R. Pred, *The Spatial Dynamics of U.S. Urban-Industrial Growth,*

1800-1914 (Cambridge: M.I.T. Press, 1966); and Allan R. Pred, *Urban Growth and the Circulation of Information* (Cambridge: Harvard University Press, 1973).

8. The two classic theories on the "rule of the mob" are articulated in Gustave Le Bon, *The Crowd* (New York: Viking Press, 1960); and Jose Ortega y Gasset, *The Revolt of the Masses* (New York: W.W. Norton, 1932).
9. The ideas in this section are based upon similar concepts expressed in Melvin De Fleur, *Theories of Mass Communication* (New York: David McKay, 1970), pp. 6-7.
10. There is still a great deal of important work to be done in this area, and only now are most social historians beginning to realize the necessity to take into account the development of mass communications as important factors in social change.
11. The best account of the growth of journalism in Canada is found in Wilfred Kesterton, *A History of Journalism in Canada* (Toronto: McClelland and Stewart, 1967). The history of journalism is not discussed in much detail here because Professor Kesterton has done so elsewhere in this volume.
12. For a detailed examination of the literature concerned with the process of innovation diffusion, see Everett M. Rogers and F. Floyd Shoemaker, *Communication of Innovations: A Cross-Cultural Approach* (New York: The Free Press, 1971).
13. A "functional alternative" is an innovation that assumes most of the functions of an existing mode of action, making the earlier innovation obsolete or forcing it to alter its current function. See De Fleur, *Theories of Mass Communication*, pp. 19, 34.
14. For an extensive examination of the problems of media ownership in Canada see the *Report of the Special Senate Committee on Mass Media*, 3 vols. (Ottawa: Queen's Printer, 1970).
15. The reasons for the popularity of the movies during this early stage are explained in Garth S. Jowett, "The First Movie Audiences", *The Journal of Popular Film*, vol. 3, no. 1 (Spring 1974), pp. 39-54.
16. The relationship between the growth of television and the decline of the motion picture audience is examined in depth in Fredric Stuart, *The Effects of Television on the Motion Picture and Radio Industries* (New York: Arno Press, 1975).
17. The age variation on motion picture audiences in Canada is discussed in Carol Kirsh et al., *A Leisure Study - Canada 1972* (Toronto: Culturcan Publications, 1973). This study points out that in 1972, 47 per cent of the movie audiences was under the age of 24.
18. See De Fleur, *Theories of Mass Communication*, pp. 49-55.
19. Frank W. Peers, *The Politics of Canadian Broadcasting, 1920-1951* (Toronto: University of Toronto Press, 1969) p.6.
20. Ibid., p. 12.
21. See Stuart, *The Effects of Television* for details on how radio was able to survive, while the movies continued to decline.
22. For a detailed discussion of radio phone-in shows see Benjamin D. Singer, *Feedback and Society* (Lexington, Mass.: Heath Lexington Books, 1973), pp. 45-56.
23. In 1974, it was estimated that 79 per cent of the viewing hours in Canada were spent viewing Canadian television. However, in some provinces, such as Ontario (38 per cent) and British Columbia (41 per cent), the time spent watching American channels was much

greater. See *The Canadian Media Directors Council Media Digest 74/75* (Toronto: Marketing Magazine, 1974).

24. For the future possibilities of cable television see Ithiel de Sola Pool (ed.), *Talking Back: Feedback and Cable Technology* (Cambridge: M.I.T. Press, 1973).
25. To arrive at a standardized diffusion chart, each medium was indexed at 100 for the year of peak audience, and the other years calculated accordingly. Although the individual media measurements are different, this allowed the diffusion curves to be compared on a single scale.

Propaganda in Canadian Society

TERENCE H. QUALTER

In the English language "propaganda" is a negative term. We tend to react defensively to the charge of being propagandists. A professor of, say, history, told that his lectures are largely propaganda, is offended by what he interprets as a challenge to his academic integrity. We struggle to create definitions which will put propaganda and education, or propaganda and truth, in exclusive compartments. Yet this pejorative connotation is itself simply the product of a successful propaganda campaign. In its origins propaganda is an entirely neutral word. It is derived from one of the organizations of the Roman Catholic Church, the *Sacra Congregatio de Propaganda Fide,* or the Sacred Congregation for the Propagation of the Faith, the body principally responsible for the Church's missionary activities.

By the last years of the First World War all the belligerents had established elaborate propaganda organizations, making the battle of words another front in the total conflict. In all cases the aims were the same: to sow disunion and defeatism among the enemy, to gain the sympathy and support of neutrals (or at least prevent that sympathy and support from going to the enemy), and to strengthen morale at home. It was at this stage that the Allies made an important decision which has affected all our subsequent attitudes to propaganda. Because the Germans had, and admitted to having, a propaganda organization to present their case, the Allies "granted" the Germans exclusive use of the term. In opposition to the German propaganda, they established Ministries of Information. To counter the lies and deceptions of the enemy's propaganda "our" Ministry of Information spread truth and reason. This association of propaganda with the cause of "them" and therefore by implication with misrepresentation, illogical argument, and appeals to people's basest instincts, has persisted to this day. Yet it is an association which is itself a dishonest misrepresentation, an attempt to destroy the credibility of an opponent or the validity of his argument by name-calling.

Propaganda and Attitudes

Propaganda, correctly, is no more than the attempt to influence people's attitudes. Simply stated, propaganda is based on a number of assumptions and propositions which are described below.

In some areas, some of our behaviour is influenced by our attitudes. The "some" in both cases is stressed, for the propagandist does not claim a *general* theory of behaviour. He simply recognizes empirically that he can sometimes influence the way people *act.* He also recognizes that there are some areas of human behaviour which no amount of propaganda can affect, and that even in those areas where he has some experience of success, he cannot touch all the people all the time.

Attitudes may be defined as habitual psychological or internal responses to external stimuli. If, for example, every report of the activities of, say, the F.L.Q. (the stimulus) produces similar internal feelings of anger, or sorrow, or elation, then there is a well-established attitude to the F.L.Q. This specific attitude may also be a manifestation of a deeper attitude to French Canadians, or to political extremism in general. The attitude is the internal feeling, even if its external expression is modified by the presence of a sympathetic or hostile audience. Of course, in fact our attitudes are the product of a lifetime of stimuli and the relationship between a single stimulus and the attitude will be much more complex and indirect than is suggested here. The main point is that we all have a "set" of attitudes which tends to change only slowly and which is aroused by the appropriate external stimuli.

Symbols and Stimuli

Most stimuli are symbolic in form. A symbol may be defined as anything perceptible to the senses which is accepted as representing something else. It is difficult to be more precise than this without excluding some form of symbolism. A symbol thus exists at two levels. It has an objective reality of its own, which the senses perceive, and a subjective, representational significance. A word has objective existence as a sequence of sounds or of marks on paper, and a flag has objective existence as a piece of coloured cloth. But not every arrangement of sounds or of marks on paper is a word, and not every piece of coloured cloth is a flag. Sequences of sounds and marks become words, symbols for ideas, or thoughts, or other realities, when those who use them agree that this or that specific combination will have this or that reference. Thus the meaning or reference of a symbol is not something inherent or internal to the symbol, but is something imposed upon it by those who use it. A thing becomes a symbol for something else when some group of people agree or accept that it shall stand for that something else.

While art, architecture, signs, uniforms, gestures, and so on, may all have symbolic significance, by far the most important group of symbols are verbal. Verbal symbols, or words, are the major conventional audio and visual representation of the images in our minds. They are conventional in that the reference or meaning of a word is attached to it, and does not come from the word itself. The sociologist Pareto described words as "mere labels for keeping track of things." In this sense the correct meaning of a word is whatever meaning its users have attached to it. Thus, if we take the sequence of black marks on white paper, STATE, we engage in a futile exercise if we try to establish its "true" meaning. Instead of asking what the symbol STATE means, we can really only ask what meaning has such and such a group attached to it at such and such a time. The reference of a symbol may, of course, change over time, and it may even be deliberately changed by redirection, by narrowing, or by expansion.

Words do not exist in isolation. For effective use they must be combined in sequences according to recognized operating rules. The set of words and the operating rules for combining them together are known as a language. A language is thus a conventional symbol system. Symbolic communication is possible only to the extent that the parties to the communication have learned the same symbol system. In the case of language this is a larger requirement than might at first appear, for a language is not a unified thing known in its entirety by all its users. The extent of vocabulary, knowledge of operating rules, and symbol references are all variables affected by region, education, and social class. Because of this, complete communication is rarely possible.

The problem of communication becomes further complicated by the fact that some symbols have, in addition to their dictionary reference, an emotional connotation. Many symbols are far from neutral in their effect and stimulate various positive and negative associations. These associations are not properties of the words or symbols themselves, but are products of the "attitudinal complexes" of those using them. As this attitudinal complex is the product of the individual's entire previous experience and psychological make-up, it will be different for each person. But members of the same social class, occupation, national group, religion and so on may share certain experiences, and may therefore develop some attitudes similar enough to respond in similar ways to the appropriate stimuli.

The Goals of Propaganda

Because a great deal of our behaviour, especially social behaviour, consists of externalized responses to internal attitudes, it follows that behaviour might be influenced by the conscious manipulation of the stimuli which arouse the attitudes. This, then, is the foundation of propaganda. It is the deliberate manipulation of symbols, with the intention of arousing attitudes which will result in behaviour desired by the propagandist.

This deliberate manipulation has nothing to do with honesty, truth, irrationality, distortion, one-sidedness, or any of the other supposed characteristics of propaganda. It may well be, as a matter of fact, that when a propagandist is trying to arouse certain attitudes in a large audience he may decide that the surest way to success is through the presentation of a grossly one-sided message (and he *may* be unsuccessful in using such an approach). It may also be generally true that when an attempt is made to influence the behaviour of a group as large as, say, the nation, it will be necessary to find some common set of attitudes, which usually means the most basic, primitive attitudes aroused through highly emotion-charged symbols. But it is not the one-sidedness or the appeals to the emotions which make the activity propaganda, but the use of symbols in the attempt to influence attitudes.

The neutral character of propaganda per se is most clearly shown by comparing it with education. There have been endless attempts to establish mutually exclusive definitions of these two activities, but none have been completely successful—largely because they are not mutually exclusive. Propaganda and education are concerned with different things, and their territories may often overlap. Education is concerned with the teaching of what is believed to be true in the light of currently available knowledge. Propaganda is concerned with the arousal of attitudes to influence behaviour. An activity which uses what is believed to be true to stimulate a favourable attitude may therefore be both propaganda and education. Thus a new history textbook demonstrating that Canadian Indians have been unfairly treated by earlier historians may have, as part of its purpose, the creation of a more sympathetic understanding of, and therefore treatment of, contemporary Indian society. To the extent that it has that purpose, it is propaganda. To the extent that it is based on an objective study of the evidence and represents the author's sincerest efforts to discover the truth, it is also education.

It is no less education by being also propaganda, and no less propaganda by being also education.

Propaganda, then, is simply the deliberate manipulation (or use) of symbols to form, control, or alter attitudes, with the intention of influencing behaviour. To this extent, therefore, almost any form of symbolic communication may be propaganda, while no form of communication is necessarily or exclusively propaganda. Propagandists are those who *deliberately* manipulate symbols to influence behaviour.

All politicians, and political activists, when they speak or write in defense of their party or its policies, are propagandists, and their role as propagandists is not in any way diminished because they may speak rationally or truthfully. To the extent that film-makers, playwrights, journalists, editors, artists, poets, professors, novelists, and folk singers intend or hope that their work will influence human attitudes and values, and therefore ultimately human behaviour, they are propagandists. And as this intention or hope must be present in a great deal of the public activity of all who deal in symbols, most of such activity is propaganda. Even the statement "Art for Art's sake" is a political statement about the social role of the artist and is therefore propaganda.

It has been necessary to develop this argument at some length because the traditional approach to propaganda as an undesirable activity indulged in only by one's enemies frustrates any serious attempt to examine it as a political/sociological phenomenon. People who do not agree on what is the truth, or on what is a rational argument, cannot agree on the identification of propaganda if it is to be recognized by the absence of truth or rationality. Here all we have said about a man when we label him a propagandist is that he uses symbolic communication to influence attitudes. Having settled this point we are then on firmer ground for asking further questions about the activities of a given propagandist in given circumstances.

In very broad categories we can look at propaganda from three perspectives: form, content, and objective.

Form deals with the type of symbolic communication (spoken word, written word, art, architecture, etc.) and the medium of communication (newspaper, radio, public platform, classroom, etc.). Content deals with what is communicated and includes any subjective evaluations of the rationality or honesty of the message. Objective deals with the goals being pursued by the propagandist, the cause for which he is a propagandist.

Propaganda in Canada

As far as form and content are concerned, we cannot identify any exclusively or uniquely Canadian characteristics. There is no evidence to suggest any distinctive style in Canadian political speech making or editorial writing. We can make no valid generalizations that Canadian newspaper propaganda is more (or less) truthful than that of any other industrial nation. We cannot even say whether there is more or less propaganda in Canadian newspapers than elsewhere. Indeed, one of the problems of any comparative study of propaganda form and content is the sheer impossibility of obtaining the relevant data. What, for example, is the "mean truth level" in the news columns of American and Canadian newspapers? In 1973, how many more political speeches were made in Great Britain than in Canada? How much propaganda is disseminated in sociology lectures in Canadian universities in any year? There are no answers to these questions or to hundreds of others of the same kind. In most cases there are no agreed units of measurement.

As a consequence there are not many useful general statements that we can make about propaganda in Canadian society. We do not know, and have no means of knowing, how much propaganda there is. The question, "How much?" is unanswerable. We cannot even identify all the propagandists. Individual politicians, political parties, editors, reporters, cartoonists, trade unions, Chambers of Commerce, manufacturers' associations, farmers' groups, organized interests of every kind, churches, artists, writers, teachers, architects, may all from time to time engage in propaganda for any number of causes. None are exclusively engaged in this activity. About the only completely correct statement that can be made, and it is not a very profound statement, is that at any one time a large number of people are using a wide variety of symbols in the attempt to influence the attitudes of a still larger number of people on a range of issues and usually in conflicting directions.

Propagandists in Canada will use whatever forms are available to them. They will write newspaper editorials, buy advertising space in the mass media, make speeches, publish pamphlets, deliver lectures, display posters, sing, parade, wear buttons, dress in a certain way, or write books, and in doing these things they will be silly, profound, fair-minded, scurrilous, and frequently incoherent. In no case, however, will they be behaving in a distinctively Canadian way. They will simply be propagandists doing what all propagandists do, but in a Canadian environment.

Canadian Propaganda

One thing we can do, however, is to draw a distinction between general propaganda in Canadian society, and one particular manifestation of it: Canadian and counter-Canadian propaganda. Canadian propaganda would be distinguished or identified by its principal objectives, rather than by its form or content. The objectives would be, by definition, the creating, preserving, or enhancing of a sense of Canadian identity. The first task of Canadian propaganda per se, would be to cultivate an awareness that Canada exists as an independent political-cultural entity. The propaganda succeeds to the extent that the inhabitants of this northern part of the continent not only perceive themselves as Canadian, but also accept that this is a fact of some significance in their lives. This is fundamentally what is meant by Canadian propaganda.

The counter-Canadian propaganda has two principal sources, external and internal. The external assault on the sense of Canadian identity comes, first of all, from the whole ideology of internationalism and the disparagement of all forms of nationalism. Any appeal to look to the world, or to humanity in general, is counter-nationalist propaganda. A more specific application of the internationalist case is the appeal, often no more than implicit, of continentalism: the whole ideology of closer socio-cultural, economic, and political ties with the United States. There is also the external threat of "alien" loyalties. At one level this may mean no more than the emotional ties of "homeland" especially for first-generation immigrants. At another level it may involve an ideological allegiance to another country: the Soviet Union, Israel, Ireland, etc. In the first case the individual, it is presumed, has not yet come to make a complete identification with Canada, and in the second case he or she might be positively hostile to such identification.

There are also internal obstacles to the propaganda for Canadian identity. Collectively these might be termed the challenge of fragmentation. It arises when loyalty to province, region, language, ethnic group, religion, political belief, and so on makes demands which inhibit or diminish exclusive loyalty to nation.

It is not suggested here that the claims of greater international co-operation, or the continued love of the country of one's origin, or the pluralistic appeals of other associations within the Canadian polity are necessarily undesirable. They may be an indication of a healty vitality in social-political life. It is simply a matter of fact that to the extent that they persist, the sense of *Canadian* identity is weakened, and the task of the Canadian propagandists is made more difficult. Their existence is the reason for there being a Canadian propaganda in the first place.

The further objectives of the Canadian propagandist are all corollaries or developments of the primary theme. Perceptions of Canadian identity grow easily and logically into all forms of patriotism and national pride. The first step is the recognition of the "apartness" of Canada. The second step is love of, and pride in, that apartness: seeing Canada not only as different from, but also superior to, other nations. Extreme manifestations of such patriotism are sometimes described as chauvinism.

Opposition to the cultivation of patriotism arises both from a general discrediting of *all* patriotism and national symbolism and from a specific negativism to *Canadian* patriotism in particular. The belittling of patriotism may thus range from apathy and disinterest to positive hostility. Some will be completely unreceptive to patriotic propaganda, being bored or unmoved by it. These may be the people who love no country. With others the reaction will be more obviously negative, especially when Canadian symbols run counter to those of an older tradition such as the British monarchy. These are the people who love other countries more.

A third related theme for Canadian propaganda might be to emphasize the particular or uniquely Canadian relevance of issues such as unemployment, capital investment, Great Lakes pollution, conservation of natural resources, urbanization, and so on. Canadian relevance would be proposed in response to the assertion that these things are merely manifestations of larger issues: for example, the socialist reconstruction of society, or the capitalist (or communist) conspiracy, which would have to be solved at a global level.

Finally, there would be the need to put forward the Canadian point of view on a number of specific issues: trade with Communist countries, the legitimacy of democratic socialism, the meaning of law and order, competition and co-operation, the standards of behaviour expected of police and public officials, the place of ethnic minorities in the society, or foreign policy. The object would be twofold: to make Canadians aware that there are or should be specifically Canadian points of view on these questions, and to impress the idea that the Canadian viewpoints are morally, or legally, or logically, or politically superior to rival views.

This is not an exhaustive catalogue of the objectives of Canadian propaganda. Obviously further subdivisions or different categorizations could be made. It is not even a classification of the "good guys" and the "bad guys." Some of what would by definition be Canadian propaganda would be offensive to a great many Canadians. Some would appear to the neutral observer, if such could be found, as rampant jingoism. Some of the counter-Canadian propaganda, especially that from internal sources, would be on behalf of that cultural diversity which is an important part of the Canadian society. In short, Canadian nationalism is a legitimate cause in Canada, but it is not the only value to be pursued.

To summarize the implications of the term "Canadian propaganda": certain policies, causes, values, ways of doing things, economic structures, social arrangements, historic traditions, political forms, art, literature, sports heroes, etc., are to be identified as Canadian, and therefore a source of pride to all Canadians. This is Canadian propaganda. Propaganda which seeks to identify such policies etc. with other polities, or as part of wider associations (or smaller associations within Canada), or which tries to denigrate such policies etc., is counter-Canadian propaganda. Any other propaganda, for example, the election propaganda of the recognized political parties, is general propaganda disseminated in a Canadian environment.

If this rather lengthy description is applied to the more technical definition used earlier, Canadian propaganda may be defined as the deliberate manipulation of symbols to form, control, or alter attitudes favourable to Canada. Counter-propaganda is propaganda which directs attitudes away from Canada.

As already described, the first-level purpose of Canadian propaganda is to create a greater awareness of all things Canadian, and a more favourable attitude to those things. There is a second-level, more fundamental purpose. This is that the attitudes, the internal responses to stimuli, be reflected in a more positive behaviour towards Canadian policies, Canadian political and social leadership, the Canadian consumer market, Canadian cultural values, and Canadian standards in general.

It is important to stress that propagandists influence attitudes in order to affect behaviour. The final test of the success of propaganda is not the affected attitude, but the consequent behaviour. The propagandist does not foster patriotism simply because love of country is a virtuous thing. He encourages patriotism because patriotic people are more likely to give positive support to the actions of their government, to fight for their country in time of war, to pay their taxes, to obey the law, to conform to social conventions, or to invest in the products of their own industry. We can illustrate with one simple example. A wider circulation of Canadian magazines might be encouraged because it would help to create a deeper sense of Canadian identity. To many this would seem an end in itself. But unless the increased sense of identity led in turn to a greater desire to read and buy still more Canadian magazines, the propaganda could not be counted a complete success.

Propaganda Media

It remains now to consider the various media as instruments for the dissemination of the symbols of Canadian and counter-Canadian propaganda. Most of the detailed data are to be found in other papers in this book and it is not necessary that they be restated here. It is more important to consider some of the implications of those data.

Television

Obviously we begin with the mass media, and of these the most important is television. This is not the place to go into a lengthy discussion of the relative merits of the several media as sources of propaganda. It is no more than reiterating a truism to state simply that television has enormous power to spread fact and opinion and to influence social attitudes and behaviour. In Canada it has vast potential as a propaganda medium. There are few homes without a television set, except by choice. There is already in existence a national, publicly-owned network accessible to some 96 per cent of Canadians. Independent networks and private stations also reach a high proportion of Canadians.

Yet television in Canada is in a most ambiguous position. Canadian nationalists are clearly not happy with it. The core of the uneasiness lies in the fact that the largest centres of Canadian population lie close to the United States border and within range of American television stations. A very large number of Canadians watch American television fairly regularly and there is no way acceptable to present Canadian society by which they could be prevented from doing so. Further, a good deal of the programming on Canadian networks originates in the United States. As American television naturally embodies American cultural values, often at odds with Canadian values, it operates as a major source of counter-Canadian propaganda. The American influence is pervasive, obvious, and clearly disturbing.

Currently the commonest counter to American influence has been to require certain minimum levels of "Canadian content" in the programs of Canadian stations. At present some 60 per cent of CBC programming originates in Canada. While any increase in this level will automatically reduce the American content, and therefore the direct American influence, we must be cautious. We must bear in mind that Canadian content is not necessarily the same thing as Canadian propaganda. A poor television program is still a poor program, whether it originates in Canada or not. If the Canadian origin of a poor program is emphasized, it will be counter-productive for other efforts of Canadian propagandists. If a Canadian program is to succeed as Canadian propaganda, it must first succeed simply as a program.

There is another barrier to television as a propaganda medium. In our society television is primarily looked to for entertainment, particularly escapist entertainment. Public affairs and news programs will attract audiences, but generally these are smaller than for a crime drama or a comedy series. The only effect of any attempts at sustained overt propaganda would be to drive viewers to another channel. Most of the propaganda on television is implicit in the social values embodied in entertainment programs: attitudes to wealth, crime control, family life, and so on. And as most of the most widely-watched entertainment shows are of American origin, American values are more widely disseminated than Canadian. This is a disturbing situation and not one that is easily remedied. Any clumsy attempt to supplant all American programs on Canadian networks would probably have the effect of driving more Canadians into watching nothing but American television, where they would get no Canadian content at all.

Radio

Radio is now a less important medium than it was in the pre-television era. Its principal function today is to provide a continuous musical background to work and leisure—a background interspersed with commercials and local news. Because most people listen to local radio, the American influence across the border is less significant than for television. Here, in the matter of Canadian content, the insistence on a minimum proportion of programs being of Canadian origin is more an economic matter of providing support for Canadian artists and technicians than providing a forum for nationalistic ideology. Technically, radio is equipped to be a more effective vehicle of Canadian propaganda. Socially and politically it is unlikely that there will be any change in its present role.

The Press

The daily newspapers are almost wholly Canadian owned, although the ownership is heavily concentrated in a few hands. The circulation of non-Canadian daily newspapers is too small to be of any significance. The Special Senate Committee on the Mass Media, in its 1970 *Report,* so thoroughly examines the Canadian press that there is little point in repeating the exercise here. The main conclusion, from the perspective of this article, is that although the resources are there, the economics of the newspaper industry, the values pursued by the owners, and the subservience of some papers to the local political establishment, reduce the potential usefulness of the daily press as a medium for Canadian propaganda. One saving factor is the dependence of most papers on the Canadian Press wire service for the bulk of their news. The Canadian Press is a co-operative owned by the papers it serves, and it provides a comprehensive coverage of Canadian news for all but a few of Canada's 116 or so daily newspapers. This means that Canadian papers are well served in Canadian news and are correspondingly less dependent on foreign sources. The CP is an unheralded, but not unimportant, unifying force in Canada.

To the extent, therefore, that Canadian news about Canadian events increases awareness of the Canadian fact, the press can be regarded as a useful instrument of Canadian propaganda. However, the press also contains a considerable amount of internal counter-propaganda (propaganda for the numerous groups and associations within Canada which inhibit unqualified loyalty to Canada as such), and a good deal of propaganda for other causes which are outside the Canada vs. counter-Canada issue. It is therefore a medium of mixed value.

One of the few significant sources of sustained American influence in the Canadian press for which there is no adequate Canadian response is the set of American syndicated comic strips carried in most papers. Some of these are heavily oriented to American cultural and political values.

Periodicals

Magazines are in a most unhappy state. The Senate Committee had a great deal to say of the unfortunate social and economic consequences of the dominating position of American magazines, especially the tax-favoured "Canadian" editions of *Time* and *Reader's Digest*. The aims of Canadian propaganda, as previously defined, would be greatly enhanced by more and better Canadian magazines on a wider variety of themes. It would be possible to do something about this, perhaps through financial concessions, subsidies, or different tax arrangements. However, we should not be too naively optimistic about the extent to which price adjustments will help Canadian magazine sales. In a democratic society, too, it is difficult to persuade people to buy a magazine just because it is Canadian, or not to read another just because it is not Canadian. If it is to attract readers, a Canadian magazine on any topic must be superior to its American rival. A Canadian *Playboy* would have to have more and prettier girls, funnier jokes, and better stories. Given the superior resources of the United States, it is an unfortunate fact that in most instances the Canadian product will not be able to compete successfully. Without censorship at the border, American magazines will continue to be a major influence in Canadian society.

Conclusion

In short we must conclude that in the area of the mass media, as long as Canada remains a democratic society, American influences will have a dominating but far from monopolistic voice. The Canadian point of view can be and is heard, but it is the quieter of the two voices. In effect, the Canadian propagandist must always play the role of the spokesman for the minority, even in Canada itself.

There are still rich fields for Canada propagandists to cultivate. The mass media are not the only forms of communication. Already a great deal is done by various people, far more than many critics would believe. Nobody has, to my knowledge, collected any serious statistical data on the miscellaneous media, so we may note only impressions and suggest possibilities.

At the school level there is increasing concern that textbooks should be Canadian. This applies not only in the obviously sensitive areas of history and social studies, but in other fields as well. I have seen elementary school arithmetic books in which exercises are illustrated with CN trains moving between Canadian cities, and reading programs with stories in Canadian settings. All this is good propaganda.

It is often assumed that all external counter-propaganda in Canada originates in the United States and that America is the sole threat to Canadian identity. Of course, this is not true. Some of the most hysterical opposition to the increasing use of distinctly Canadian symbols on flags, postage stamps, coins, mail-boxes, and so on has come from the most anti-American of all Canadians, the neo-Empire Loyalists who would not have us forget our British traditions. Yet it is through such symbols that the perception of a distinct Canadian identity will develop and spread. Even those Canadians who read no magazines or daily newspapers, who speak little of either English or French, and who might watch only hockey on television, will handle Canadian money, notice a Canadian flag, and perhaps stand for the Canadian National Anthem.

Canadian values can also be propagated through greater publicity for Canadian art and literature, holidays in Canada, the achievements of famous Canadians, and such events as Expo 67. On this latter, it is interesting to note the importance now attached to the political implications of such events. The American Pavilion at Expo 67 was sponsored by the U.S. Information Agency (the American International propaganda organization) and not, as in previous expositions, by the Commerce Department.

We can conclude this brief survey with a few propositions and summary statements, some admittedly general, but necessary to dispel confusion.

1. A great many people are disseminating a great deal of propaganda for a great many causes.
2. We do not know and cannot easily hope to know how much or how many.
3. We can usefully distinguish Canadian propaganda from

general propaganda in Canada. Canadian propaganda is propaganda for Canadian national identity.

4. There is no single authority responsible for the dissemination of Canadian propaganda or for defining the objectives of such propaganda.
5. Many people engage in Canadian propaganda. Their work is unco-ordinated and they are unlikely to be agreed on the specifics of the ends they are seeking to achieve or the means of achieving them. Canadian propaganda will, therefore, often be self-contradictory, much of it will be repetitious, and a good deal of it, undertaken by well-meaning but unqualified amateurs, will be self-defeating.
6. Counter-Canadian propaganda is propaganda which frustrates the objectives of Canadian propaganda.
7. Some counter-Canadian propaganda arises outside Canada and stresses loyalty to, or the values of, other societies.
8. Some counter-Canadian propaganda also arises from the pluralistic nature of Canadian society. It is an internal counter to a monolithic Canadian propaganda.
9. The media are very uncertain instruments for Canadian propaganda. None are under the exclusive control or influence of Canada propagandists. All are accessible to counter-Canadian propaganda and disseminate a great deal of it. Some media, such as television, are even more open to counter-Canadian propaganda, especially external, than to Canadian propaganda.

Public Opinion and the Study of Canadian Society

MILDRED A. SCHWARTZ

Loyalty, Solidarity, and Commitment

Newspaper headlines such as "Public Divided on Increase in Welfare Benefits," make statements about public opinion. While considerable variation exists on the definition of public opinion, such a headline captures several widely accepted themes.[1] It makes clear that public opinion deals with issues of more than individual concern, affecting significant (though unspecified) numbers. It suggests that the issue is controversial, with two or more possible positions. In this way it affirms what is sometimes lost in popular conceptions of public opinion, that is the absence of total unanimity. It is, however, most vague in conveying the meaning of "public." In this regard, statements in the press reflect a difficulty shared with more serious students of the public, who recognize that there are no clear boundaries distinguishing public from private issues, or the public itself as a coherent body.[2] Yet if later we were to see that the Gallup Poll had found support for welfare benefits from 60 per cent of those over fifty years of age and 45 per cent under fifty, while opposition came from 30 per cent of the older respondents and 40 per cent of the younger, with the remaining 10 and 15 per cent respectively undecided, we would begin to discern some characteristics of the public. There appear to be many publics, rather than a single undifferentiated one, and these are mobilized to express their opinions depending on the ex-

---

This paper benefited from many helpful suggestions by Maurice Pinard, John Johnstone, and the editor of this volume, Benjamin Singer. The author assumes full responsibility for her selective attention to their criticism.

tent of their own involvement. Opinions are public to the extent that they are able to be expressed, even if not everyone has an opportunity to give his views to interviewers. Survey research methods used for public opinion polling, in any event, are an important development in making opinions public and in providing more or less precise means for measuring their incidence. [3]

Public opinion has two characteristics that give it relevance to the study of society, its *organizing quality* and its *differentiated nature*. Public opinion is more than a collection of individual opinions, discrete and unorganized. It has a kind of incipient organization and potential for relating individuals and groups. Early definitions of public opinion viewed its emergent qualities as a translation of Rousseau's notion of the General Will. Such near-mystical formulations have been abandoned, but we still cannot speak of the public without having a conception of a collective product.[4]

As our imaginary newspaper headline suggested, public opinion has a differentiated character that enables it to be isolated as a characteristic of society, in a fashion analogous to rates of morbidity or mortality. For example, information on the health of individuals is aggregated to show disease rates for particular diseases, populations, locales, and time periods. Comparisons can then be made in the distribution of rates both within and across societies. Information on public opinion is not normally communicated in terms of rates, but public opinion can usefully be viewed as a product of individual opinions with a given distribution, dependent on the issue, population affected, geographic setting, or time period. It is such distributions which can be treated as societal characteristics, amenable to internal and external comparisons.

To use public opinion research in the study of society, we must begin with an appreciation that the issues about which we wish to ascertain opinions will be highly variable in salience. The salience of issues is associated with people's knowledge of them, which in turn hinges on such issue characteristics as complexity, specificity, and currency. The less complex and more general issues are more likely to produce some opinion, as are those most open to discussion and debate through the mass media.[5] Salience is also related to the extent to which the resolution of issues appears to directly affect the public. More salient issues are those perceived to concern people's well-being, either as individuals or members of solidary groups. Issues will also vary in the degree to which they arouse intense feeling. And finally, even when significant segments of the public recognize their stake in an outcome and feel strongly about it, our evaluation of the issue must still take into account the available alternatives, both in the expression of opinions and in the ability to act on them.

The inclination to disparage public opinion where it is not linked with behaviour is understandable, but should not distract us from its intrinsic usefulness to the concerns of sociology. Public opinion has a value in its own right, stemming from the link between its distributive features and society conceived of as a system held together by common values, ties, and interests. Public opinion research then becomes an important assay of this mother lode of social cohesion. The disparagement of interest in mass levels of society, sometimes encouraged both by conservatives and radicals of the left, may have served to obscure the connection between public opinion and the study of society. By downgrading what they see as the pluralist, liberal conception of society for a more "realistic" emphasis on élite decision-makers and the coercive mechanisms of social order, they may feel that they have righted an undue concern with an irrelevant epiphenomenon.[6] And it may be that they have provided a needed corrective to those who have slighted the degree to which most social systems are held together through the constraints of superior power, wealth, and prestige. But this is hardly the whole picture, and those who deny some independent importance to the public and its views are also denying that even the most coercive regimes take some account of the opinions of those they rule.

> Governments must concern themselves with the opinions of their citizens, if only to provide a basis for repression of disaffection. The persistent curiosity, and anxiety, of rulers about what their subjects say of them and of their actions are chronicled in the histories of secret police. Measures to satisfy such curiosity by soundings of opinion are often only an aspect of political persecution; they may also guide policies of persuasion calculated to convert discontent into cheerful acquiescence. And even in the least democratic regime opinion may influence the direction or tempo of substantive policy. Although a government may be erected on tyranny, to endure it needs the ungrudging support of substantial numbers of its people. If that support does not arise spontaneously, measures will be taken to stimulate it by tactical concessions to public opinion, by the management of opinion, or by both.[7]

To us, the most dramatic point of this quotation is the reality of public opinion to rulers. It should have a similar reality to social scientists, eager for additional approaches to the study of society.

Not all concepts of society give a place to public opinion, nor is it necessary that they do so. But if they wish to place some stress on the importance of the social bonds that sustain social systems, then public opinion should be seen as an active force in the maintenance of social cohesion.

We can study social cohesion by using the concepts loyalty, solidarity, and commitment, which have played a leading role in the theories of society of thinkers such as sociologist Talcott Parsons. As manifested in public opinion, loyalty refers to the expression of feelings of allegiance, solidarity to a sense of unity, and commitment to an attachment to a home territory.

Although we can understand loyalty, solidarity, and commitment as evident in supportive acts, such as membership in groups upholding dominant values, participation in patriotic activities, and acquiescence in decisions made by authorities, yet some acts—such as patriotic observances—do not occur frequently enough to be useful as indicators, and others are too widespread and unspecific—such as acquiescence with the status quo—to be easily interpreted. It is probably easier to find signs of *lack* of loyalty, commitment, or solidarity in acts such as emigration, support for revolutionary movements, and participation in subversive groups; of course, when these acts become widespread, they are signs of the imminent disintegration of the political community. Thus, it is appropriate to seek measures of opinion in order to produce an independent measure of the state of social cohesiveness. Such opinions are analogous to rates of disease as indicators of the health of a society. However, in the case of social cohesiveness, there is an upper limit, even if we cannot attach a quantitative level to it, for excessive social cohesiveness is a sign of a rigid, over-conforming society in which there is little room for innovation or change. It is important to keep this in mind when studying data on loyalty, solidarity, and commitment in Canada.

Data Sources

The sources for this analysis are four major national surveys and one regional survey, all conducted during the 1960s. We have a sample of 2,727 respondents, obtained from a study conducted after the 1965 general election by Philip Converse, John Meisel, Maurice Pinard, Peter Regenstreif, and Mildred Schwartz. This is identified throughout as the 1965 Election Study.[8] Following the 1968 election, 2,767 respondents were interviewed under the direction of John Meisel (1968 Election Study).[9] The Royal Commission on Bilingualism and Biculturalism stimulated two studies, one of the adult population and the other of adolescents. Le Groupe de Recherche Sociale directed the adult study in 1965, with a sample of 4,071. [10] We identify this as the Ethnic Study. Within the same sampling framework, questionnaires were distributed to 1,365 young people, between the ages of 13 and 20. The study was directed by John Johnstone, and we refer to it as the Youth Study.[11] The regional study was done in 1969 when 1,046 respondents in the provinces of Nova Scotia, New Brunswick, and Prince Edward Island were interviewed concerning Maritime union (the Maritime Union Study).[12] These data are supplemented by local studies and public opinion polls conducted by the Canadian Institute of Public Opinion, the Canadian affiliate of the Gallup organization. Most samples consisted of about 700 respondents selected through quota sampling methods.[13]

Because the link between an abstract theory of social cohesion and specific opinion items is not straightforward or unambiguous, particularly when based on data collected through surveys designed for other purposes, we have focused only on those items which have a recognized bearing on the life of most Canadians, and about which there should be a high level of awareness. The result is intended as a convincing argument for the use of opinion indicators to measure the state of loyalty, solidarity, and commitment in the Canadian political community, and to suggest the possible feedback or communications function of public opinion studies.[14]

Loyalty

Loyalty is generally understood as faithfulness to constituted authority, equated with allegiance, and manifested in such statements as "my country, right or wrong." Since it is the political community that is the object of loyalty in this discussion, we put aside those meanings of loyalty that concern norms of government or authorities. Loyalty is treated as "allegiant attitudes"[15] to the political community as it is set off by physical boundaries. In this sense, there exist in Canada a number of different, physically distinct political communities. Our focus will be on two kinds, the provincial and national. In a federal system, loyalty to one community does not necessarily involve disloyalty to another, and, indeed, federalism rests on the premise that there will be simultaneous loyalties. Loyalty is conceived as allegiance to the status quo, but without making the further judgment that this is necessarily "good."

At the provincial level, loyalty has been called into question in two areas, through advocacy of Maritime and of Prairie political union. Maritime union has a lengthy history, and the move to bring it about was one of the stimuli to the larger union established with Confederation.[16] Most recent interest in the subject was manifested in 1965, when the legislatures of New Brunswick, Nova Scotia, and Prince Edward Island commissioned a Maritime Union Study. The 1969 opinion survey found 64 per cent who said that they would vote in favour of union, and 25 per cent opposed.[17] Approximately one year later, the Canadian Institute of Public Opinion inquired of a national sample their feelings about such a union. In total, 44 per cent approved, 38 per cent disapproved, and 18 per cent were undecided.[18] In the Maritimes alone, 4 per cent were undecided. Compared with the Maritime Union Study, results in the Maritimes showed a marked change of opinion—44 per cent in favour and 52 per cent opposed—though one wonders how much of it is an artifact of the methods used and how much is a genuine shift in opinion. With the information available, there is no way of making precise estimates. It would seem that there has been some decline in support for Maritime Union, though probably not as great as these figures suggest.

In the Maritime Union Study, respondents were asked, "If it came to a vote would you yourself vote in favour of having complete economic and political union for New Brunswick, Nova Scotia, and Prince Edward Island which would see the three provinces joining together to form a single province?" The Gallup Poll a year later asked, "Some people believe that it would be a good thing for the Maritimes, and for Canada, if the eastern provinces united to become one province. Do you agree with this or not?" We can assume this was a more abrupt way of directing respondents to think of new political arrangements. Under the circumstances, it was much easier to express disapproval, or more precisely, commitment to the status quo. Yet we also believe there were some genuine shifts in the direction of disapproval of union, and these were related to changed circumstances. In the fall of 1969, there was an excitement about the possibility of union, as a new approach to the economic problems of the region, and this was communicated to the residents. As it was discussed, studied, written about in newspapers, and scrutinized by politicians (many of whom would be out of a job with union), it began to look less attractive. It was this awareness that most likely accounted for the later Gallup Poll results.

The implications of these findings for loyalty can best be seen when counterposed with similar questions about the political union of the three Prairie provinces. Prairie union has not, thus far, had the same official sanction as Maritime union, but it too has been the subject of serious discussion and study.[19] We do not have comparable survey data from a prairie sample, but attitudes toward union were ascertained in Alberta in 1968. Views were mainly negative, with only 23 per cent agreeing that "The three western provinces should join together and form one large province."[20] In 1970, the Gallup organization asked a national sample their opinions of Prairie union. The western sample, which included British Columbia as well as the three Prairie provinces, was, compared with other Canadians, most disapproving. Sixty-three per cent of the Westerners disapproved, compared with 44 per cent of the Martimers and 37 per cent in Quebec. In those latter regions, however, a relatively large proportion had no opinion, unlike the situation in the West, where almost 90 per cent held an opinion. From the positive side, 26 per cent of the Westerners approved of union, not unlike the percentage found by Elton in Alberta.[21]

These results tell us that Maritimers have less loyalty to the existing provincial community than do Westerners in the Prairies. Yet, given the serious economic problems of the Maritimes, we may be tapping both a strong sense of political realism and a form of local loyalty willing to consider alternative political arrangements and even new political boundaries in order to increase the viability of the local community. This is a possibility, however, for which one can find neither support nor refutation. We can only conclude, then, that provincial loyalty is stronger in the

Prairies than in the Maritimes.

Other issues pertaining to loyalty raise more serious questions about the continuity of the political community. This occurs where the sense of allegiance to the existing state is weak and where there is a preference for its dismemberment in order to attain local independence, as in separatism, or to join with another political entity, as in annexation to the United States. Both of these preferences, either for regional independence or for joining with another political state, go to the heart of the meaning of political loyalty, and have been recurring issues in the history of Canada.

A weakened sense of allegiance to Canada, motivated by a strong attraction to the United States, has probably affected some proportion of the Canadian population that has moved to the neighbouring country. Some of this movement has no doubt been motivated by other reasons, but in any case, we would consider such emigration as an individual concern, and not a collective attribute. For the latter, we look to opinions advocating political union, whereby the boundaries of the political community would drastically alter, and Canadian nationhood would be lost. The Canadian Institute of Public Opinion has asked respondents, "On the whole, do you think Canada should join the United States, or remain independent? "In 1964, 13 per cent favoured joining the United States, 81 per cent advocated independence, and a mere 6 per cent were undecided. Attraction to the United States ranged from 20 per cent in the East (including Quebec), 11 per cent in Ontario, and 8 per cent in the West.[22] In that same year, the Groupe de Recherche Sociale asked a national sample directly about political union with the United States. Twenty-nine per cent reported being in favour of such union; 12 per cent strongly and 17 per cent moderately.[23] This issue has also been approached by the CIPO, offering respondents a choice among three alternatives: remain in the Commonwealth, become independent, or join the United States. Since currently membership in the Commonwealth and political independence are not incongruent, while feelings toward the modern Commonwealth have been largely positive, we focus only on those who advocated joining the United States. This averaged about 20 per cent from 1943 to 1950, and dropped to 10 per cent according to five surveys conducted between 1952 and 1962.[24]

Union with the United States apparently has different meanings, depending on the region. In the Maritimes, for example, political union was favoured by 25 per cent, according to the Maritime Union Study. Most attraction came from older respondents, men, those in the lowest income groups, and French-speaking.[25] Maritimers were also asked their opinions of complete separation from Canada in 1969. Only 10 per cent said they would vote for such a policy, with no appreciable difference among population subgroups.[26]

In contrast to the Maritimes, the issue of separatism in Quebec appears as a more viable alternative. With the emergence of separatist movements, residents of Quebec have had organizational channels through which to work, and with their entry into electoral politics, they have given voters new choices. In the 1973 provincial election, the separatist Parti Québécois became the official opposition. Yet separatism, while it might generate large-scale support under the right circumstances, has not done so. In the 1968 Election Study, respondents were asked, "There has been quite a bit of talk recently about the possibility of Quebec separating from the rest of Canada and becoming an independent country. Are you in favour of separation or opposed to it? Please tell me whether you are strongly in favour of separation, slightly in favour, undecided, slightly opposed, or strongly opposed to separation." Of those of French origin, 4 per cent gave strong support to separation and 6 per cent mild support.[27] Mild support increases one percentage point if the focus is on French-language speakers in Quebec, while strong support remains the same.[28] Support, then, is low even among those who would be anticipated to be most favourable. In addition, only 2 per cent of other highly affected groups—the French-speaking outside of Quebec and the English-speaking within Quebec—saw even slight merit in separation.[29]

When we deal with an issue as salient as the dismemberment of Canada, we anticipate that relatively few respondents will be uncertain, and almost everyone will have an opinion.[30] But we see in Table 1, that on the question of separation, 21 per cent of French-speaking Quebeckers were undecided, compared with a general average of 14 per cent. Only in the Maritimes was indecision higher. Similarly, in a 1968 Gallup Poll survey, specific opinions about separation were expressed by all but 11 per cent of a national sample, whereas 17 per cent of Quebec respondents were undecided.[31] Such rates of indecision are not uncommon in public opinion surveys, especially when respondents are asked about issues that are of primary concern to élites, difficult to understand, and beyond the experience of the ordinary citizen.[32] This is definitely *not* the

Table 1 PER CENT UNDECIDED ABOUT THEIR REACTIONS TO THE POSSIBLE SEPARATION OF QUEBEC, BY LANGUAGE SPOKEN

	% Undecided		*Number*	
French-speaking:	18		716	
Quebec		21		632
Outside Quebec		12		84
English-speaking:	11		1907	
Maritimes		23		249
Quebec		6		90
Ontario		10		868
Prairies		11		462
British Columbia		6		238
Other languages	12		144	
Total	14		2767	

Source: 1968 Election Study, cited in Ronald Manzer, *Canada: A Socio-Political Report* (Toronto: McGraw-Hill Ryerson, 1974), p. 166.

case here, as evident by the low level of no opinions among Canadians outside of Quebec. We would suggest instead that a combination of cultural values and structural conditions tend to make the French-speaking more reluctant than other Canadians to express political opinions or reveal electoral choices.[33] On this particular issue, we would suggest that the reluctance to express opinions, linked to experience as a minority group with lower status and power, is augmented by the cross-pressures set up by the nature of separation. That is, as Maurice Pinard has suggested, pressures for advocating separatism which stem from strong ethnic identification may be offset by fears of the economic costs. The very salience of the issue then increases immobilizing cross-pressures, as well as otherwise contributing to a reluctance to indicate where one's sympathies lie.

The survey data available indicate that there are only minor pockets, of relatively small magnitude, where loyalty to the existing political communities is not general. Low levels of loyalty were most apparent in the Maritimes, where there was instead a willingness to consider alternatives to existing provincial boundaries. More serious gaps in politically sustaining attitudes are not evident, but, as in our discussion of the incidence of no opinions among French-speakers in Quebec, there were clues that such opinions may exist with greater frequency than could be measured by ordinary methods of public opinion polling.

Solidarity

We see solidarity expressed as a sense of unity, a feeling of oneness with respect to interest and goals. Such solidarity may stem either from similarities among people or from their interdependence.[34] In a country with the diversity of Canada, the existence of solidary feelings across provincial, ethnic, and religious lines is a recurring issue. In addition, because of Canada's continuing ties with other countries—Britain and France as colonial progenitors, and the United States as an overwhelmingly proximate neighbour—one must also evaluate Canadian feelings towards these countries in relation to the affinities with their own countrymen.

The 1968 Election Study included a series of questions on cross-linguistic, cross-national ties. In each instance, respondents were asked who had most in common, with one comparison always between English-speaking Canadians and French-speaking Canadians. In two questions, the comparison was also between English-speaking Canadians and Americans or British, and in the third, between French-speaking Canadians and French. The major findings are summarized in Table 2, and indicate a general recognition of close ties between English Canadians and Americans, superceding those between the two linguistic groups within Canada. Opinion is evenly divided when comparing Canadians to the British, while a clear majority emphasize French-English ties in Canada rather than ties between French Canadians and the French. The sharpness of difference in opinion within Canadian society emerges when comparisons are made among regions and linguistic groups. In each instance, the French-speaking, particularly those outside of Quebec, are most often of the opinion that Canadians have most in common, regardless of their language. This is a view shared by other Canadians only with regard to the affinities between the French-speaking in Canada and France. In this instance, English Canadians seem to have a stake in denying, certainly much more so than the French, that their compatriots have more in common with the people of another country.

This evident lack of solidarity across linguistic lines within Canada is also manifested by young people in a single question comparing both language groups and English Canadians and Americans. Results are presented in Table 3 so that comparisons can be made among linguistic groups for both young people and adults. What is most striking is the greater sense of difference among all young people compared with the adult sample of the same language group. Fortunately, this does not seem to be a harbinger of a greater distance among language groups, but

Table 2 OPINIONS OF GROUPS WITH MORE IN COMMON

		%
	English Canadians and French Canadians	33
or	English Canadians and Americans	49
	English Canadians and French Canadians	41
or	English Canadians and British	41
	English Canadians and French Canadians	58
or	French Canadians and French	24

Source: 1968 Election Study, cited in Ronald Manzer, *Canada: A Socio-Political Report* (Toronto: McGraw-Hill Ryerson, 1974), pp. 175-77.

rather of maturational differences. In the Johnstone Youth Study of 1965, less sense of commonalty was expressed with Americans for older respondents. This suggested to Johnstone that "over the adolescent years English youth perhaps become slightly more aware of the fact that one of the main things they do share with French Canadians is a common national identity."[35] The research does not tell us what these maturational influences might be, but at this time, we would expect that the greater nationalist sentiment expressed in the media and by élites would have an impact on the younger generation.

In the same study, young people were asked their perceptions of the extent of agreement in the society, and

Table 3 OPINIONS OF GROUPS WITH MORE IN COMMON, BY LANGUAGE SPOKEN IN THE HOME.

	More in Common[a]	
	English Canadians and French Canadians %	*English Canadians and Americans* %
Adult Sample[b]		
English	28	56
French	45	33
Other	28	33
Youth Sample[c]		
English	20	68
French	39	41
Other	9	69

[a]Other answers have been omitted.

[b]Source: 1968 Election Study.

[c]Source: John Johnstone, *Young People's Images of Canadian Society* (Ottawa: Queen's Printer, 1969), p. 33. Reproduced by permission of Information Canada.

their answers are summarized in Table 4. According to these young people, the sharpest lines of cleavage are between English- and French-speaking, and between Eastern and Western Canadians. We find these views most evident among English-speakers and those of "other" languages. The latter, however, seem more uncertain than other respondents, displaying a high rate of no opinion. Yet it is still clear that the French-speakers have the most optimistic views of the extent of national consensus.

The generally more open-minded view of French Canadians is further documented by a study of the adult population. The Ethnic Study found that 57 per cent of the French Canadians would like to have English Canadians among their best friends, and 50 per cent would similarly like English Canadians among their close relatives. This compared with 48 per cent of the English Canadians who

Table 4 PER CENT PERCEIVING AGREEMENT ON MOST THINGS AMONG CANADIANS

Population Group in Agreement:	*Language in Home* English	French	Other
Canadians in General	44	37	34
Eastern and Western Canadians	28	30	15
Roman Catholics and Protestants	44	46	33
French- and English-speaking Canadians	18	36	5
Native and Foreign-born Canadians	43	49	40
Rich and Poor Canadians	33	36	28
Urban and Rural Canadians	35	44	35

Source: John Johnstone, *Young People's Images of Canadian Society* (Ottawa: Queen's Printer, 1969), pp. 45-47. Reproduced by permission of Information Canada.

felt such cross-ethnic friends would be desirable, and 38 per cent who wished such relatives.[36]

This openness to interpersonal relations across ethnic lines is apparently distinct from general levels of tolerance, at least at the aggregate level. In the 1968 Election Study, respondents were presented with the statements: "Canada would be a better place if all people had the same national origin," and "Canada would be a better place if all people had the same religion." The ethnic and religious tolerance tapped by these statements was most in evidence for English-speaking Canadians. Eighty-six per cent of the English speakers disagreed with the statement on ethnic homogeneity compared with only 59 per cent of the French. There was slightly less difference between groups with regard to religious tolerance, but here there appeared to be some impact from respondents' religious affiliation. Eighty-one per cent of the English Protestants disagreed with the desirability of religious homogeneity, compared with 76 per cent of the English Catholics, and 65 per cent of the French Catholics.[37]

Solidarity of outlook, then, is rather limited, and these limits are anticipated from at least adolescence. The

French-speaking express greater solidarity with other Canadians than do the English, and greater willingness to cross ethnic lines for interpersonal relations. Yet they are also, perhaps because of the problems they recognize to inhere in their own continued existence, less willing to concede that ethnic and religious heterogeneity are desirable attributes for Canada.

Commitment

Commitment as an aspect of social cohesion is manifested as an attachment to a geographically-bounded home. Love of a home territory is a basic human characteristic. Anthropologists have described territorial ties as one of the primordial forms of human attachment. It is easy to see how this would occur in small, relatively simple, and basically immobile societies, but it is also true that the mobility of the modern world has not destroyed the social relevance of territory.[38] Yet recognizing the significance of territorial attachments in the modern state is complicated by its size and complexity. It is not territory per se that is at issue, but the physical location it gives to a political community, and it is the boundaries of this community which may vary. The consequences of differential commitment are then also varied. If commitment is exclusively to the smallest territorial unit, a village for example, we would expect this to be associated with an immobile population, strong traditionalism, and possibly a fragmented state. In any event, there would be little sense of a broader political community, and nationhood would be expressed by only a small élite. If, in contrast, there is a lack of commitment to the local community, we can anticipate a highly mobile population, fluid in its ties, and ever ready to move on to new opportunities. Even if this meant a strong sense of nationhood, it would be accompanied by weak local organizations and institutions, unable to provide the infrastructure for the state. The first situation is resistant to change; the second is indifferent to change.

Some degree of attachment to various levels of the political community would appear to be ideal, but to what extent is not evident. In Canadian society, we can readily imagine the benefits from a sense of commitment to local, provincial, and national levels. This subject has not been explored in exactly these terms, but some evidence is available on the provincial or regional level. In the 1965 Election Study, respondents were asked, "In which Canadian provinces do you think you might like to live?" This was followed by the query, "In which Canadian provinces would you definitely never want to live?" The survey permitted respondents to name as many provinces as they wished, including the one in which they lived. An analysis of the results, in which data are grouped for the Atlantic and Prairie provinces, is reproduced in Table 5.[39] At least three findings are worthy of note.

Looking at the cells in the diagonal of Table 5, it is evident that an overwhelming majority of the respondents preferred their own region. This was a choice made by about three-quarters of those in the survey, in all regions

Table 5 PREFERRED PLACE OF RESIDENCE, BY REGION (PER CENT)

Region of Residence	*Preferred Region*[a]					
	Ontario	*B.C.*	*Prairies*[b]	*Atlantic Provinces*[b]	*Quebec*	*Number*
Ontario	76	42	19	7	6	1054
B.C.	10	97	16	4	2	256
Prairies	14	49	80	5	1	395
Atlantic Provinces	20	14	15	75	4	229
Quebec	18	13	4	3	77	793

[a]Respondents could mention more than one province.

[b]Combination of individual provinces.

Source: Mildred A. Schwartz, *Politics and Territory* (Montreal: McGill-Queen's University Press, 1974), p. 89.

except British Columbia, where self-selection was almost unanimous. While more detailed breakdowns are not given here, further analysis of the data revealed that within the Atlantic provinces, choices were mainly confined to respondents' own province and not to other parts of the region. In the Prairies, however, Alberta was an important third choice, selected after British Columbia by residents of Saskatchewan and Manitoba. Albertans, in contrast, did not reciprocate the feelings of their Prairie neighbours.

A second point of interest concerns the relative frequency with which regions other than home territory were selected. For non-residents, the two most popular choices were Ontario and British Columbia. Ontario was viewed as a desirable place to live with a frequency next to one's own province by those in the Atlantic provinces and Quebec, and was mentioned third most often by the Prairies; British Columbia was placed second by the Prairies and Ontario, and third for Quebec. No other areas of the country were seen as particularly attractive, and Quebec was notably rejected by non-residents.

Our third point is the general lack of interest in other parts of Canada as places for possible residence. (This says nothing, of course, of actual migration patterns.) Only residents of Ontario were willing to name other desirable provinces to even a moderate degree, while the Prairies looked with favour only on British Columbia.

Before attempting to interpret these findings, we can look at a related set of data from a sample of young people. They were asked, "In which Canadian province —including your own—do you think you might like to live at some time in the future?" and, "In which Canadian province would you definitely never want to live?" An index was computed based on both questions, ranging from a possible +100 for entirely positive views to -100 for entirely negative views.[40] The differences in population sampled, procedures for administering questionnaires, question wording, and methods of analysis can all be expected to result in differences between the 1966 adult sample and the sample of young people. By some extrapolation, including summing reactions to individual Atlantic and Prairie provinces, and taking into account only French-speaking Quebec youth, comparisons are possible, though hardly precise, if frequencies for both samples are converted into ranks, as we have done in Table 6. In general, young people anticipate adult reactions by their favourable reaction to British Columbia and secondly Ontario, and by

Table 6 RANKING OF PREFERRED PLACE OF RESIDENCE

Region of Residence	*Preferred Region Adult Sample*				
	Ontario	*British Columbia*	*Prairies*	*Atlantic Provinces*	*Quebec*
Ontario	1	2	3	4	5
British Columbia	3	1	2	4	5
Prairies	3	2	1	4	5
Atlantic Provinces	2	4	3	1	5
Quebec	2	3	4	5	1

Source: Mildred A. Schwartz, *Politics and Territory* (Montreal: McGill-Queen's University Press, 1974), p. 89.

	Youth Sample				
	Ontario	*British Columbia*	*Prairies*	*Quebec*	*Atlantic Provinces*
Ontario	1	2	3	4	5
British Columbia	2	1	3	4	5
Prairies	3	2	1	4	5
Quebec[a]	2	3	4	1	5
Atlantic Provinces	2	1	4	5	3

[a]French-speaking only.

Source: Adapted from John Johnstone, *Young People's Images of Canadian Society* (Ottawa: Queen's Printer, 1969), p. 93. Reproduced by permission of Information Canada.

their negative assessment of Quebec and the Atlantic provinces, although Quebec is not as uniformly ranked low by youthful non-residents. Looking at actual results of evaluations suggests as well that young people outside of Quebec are somewhat more positive in their feelings about other provinces than are adults.

These opinions are useful indicators of feelings of commitment. They suggest a form of regional enthnocentrism which is part of the socializing experiences of Canadians, at least from adolescence. Moreover, they suggest considerable consensus on which are the most attractive parts of the country, and which the least. Young people appear somewhat more flexible in their assessments than their elders, which may mean some growing commitment to a broader political community than that represented by the home province.

The Social and Political Meaning of Public Opinion

For political scientists, the study of public opinion continues to be an important and independent avenue of research into a phenomenon that indicates something about consensus for the continuity of legitimate rule, as well as providing the subject matter for the formulation of public policy.[41] For the sociologist and social psychologist, however, public opinion seems to have become a less interesting field of study.[42] In recent compendia of these disciplines, the *Handbook of Modern Sociology* and *The Handbook of Social Psychology*,[43] there are no separate entries for public opinion, and in the former, the subject is discussed only incidentally in a chapter on political sociology.[44] Only in the *Handbook of Communication* does a political scientist devote a chapter to the topic.[45] We may take these as signs of unwarranted neglect which this chapter has attempted to remedy through an examination of the way in which public opinion can give us useful insights into the nature of society.

This review of existing survey data has allowed us to ascertain the climate of opinion associated with the social cohesiveness of Canadian society. Social cohesiveness has been approached through the concepts of loyalty, solidarity, and commitment. For most Canadians, these concepts have acted as stabilizing influences, tying people to their local community. It can also be said that the forms of stability that exist as expressions of public opinion about social cohesiveness have been achieved at the cost of developing broader, national ties. While studies of public opinion make possible such an analysis, because public opinion is an indicator of a social state, one can in a manner of speaking step back from the substantive analysis made possible by such Canadian public opinion studies and see this tool—the public opinion inquiry—as a form of communication, as a mode of feedback by which the Canadian population can, by such characteristics, be linked to policy decisions as well.

1. W. Phillips Davison, "Public Opinion. I, Introduction, " *International Encyclopedia of the Social Sciences,* vol. 13 (New York: Macmillan and Free Press, 1968), p. 188; Bernard C. Hennessy, *Public Opinion* (Belmont, Calif.: Wadsworth, 1965), pp. 94-97.
2. Kurt Lang and Gladys Engel Lang, *Collective Dynamics* (New York: Crowell, 1961), p. 371.
3. For a brief review of the strengths and limitations of public opinion data, see John E. Mueller, *War, Presidents and Public Opinion* (New York: Wiley, 1973), pp. 1-19.
4. Davison, "Public Opinion," p. 192.
5. Mildred A. Schwartz, *Public Opinion and Canadian Identity* (Berkeley: University of California Press, 1967), p. 217.
6. For a review of some of the arguments, see Milton Mankoff, "Power in Advanced Capitalist Society: a Review Essay on Recent Elitist and Marxist Criticism of Pluralist Theory," *Social Problems,* vol. 17 (Winter 1970), pp. 418-30.
7. V.O. Key, Jr., *Public Opinion and American Democracy* (New York: Knopf, 1961), p. 3.
8. For a description of the sample design and procedures, see John Meisel and Richard Van Loon, "Canadian Attitudes to Election Expenses 1965-6," in Committee on Election Expenses, *Studies in Canadian Party Finance* (Ottawa: Queen's Printer, 1966), pp. 32-41; and Mildred A. Schwartz, *Politics and Territory* (Montreal: McGill-Queen's University Press, 1974), pp. 84-85.
9. John Meisel, *Working Papers on Canadian Politics* (Montreal: McGill-Queen's University Press, 1972), p. 60. No description of the study

design is given, but it is known to have followed well-established procedures.

10. Le Groupe de Recherche Sociale, *A Study of Interethnic Relations in Canada* (Montreal: mimeo, 1965), pp. 297-325.
11. John C. Johnstone, *Young People's Images of Canadian Society* (Ottawa: Queen's Printer, 1969), pp. 105-11.
12. Market Facts of Canada Ltd., *The Maritimes and Maritime Union: An Opinion Study* (Fredericton: Maritime Union Study, 1970).
13. In evaluating all the data used here, the reader unfamiliar with the techniques of survey research may wish to consult a book designed for both research users and consumers, particularly the section on research design. See Earl R. Babbie, *Survey Research Methods* (Belmont, Calif.: Wadsworth, 1973).
14. For a discussion of the consequences of various approaches to asking questions, including the form of the question, see Seymour Sudman and Norman Bradburn, *Response Effects in Surveys: A Review and Synthesis* (Chicago: Aldine, 1974), chapter 2.
15. Opinions are often described as issue-linked, flexible, and shifting in relation to events, while attitudes are seen as more stable, part of an individual's cognitive map, and tied to basic personality dispositions. These distinctions are sometimes useful, and indeed we speak here of allegiant attitudes, in preference to opinions, as a more precise way of subsuming what is likely to be a series of particular issue-related opinions which bear on the general topic of loyalty. For the most part, however, we agree with McGuire that the distinction has little merit. William J. McGuire, "The Nature of Attitudes and Attitude Change," in G. Lindzey and Elliot Aronson (eds.), *The Handbook of Social Psychology*, vol. 3, rev. ed. (Reading, Mass.: Addison-Wesley, 1969), p. 152.
16. J.M. Beck, *The History of Maritime Union: A Study in Frustration* (Fredericton: Maritime Union Study, 1969).
17. Market Facts, *The Maritimes and Maritime Union*, p. 28.
18. Canadian Institute of Public Opinion, The Gallup Report, September 9, 1970.
19. Prairie political union was the subject of a conference sponsored by the University of Lethbridge and the Lethbridge *Herald* in May 1970. The papers presented and a transcript of the discussion were published in David K. Elton (ed.), *One Prairie Province? Conference Proceedings and Selected Papers* (Lethbridge, Alta.: Lethbridge Herald, 1971).
20. David K. Elton, "Electoral Perceptions of Federalism: A Descriptive Analysis of the Alberta Electorate," in Elton, *One Prairie Province?*, p. 145. We note that the province names were not specified.
21. Canadian Institute of Public Opinion, The Gallup Report, September 11, 1970.
22. Canadian Institute of Public Opinion, The Gallup Report, October 3, 1964. This report also indicates that in 1950, and again in 1960, 10 per cent were in favour of union with the United States.
23. "Who's for Canada—and Who's for the USA," *Maclean's*, June 6, 1964, pp. 12-13.
24. For details, see Schwartz, *Public Opinion and Canadian Identity*, pp. 73-77.
25. Market Facts, *The Maritimes and Maritime Union*, p. 73.
26. Ibid., p. 77.

27. Meisel, *Working Papers on Canadian Politics,* p. 216.
28. Data from the 1968 Election Study cited in Ronald Manzer, *Canada: A Socio-Political Report* (Toronto: McGraw-Hill Ryerson, 1974), p. 166.
29. A review of trends in favour of separatism among French-speaking Canadians in Quebec indicates that, since 1962, this has ranged from 7 to 19 per cent. The highest level was reached at the time of the 1973 election, and in general, greatest support for separtism appears related to the mobilizing activities associated with provincial elections. See Maurice Pinard, "La Dualité des loyautés et les options constitutionnelles des Québécois francophones," *Choix,* forthcoming issue.
30. Schwartz, *Public Opinion and Canadian Identity,* pp. 218-23.
31. Canadian Institute of Public Opinion, The Gallup Report, October 16, 1968.
32. Philip E. Converse, "The Nature of Belief Systems in Mass Publics," in David Apter (ed.), *Ideology and Discontent* (Glencoe: Free Press, 1964), pp. 206-61; Philip E. Converse, "Comment: The Status of Nonattitudes," *American Political Science Review,* vol. 68 (June 1974), p. 650.
33. Mildred A. Schwartz, "Canadian Voting Behavior," in Richard Rose (ed.), *Electoral Behavior: A Comparative Handbook* (New York: Free Press, 1974), p. 579; Robert R. Alford, *Party and Society* (Chicago: Rand McNally, 1964), p. 228; Schwartz, *Public Opinion and Canadian Identity,* pp. 223-26. Studies from 1962 to 1973 indicate that the average rate of undecided or qualified answers among French-speakers in Quebec has been about 18 per cent when faced with a question on separation from Canada. See Pinard, "La Dualité."
34. Talcott Parsons, "Durkheim's Contribution to the Theory of Integration of Social Systems," in Parsons, *Sociological Theory and Modern Society* (New York: Free Press, 1967), pp. 3-34.
35. Johnstone, *Young People's Images,* p. 34.
36. Le Groupe de Recherche Sociale, *A Study of Interethnic Relations in Canada,* p. 241.
37. John Meisel, "Cleavages, Parties and Values in Canada", *Sage Professional Papers,* vol.1 (1974), p. 16.
38. For a discussion of early views of territoriality, see Schwartz, *Politics and Territory,* pp. 2-3.
39. Ibid., pp. 88-91.
40. Johnstone, *Young People's Images.*
41. For example, Avery Leiserson, "Political Opinion. II," *International Encyclopedia of the Social Sciences,* vol. 13, pp. 197-204; Robert E. Lane and David O. Sears, *Public Opinion* (Englewood Cliffs, N.J.: Prentice-Hall, 1964), p. 1.
42. A recent exception is Rita James Simon, *Public Opinion in America: 1936-1970* (Chicago: Rand McNally, 1974).
43. Robert E.L. Faris (ed.), *Handbook of Modern Sociology* (Chicago: Rand McNally, 1964); Lindzey and Aronson (eds.), *The Handbook of Social Psychology.*
44. Scott Greer and Peter Orleans, "Political Sociology," in Faris (ed.), *Handbook of Modern Sociology,* pp. 812-13.
45. Ithiel de Sola Pool, "Public Opinion," in Ithiel de Sola Pool and Wilbur Schramm et al. (eds.), *Handbook of Communication* (Chicago: Rand McNally, 1973), pp. 779-835.

Social Problems and Communication

It is, of course, obvious that mass media play an essential role in our attempt to cope with modern life, and the consequences of this role may not be all positive. There have been a growing number of suggestions, backed up by some laboratory experiments, that the increase in individual and collective violence (as well as in other forms of deviance such as drug-taking) in such places as the United States, may be generated in part by the mass media.

Singer's article provides data on the first comparison of television news programs of Canada and the U.S. and suggests the possibility that American television may not only reflect actual events in a social system but may in fact emphasize certain kinds of events, in this case, those dealing with aggression. If "through repeated emphasis of certain categories of events" social reality is distorted, it follows that standards of judgment and frames of reference toward what is normal and expected in a society may be altered, as the article suggests. The policy implications, then, of continuing to make available massive amounts of American television in Canada, may need to be examined from this point of view, as well as from a point of view emphasizing the problem of Canadian identity.

McCormack, in "Censorship and 'Community Standards' in Canada," asks where responsibility for Canadian standards vis à vis "pornography" shall be located and suggests a discomforting thought to conventional civil libertarians: that what appears to be a liberalizing trend with respect to obscenity and/or pornography, may in fact be a neoconservative redefinition of pornography which approves middle and upper class forms of sexuality in literature but continues to ban the "pornography of the people," labelling it "hard core" and not socially redeeming. Censorship, she suggests, should be seen as a sociological phenomenon which reflects neither attitudes nor tolerance but rather the way in which a society chooses to organize its system of social control.

The excerpt of the report of the Committee chaired by Professor Maxwell Cohen, "Hate Propaganda in Canada," indicates that much of the group-defiling literature found in Canada in the 1960's was brought in from the United States. The report suggests that radio and television have, unintentionally, been promoting hatemongering and advocacy of genocide by giving platforms to hatemongers. The document is of historical significance, not only because Pierre Elliott Trudeau, then a professor of law, helped to draft the report, but because by 1970 its recommendations curbing hate propaganda had become law, in spite of well-intentioned opposition by civil libertarians.

Latouche, in "Mass Media and Communication in a Canadian Political Crisis," provides us with a communications model for interpreting the events of the FLQ crisis of October, 1970. He suggests that "the entire crisis was a battle for the temporary control of the communication system in Quebec." Nielsen, in "The Media: Must We Serve as Tools for Terrorists?" does not disagree with this approach. In fact, he suggests that Canadian broadcasting may have transformed its audience into a "mob demanding immediate satisfaction of its desires." Nielsen agrees with many other authorities in recommending that radio and television should restrict the kinds of coverage given political terrorism in the future in order to remove some of the profit from such acts. Implicit is the belief that part of the reason for such acts of violence is the assurance of dramatic coverage of the kind that may help destroy a people's faith in its democratic institutions.

Given that the enormous revolution in communications has increased the potential for the serial commission of individual and collective violence, should our perspective toward communications channels be oriented toward restrictions or are there inconsistencies in the opposite direction as well—that is, a lack of communications chan-

nels which causes the malaise of modern man to increase? Is it possible that there exists an oversupply of mass one-way channels, such as television, but a deficiency of two-way channels of the kind that are necessary to cope with rapidly changing, complex society? This is in fact one of the major dilemmas of modern, industrialized societies. Claxton and McDougall investigate this theme through their empirical research into information and complaint channels in London. Their study informs us about available channels in a typical city; their approach was to study the concerns handled by each kind of channel, the volume of such concerns in each kind of channel, the channel procedures (communication means) and the action resulting. Suggested for further study are the function of such channels, the means of contact available and finally the public awareness of channels for information and problem solving.

Sandra Gwyn's article describes the efforts made towards establishing two-way communication through the use of mass media. Technology has made possible the "massification" of the media, but it has also created techniques by which citizens can communicate very effectively with fellows and leaders, as well as with themselves through the ensuing crystallization of self-image. Mrs. Gwyn explores the sociological consequences of such communication, particularly the possible effects on social change.

The role of communication in making it possible to cope with sudden events in the larger social system is suggested by the classical studies of rumour. Research in the past has shown that rumour possesses a psychological function — it provides some kind of orientation during times of great stress. The pioneering Canadian studies into crisis communication conducted by Scanlon and his associates at Carleton University show us that such communication follows normal social structural channels. Communication in such circumstances can be a socially directive force, rather than a disruptive one. Studies such as these help us to understand more about the positive potential of communication during crises.

Violence, Protest, and War in Television News: The U.S. and Canada Compared

BENJAMIN D. SINGER

Reprinted from THE PUBLIC OPINION QUARTERLY, *Volume 34, Winter 1970-1971.*

An analysis of the manner in which a nation's major news media portray the nation's events may tell us a great deal about the actual distribution of events in that nation; it may be a reflection of the values of the audience toward news; or it may reflect the social system of the medium itself.

Until now, there has been a great deal of attention paid to the role of television drama in presumably stimulating violence, while the newscasts, with their huge, heterogeneous audiences, have escaped close attention. Television news may be a more sensitive barometer of the central values of a culture than printed media because television time is scarce—a national news show may have the time to carry perhaps twenty items compared with several hundred by its news counterpart, the daily newspaper.

While an analysis of the content of popular American newscasts would provide us with some notion as to the kind of reality being portrayed to audiences, it would be of even greater interest if American newscasts could be compared with those of another society which possessed similarities. We could thus begin to find out if American newscasts tend to favor the presentation of violent news.

This analysis was aided by Canada Council Grant No. 69-1005. The author would like to acknowledge the valuable assistance of Andrew Cameron, John Hannigan, Catherine Kopinak, and Christine MacLeod.

Canada is probably the ideal comparison society, for, in addition to being largely English-language speaking and possessing a similar social structure, Canada is a client of American news services, directly receiving American stations and rebroadcasting a substantial amount of American television material, both entertainment and news.

The "National News," a Canadian Broadcasting Corporation program, is received in London, Ontario at 11 p.m. The CBC has a purchase arrangement with CBS-TV and NBC-TV which permits them to pick up and use any news stories carried by either network. The CBC program does carry a substantial number of American stories. During the test period April 20 to May 10, 1970, approximately 20 per cent of all items carried on the CBC National News were stories about the United States. London, the site of the present research, receives seven American television stations by cable and three Canadian stations, two by cable.

The objective of the present research was to compare a leading American television news program, "CBS Evening News," with its Canadian counterpart, "National News," on a daily basis. While it could be argued that a comparison between two noncommercial news programs or two commercial programs would be more appropriate, the CBC National is the only Canada-wide television news program that represents all areas, and there is no equivalent American non-commercial national news program.

The research focuses upon three major areas of concern which have been the subject of a substantial amount of comment because of their purported influence on viewers: the presentation of material dealing with violence, protest, and war. The research attempts to provide a breakdown of the amount of such "aggression items" presented on a typical national news program in the U.S. and by its Canadian counterpart. The working hypothesis to be explored is that American television presents a higher proportion of news items of an aggressive nature, even where the foreign station has full access to the same materials and is accustomed to utilizing a substantial amount of American materials.

If the hypothesis is supported, it may be an indication that U.S. culture has a larger number of such events which the media rather passively reflect; that the culture's value system is such that there is more interest by the population in such items; or that American news institutions, particularly television, choose to emphasize these aspects of social reality. It cannot, of course, point up which of the factors is most responsible—a project far beyond the ability of the present research.

Method

The research was conducted between April 20 and May 10, 1970, the time being fortuitously chosen as a result of the availability of graduate student assistance. Research workers monitored the programs with the aid of tape recorders; the materials were then transcribed, coded, and tabulated. A test of coder disagreement based on a sample of several days was computed. The range of disagreement reported was from 2 to 11 per cent, with the mean being 4.6 per cent. The coding scheme involved the news locale (Canadian, U.S., international) as well as its substantive concern (labor, war, space, business, politics or government, protest, violence, etc). The coding was straightforward with the exception that protest includes events of the contemporary protest variety—such as civil rights, women's liberation, anti-Vietnam, student protest—and excludes such labor activities as strikes. Because of the treatment of the latter, findings on aggression items ought to be considered conservative. The amount of time occupied by each news item was also recorded.

Results

The major finding is indeed striking. The American television news show exceeds the Canadian program in aggression items for every one of the 21 consecutive days monitored. CBS-TV has carried as much as 78 per cent aggression items (on April 30), compared to 38 per cent for CBC-TV. The smallest differential was on May 2, when CBS-TV carried 50 per cent compared to 46 per cent for the CBC, but most typically the differential was on the order of more than twice as much.

The grand total for the three weeks indicates CBC with 25.9 per cent and CBS with 49.5 per cent, a nearly two-to-one difference in favor of the American news shows.

Table 1 AGGRESSION TIME TOTALS AND PERCENTAGE OF TOTAL TIME ON CBC AND CBS TELEVISION NEWS SHOWS

		CBC		*CBS*	
Date	*Subject*	*Time in Minutes*	*Per cent of total time*	*Time in Minutes*	*Per cent of total time*
April 20-April 26	Violence	12.5	11.2%	10.0	6.3%
	Protest	8.0	7.2	11.25	7.1
	War	10.75	9.6	46.25	29.3
	Aggression Totals	31.25	28.0%	67.50	42.7%
	Total Newscast Minutes	111.75		158.00	
April 27-May 3	Violence	4.7	4.7%	15.75	8.7%
	Protest	0.2	0.0	17.25	9.5
	War	23.4	23.5	53.00	29.4
	Aggression Totals	28.3	28.2%	86.00	47.6%
	Total Newscast Minutes	133.25		180.50	
May 4-May 10	Violence	12.25	11.1%	19.25	12.2%
	Protest	16.25	14.7	49.75	31.4
	War	7.00	6.3	31.75	20.1
	Aggression Totals	35.50	32.1%	100.75	63.7%
	Total Newscast Minutes	110.75		158.25	

Table 2 AGGRESSION ITEMS ON CBC AND CBS TELEVISION NEWS SHOWS, FREQUENCY AND PERCENTAGE OF ITEMS (ITEMS ON WAR IN SOUTHEAST ASIA REMOVED)

		CBC		CBS	
Date	*Subject*	*No. of items*	*Per cent*	*No. of items*	*Per cent*
April 20-April 26	Violence	8	7.0%	18	18.8%
	Protest	4	3.5	8	8.3
	War	4	3.5	4	4.2
	Aggression Totals	16	14.0%	30	31.3%
	Total Newscast Items	114		96	
April 27-May 3	Violence	8	9.4%	14	13.8%
	Protest	1	1.2	12	11.8
	War	4	4.7	10	10.0
	Aggression Totals	13	15.3%	36	35.6%
	Total Newscast Items	85		101	
May 4-May 10	Violence	10	11.1%	16	16.2%
	Protest	12	13.3	19	19.2
	War	0	0.0	5	5.1
	Aggression Totals	22	24.4%	40	40.4%
	Total Newscast Items	90		99	
April 20-May 10 (TOTAL)	Violence	26	9.0%	48	16.2%
	Protest	17	5.9	39	13.2
	War	8	2.8	19	6.4
	Aggression Totals	51	17.7%	106	35.8%
	Total Newscast Items	289		296	

Comparative data were available for some days on NBC-TV. During the period April 20-April 25 inclusive and April 30-May 1 (a total of eight days), CBS-TV exceeded the NBC-TV aggression item percentage five days, was exceeded by NBC-TV two days, and tied one day. The summary total was: CBS-TV 53.4 per cent and NBC-TV 40.9 per cent.

Since item counts may be disputed as a measure of emphasis, the proportion of time spent on such stories was calculated. The daily pattern was much the same as for item counts. Table 1 summarizes the findings on a weekly basis (the daily basis was similar).

Some may argue that the war in Southeast Asia is of such overwhelming concern, is such a part of the inherent event environment in North America, that its coverage is mandatory, thus removing choice on the part of audience and medium. If this is true, it would be most true for the U.S. Thus, inclusion of the war in Southeast Asia may explain why so many more aggression items are found on the American program. To answer this argument, the tables have been reconstructed in order to cancel out the effects of the Southeast Asian war in both cases. Weekly summations are shown in Tables 2 and 3.

As can be seen from these tables, when war items are removed, not only do "aggression items" continue to represent a substantial proportion of CBS items and time (36 per cent and 40 per cent, respectively), but on a comparative basis the American station continues to be significantly ahead on such items—the CBC figures are 17.7 per cent and 19 per cent respectively.

In societies where the media are not controlled and news presentations are free to vary, periodic monitoring of such media as television in a comparative perspective is important, particularly where scarcity of time intensifies the selective process. One of the assumptions underlying traditional press freedoms is that, within limits, all news will be published. This is hardly the case with our dominant medium, television; in fact, the reverse is true: very little of the news is used. Hence, such a medium has en-

Table 3 AGGRESSION TIME TOTALS AND PERCENTAGE OF TOTAL TIME ON CBC AND CBS TELEVISION NEWS SHOWS (ITEMS ON WAR IN SOUTHEAST ASIA REMOVED)

		CBC		CBS	
Date	*Subject*	*Time in minutes*	*Per cent of total time*	*Time in minutes*	*Per cent of total time*
April 20-April 26	Violence	12.5	11.8%	10.0	14.1%
	Protest	8.0	7.5	11.25	15.9
	War	5.0	4.7	0.0	0.0
	Aggression Totals	25.5	24.0%	21.25	30.0%
	Total Newscast Minutes	106.0		70.7	
April 27-May 3	Violence	6.25	6.1%	15.75	11.5%
	Protest	0.25	0.3	17.25	12.6
	War	0.0	0.0	9.25	6.8
	Aggression Totals	6.50	6.4%	42.25	30.9%
	Total Newscast Minutes	102.0		136.75	
May 4-May 10	Violence	12.25	11.8%	19.25	14.7%
	Protest	16.25	15.7	49.75	38.1
	War	0.0	0.0	4.0	3.1
	Aggression Totals	28.5	27.5%	73.0	55.9%
	Total Newscast Minutes	103.75		130.50	
April 20-May 10 (TOTAL)	Violence	31.0	9.9%	45.0	13.3%
	Protest	24.5	7.9	78.25	23.2
	War	5.0	1.6	13.25	3.9
	Aggression Totals	60.5	19.4%	136.5	40.4%
	Total Newscast Minutes	311.75		338.0	

ormous power to affect the perceived environment of viewers through repeated emphasis of certain categories of events. This process, by distorting the social reality perceived by individuals in a society, alters their standards of judgment and hence frame of reference toward what is normal and expected in such a society.

The present research raises questions that are not easily answered. The questions are relevant to much of the controversy that has raged with increased vigor since the advent of television. It is of course possible that such newscasts reflect a true state of affairs, i.e., differential amounts of violence in each social system. Another possibility involves both differential rates of known occurrences along with variations in selection, i.e. a system with greater violence may still overreport it on television when compared to a system experiencing less violence. It is possible, in addition, that a system whose television newscasts report a higher number of such items, is, nevertheless, underreporting in terms of the population of known events.

There is also the policy question of whether it necessarily follows that high incidence of violence need be reported if it is believed that reportage—particularly television reportage—plays a crucial causal role in serial violence. Some would and have argued that reportage of such events, particularly the dramatized reportage so prevalent on television, is a determinant of such serial events as air hijacking, arson, bombings, mass murders, campus disturbances, and urban riots. The policy implications of this question are enormous and ultimately become matters of political philosophy.

Some methodological issues may be answered in the future by the development of new and imaginative research designs, particularly dealing with the problem of ascertaining the relationship of reportage, viewed as a sample selected from a population of events, to the population of events. One purpose of the present research has been to establish a base from which such questions may be explored in the future.

Censorship and "Community Standards" in Canada

THELMA McCORMACK

> "The most difficult problem for me in applying the definition of obscenity in this case is determination of contemporary community standards."[1]

> "It does seem to me that since the standard of acceptability . . . is to be contemporary . . . that those charged with the enforcement . . . should receive special training . . . and that the enforcing authorities should not be hesitant to consult with those in the field who have the experience, expertise, knowledge and training to give advice . . ."[2]

The first quotation is from Mr. Justice Laskin's dissenting opinion in the Dorothy Cameron case, a case involving an exhibition of drawings which the Court found had shown "undue exploitation of sex." The second is from a decision by Judge Lyon in which he found for a theatrical company presenting *An Evening with Futz.* Both opinions reflect the difficulties judges have when our Criminal Code requires them to make empirical sociological assessments. In the opinion of Judge Lyon quoted above, there is an invitation to social scientists to provide their expertise.

What could be simpler? The law defines "obscene" as "undue exploitation of sex," and "undue" means exceeding "community standards." Now if there is one thing social scientists have learned to do and do well over the past half-century, it is to conduct a public opinion poll. The hardware has become better and the cost cheaper so that if all the courts want are measures of central tendency, the matter could be disposed of quickly. But it is the concept of "community standards" itself which requires careful scrutiny to determine its meaning, its relation to other concepts such as "obscenity," and these other concepts in relation to a more general theory of censorship in the arts.

"Community standards," however, is the pivotal concept, for it is emphatically rejected by all good civil libertarians on two grounds. First, it is inconsistent. They see no reason to distinguish between freedom of expression in the area of political ideas and freedom of expression in the arts. If it is only under the most exceptional circumstances that we accept censorship in political ideas, why do we accept it as normal in the arts? Second, it is incorrect. Freedom of expression means the protection of minority opinion, of dissent, whereas "community standards" is an attempt to impose conformity. The effect of introducing "community standards" is to create, in the words of Mr. Justice Douglas of the U.S. Supreme Court, "a regime where in the battle between the literati and the Philistines, the Philistines are certain to win."[3]

In the comments that follow, I would like to examine the censorship controversy with a view to proposing a more sociological perspective on censorship generally, and on the concept of "community standards" in particular.

Censorship, however, takes many forms, some more pleasing or offensive to the modern mind than others. Plato's censorship which exiled all poets shocks us more than the Kremlin's which selects only certain poets. And there is a significant difference between imprisoning artists in Siberia and withholding a licence for the showing of a particular film. And finally, whatever one may think about censorship in the abstract, modern censorship which repudiates the principle of "prior restraint" or pre-publication censorship must be considered a liberal step. (The exception is censorship of motion pictures where "prior restraint" still operates.)

It is sometimes said that censorship is only as good as the censors. If this were true, three hundred years of effort to devise better law would have been wasted.

Happily, it is only one of those half-truths. In any case, for purposes of this discussion we are concerned with censorship and not with censors, and with the most modern forms of censorship; that is, with censorship that has developed within the framework of democratic institutions and which in the opinion of most, including some of the most sophisticated legal minds, does not contravene either the letter or the spirit of democratic freedoms.

Censorship is a form of social control, an evaluative system which assigns approval and disapproval. A Governor General's Award, a Provincial Government commission for sculpture, subsidies for composers, the inclusion of certain paintings in the permanent collection of a prestigious art gallery are all as much a part of a system of censorship as the regulations which ban the use of certain four-letter words on television. Like other forms of social control, censorship is both an incentive and a deterrent to the performance of certain kinds of behaviour and the expression of certain kinds of attitudes. Many people who oppose censorship oppose it only in its negative form, arguing that it is wiser, more productive and more humane to emphasize reward than punishment. But on this point the findings of social psychologists offer no clear-cut directive.

"Without some form of censorship," Walter Lippmann once wrote, "propaganda in the strict sense of the word is impossible."[4] By this he meant that censorship controls behaviour indirectly by structuring how we perceive reality, how we regard our own behaviour and the behaviour of others. These mental sets are transmitted from one generation to the next in so many and such subtle ways that we are barely conscious of the process. Children, however, start to learn early in life what kinds of behaviour are considered right and wrong, good and bad; what will be admired as "decent" and scorned as "indecent;" whom to welcome and whom to avoid. They learn to evaluate not only behaviour, but attitudes and belief systems as well: whether ideas are moral or immoral, subversive or patriotic, just or unjust, ugly or beautiful. Finally, they acquire through the processes of socialization a method, rules to guide them and assist them in making judgments when they are not self-evident or a matter of "common sense." Whether we turn to horoscopes, sacred texts, historical precedent or scientific knowledge is very largely a matter of which of these we have been taught to trust.

Two things are special about systems of social control in individualistic and democratic societies like ours. First, the greatest emphasis is placed on internalized systems of censorship, that is, on the learned form of censorship we call "conscience." We acknowledge the necessity of external systems, but not with enthusiasm. These are seen as a protection for the young, a crutch for the weak. Ideally, we believe that every person ought to be his own censor, that individuals should be self-accountable, capable of knowing the difference between right and wrong. To that extent, censorship is seen as a necessary evil.

Second, we are more concerned with controlling what people do than with what they think. And where political expression is concerned, we have been extremely careful, even in wartime, in considering moves to impose censorship. We have been less cautious in the arts, for reasons we will examine later, but, in any case, in that censorship attempts to control expression rather than action, it is contrary to our convictions.

Ideology and legal fictions aside there are, in any organized society, at least two systems of social control or censorship operating simultaneously and more or less in harmony. Whether it is the law or the voice of conscience, the function of such control is the same: to structure behaviour and attitudes in a way which expresses our values and makes orderly, sustained social interactions possible. Abolishing censorship, then, does not eliminate problems of social control; it merely locates them elsewhere.

Elsewhere is either within ourselves or with the authorities we choose to trust. As issues become more complicated, we become more uncertain and more dependent on the advice of others whom we regard as both trustworthy and competent. Increasingly these intermediaries, these authorities or advisers are secular rather than religious, and they are "experts," "specialists," university-educated professionals rather than neighbours, relatives and others whose qualifications are "likeness" or social affinity. One of the distinctively contemporary problems for a modern democracy revolves in part around a conflict about authorities. To which set of authorities do we defer?

Some sociologists believe that the handwriting is on the wall, that we live in an age of experts, and that leadership based on social affinity is a thing of the past; it is only a matter of time before the urban, sophisticated, cosmopolitan cast of mind triumphs over the rural, provincial, fundamentalist cast of mind. Others are less confident that there is such an evolutionary process or that it is moving inexorably in this direction, and point to the periodic resurgence of nationalism, ethnocentrism, distrust of foreigners and suspicion of scientific experts.

Still others question whether such a meritocracy would be desirable. Are the judgments of experts—in this case art and literary critics—unbiased? Are they made freely and with sufficient detachment to stand up for future generations? If all censorship disappeared tomorrow would the critics, the experts, constitute a new Establishment, no less and possibly more repressive than the old? And who among the critics will be the final arbiters—the daily newspaper reviewers who, according to one study, remain very close to prevailing taste,[5] or the prestige critics of the universities and "little mags"? These questions—to which set of authorities do we turn, and what are the social consequences of the choice—are at the very center of the drafting, interpretation, and application of anti-obscenity legislation. Judges may perhaps be pardoned if they are no more able than any of the rest of us to resolve the dilemma. Those who are sceptical of the testimony of expert witnesses and who give higher priority to "community standards" are cast among the Philistines, while those who weigh the opinions of art critics and professors of literature more heavily place themselves on the side of the élites.

Mr. Justice Laskin, in the Cameron case referred to earlier, attempted to break through this impasse by redefining "community standards." It is not Mr. Justice Freedman's median[6], or Judge Woolsey's *"l'homme moyen sensuel"*[7] but rather the relevant public; not the public-at-large but the reading public; not all Canadians or even all Canadians in a certain locale, but the subgroup in an area which participates in and which is regularly exposed to art. In "seeking a Canadian community standard based on the average appreciation of art," he writes, "the Court, in my opinion, is not limited to a settled national consensus. The average in community attitudes is better struck according to the range of exposure that particular art or art forms have had in the localities of Canada where art is exhibited."[8] Thus responsibility is removed from the hands of the self-appointed decency crusaders who are more concerned with morality than art, and from the hands of a narrow group of experts who may have their own axes to grind. Responsibility then rests with the subculture of artists and dealers and the publics they influence.

But does this not beg the question? For if writers and artists were *maîtres chez nous,* if they were in control of what is produced, where and how it is marketed, there would be no censorship. They would be in the same position as other professionals. It is precisely the failure of artists to adopt the model of the professions that leaves them so exposed and vulnerable to censorship, vigilante groups and the least-informed public opinion, not to mention the tyranny of critics who have their own intellectual vested interests.

If it were not for professionalization, the sciences, especially the social sciences, would be in the same position as the arts. Customs officers would confiscate their books at national borders; morality squads would raid university bookstores, the local police would attend their seminars, and the post office would suspend the mailing privileges of learned journals. They are spared these indignities by the existence of a well-organized subsystem which acts as a mediating buffer between themselves and the state, or between themselves and a lay public.

Professionalization involves three principles. First, there is a tacit agreement with the state to respect, and to subordinate scientific interests to, a core of values which may not be universal but extend further than the boundaries of any given society or locality at any particular moment in history. The recent controversy within the medical profession about the ethics of heart transplant surgery is a good example of the strain and the constant effort to redefine the line which divides scientists from the human experiments of Dachau. In other words, the first condition of professionalization is that professionals voluntarily deny themselves the absolute freedom of inquiry which an ideal model of scientific growth requires. To artists and writers, however, this condition is unacceptable; if freedom is not total, it is servitude. Any concession leads inevitably to submission to a society ruled by cultural commissars.

Professionalization also involves self-government. Professions set and administer the conditions for eligibility, screening out quacks and charlatans as well as expelling from their ranks those who disregard their tenets. The procedures are far from perfect, and they occasionally reflect extraneous considerations; for example, there are quotas based on sex, race, religion. Moreover, anyone familiar with professional organizations knows that there are forms of internal censorship such as admission to graduate training and editorial control of journals which may be more counter-productive than anything the state might do. Nevertheless, with all its faults and grievous errors, with all its tendencies to develop the rigidities of a medieval guild, the professional organization through its self-government creates a *cordon sanitaire* around itself which makes external systems of censorship redundant, the exception being during special emergencies such as wartime.

In the arts, however, there is no organization and no effective self-policing. If one thinks of certain pornographers standing in relation to serious writers and filmmakers as quacks do to doctors, the difference is clear: there is no action that can be taken against the pornographers. Hence, the intrusion of the state.

Writers and artists do get together at conferences or at meetings from time to time, but when they do they are, understandably, most concerned with their economic plight. And they are anything but *effete* aesthetes on these occasions. Indeed, they sound more like the Canadian Association of Manufacturers or like a hard-headed group of trade unionists,[9] and lately they have adopted the fashionable rhetoric of the militants in speaking about "artist power."[10] But except for these occasions they nurture and keep alive an image of themselves as free independent spirits; persons mysteriously endowed by nature with delicate sensitivities which can be fatally damaged by organization, over-training, degree-granting procedures and anything comparable to licencing. Until writers and artists give up some of their romanticism about spontaneity, some of their mystique about creative insight and the conditions that are hostile to it, censorship or the possibility of it will continue to hang over their heads.

Finally, the notion of professionalization and the claim against government regulation rest on the assumption that the professional, unlike the entrepreneur, is not motivated by economic self-interest; rather, he is motivated by public service. And this is reflected in the system of payment (fees geared to need rather than prices geared to the market) and in other ways. The abuses are legion and will become more so as recruitment into the professions reaches down in the stratification system to those who do not inherit wealth. But the dangers in these abuses are well recognized as professionals steer a course between the entrepreneur and the proletarianized wage earner.

People in the arts, however, almost never assume any control over the marketing of their work. Just why this should be, I do not know, but would guess it goes back to the patron-artist relationship. For the present, however, as long as publishing and other forms of distribution remain a form of free enterprise, the suspicion exists that writers or publishers of pornography are disingenuous when they appeal to liberal values, that behind their maudlin self-pity they are (or hope they will be) enriching themselves in the most contemptible way there is, by exploiting what most people regard as a human weakness. Studies have shown that pornography is not a multi-billion dollar business, but I have yet to find anyone who believed that pornographers were motivated by anything but the desire to get rich. Just as we have no respect for doctors who remain within the law but grow rich by prescribing diet pills, so we have no respect for the liberalism of writers, film producers and others who make it big with pornography. In short, if people in the arts want to be taken seriously as professionals and claim exemption from censorship, they must develop parallel or alternative economic structures which they themselves control. Otherwise, their integrity remains under a cloud.

Professionalization continues to be an anathema to writers and artists, while publishers are hardly enthusiastic about the development of non-profit co-operatives. Together they live in the hope that censorship will die of its own accord as the "sexual revolution" advances. Patience is all that is needed.

Behind this confidence in the sexual revolution is the assumption that constraints on sexual behaviour are historical rather than functional, that laws which prohibit certain forms of sexual activity correspond to feudal or mercantile regulations on economic behaviour. The same "invisible hand" that can be counted on to regulate a laissez-faire economy can be counted on to regulate our sexual relations. To legislate sexual morality, in life or in literature, is a cultural lag, an obstacle impeding a natural evolutionary development. This essentially is the view of Wayland Young in *Eros Denied*.[11] Social history, he argues, is moving toward greater sexual individualism, "a time of perfect sexual freedom." By freedom he does not mean promiscuity any more than Adam Smith meant economic anarchy. Freedom for Young is freedom of choice, a "time when men can be faithful husbands, unfaithful husbands, stakhanovites, orgiasts, homosexuals, whoremongers, kinkies or monks, and women can be faithful wives, unfaithful wives, stakhanovites, orgiasts, Lesbians, whores, kinkies or nuns, exactly as they choose, when this will rate the same sort of interest . . . as whether they are parsons, journalists, school teachers, miners, electronic engineers or shorthand typists."[12] Censorship stands in the way of realizing this sexual individualism.

Traditionally, the opposing view has been based on a more Hobbesian view of human nature and a more Freudian view of sex. Natural sexual energy is an overwhelming force, and, unless regulated, a destructive force. It must be sublimated to ensure safety and order as well as to preserve the family as a social institution. Victorian standards may be excessive, even detrimental to mental health, and therefore in need of reform, but to have no restraints, no laws, no guidelines, no taboos would make civilization impossible.

Fear of sex and sensuality generally lies at the basis of arguments that freedom of expression in the arts is different from freedom of expression in the realm of political ideas. To lump them together as civil libertarians do would undermine political freedom. We cannot enjoy both since the exercise of political citizenship requires a certain kind of character structure which is built around rationality and self-discipline.

The most recent exposition of this view is by Clor,[13] who points out that political responsibility in a democracy places a great burden on the citizen. He is called upon to reflect carefully, to examine the long- and short-range consequences of various alternatives, to comprehend exceedingly complex problems. These processes require a willingness to defer or postpone immediate gratification of emotion or desire. If and when citizens cease to carry out their duties by surrendering to passion, they forfeit democracy, for their intellectual apathy and indifference will inevitably deliver power into the hands of the few.

Sensuality in and of itself does not erode the citizen's capacity for political judgement. But when it is combined with norms of self-indulgence and the idealization of spontaneity, the personality structure for democratic participation is crippled. Unless we are prepared, then, to resist the temptations of hedonism, unless we are prepared to discipline ourselves with regard to sexual behaviour in practice, and to sexual experience vicariously in the arts, political freedom may decline. Art may flourish, Clor suggests, but not democracy. "To the extent that individuals do not govern themselves, they must be governed by some external agency," he writes. "Such men may be perfectly satisfied to let the government manage all public affairs, and many private affairs, as long as it provides them with opportunities for their personal pursuit of pleasures. This state of affairs would not be 'actual democracy,' though it might be 'sexual freedom.' "[14]

Neither of these positions, Young's or Clor's, is tenable from a sociological point of view. Sexual regulations, whether they are folkways or mores enacted into law, exist in modern societies not because sex is a dangerous wayward impulse, nor because the family is an indispensable institution, nor because erotic passion conflicts with political rationality. They exist because certain values which are only indirectly connected with sex are at stake. For example, it is an offense for an adult to stimulate a child sexually, a practice which was normal in the middle ages and acceptable still in parts of the world.[15] But it is a criminal offense in our society because of our conception of childhood, our overriding belief that the dependency of children should not be exploited for the benefit or pleasure of adults. So long as this remains one of our values, we will continue to have the state in the bedrooms, washrooms, parks and automobiles of the nation.

Any change taking place, then, in our sexual mores is *selective*. And the direction which the changes take will be influenced by changes in the social structure and mediated by the formation of new constituencies. Supporters of Women's Liberation movements, for example, are not likely to equate the freedom to be a whore, as Wayland Young does, with revolutionary social progress. Young's revolution is Kate Millett's counter-revolution.[16] In any event the hope that censorship will die as Victorian prudery fades is a false one. Short of professionalization all that writers and artists can do is gamble on pornography becoming fashionable.

And at the moment pornography *is* fashionable. Conspicuous liberation has replaced conspicuous consumption for a new generation of bourgeois *arrivistes.* What mink coats and cadillacs were to another generation, tickets to *Hair* and *O Calcutta* are to the current one. The old hardcore pornography is becoming middlebrow *kitsch.* Small bookstores are still having troubles with zealous morality squads, but when a Judge can agree with an author that the sexual relationship between a farmer and his pig is not "bestiality" but a "strange passion,"[17] the operators of skin shops whose patrons are not the arty set have grounds for thinking that they are being discriminated against. Later in this discussion I will deal with this question. The point I would like to make now is that fashion is unstable and no substitute for structural autonomy. Without that autonomy censorship will persist.

Pornography is likely to disappear before censorship does. The growth of psychology, sociology and anthropology in the past half-century, and the diffusion of this knowledge throughout society have created levels of information about sex, sex roles, sexual development, patterns of family life and so on which cumulatively have changed the intellectual environment in which people are exposed to pornography. A person going to the most vulgar stag film today brings with him a knowledge about sex which changes the nature of prurient experience. If such an entity as prurient thought does exist, it has never been that and only that, but always modified by the whole mind. Thus, it is one form of prurient thought to observe masturbation on the stage if one believes that masturbation is evil or dangerous to health; it is quite another, if one believes it is normal and harmless. Similarly, it is one experience to read a pornographic book with little education in literature; another, if one has read widely.

Bearing in mind, then, that the revolution that has taken place is not in our sexual mores but in our knowledge and in the democratization of our educational system, pornography has ceased to be a dangerous influence on behaviour, but has become instead a form of entertainment, a diversion which does not require any grandiose explanation. This is another way of saying that if the law is concerned with "community standards," the first reading it must take is of community standards with respect to levels of general knowledge and education. A public opinion poll on whether people are shocked by erotic drawings or four-letter words on television is, in this sense, misleading.

Neither legislators nor judges in North America have given artists and writers any grounds for hope that anti-obscenity statutes will soon disappear. But it is commonly believed that there is a liberalizing trend which may be even wiser, for this trend will eliminate some of the absurdities which require writers to use asterisks for words heard on any school playground, and at the same time it will prevent the blatant promotion of extreme forms of pornography. Although the Commission on Pornography and Obscenity recommended that adults be free to read and see what they wish,[18] and civil libertarians share this view, it takes, as I have indicated, more than recommendations and legal reasoning. Besides, these are conservative times. But since the Canadian government is now about to undertake a review of the Criminal Code, it is worth looking at the trend in censorship.

In 1928 when D. H. Lawrence was writing *Lady Chatterley's Lover*, the prevailing doctrine was known as the Hicklin rule. Enunciated in 1868 by Lord Chief Justice Cockburn, it stated that the test of obscenity was "whether the tendency of the matter charged as obscenity is to deprave and corrupt those whose minds are open to such immoral influences, and into whose hands a publication of this sort may fall."[19] Apart from the difficulties in defining "deprave and corrupt," the Hicklin rule meant that isolated passages in a book could be introduced as evidence of obscenity, and on that basis the book could be found obscene. The Hicklin rule also meant that the work in question would be judged by its putative effects on the minds of young persons or adults whose moral fortitude was wanting.

Critics have pointed out that what worried the Victorians was not impressionable youth, but the spread of literacy among the British working class. This is a serious charge, and, if true, it would support those who suspect that anti-obscenity statutes are part of a class conspiracy. I want to come back to this interpretation later.

For almost a hundred years judicial decisions nibbled away at the Hicklin doctrine in Britain, Canada and the United States. Then, almost simultaneously, the three countries buried its remains. In 1957, the U.S. in the Roth decision held that if a publication is to be considered obscene, it must appeal to "prurient interest" and be "utterly without redeeming social importance," and that the standards to be applied were those of the "community" or "the average person."[20] In 1959 the British passed the Obscene Publications Act which required that a book be looked at as a whole. Even if it was then found obscene in the sense of having a tendency to "deprave and corrupt" persons likely to read it, publishers could *not* be convicted "if it is proved that publication . . . is justified as being for the public good on the ground that it is in the interests of science, literature, art or learning or of other objects of general concern."[21] In the same year Canada amended the Criminal Code so that obscenity was defined as "the undue exploitation of sex, or of sex and any one or more of the following subjects, namely, crime, horror, cruelty and violence."[22] "Undue" was to be interpreted as exceeding "community standards." The exemptions were not as specific as the British act; the Criminal Code merely provided that "no person shall be convicted of an offense . . . if he establishes that the public good was served by the acts that are alleged to constitute the offence and that the acts alleged did not extend beyond what served the public good." Despite the differences among the three countries, *Lady Chatterley* (who was not a lady, according to the Crown prosecutor in England where the case was tried under the new legislation) became part of the literary experience of the British, Canadian and American populations.

In 1966 the U.S. Supreme Court upheld the conviction of Ralph Ginzburg, a publisher of magazines, for the way he promoted his publications.[23] Ginzburg had attempted to have *Eros* mailed from such places as Intercourse, Pennsylvania and Blue Ball, Pennsylvania, succeeding finally in Middlesex, New Jersey. The Court was concerned less with the content of the publications than with their advertising, publicity and promotion. The reaction among lawyers to the Ginzburg decision was mixed, but it was generally felt that the precedent set by prosecuting the "conduct of the purveyor" represented a new direction.

In spite of the liberal trend in interpretation, the courts, whether in England, Canada or the U.S., have never held that censorship is in principle wrong or unconstitutional. At most, all they have done is to allow a new type of defense against the categorizing of material as obscene, or to accept new conditions for exemption. But to this day, the protection given to the arts is considerably less than that given to political expression. If a neo-Nazi group in the U.S. had sought to have its mailing address in

Berlin, Ohio, it would have done nothing more or less than Ralph Ginzburg did in attempting to have *Eros* mailed from Intercourse, Pennsylvania. Yet it is doubtful if the U.S. Supreme Court would have upheld a conviction of the publishers of such "hate literature." Apparently, pandering to paranoid interests is less culpable than pandering to prurient interests.

Modern social psychology which has given us new insights about the nature of political extremism, and which does not support the view that sensuality is the enemy of reason, makes this inconsistency in judicial interpretation absurd. Many of our judges and legislators must be aware of this, but the question is whether they will argue for the elimination of all forms of censorship or for the extension of it to political expression. What will they make of the title of a recent book by Professor Lionel Rubinoff, *The Pornography of Power*?[24] One thing is certain: whatever arguments social scientists may offer for abolishing or extending censorship, these arguments will apply to both politics and art.

When we examine more closely the liberalizing trend of judicial opinion, what we see is an elitist bias that sympathizes with art historians, university students, literary critics, sophisticated consumers. These cultural elites may not correspond exactly to class elites, but from the point of view of democratic theory, the discriminatory principle is the same. Without intending to, those who have attempted to liberalize the law have reflected the more general shift in modern societies from class stratification to functional inequality. The letter of the Hicklin rule has changed, but has the spirit behind it?

The older problem of a class bias still remains in the distinction which is sometimes made on aesthetic grounds between "erotic art" and hardcore pornography.[25] In Britain and in the United States, though to a lesser degree in Canada, there has been a tendency to limit application of the law to hardcore pornography, especially to materials which have a homosexual or fetishistic content. Erotic art may, in the past, have been a peoples' art, but this is not the case today. In a society where a large majority of people do not read the books or see the plays and art exhibits that meet the criteria for erotic art, any distinction made on aesthetic grounds tends to be discriminatory. In other words, here as elsewhere there is one law for the rich and one for the poor, with additional discrimination against the sexual deviate: one law for the normal and one law for the abnormal.

The trend, then, has not been a liberalizing one; it has just been a change. But academics and intellectuals generally are not about to bite the hand that has given them access to Henry Miller, Kenneth Tynan and the Kinsey library. As long as the term "community standards" is defined broadly enough to satisfy their tastes, they have no serious objection to barring trash which has no aesthetic merit. Their complacency, however, may be shaken by the new radicalism with its cult of "community," its distrust of cultural elites, and its anti-intellectualism. In the name of radical egalitarianism, the New Left may insist on a more literal interpretation of the "community" in community standards (namely, as the urban ghettos), and a more politically relevant, (that is, anti-bourgeois) interpretation of "art." We are back then to the question of "community standards." Can this criterion be used intelligently to counteract the tendency toward elitism and discrimination without acquiescing to a Philistine majority?

The New Left is divided on the subject of censorship. On the one hand, it regards censorship as a class conspiracy, a form of police authority, the legal arm of a repressive state. (Legal difficulties encountered by their own underground media with its porno-politics have gone far toward making this a self-fulfilling prophecy.) Censorship is seen as part of a larger system of exploitation in which a ruling class imposes its own language, life style, education and art expression on the underprivileged, the poor and the dispossessed in order to destroy self-esteem and incipient class consciousness.[26] Thus, the proletariat and indigenous populations come to regard their own natural language as improper and illiterate; their respect for the body, physical labour and natural functions as uncouth and inferior. Censorship, then, is a way of intimidating the poor and maintaining class distinctions. That being the case, it follows that censorship must be exposed and destroyed so that the proletariat may recover its sense of dignity and develop a revolutionary class consciousness.

On the other hand, the New Left has also been critical of the classical civil liberties doctrine with its judicial neutrality, its atomistic emphasis on individual rights, its failure to discriminate between human progress and regression.[27] Mr. Justice Douglas, who has been one of the most distinguished and consistent civil libertarians and who has argued that pornography is a matter of taste like a preference for Chopin or "rock" music,[28] is not their champion. To members of the New Left, saying that pornography is a matter of taste is tantamount to saying that racism is a matter of taste. Permitting or encouraging pornography, then, is not freedom; it legitimates a reactionary exploitative concept of sexual relationships. Whatever one thinks of this critique, it at least makes clear that the opposition to the civil libertarian position is not confined to the radical Right, to the strident voices who claim that Toronto is the smut capital of North America,[29] to the latter-day Comstocks who would censor not only pornography but sex education as well.

In the final analysis the debate on censorship is a debate between humanists with their organic view of society and liberals with an atomistic view, between moralists and behaviouralists. It will remain there until we look at the arts and creativity in the arts in a new way. If what were being discussed were knowledge and intelligence rather than art and creativity, the argument would quickly collapse. For we have long ago given up the idea of intelligence as an inborn characteristic and have recognized it as a capacity shared by all in the human race, a capacity which is only realized through social experience and education. Its expression is not a product, a thing, a form of property; it is a process by means of which a society may think and plan ahead in order to control its own destiny. As Dewey pointed out so many years ago, intelligence is a cooperative method which is essentially instrumental. Perhaps this is what Mr. Justice Laskin had in mind when he said:

> "We espouse this freedom [of expression] because of a conviction, supported by experience, that individual creativity whether in the arts or in the humanities or in science or in technology, constitutes our social capital."[30]

If art is regarded as social capital, education becomes the critical variable; education not just about the arts but in the arts. If Canadians had such an educational system, the Courts would no longer be forced to choose between the Philistines and the literati, alternatives which any sociologist knows are the consequences of inequities in education. "Community standards" could be trusted, as of course they must be in a democratic society.

In summary, what I have tried to suggest in these remarks is that censorship is not a question of attitude, of more or less tolerance, but of how a society chooses to organize its system of social control. Our liberal tradition with its dichotomy between the state and the individual oversimplifies and obscures how social control operates. The dynamic conflict in modern societies is not between the state and the individual but between different types of authority: one based on social affinity; the other, on expert knowledge. This tension is reproduced in discussions about who should determine "community standards": Philistines or literati; the majority or the minority; the traditionalists or the experts.

What we seldom ask ourselves, however, is why the majority is Philistine in its taste, why it cannot be trusted to recognize quality and appreciate innovation in the arts. It is an extremely conservative view of human nature to accept this distinction as a given, as an inevitable fact. Our evidence from the social sciences suggests otherwise, that taste in the arts is learned, that critical appreciation is acquired, that what appears to be hereditary or genetic inability is the result of differential access to educational opportunity as well as the nature of the educational process itself. Consensus may be difficult to achieve; it may even be impossible in a heterogeneous society. But the difficulties in achieving consensus should not be confused with incompetence. Incompetence, like competence, is social, and this applies to artistic evaluations as well as any other.

Our dichotomy between state and individual is misleading for still another reason in that it fails to account for the operation of intermediary organization. As I have indicated here, if the social sciences whose literature deals with every known form of deviant behaviour have escaped censorship, it is not because of individual social scientists, but rather because of a collective response, i.e. professionalization. The unwillingness of people in the arts to adopt this model is due in part to a belief on their part that artists are born, not made, and that anything vaguely suggesting bureaucratization must destroy the delicate gift. Thus, unlike the sciences, they invite regulation by the state. The alternative to censorship is professional self-government.

The expectation that the sexual revolution will sweep censorship away is, I have suggested, wishful thinking, a failure to understand social change generally and sexual change specifically. The revolution, if that is the appropriate word, that is likely to have any impact on this problem is the growth of our knowledge about sexuality, the range of sexual practices, the function of sexual taboos, and the diffusion of this knowledge throughout our society. Against this background pornography has become largely irrelevant; enjoyable, but irrelevant; entertaining but of no consequence. Army Generals may enjoy a performance of *The Chocolate Soldier,* but they do not take it seriously. So, too, with pornography in the twentieth century.

Examining the trend in anti-obscenity legislation and judicial interpretation, I have suggested here that contrary to the popular view that it has been a liberal trend, it has been conservative. By that I mean that the liberalization has been to the benefit of the cultural elites. Hardcore pornography is pornography which the critics have declared is without artistic merit; it is the pornography of the inner city, of the slum, and of the deviant subcultures. If I am right about this, and if I have understood the philosophy of the new radicals, it will not be long before this flaw is discovered, and used to the embarrassment of the liberal Establishment.

Equally disturbing in my view is that the door is now wide open for an extension of censorship to political ideas. The compartmentalization and separation of freedom of expression in political ideas from freedom of expression in the arts, was based on the idea that censorship in the arts was desirable for political freedom of expression; this theory has no support whatsoever in our contemporary understanding of human behaviour. Man is both rational and irrational; thinking and feeling; sensual and analytic. And what he creates are symbolic systems of communication which combine all of these.

As Canadians review the Criminal Code, they will have to ask themselves a series of questions: to censor more or to censor less? And if to censor less, will this mean that the arts lose or gain? Will they lose the protection of the state only to become the victims of vigilante groups? Of the intellectuals? These alternatives are surely more destructive to creativity in the arts than professionalization.

1. *Regina* v. *Cameron* (1966) 4 c.c.c. 303.
2. *Regina* v. *Trio Productions Limited et al.*
3. *Roth* v. *United States* 354 US 476 (1957).
4. Walter Lippmann, *Public Opinion* (New York: Free Press, 1946), p. 31.
5. Jules J. Wanderer, "In Defense of Popular Taste," *American Journal of Sociology*, 76, no. 2, pp. 262-272.
6. *Regina* v. *Dominion News and Gifts* (1961) *Ltd.* (1963) c.c.c. 103, 40 C.R. 109, 42 W.W.R. 65, p. 116.
7. *United States* v. *One Book Called "Ulysses"* 5 F. Supp. 182 (1933).

8. *Regina* v. *Cameron.*
9. Writers' Conference, Queens University, 1955.
10. Richard Johnston, ed., *The Artists—a New Power,* Reports from the Canadian Conference of the Arts, Proceedings and Recommendations of the Calgary Conference on the Visual Arts, January, 1969.
11. Wayland Young, *Eros Denied* (New York: Grove Press, 1966), pp. 268-269.
12. *Ibid.*
13. Harry M. Clor, *Obscenity and Public Morality* (Chicago: University of Chicago Press, 1969).
14. *Ibid.*, p. 201.
15. Philippe Ariès, *Centuries of Childhood,* trans. Robert Baldick (New York: Vintage, 1962).
16. Kate Millett, *Sexual Politics* (New York: Doubleday, 1970).
17. *Regina* v. *Trio Productions.*
18. *Report of the Commission on Obscenity and Pornography* (New York: Bantam Books, 1970).
19. *Regina* v. *Hicklin* (1868) L.R. 3 Q.B. 360.
20. *Roth* v. *United States.*
21. C.H. Rolph, *The Trial of Lady Chatterley* (London: Penguin Books, 1961).
22. Canada Criminal Code, 1959.
23. *Ginzburg* v. *United States,* 383 U.S. 463 (1966).
24. Lionel Rubinoff, *The Pornography of Power* (New York: Ballantine, 1967).
25. Drs. Eberhard and Phyllis Kronhausen, *Pornography and the Law* (New York: Ballantine, 1959).
26. Malay Roy Choudhury, "Censorship: F*ck Censorship" in Jerry Hopkins, ed., *The Hippie Papers* (New York: Signet, 1968), pp. 123-127.
27. Herbert Marcuse, "Repressive Tolerance," *A Critique of Pure Tolerance* (Boston: Beacon, 1969).
28. *Ginzburg* v. *United States.*
29. Gordon Carton, MPP (Armourdale), quoted in *Toronto Globe and Mail,* 23 October 1969, p. 4.
30. *Regina* v. *Cameron.*

Hate Propaganda in Canada

MAXWELL COHEN

Reprinted from the Report of the Special Committee on Hate Propaganda in Canada *by Maxwell Cohen, 1966. Reproduced with the permission of Information Canada.*

How extensive is the Hate Propaganda problem in Canada? What forms does it take? What media does it employ? Who are responsible for its recent recurrence? Are the men and materials Canadian in origin or do they have links with sources and persons outside of Canada? These are questions to which this Chapter, surveying hate propaganda in Canada, addresses itself.

Introduction and Background

The term "hate propaganda" is a very difficult one to define, but this Committee has tended to restrict its attention to the kind of materials discussed in this chapter—significant samples of which are included here—and the main characteristics of which are a generally irrational and malicious abuse of certain identifiable minority groups in Canada. Several themes seem to run through most of this propaganda, among them the assertion that "Communism is Jewish"; that Hitler was right in his policy of racial extermination; that a Jewish conspiracy exists to get control of the Canadian as well as of the world economy; that the Negro race is an inferior one which can weaken our society; that there is a deliberate campaign to mongrelize the races; and that Negroes should be returned to Africa. Such propaganda has been expressed both orally and by the written word, the former in public meetings of extremist right wing groups, on "open line" or "hot line" radio broadcasts and by interviews on radio or television of certain well-known persons of extreme views. In this connection the development and extension of "open line" or "hot line" broadcasting represents a new and peculiar problem (although originally only two private radio stations in Vancouver and Montreal seemed to offer this kind of program, it is becoming more widespread and the Board of Broadcast Governors has announced that enquiries are now under way into the nature of these programs.) As far as written propaganda is concerned, hate material has been distributed by mail, by hand, and even on several occasions by being dropped from the top floors of downtown buildings in Toronto.[1] During the past two or three years the activity of hate promoters has received much publicity in Canadian newspapers as well as by means of broadcasting, particularly C.B.C. television programs.[2]

Although the Committee has concerned itself with the distribution of hate propaganda in Canada within the last four or five years, and more particularly within the last two to three years, this is not a new problem in this country. Hate activity extends back prior to 1960 and probably it antedates even the distribution of hate propaganda that occurred in the latter nineteen thirties.

Without treating the pre-1960 period in great detail, it should be pointed out that during the period of 1937 to 1939 a good deal of hate materials were distributed across Canada.[3] Most of the propaganda at that time was anti-semitic in nature, stressing such themes as "Communism is Jewish", and much of the activity centered on two individuals, Adrien Arcand and John Ross Taylor. Arcand was the founder and leading figure of the "National Unity Party" in the Province of Quebec, and Taylor operated at that time in the Toronto area.

Both were interned during World War II. Although there were other persons involved in the distribution of hate literature in this prewar period, Arcand and Taylor are the only ones whose names also have been linked to the current hate campaign in Canada.

Immediately following the Second World War, Arcand's group was revived in the Montreal area. Although Arcand has been in a state of virtual retirement for some time, and has referred to the small group around him as nothing more than a "study group", he has held some reorganization meetings recently and there is evidence of renewed activity by him in the Montreal and Quebec City areas, although his following remains small.[4]

Taylor resides in Gooderham, Ontario, from where he operates the organization "Natural Order" as well as one called "Canadian Publications". Natural Order and Canadian Publications seem to have participated prominently in recent distributions of hate propaganda.

The current hate campaign dates from early 1963, when it began in the Toronto area. Since then it has extended to several other centres in Ontario, and to at least seven other provinces: British Columbia, Alberta, Saskatchewan, Manitoba, New Brunswick, Nova Scotia and Quebec; but the main activities have been essentially in Ontario and to a lesser extent in Quebec and in British Columbia. From 1963 on there was and continues to be a steady dissemination of hate propaganda, mainly anti-Jewish, anti-Negro and neo-Nazi in nature. The propaganda has been plastered and displayed in conspicuous places, distributed at public gatherings, placed in apartment mailboxes, sent through the regular mails, and scattered from the upper floors of downtown buildings to the streets below.

The printed, mimeographed and other written materials seem to be obtained in large measure, although not exclusively, from American sources. In many instances it is mailed directly from Arlington, Virginia, the headquarters of the American Nazi Party and the World Union of National Socialists, and from Birmingham, Alabama, the headquarters of the National States Rights Party and its organ "Thunderbolt", as well as of "World Service." In other instances these materials are imported in bulk by mail or otherwise from the United States or abroad and then distributed in this country. Several of the publications were distributed for a time by David Stanley, a young Canadian of extreme views, whose activities have been publicized by the C.B.C. and by the press. Stanley has now published a statement recanting his former extremist and anti-semitic positions and charging that certain of his former colleagues are pursuing policies that he could no longer support.

Since a large proportion of hate propaganda stems ultimately from American sources, a word should be said about them. The National States Rights Party, which is both anti-Negro and anti-semitic, was launched in 1958. The party headquarters, formerly located in Kentucky, are presently located in Birmingham, Alabama. The organization has branches in New York, California and Ohio. Its official monthly publication, "The Thunderbolt", has been the subject of two recent prohibitory orders issued by the Postmaster General of Canada. The National States Rights Party recently absorbed the National White Americans Party, whose name has appeared on some of the recent hate materials. The Thunderbolt recently expanded from 8 to 12 pages, boasts that its circulation is now over one hundred thousand, with claims to readership in fifty states and scores of foreign countries. In addition to The Thunderbolt, the National States Rights Party maintains a depot of hate literature and promotes the sale of the writings of both American and foreign authors specialising in bigotry and racist material. For example, it has revived the distribution of "Jewish Ritual Murder" by Arnold Leese, a British fascist, which was originally published 25 years ago, and of Julius Streicher's "Der Stürmer" which includes obscene and scurrilous illustrations designed to project the ritual murder allegations therein contained.

Another important source of hate propaganda being distributed in Canada is the New Jersey publishing group composed of followers of Conde McGinley, whose semimonthly publication "Common Sense" has a claimed circulation of ninety-one thousand. Common Sense persistently repeats the charge of a "Jewish conspiracy" to rule the world and the charge that the Communist Party in the Soviet Union and elsewhere is an instrument of this Jewish conspiracy. The United Nations Organization is described as a front created to establish Israel as the seat of world domination. The campaign for racial desegregation is viewed as a Communist-Jewish plot to mongrelize the nation. The group even opposes mental health legislation and water fluoridation programs in racial terms, the former being seen as a plot by Jewish conspirators to "put their enemies away".

The two sections that immediately follow comprise: *first,* an assessment of the extent of the problem and the numbers of individuals and groups involved in the dissemination of hate propaganda in Canada in recent years; and *second,* a brief summary of conspicuous cases of hate material distributions.

Persons and Groups Involved in Hate Propaganda Activities in Canada

The Committee has had the opportunity of surveying the files of the Department of Justice and of studying extensive newspaper reports covering a period of several years as well as other private and public materials describing persons and organizations involved in hate propaganda activities.

The Committee is satisfied that the number of organizations involved, although often with small membership, is somewhat larger than perhaps generally publicized but that the individuals directly concerned are relatively few in number and many of them are involved in more than one of these right-wing, extremist "hate" groups. The Committee has been made aware of about fourteen organizations, several of which, however, are splinter groups derived from now expelled elements of the Social Credit movement; a few are outright Nazi-type parties; and a few are indigenous Canadian-fascist associations. One or two are simply "extremist" with little ideological content. However odious the behaviour of these groups and however offensive the materials they distribute, the Committee believes that none of the organizations represent today a really effective political or propaganda force and that, in any case, very few individuals as such are involved.

Nevertheless, however limited may be the numbers of persons involved, or the political and administrative significance or effectiveness of many of the organizations responsible for the printing and distribution of hate materials, it would be very unwise, in the Committee's opinion, to ignore them. Not merely are these activities and materials deeply offensive to many Canadians, whether targets of the material or not, but it would be a mistake to ignore the potential of prejudice developed by these groups and their continuing "hate" activities.

Some idea of what these materials attempt to promote by way of malice and prejudice will be evident from the list of pamphlets etc. distributed in Canada, and from samples. Some examples are reproduced below:

NATIONAL WHITE AMERICANS PARTY

P.O. Box 2013 — Atlanta 1, Georgia.

P.O. Box 431,
Scarborough, Ont.,
Canada.

February, 1964.

Dear Sir/Madam,

A mutual friend has informed us that you are a strong believer in segregation and a dedicated opponent of Jewish Communism.

To avoid delay we are enclosing a membership card to the NATIONAL WHITE AMERICANS PARTY. All you need to do is sign it and you are an official member. Then, drop us a line to inform us of your decision and an organiser will visit you to explain our activity here in Toronto.

You may consider this procedure presumptuous or an imposition on your privacy, but my friend, in this struggle against International Jewish Communism every minute counts. So, to avoid wasting time we are mailing out thousands of cards and leaflets to obtain a mass membership. Your signing the card does not obligate you in any way, although you will be asked to vote for anti-Jewish candidates, boycott Jewish goods, etc. There are no dues or fees.

You may wonder why you are being asked to join an American based organization. The NWAP is a party of the Whiteman and therefore supersedes national boundaries. We believe in the superiority of the Aryan race as proved by *his* great culture and civilization. The negro races have *never* developed a civilization, discovered any new invention, written a great symphony, or even originated an alphabet. They are on a MUCH lower level to the Whites. We believe in sending all negroes back to Africa whence they came.

On the Jewish Question our policy is much stricter. We *demand* the arrest of all Jews involved in Communist or Zionist plots, public trials and executions. All other Jews would be immediately sterilized so that they could not breed more Jews. This is vital because the Jews are CRIMINALS as a race, who have been active in anti-Christian plots throughout their entire history.

We are moving ahead to victory. We have a positive, active program. Truth is on our side. But to win, we need your help. Help us distribute a million anti-Jewish leaflets during 1964. Let us hear from you real soon, so we can start laying out our plans for the next election.

Yours for a White World,

(Sgd.)
Col. J.P. Fry,
National Organizer (Canada)

....

THE THUNDERBOLT

The White Man's Viewpoint

Issue 49 February 1963

COMMUNIST PARTY MEETS IN NEW CENTERS

Just as the NAACP, Martin Luther King and other extreme left-wing elements use Negro churches as protective fronts to hold their subversive meetings, the U.S. Communist Party uses Jewish Religious Centers for their secret dens of Anti-American plotting. On this page we picture the Los Angeles "Jewish Cultural Center," which Communist Jews are going to use to celebrate their release by the U.S. Supreme Court. What the public does not know is that the Communists frequently announce in their publications meetings in Jewish religious centers. Many also do not know that the only daily Communist newspaper left in America today is not the so-called "Daily Worker" (it only comes out twice a week now), but the "Morning Friheit"—A YIDDISH DAILY, PUBLISHED BY THE OFFICIAL JEWISH SECTION OF THE COMMUNIST PARTY. And that they have an official magazine for the Communist Party named "Jewish Currents" also published at the same address. While all Jews in America may not be Communists, it is a fact that Jews make up the majority in the U.S. Communist Party today. In other words, if the Jews would in mass resign from the U.S. Communist Party, the Party would cease to exist. Ninety-five percent of all Jews in America can be classified as either, Socialists, leftists, or Liberals—regardless, they are on the left—and are the main force moving this nation leftward into the camp of International Communism.

Whenever these facts come to light, the Jews always fall back on the old defensive smear word "Anti-Semitic", and condemn all who would expose them. Therefore, we continually find Communists announcing that their next meeting will be held at a synagogue, Jewish Community Center, Jewish Cultural Club, Yiddish School, etc. Our leaders are afraid to oppose these dens of treason, for fear of being called "Religious Bigots." Time is running out, and we must soon awaken our people to the complete realization of just who is behind and promoting Communism in America.

NATIONAL SOCIALIST MOVEMENT

74 Princedale Road, London, W.11

"Britain Reborn" - the National Socialist Policy.

Despite the Jewish lie machine -

HITLER WAS RIGHT

Democracy means - Jewish Control
National Decline
Racial Ruin

Hitler raised Germany from the depths of Democracy. He sought the friendship of Britain in creating a new Europe based on national unity, social justice, racial betterment and defence against Communism; but the Jews forced Britain to declare war on their behalf.

Hitler fell, but National Socialism lives on, and is today the only force which can save our nation and race from ruination and build a new and greater Britain for the British.

....

SPECIAL BULLETIN

By World Service

We do not say every Jew is a Communist, but that the majority of the Communist leaders and spies were and are Jews. Therefore:

COMMUNISM IS JEWISH

At present we have no means of bringing the truth to the people, except our leaflets etc. To expose ourselves now would be suicide. We would be smeared or even assassinated as countless other patriots were: The Czar and his family; Count Folke Bernadotte (1st U.N. Secretary); and the British Governor of Palestine - all murdered by Jews; Moise Tshombe, Katangan Christian leader - also martyred!

Over 1000 British officers and men blown to pieces, knifed or hanged by Jewish terrorists in Palestine. Thousands of defenseless Arab women and children! Through the Jewish stranglehold on money, business and press, the German, Italian, Hungarian and Slavic peoples are blamed for alleged war crimes. The Jews should take action against the criminal and communistic elements in their midst before crying persecution. Are they trying to divert attention from their own atrocities?

Instead of producing anti-communist films, Jewish-controlled Hollywood continues to pour forth anti-nazi and anti-christian films (e.g. the latest "Cardinal" by Otto Preminger, another Zionist Jew).

Christians unite, boycott Jewish filth. Nazism is dead, but Communism lives.

FIGHT COMMUNISM OR DIE A SLAVE.

The grossly repulsive character of the above needs no further comment.

Finally, a word must be said about the links that the Committee has observed between Nazi-fascist-extremist movements in the United Kingdom, Sweden, the United States and some of the organizations concerned with hate activities in Canada. These activities, often international in character, thus continue to stimulate home-grown varieties of the same character. Again, although the Canadian numbers may be small, the effects are likely to be a great deal more dangerous than present numerical estimates would suggest. The continuing harassment of any minority groups and the uncontrolled repetition of fabrications and pseudo-facts may leave behind a residue of actual or pending belief that becomes the seedbed from which a more dangerous and more widespread prejudice can flower tomorrow.

Hate Propaganda Materials and Their Distribution 1963-1965

The following is a selective summary of some of the leading instances of hate propaganda disseminated in Canada during the past two years, set out chronologically, province by province.

1. Ontario

The current hate propaganda dissemination can be traced back to an advertisement placed in the Toronto Globe and Mail on April 1, 1963, asking persons interested in collecting Nazi propaganda leaflets "as a hobby" to write for a free sample to a postal box in Scarboro, Ontario.

Evidence then mounted of distribution in a number of areas in the Province.

1963

In April 1963, a pamphlet entitled "Program of the World Union of Free Enterprise National Socialists" (American Nazi Party, Arlington, Virginia) was posted at a construction site on Yonge Street in Toronto, and a sticker reading "Hitler was right" was placed on store windows in the Kingsway district of Toronto.

On July 2 an anti-semitic tract was distributed outside Massey Hall at a Martin Luther King fund raising performance.

In the same month four different "hate" pamphlets, emanating from the United States, Sweden and Canada were distributed by mail in Toronto.

In September, various pamphlets emanating from Union, New Jersey, Norrviken, Sweden and Arlington, Virginia were distributed by mail to residents of Toronto.

In October, a pamphlet entitled "Stop This Jewish Cruelty", published by the National Socialist Movement of London, England, was placed on store windows in the Islington area of Toronto.

In the same month residents of Ottawa received issues of "Common Sense", published by the Christian Education Association of Union, New Jersey, by mail.

During the week of October 20, anti-semitic material was distributed on a door-to-door basis in St. Catharines, Ontario.

On October 2 construction fences in Toronto were labelled with stickers reading, "We, The Jews, The Destroyers".

On November 7, the Canadian Jewish Congress at its offices on Beverley Street in Toronto received by mail an envelope containing "Common Sense" and other anti-semitic material.

On November 9, a swastika was found painted on a fence at Wellington and Walnut Streets on Stanley Park Soft Ball Stadium in Toronto. The words "Hitler Was Right" were also found painted on fences. On the same day swastikas were found on various fences along with "Juden 'raus"[5] and "Hitler Was Right" stickers near the Forest Hill area of Toronto.

On November 11, the words "Communism is Jewish" were repeated twice, with swastikas, on a wooden boarding at the Queen Street Bridge in Toronto.

On the same day, leaflets entitled "Communism is Jewish" and "Hitler Was Right" were scattered in considerable quantities from the upper floors of buildings in downtown Toronto. The leaflets were published by the American Nazi Party, Arlington, Virginia.

On November 27 and 28 pamphlets entitled "World Service, Special Bulletin—White Men Awake" (World Service, Birmingham, Alabama) were attached to poles and stuffed in mail boxes in Toronto.

On December 3 the same leaflet was distributed to stores at Dufferin Plaza in Toronto.

On December 11 and 12 the leaflet "White Men Awake" was distributed to various apartment houses in the Queen Street area of Toronto in the early morning hours. On the same day several Rabbis in Toronto received the leaflet with a handwritten notation "More to come!"

On December 12, copies of "Thunderbolt" were mailed to members of the German Club in Niagara Falls, Ontario.

On December 20, the leaflet entitled "Special Bulletin" (World Service) was stuffed in apartment house mailboxes in Scarboro.

During the week of December 23, handwritten postcards were received by several Rabbis bearing the message "Hitler Was Right—Communism is Jewish". The cards were postmarked December 15, from Amos, Quebec.

On December 27, copies of "The World Service Bulletin" were stuffed in apartment house mailboxes on Thorncliffe Park Drive in Toronto.

1964

On January 15, five hundred leaflets entitled "Special Bulletin" were picked up by an apartment administrator from tenants' mailboxes in apartment houses along Don Mills Road, Victoria Park Avenue and Eglinton Avenue East in Toronto. The leaflets all had special "hate" messages typed on the reverse side.

The same leaflet was received by mail by persons in Toronto whose names begin with the syllable "Rosen—" (Rosenblatt, Rosenbloom, etc.)

On February 17, prepaid five cent envelopes containing a letter from the "National White Americans Party", an Einar Aberg multi-lingual leaflet and a membership card in the NWAP, were received by several hundred residents in the city of Toronto including a) most synagogues and Jewish organizations, b) leaders in Jewish community activities and professional workers in Jewish agencies, and c) the UN Association and certain trade unions. Similar materials were received at about the same time by a

County Court Judge, an Ontario Chief Justice, and the Chairman of the Metropolitan Toronto Police Commission.

In January and February, several Jewish public figures in Toronto received neo-Nazi and anti-semitic materials in envelopes post-marked Victoria, B.C. In some cases these arrived frequently and consistently with ever-increasing offensiveness.

In July a pamphlet entitled "Mind Twisters" was found posted in Toronto parks.

In September the same pamphlet was distributed by hand by several people in Toronto.

On September 7 and 8, the dates of the Jewish New Year, one of the most solemn of Jewish religious holidays, a green card was received in the mail by many members of the Jewish Community in Hamilton and Toronto. The card, mailed from Toronto, depicted a Jew fleeing a large swastika, and contained the words "THITH ITH THE END". The cards apparently were published by the "Canadian Nazi Party".

In approximately the same period, various pamphlets were distributed in Sault Ste Marie, including the notorious "Protocols of the Learned Elders of Zion".

In November, a pamphlet published by the "Nazi Party of Canada" entitled "This is a kike (Jew)" was placed on the campus of the University of Toronto.

On December 5, several pamphlets published by the World Service, in Birmingham, Alabama, and entitled "Communism Is Jewish", "Program of Canada Youth Corps" and "The Mind Twisters" were distributed on Toronto streets.

1965

In January, various pamphlets emanating from the United States and including "Common Sense" and "Protocols of the Learned Elders of Zion" were distributed by a man and woman in downtown Sudbury.

In the months of January and February, a number of anti-Jewish publications were circulated in Port Arthur and Fort William by persons residing in Sault Ste Marie. Most of the material was published in Philadelphia, Pennsylvania, but some bore the postmark of Gooderham, Ontario.

During the same period various hate materials were delivered to homes in Wawa, Ontario by persons from Sault Ste Marie. One of the leaflets proclaimed that "Communism is Jewish" while another expounded on the "Bombing Atrocity of Dresden". One of the pamphlets told of alleged atrocities committed by allied troops during the second World War and another was entitled "The Falsehood about the 6 Million Jews Said to be Gassed by Hitler".

Early in February, residents of Stratford, Ontario, received hate literature from Union, New Jersey.

On February 19, 1965, it was reported that hundreds of anti-semitic and anti-negro leaflets were found strewn in cars parked on the main streets and in parking lots in North Bay, Ontario. Others were reported found in the doorways of retail shops.

On February 13, various hate leaflets published by World Service of Birmingham, Alabama, were distributed in Oshawa, Ontario.

In Sault Ste Marie, Ontario, the distribution of hate literature began in the Fall of 1964 and is still continuing (February 1965).

In February, copies of "Common Sense" (Christian Education Association, Union, New Jersey) were distributed from door to door in Port Arthur, Ontario.

In March, pamphlets mailed from the southern United States were received on the campus of McMaster University in Hamilton.

In July, a pamphlet entitled "Help Free Canada from Jewish Control, Join the Canadian Nazi Party, Free Speech for Beattie" were scattered from the air and found at King and Yonge Streets in Toronto.

In May and in July meetings and demonstrations at Allen Gardens, Toronto, led to disorders and arrests.

2. Quebec

1964

In January of 1964, students at McGill University and Loyola College in Montreal received by mail a variety of hate pamphlets, published in New Jersey, Alabama, California and Sweden.

1965

In Montreal, a pamphlet entitled "World Union of National Socialists Press Release re Formation of Union of Fascists", signed by "Helmut F. Dieskau, commander, Union of Fascists (Canada)" was left on steps, lawns and mailboxes of Jewish residents.

In June and July, a pamphlet entitled "Renaissance", apparently published by the Canadian National Socialist Party, was distributed by mail to residents of Montreal.

In September, Adrien Arcand published a restatement of his views in a book entitled *A Bas La Haine.*

3. British Columbia

1964

In March, 250 copies of the pamphlet entitled "Communism is Jewish" were distributed by a juvenile in Victoria.

During the same month, another pamphlet entitled "National White Americans Party" and signed by "Col. J. P. Fry, National Organizer (Canada)", bearing P.O. Box 431, Scarborough, Ontario, was distributed by mail in Vancouver. The pamphlets had a Victoria postmark.

In May, a pamphlet that included a membership application in the National White Americans Party and bearing a return address in Atlanta, Georgia, was mailed in Squamish, B.C. The pamphlets bore a Birmingham, Alabama postmark.

In September and October of 1964, pharmacists in British Columbia received a publication entitled "Ottawa Anti-Communist Report" which had been mailed from

Ottawa, Ontario. Among the items included in the publication was one headed "Jews in Pharmacy" which stated that the Jews were attempting to get control of the pharmaceutical trade in Canada, and which alerted readers to the grave menace to the National welfare if the Jews were allowed to succeed in these efforts. The publication spoke of the "Rokeah" which it described as a Jewish organization designed to gain control of important segments of national-economic life. It linked the deliberate efforts to get control of vital areas of the economy with international Communism.

1965

In February, a pamphlet entitled "Money Creators" published by Canadian Publications in Gooderham, Ontario, was mailed from Alberni Street in Vancouver, to residents of Victoria. Several other pamphlets emanating from the United States and Sweden were mailed as well.

In March a pamphlet from the House of Free Speech in Vancouver to the Members of the House of Commons in Ottawa defended "so-called hate literature" and attacked Jews.

4. Alberta

A certain amount of hate literature distribution occurred in December of 1964 in Calgary.

5. Saskatchewan

In April of 1965, a number of pamphlets were mailed from the Vancouver branch of Natural Order to residents of Saskatoon.

6.˙ Manitoba

In September of 1964, several pamphlets, including one entitled "Communism is Jewish" were mailed to the principal of a high school and others in Winnipeg.

7. New Brunswick

April 1965, pamphlets were mailed from Fredericton, New Brunswick, to people in Moncton and St. John.

8. Nova Scotia

In May of 1964, a number of pamphlets were mailed to people in Dartmouth. The pamphlets bore the return address: National White Americans Party, P.O. Box 2013, Atlanta, Georgia. The pamphlets were postmarked Birmingham, Alabama.

Pamphlets bearing the same return address and postmark were sent to Musquodobit Harbour and Halifax.

In January 1965, the "Press Release re: Formation of Union of Fascists (World Union of National Socialists)" was mailed from Ottawa to addresses in Halifax.

Conclusions With Respect to Hate Materials in Canada

It is evident from the foregoing that there exists in Canada a small number of persons and a somewhat larger number of organizations, extremist in outlook and dedicated to the preaching and spreading of hatred and contempt against certain identifiable minority groups in Canada. It is easy to conclude that because the number of persons and organizations is not very large, they should not be taken too seriously. The Committee is of the opinion that this line of analysis is no longer tenable after what is known to have been the result of hate propaganda in other countries, particularly in the 1930's when such material and ideas played a significant role in the creation of a climate of malice, destructive to the central values of Judaic-Christian society, the values of our civilization. The Committee believes, therefore, that the actual and potential danger caused by present hate activities in Canada cannot be measured by statistics alone.

Even the statistics, however, are not unimpressive, because while activities have centered heavily in Ontario, they nevertheless have extended from Nova Scotia to British Columbia and minority groups in at least eight

Provinces have been subjected to these vicious attacks. The Committee firmly believes that Canadians who are members of any identifiable group in Canada are entitled to carry on their lives as Canadians without being victimized by the deliberate, vicious promotion of hatred against them. In a democratic society, freedom of speech does not mean the right to villify. The number of organizations involved and the numbers of persons hurt is no test of the issue: the arithmetic of a free society will not be satisfied with over-simplified statistics demonstrating that few are casting stones and not many are receiving hurts. What matters is that incipient malevolence and violence, all of which are inherent in "hate" activity, deserve national attention. However small the actors may be in number, the individuals and groups promoting hate in Canada constitute 'a clear and present danger' to the functioning of a democratic society. For in times of social stress such "hate" could mushroom into a real and monstrous threat to our way of life. Nor does giving some of these hate promoters a radio or television platform serve any valid debating purpose. The Committee is aware that radio and particularly television may expose malice and fraud for what it is, but such a view of affording an electronic audience to hate promoters does not take into account the effects of hate arguments and pseudo-facts on uncritical and receptive minds. The broadcasting of "hate", therefore, whether for news or exposure purposes, should be carefully disciplined by those in charge. Indeed, the Committee feels that in recent years some radio and T.V. producers, with the best of intentions, have been mistaken in their belief that exposure of this kind will destroy the virus. But whatever the validity of these views they do not justify giving propagandists a mass platform as if what they had to say was normal debate on real issues. Plainly it is not.

In the Committee's view the "hate" situation in Canada, although not alarming, clearly is serious enough to require action. It is far better for Canadians to come to grips with this problem now, before it attains unmanageable proportions, rather than deal with it at some future date in an atmosphere of urgency, of fear and perhaps even of crisis. The Canadian community has a duty, not merely the right, to protect itself from the corrosive effects of propaganda that tends to undermine the confidence that various groups in a multicultural society must have in each other. The Committee therefore concludes that action by Government is necessary.

Principal Conclusions

Our study of the problem of hate propaganda in Canada (and elsewhere), in its factual, psychological, legal and more general dimensions, has brought us to four principal conclusions:

(1) *A serious problem.* As this report has already made abundantly clear, over the past several years there have been a number of groups engaged in the distribution of hate propaganda in Canada. While the principal area of distribution has been the Province of Ontario, there also has been some dissemination of materials in urban centres such as Victoria, Vancouver, Montreal, Moncton, and Halifax, as previously described. The propaganda distributed has attacked various racial, religious and ethnic groups, particularly Jews and Negroes, in abusive, insulting, scurrilous and false terms, and these pamphlets, handbooks, booklets etc., could not in any sense be classed as sincere, honest discussion contributing to legitimate debate, in good faith, about public issues in Canada. For those identifiable groups so attacked these offensive tracts have been deeply provocative and in particular the Jewish community of Canada viciously has been made the special target of the whole hate program. It is not to be wondered at that men of good-will should be repelled by these malicious and ignorant pretensions and that Canadian Jews, remembering the debasement of all Judaeo-Christian values by Nazi policy, should be especially sensitive to these abuses of the freedom that a democratic society must possess and protect.

The amount of hate propaganda presently being disseminated and its measurable effects probably are not sufficient to justify a description of the problem as one of crisis or near crisis proportions. Nevertheless the problem is a serious one. We believe that, given a certain set of socio-economic circumstances, such as a deepening of the emotional tensions or the setting in of a severe business recession, public susceptibility might well increase significantly. Moreover, the potential psychological and social damage of hate propaganda, both to a desensitized majority and to sensitive minority target groups, is incalculable. As Mr. Justice Jackson of the United States Supreme Court wrote in *Beauharnais* v. *Illinois,* such "sinister abuses of our freedom of expression . . . can tear apart a society, brutalize its dominant elements, and persecute even to extermination, its minorities".

(2) *Inadequate legal remedies.* Canadian law clearly is inadequate with respect to the intimidation of and threatened violence against groups, and almost wholly lacking in any control of group defamation. There is no longer any valid legal reason for continuing to exclude "groups" from the protection of the law. The present state of the rules with respect to groups is merely a reflection of the fact that our law developed in a more individualistic age. But the twentieth century has been marked by a growing sense of social inter-dependence, of the importance of group activity, and legal policy already has reflected this change of climate in many sectors. Most other modern states have already expanded their legal systems to provide for group intimidation and defamation.

(3) *Law: A Solution.* Democratic society no longer accepts, if it ever did accept, the notion that freedom of expression is an *absolute right* which must exist wholly independent of qualification. Our Anglo-Canadian political and legal traditions reflect generally the long struggle to free society from the absolutism of sovereign or the oligarchy of the privileged. Freedom of expression became the most conspicuous index of the movement from government by the few to self-government by the many. But even at its highest point of historical and political accep-

tance, freedom to speak and to publish was circumscribed by law. The prevailing view in Canada is that freedom of expression is a qualified right, representing the balance that must be struck between the social interest in the full and frank discussion necessary to a free society on the one hand, and the social interests in public order and individual and group reputation on the other hand. The Board of Review which recently upheld an interim prohibitory order of the Postmaster General against the National States' Rights Party adopted a succinct statement to this effect by the late Chief Justice of Canada, Sir Lyman Duff:

> "The right of public discussion is, of course, subject to legal restrictions; those based upon considerations of decency and public order and others conceived for the protection of various private and public interests with which, for example, the laws of defamation and sedition are concerned."

There is an evident distinction between "*legitimate*" and "*illegitimate*" public discussion, and the state has as great an obligation to discourage the latter as it has to maintain the former. Concededly there are borderline areas of delicate ambiguity between the two spheres, and the most that law can hope to accomplish is to balance the conflicting interests with as much ingenuity and wisdom as possible.

(4) *Priority to freedom of expression.* Because of these wide borderline areas where vigorous rough and tumble debate shifts into the brutal, the vicious and the illicit, the general preferences with which one approaches the task of balancing interests is of crucial importance. For the crucial issue in striking a balance between conflicting interests is the weight to be assigned to the interests in question. As a sheer matter of drafting, for example, legislation easily could be framed which would catch all instances of hate dissemination, without exception and however subtle, but this might be accomplished at the expense of including the whole borderline area within the

statutory proscription, with detriment to many instances of legitimate, even if very rough, public debate.

It is our opinion that the Canadian people already have made the decision that as among conflicting values, preference must always be given to freedom of expression rather than to legal prohibitions directed at abuses of it. This is not to say that freedom of expression is regarded as an absolute, but only to insist that it will be esteemed more highly and weighted more significantly in the legislative scales, so that legal markings of the borderline areas will always be such as to permit liberty even at the cost of occasional licence. But at some point that liberty becomes licence and colours the quality of liberty itself with an unacceptable stain. At that point the social preference must move from freedom to regulation to preserve the very system of freedom itself.

(5) *Specific Conclusions.* The four general conclusions above became, therefore, two specific ones. First: there should be new legislation in Canada because of the present deficiencies in the law, so as to forbid the following: (a) advocacy of genocide, (b) incitement to hatred of groups that is likely to occasion breach of the peace, and (c) group defamation. Second: the legislation should be so drafted as to permit the maximum freedom of expression consistent with its purpose and the needs of a free Society. It is necessary to comment on these specific conclusions in some detail.

Genocide

In our opinion there should be Canadian legislation to prevent any advocacy of genocide. So abhorrent is such advocacy that it can have no standing whatever as argument in a democratic society.

For purposes of Canadian law we believe that the definition of genocide should be drawn somewhat more narrowly than in the international Convention so as to include only killing and its substantial equivalents—deliberately inflicting conditions of life calculated to bring about physical destruction and deliberately imposing measures intended to prevent births. The other components of the international definition, viz., causing serious bodily or mental harm to members of a group and forcibly transferring children of one group to another group with intent to destroy the group, we deem inadvisable for Canada—the former because it is considerably less than a substantial equivalent of killing in our existing legal framework, the latter because it seems to have been intended to cover certain historical incidents in Europe that have little essential relevance to Canada, where mass transfers of children to another group are unknown. We consider that the groups to be protected against genocide should be readily identifiable groups, distinguished by religion, colour, race, ethnic or national origin.

To our minds it is hard to exaggerate the importance of Canadian legislation against advocacy of genocide. Clearly, it would be the fulfilment of an international obligation Canada undertook as a signatory to the Genocide Convention. It would be an emphatic public declaration of our total commitment to the elimination of this most inhuman manifestation of prejudice and a reassurance to any minority groups in our midst that promoting such a concept in public discussion is beyond the pale. At the same time it would be one more potent instrument in the education of the people of Canada as to the awful consequences of racism and prejudice.

But because existing Canadian law already forbids most substantive aspects of genocide in that it prohibits homicide or murder vis-a-vis individuals, and because it may be undesirable to have the same acts forbidden under two different legal categories, we deem it advisable that the Canadian legislation which we urge as a symbol of our country's dedication to the rights set out in the Convention should be confined to "advocating and promoting" genocide, acts which clearly are not forbidden at present by the Criminal Code.

Canadian law generally has not gone to the length of prohibiting mere intellectual advocacy of a forbidden act, but has contented itself with proscribing conduct which incites to illegal action in a present, immediate way. However, we are convinced that, in the one case of the urging of physical violence against identifiable groups, to the point of genocide, there is no social interest whatever in allowing advocacy or promotion of violence even at the highest level of abstract discussion. It is odious and unacceptable at any level.

We would stress the difference between advocacy and promotion of revolution against constituted authority in the state and the advocacy of annihilation of identifiable groups for no reason other than that they are what they are. We would concede as a philosophical argument that there may be a genuine social interest in not totally excluding advocacy and promotion of violence against state authorities, in that otherwise there would be little possibility of overthrowing tyrannical governments.

But the case is wholly different with respect to the advocacy and promotion of violence against identifiable groups, which are defined, not by their political power, but by natural facts such as race or colour, or fundamental personal choices such as religion. The serious discussion, even at the most abstract level, of genocide as a conceivable political or social policy, is simply not tolerable in a civilized community; it has no social value whatever.

This is not open to the objection that can be urged against the jurisprudence of many American courts in cases involving freedom of expression, viz., that there is no substantial public interest in permitting certain kinds of utterances—the lewd and obscene, the profane, the libellous, and the insulting or fighting word—for these categories beg the question as to what is lewd, obscene, profane, etc., since often there is no readily ascertainable consensus as to their definition or application. There can, however, be no misunderstanding as to what is meant by "*genocide*", for it can be defined precisely—as the Convention has done—in a manner that leaves no room for uncertainty. There is, therefore, no ambiguity and no begging of the question in the stand we take, namely that any form of advocacy or promotion of genocide is outside the bounds of legitimate public discussion. In our opinion there is no need for any exempting clause in the application of legislation against advocacy of genocide, because there is no social interest in protecting any variety of such advocacy. The prohibition should be absolute because the act is wrong absolutely, i.e., in all circumstances, degrees, times, and ways.

Disturbance of the Peace Through Incitement to Hatred of Groups

With respect to incitement to hatred or contempt of identifiable groups, where linked with disorder, we also conclude here that new legislation is necessary. It is readily apparent that it should be unlawful to arouse citizens deliberately to violence against an identifiable group, and in our understanding of Canadian law this already may be proscribed by the present rules in the Code governing sedition (although this is not absolutely certain). But the social interest in the preservation of peace in the community is no less great where it may not be possible for the prosecution to prove that the speaker actually *intended* violence against a group, or where the wrath of the recipients is turned, not against the group assailed, but rather against the communicator himself, and the breach of the peace takes a different form from that which he was *likely to intend.* In neither case, of course, do we wish to suggest that the attackers who themselves commit a breach of the peace should not be criminally liable, and there is little doubt that they are already liable under existing criminal law. But the gap in the law today derives from the fact that it does not penalize the initiating party who *incites* to hatred and contempt with a likelihood of violence, whether or not intended, and whether or not violence takes place.

To our minds the social interest in public order is so great that no one who occasions a breach of the peace, whether or not he directly intended it, should escape criminal liability where the breach of the peace is reasonably foreseeable, i.e., likely; and we believe that this should be the law regardless of whether the incitement to hatred or contempt against an identifiable group is spoken, written, or communicated in any other way.

We recognize that such legislation may pose some dangers for legitimate freedom of expression, in that, if unqualified, it would make it possible for any unreceptive audience by their negative or violent response to determine whether or not the speaker addressing them would be liable to go to jail. But we believe that such dangers can be minimized by drafting the legislation narrowly in the following respects: (1) its application should be restricted to statements communicated in a "public place"; (2) the statements must be such as to create "hatred or contempt" of an "identifiable group", so that the speaker must be the author of his own misfortune and not merely the victim of a hostile crowd; (3) the "identifiable group" that is protected must be limited to sections of the public distinguished by religion, colour, race, or ethnic or national origin, so that sharp attacks on such other groups as political parties will clearly be outside the prohibitions of the legislation; and (4) the statements must be of such a character as to be "likely" to lead to a "breach of the peace". We firmly believe that such qualifications will protect fully all legitimate discussion.

Group Defamation

The "sticks-and-stones" assumptions of our criminal law traditionally have tolerated few exceptions, and group defamation has not been one of them. Even the recognized offence of defamation of an individual has a somewhat tenuous place in our present criminal law, for often it is applied in practice only in situations where the libel gives rise to a threat to the peace. There is some justification for this limitation in the light of the civil remedy available to an injured party, but group defamation is in no way parallel in this respect, for it is as unrecognized generally by civil as by criminal law.

We do not think, however, that a civil remedy for group defamation is an adequate solution. A civil action for damages likely would be unworkable, because the law could not permit an indefinite number of members of the defamed group to bring actions nor could it tolerate a limited number of suits that would lead to a scramble to sue first among the group members. A civil action for an injunction as provided in Manitoba might be workable, but when enacted by the provinces it could raise constitutional issues of some difficulty. As federally enacted (if within federal criminal law jurisdiction), it would raise issues of the desirability of prior restraints on expression and of depriving the defendant of the traditional protection of a jury, since injunctions are heard and determined by a judge alone. No civil statute can create a moral standard equivalent to that of criminal law.

We therefore have come to the conclusion that there is needed a criminal remedy for group defamation that would prohibit the making of oral or written statements or of any kind of representations which promote hatred or contempt against any identifiable group. Identifiable group we propose to define (as above) as any section of the public distinguished by religion, colour, race, language, or ethnic or national origin.

We have concluded that this new offence is desirable even though we realize that it goes beyond what has hitherto been thought by many to be the proper sphere of criminal law, for such group defamation requires no breach of the peace and no showing of likely injury to the reputation of any person. In effect, it sets out as a solemn public judgment that the holding up of identifiable groups to hatred or contempt is inherently likely to dispose the rest of the public to violence against the members of these groups and inherently likely to expose them to loss of respect among their fellow men. We are convinced that the evidence justifies this policy judgment and that in our present stage of social development the law must begin to take account of the subtler sources of civil discord.

Because so much of legitimate public debate is admittedly persuasive in intention and often cast in negative statements as well as in positive ones, and also because stereotyping seems to be an inevitable method of generalizing about groups, we realize that to recommend legislation against group defamation, without providing adequate safeguards for proper public discussion, could raise in question our very commitment to the essential democratic value of free expression. On the other hand, we do not believe that our liberties would be endangered by the mere fact of novel legislation provided that effective defences are included. In other words, it is our view that the test as to whether our recommendations about group defamation adequately safeguard free expression will be whether the exemptions we suggest leave sufficient latitude for the fullest legitimate public discussion however rough and tumble it may be.

It has appeared to us that at a minimum we must provide the principal defence already present in the Criminal Code in Section 259 for the offence of defamatory libel against an individual:

> No person shall be deemed to publish a defamatory libel by reason only that he publishes defamatory matter that, on reasonable grounds, he believes is true, and that is relevant to any subject of public interest, the public discussion of which is for the public benefit.

The test thus established as a defence to defamatory libel is public benefit and *reasonable* belief in the truth of the assertion. In the words of Mr. Justice Brennan of the Supreme Court of the United States even "erroneous statement is inevitable in free debate, and . . . it must be protected if the freedoms of expression are to have the 'breathing space' that they 'need . . . to survive' ". We are also desirous of keeping the other defences established by the Criminal Code for defamatory libel, but we believe that by limiting the scope of the offence to the *wilful promotion* of hatred or contempt against "identifiable groups" we can exempt legitimate reporting of information without the necessity of spelling out in detail all the defences contained in Sections 255 through 266 of the Code.

It is, however, in our opinion, insufficient protection for legitimate debate merely to allow the same defences for group defamation as for individual defamation. Generalizations about groups play a more vital role in public discussion than do statements about individuals. There may be no public benefit whatever even from true disclosures about individuals, whereas there will almost always, if not always, be a public benefit to be derived from *true* statements about groups. In our opinion, therefore, it is necessary to provide the unqualified defence of truth in order adequately to protect all legitimate dialogue from legal restraints.[6] Indeed this is the traditional common-law defence to civil actions of defamation and has recently been established by the United States Supreme Court as a defence for criminal defamation in all cases where discussion of public affairs is involved.

The two defences of unqualified truth, and reasonable belief in the truth coupled with public benefit, provide considerable, and we believe adequate, latitude for legitimate public examination of all matters of concern to it, from the rough and tumble of the political hustings to the riposte of more elegant forms of dialectical needling. There may even be those who believe that we have gone too far in attempting to protect free expression, or that it is undesirable that courts should be charged with the responsibility of finding "truth". To the first we would reply that we have stated from the outset the priority and preference which we believe the Canadian people rightly attach to the freedom of expression, and that it is vital to give the benefit of any doubt to liberty rather than to repression. To the second we would answer that we believe that one of the main effects of the exemptions we recommend will be to keep from the courts all cases where the statements are true patently in fact or could on "reasonable grounds" be thought to be true. Hence while courts often will function in practice as inhibitions on reckless prosecution they will also have the power and the duty to place the burden of proving truths on the accused libeller, where it belongs. Indeed this conclusion must follow since the burden of proof before the Court must rest upon those who allege the truth of the statement complained about.

In those cases where it is apparent to men of good will that the statements are an abuse of legitimate public discussion, we believe that Canadian courts will have little difficulty in so finding and in dealing summarily with malicious or fraudulent or abusive documentation. For there can be little truth in abuse as such. We are strengthened in this opinion by the example of the Post Office Boards of Review which entertained the defence of truth raised at their hearings and had no difficulty in finding that the claim to truth was entirely spurious. Indeed the first Board wrote of the statements there in question that "their abusive quality is heightened by the knowledge that they are, in the face of obvious facts and repeated demonstrations of their falsity, represented as the 'truth'." For these reasons also and so as not to severely encumber the prosecution with the necessity of adducing evidence against palpable falsehoods, we have decided to recommend that the burden of proving the truth of abusive statements should be placed upon the persons charged rather than resting upon the prosecution to disprove. For the accused was first an accuser and his accusations must be for him to prove.

In our view these exemptions adequately protect the public interest in all legitimate discussion without reducing to impotence the substantive recommendation for the control of abusive statements defaming any identifiable group.

The history of law and opinion as concurrent developments is replete with instances, as A. V. Dicey long ago indicated, not only where law reflected the state of opinion but where a fluid opinion was itself crystallized by law. This generation of Canadians is more sensitive to the dangers of prejudice and vicious utterances than ever before. Such public opinion, therefore, should now be prepared to crystallize these sensitivities, fears and doubts into positive statements of self-protecting policy—namely statements of law.

1. The most recent illustration was thousands of pamphlets dropped to young people waiting to see the Beatles at Maple Leaf Gardens, Toronto, Ontario, on August 17, 1965 (*Montreal Gazette*, August 18, 1965, page 2).
2. For a detailed summary of all programs, radio and T.V., 1963-1965, dealing with "hate" materials or giving hate promoters a platform, see Appendix III of the Report.
3. See a report in *Globe and Mail*, Toronto, December 8, 1937.
4. See also his recent publication restating his views, *A Bas La Haine*, Edition La Verité, 1965.
5. "Juden 'raus"—a Nazi-German slogan (slang) dealing with expelling Jews from Germany.
6. Mr. Hayes, while agreeing with these conclusions and recommendations, would have wished the recommendations to go further by excluding truth as a defence.

Mass Media and Communication in a Canadian Political Crisis

DANIEL LATOUCHE

Introduction

One of the most substantial concerns of communications researchers for the past few decades has been the issue of communications effects. The emphasis has been on the direct stimulus-response relationship between portrayed events and human behavior. In such cases, media can be said to do more than reflect the outer reality: they are intervening, becoming actors in social systems, rather than merely reporting events.[1] While there has been a great deal of research dealing with media's role during "normal times," there have been situations in which media are drawn into an active role in the events themselves; these situations (usually of an emergency or crisis nature) have received very little analytic attention. Included in such categories are the natural emergency (e.g., tornadoes, floods, hurricanes) and the man-made crisis. It is the purpose of the present essay to discuss the latter kind of situation, using the events transpiring in Canada during the fall of 1970 for our data, and to speculate on some of the effects on the population and on the media themselves.

Those events which surrounded the demands, kidnapping, and murder by the Front de Libération du Québec in 1970, constituted a crisis in which the communications system (the mass media) of Canada was drawn in as an important actor. While the term "crisis" has been utilized by political scientists, psychologists, economists and sociologists in a variety of ways,[2] here it is used to define a situation when the following four elements are present: (a) a *threat*[3] which is recognized as such by the actors, and which imperils the organizational status quo or the stability of the interactive relationship between actors;

(b) a restricted period of *time* during which the decision-making agents must formulate and implement a response to the threat; (c) an element of *surprise* which modifies the definition of the situation; (d) an escalating level of *risks* which increases the likelihood of an outbreak of violence or of a breakdown in the political system. Each of these elements were present in the fall of 1970 when the F.L.Q. launched its actions.

Summary of the Events

On October 5th, 1970 at 8:30 a.m., four men, later to be identified as members of the F.L.Q., kidnapped Mr. James Cross, the British Trade Commissioner in Montreal. At 9:30 a.m., the terms set by the F.L.Q. for the release of Mr. Cross were made public. They were (1) the cessation of all police activities; (2) the publication of an F.L.Q. manifesto in Quebec newspapers and its broadcast on national radio and television; (3) the liberation of 23 individuals described as "political prisoners"; (4) their transport to Cuba or Algeria; (5) the reintegration in the ranks of the Canadian Postal Service of the strikers formerly employed by the Lapalme Mail Trucking Service; (6) a "voluntary" income tax of $500,000 to be paid to the prisoners; (7) the name and picture of the individual who had recently informed on the F.L.Q. A time limit of 48 hours was specified for the "autorités en place" to meet these demands. At 10:30 a.m., External Affairs Minister Mitchell Sharp expressed the first governmental reactions:

> Clearly, these are wholly unreasonable demands and their authors could not have expected them to be accepted. I need hardly say that this set of demands will not be met. I continue, however, to hope that some basis can be found for Mr. Cross' safe return. Indeed, I hope the abductors will find a way to establish communication to achieve this.[4]

On Wednesday the 7th, Robert Lemieux, a defense lawyer in previous F.L.Q. cases, was allowed to visit the prisoners in jail in order to ascertain their willingness to participate in an eventual government-F.L.Q. deal. Meanwhile, an F.L.Q. communiqué pressed the authorities to acquiesce to demands (1) and (2) as a sign of their good faith. A similar demand was again made on October 8th, but with a time limit of 12 hours attached to it. On the same night, in an apparent gesture of compliance by the Government, the F.L.Q. manifesto was read on the radio and television networks of Radio-Canada. In its next communiqué, released on October 9th, the F.L.Q. acknowledged the gesture and temporarily suspended its threat to kill Mr. Cross. The terms for his release were scaled down to the liberation of the "political prisoners" and the cessation of police activities. In a response which apparently confirmed their willingness to negotiate, the authorities asked for a proof—which the F.L.Q. provided—that Mr. Cross was still alive, and for a place and time for his liberation. Hopes for successful negotiation were short-circuited on the next day when the Quebec Minister of Justice, Mr. Jérôme Choquette, made known the government's refusal to meet any of the additional F.L.Q. terms. In his press conference, Mr. Choquette indicated the dilemma in which the governments found themselves.

> No society can accept that the decisions made by the government and the judiciary be put into question or put aside because of blackmail by any particular group, because that means the end of all social order, which is nothing less than the denial of the liberty of individuals and groups, for this liberty can only be exercised within the framework of institutions which arbitrate between the conflicts and the interests of the groups in question.[5]

Instead, he offered the kidnappers a safe-conduct to a foreign country of their choice. Eighteen minutes later, Mr. Pierre Laporte, the Quebec Minister of Labour and Immigration, was kidnapped by a second F.L.Q. cell. Through a series of communiqués released on the following Sunday and Monday, the new F.L.Q. cell redefined the situation in the following terms: (a) if the governments persisted in their refusal to meet any of the F.L.Q. initial demands, both hostages were to be killed; (b) if the governments met the first two demands, Mr. Cross was to be set free; (c) if instead the governments met all demands, both hostages were to be set free within twenty-four hours.

On Monday, October 12th, the authorities named lawyer Robert Demers as their representative in the negotiations with Robert Lemieux who, although himself in jail, was to represent the F.L.Q. On the following day, a group of eleven prominent Québécois[6] expressed its full support of the Quebec government in its efforts to negotiate the release of the two hostages. These new hopes for a compromise solution were definitely crushed within twenty-four hours as the negotiations formally broke down, and the Quebec government reaffirmed its initial decision to stand firm in its refusal to meet any of the F.L.Q. demands. In the early hours of the morning of Friday the 16th, the War Measures Act was implemented, suspending all civil liberties and providing the law enforcement agencies with total powers of search, arrest and detention.[7] At 6:00 p.m. on the following day, the F.L.Q. carried out its threat and killed Mr. Laporte.

The next step in the crisis occurred on December 3rd when the hide-out of the first F.L.Q. cell was discovered, Mr. Cross liberated and his kidnappers flown to Cuba. On December 28th, three F.L.Q. members suspected of being involved in the kidnapping and death of Mr. Laporte were arrested on a farm near Montreal.

The Importance and Impact of the Communication Function in the Crisis

From one point of view, the October crisis can be seen as a battle for the temporary control of the communication system in Quebec. The kidnappings had a purpose that went beyond publicity for the terrorist organization and in fact generated channels with which to communicate their ideas to the population. This theory is supported by the importance with which the F.L.Q. regarded the public airing and publication of its manifesto: its publication was one of the two necessary conditions for the suspension of Mr. Cross' death sentence.

This communication dimension was also clearly present in the other F.L.Q. demands. For example, their fourth demand required that at least two correspondents from Quebec newspapers accompany the political prisoners on their trip to Cuba or Algeria. The fifth demand insisted on a public meeting in the presence of journalists to oversee the reinstatement of the Lapalme strikers. So important was this dimension that eventually a "communication" cell was established within the F.L.Q.

To successfully achieve this objective, it was imperative that the F.L.Q. impose on the political authorities and the mass media its own strategy of information throughout the crisis. This strategy included the following tactical objectives: (a) *to retain at all times the initiative in the communication process and to set the terms of the debate with the authorities* (the purpose here was to communicate the impression, valid or not, that the governments were responding to the F.L.Q. demands and not vice versa); and (b) *to have all their communiqués published immediately and uncensored.*

On the other hand, the political objectives of the government were: (a) to show conclusively that it was not engaging in a political debate with the F.L.Q.; (b) to prevent panic in the population; (c) to obtain the safe release of the two hostages; (d) to prevent any further kidnappings or other forms of escalation in the crisis; (e) to demonstrate that there were certain principles on which the governments could not compromise since they were considered to be the foundations of Canadian society.

The major thrust of the governments' efforts was to force the F.L.Q. to communicate with them so that they could gain time, learn more about the kidnappers, force them into making an error, and save the lives of the two hostages by keeping the kidnappers "talking." This tactical objective implied that the authorities did not block off any routes of communications, but deliberately avoided a clarification of their positions and intentions. They rejected the F.L.Q. *demands* but expressed a desire to achieve an acceptable *compromise;* they made it clear that the governments could not *negotiate* with a terrorist organization under the threat of political blackmail but that they were nevertheless anxious to *discuss* the issue with the F.L.Q. They never accepted formally the principle of negotiation but nevertheless gave the impression that this was the case by directing questions to the F.L.Q. which presupposed the acceptance of the principle of negotiation.

What is the verdict of this contest which included a conflict for the control of the communication process? In the short run, the governments probably emerged as the victors. Although the manifesto and communiqués of the F.L.Q. were widely distributed, the F.L.Q. could not marshall widespread and open support in the population. Only one movement, the Front d'Action Politique (a new municipal political party), expressed its solidarity with the aims of the F.L.Q. But this expression of support only served to further divide the new party and eventually contributed to its electoral defeat.[8]

On the other hand, the governments did not succeed in one of their major objectives, that of convincing the population that the F.L.Q. constituted a menace to their individual security as well as to the stability of the government process. A recent survey has shown that only 30 per cent of the population believed in the possibility of an insurrection, while a large percentage felt themselves threatened more by the police forces than by the F.L.Q. (21 per cent compared with nine per cent). The same survey also indicates the political consequences that may have resulted from the crisis. Some five months after the crisis, 74 per cent of those who voted for the separatist Parti Québécois in 1970, would have made the same choice after the crisis, while only 58 per cent of those who voted for the Liberals would again do so.[9]

The question can then be raised in view of these data: did what appeared to be a victory by the government actually obscure a breakdown in support for the government by Quebec's population? Surely the governments did not communicate effectively their own message concerning the dangerous nature of the F.L.Q. threat and, implicitly, the illegitimate nature of separatism. Since all of these messages were mediated by the communication system—both during and after the crisis—it is possible that the disaffection from the Liberal Party revealed by the survey, is in great part a result of the image of the government's credibility as it was generated by the media during the dialogue with the F.L.Q.

The Performance of the Mass Media During the Crisis

In Quebec, the North American tradition of aggressive mass media, i.e., the muckraking press and "action radio," have never taken root. However, an immediate consequence of the crisis was to catapult the media into active roles in the interaction between governments and the F.L.Q., for in addition to reporting on events, the mass media became intermediaries and actors in the crisis. Two radio stations acted as mail boxes for the F.L.Q. communiqués and hence as communications intermediaries between the F.L.Q. and the authorities, as well as between the F.L.Q. and the public and between various F.L.Q. cells. The Montreal daily *Le Devoir* soon became a key protagonist in the crisis as well, when it was the only daily newspaper to suggest that the governments should negotiate "in good faith" with the F.L.Q. in order to ensure the safe release of the hostages. In addition, because of its unique position as a link between the various segments of the Quebec intellectual community, *Le Devoir* also became a focal point for the generation and distribution of information among Quebec intellectuals, technocrats and public figures both in and out of the government. The conjunction of these two factors was sufficient to isolate *Le Devoir* from other Quebec newspapers and to give an apparent credibility to the rumour, born in Toronto, that the publisher, Mr. Claude Ryan, had joined a conspiracy aimed at replacing the present provincial cabinet with a new ministerial team.[10]

While *Le Devoir* was apparently acting as a protagonist the relative positions of television and radio were being shifted. Most research to date has indicated that television is the most preferred and trusted medium for bringing the news to people, for what they can see, they believe, and what they can see appears to be happening in the present. However, during this crisis, radio became the dominant medium for news of the crisis. There were two reasons for this shift in roles: first, as indicated earlier, was the decision of the F.L.Q. to use radio stations CKAC and CKLM as mail boxes for their communications because of the alleged "objectivity" of their announcers. In addition, the frenetic rhythm of events during the early weeks of the crisis provided radio with a clear superiority over television or the printed media. A television crew could not compete with a radio station dispatch-car for getting information on the air as quickly as possible. This coincides with findings by Benjamin Singer on the crisis in Detroit in 1967 when radio proved to be the preferred medium for gaining riot information.[11] Newspapers, of course, take more time to transform and distribute such information in printed form. Meanwhile, part of the crisis was unfolding right in the radio station studios—station personnel were playing the role described by social scientists as participant observers. Throughout most of the crisis, there was no visual element on which television could capitalize, in any case.

Clearly, then, by their own choosing, the F.L.Q. restructured the traditional roles of the media, causing them to become protagonists as never before in Quebec's history and shifting important functions from television and newspapers to radio.

The Impact of the Crisis on the Media

While the crisis affected the relative roles of the media at the time, it was also to have a delayed impact on these institutions in another sense. There is a greater concern now with the kind of role the mass media should play in the collective life of Quebec. Newsmen have been placed in the ambivalent position of regarding their work with increased importance while they have become more aware of possible constraints imposed by their political environment. In addition, there were a great number of attacks made on the press after the crisis, suggesting that the media were irresponsible in the way in which they amplified rumours during a time of severe threat.

A new awareness of their sensitive position is suggested by the two colloquia organized by Quebec journalists on the role of the media in times of crisis and in the repeated demands made by the Journalists Federation to re-convene the Quebec Parliamentary Committee on Freedom of the Press which had not met since 1968.[12] In addition, some self-questioning has taken place in the publication by journalists of a number of articles and books dealing with their role in society.[13] The two questions that have dominated the discussion have been, first, the degree to which journalists should allow themselves to be drawn into such crises as actors or intermediaries and second, the extent of their responsibility to the public, to their employers and to the government.

For governments and those who control the mass media, the crisis has revealed the precariousness of their usual forms of control. Direct control exists in the power of hiring, promotion and self-censorship; in addition, there is a more subtle form of control created by the news environment which surrounds matters of crucial political importance: that environment consists of a great deal of trivia and entertainment which some social scientists believe has a "narcotizing" function for the masses. Thus, important elements can become lost in a maze of details.

While in the beginning the media's perspective indicated the F.L.Q. actions were the work of madmen and criminals, after the government entered into a dialogue with the F.L.Q. and agreed to the reading of their manifesto over radio and television, the media came to take a political view of the events. However, this view has been short-lived for since the fall of 1970, there has been a deliberate move by the owners of media to again depoliticize the message carried by the media. One way in which this can be achieved is through the process of direct control—*retribution*. There appears to be evidence that some retribution has taken place:

Michel Bourdon was suspended on November 3, 1970 and then fired on November 9 from his job at Radio-Canada for "insubordination." On December 12, 1970, Louis Martin, host of Format 60, Radio-Canada, resigned, claiming his freedom was being increasingly curtailed. On February 12, 1971, fifteen journalists of F.L.Q. mail box CKAC were fired, followed in the spring by the dismissal of another key mail box figure, Jean Levesque. At the Montreal weekly, *La Patrie,* journalists on October 21, 1971 protested five cases of alleged political censorship. Then there was the elimination of newsmen Richard Guay, Robert McKay and Michael McAndrew from the Radio-Canada News Service for alleged "lack of objectivity."

Conclusion

Actions such as these, following from the media's active role during the crisis; the possibility of instantaneous change in function generated by the F.L.Q. actions; the new self-questioning that has taken place among Quebec's newsmen since the crisis; all these factors suggest that the mass media in French Canada will never return to "normal" in the sense that normal was considered to be stable and unchanging, and a passive reflection of events external to the media.

1. See, for example, R.K. Baker and Sandra S. Ball, *Violence and the Media* (Washington, D.C.: Superintendent of Documents, 1967).
2. In the sociological literature, the notion of crisis is analyzed in the following contributions: Charles F. Hermann, "Some Consequences of Crisis which limit the viability of organizations," *Administrative Science Quarterly,* VIII, 1, (1963), 61-82; Amitai Etzioni, *Complex Organizations: A Sociological Reader* (New York: Holt, Rinehart and Winston, 1961); R. I. Kulak, "Sociology of Crisis: the Louisville Flood of 1937," *Social Forces,* XVII, 1,

(1938), 66-72; J. A. Robinson, "The Concept of Crisis in Decision-making," in National Institute of Social and Behavioral Science, *Series Studies in Social and Economic Sciences* (Washington, D.C.: 1962); Lewis Coser, *The Social Functions of Conflict* (Glencoe: Free Press, 1956).

For examples of its use by political scientists, see Ole R. Holsti, "The 1914 Case," *American Political Science Review*, LIX, 2, (1965), 365-378; "Perceptions of Time and Alternatives as Factors in Crisis Decision-making," *Peace Research Society Papers,* III, (1965) 79-121; Charles McClelland, "Action Structures and Communication in two International Crises: Quemoy and Berlin," *Background,* VII, (1964), 201-215; "The Acute International Crisis," *World Politics*, XIV (1961), 182-204, O. R. Young, *The Intermediaries: Third Parties in International Crisis* (Princeton: Princeton University Press, 1967); R. C. North, "Decision-Making in Crisis: An Introduction," *Journal of Conflict Resolution,* VI, 3 (1962), 197-201.

In their definition of crisis, psychologists have insisted on different traits. For Miller and Iscoe, a crisis situation (1) is acute rather than chronic; (2) results in behavior that is frequently pathological; (3) threatens the goals structure of the person; (4) causes tension; (5) is a relative; what is defined as crisis for one individual may not be by another. See Kent Miller and Ira Iscoe, "The Concept of Crisis: Current Status and Mental Health Applications," *Human Organization,* XXII, (1963), 195-201.

In economics, the concept of crisis has been used mostly in connection with the 1929 events and with the theory of business cycles; see Robert A. Gordon, *Business Fluctuations,* 2nd ed. (New York: Harper and Row, 1952); Léon H. Dupriez, *Des Mouvements Economiques Généraux,* 2ième éd., Louvain, E. Nauwelae Rts, 1951; Mentor Bouniatian, *Les Crises Economiques*, 2ième éd., Paris, Marcel Giard, 1930.

3. Some authors refer more specifically to threats to the high-priority values of the organization; see H. H. Lasswell, "Style in the Language of Politics" in H. D. Lasswell et al., *Language of Politics* (New York: George W. Stewart, 1949), 20-40; H. B. Williams, "Some Functions of Crisis Behavior," *Human Organization,* XVI, 1, (1957), 15-19; A. R. Ferguson, *Tactics in a Local Crisis* (Santa Monica: Rand Corporation, Memorandum RM-3034-15A, 1962).
4. *Debates of the House of Commons,* October 6, 1970.
5. Quoted in Jean-Claude Trait, *F.L.Q. 70: Offensive d'automne* (Montréal: Editions de l'Homme, 1970), p. 74. Translation.
6. Included in this group were Mr. Claude Ryan, editor of *Le Devoir*, Mr. René Lévesque, Mr. Camille Laurin and Mr. Jacques Parizeau of the Parti Québécois, Mr. Louis Laberge and Fernand Daoust, president and secretary-general of the Quebec Federation of Labour; Mr. Marcel Pépin, president of the Confederation of National Trade Unions, Mr. J. M. Kérouac, secretary-general of the Union Catholique des Cultivateurs, Mr. Yvon Charbonneau, president of the Quebec Teachers Corporation, Mr. Mathias Rioux, president of the Montreal Teachers Alliance and Mr. Alfred Rouleau, president of l'Assurance-Vie Desjardins.

7. According to an official version of the police operations, 453 individuals were arrested and 3,068 raids carried on through the War Measures Act. Of those arrested, there were 139 students, 45 unskilled workers, 42 unemployed, 25 teachers, 17 journalists, 15 clerks and 14 technical specialists. During the raids, 4,692 bullets were seized, 912 detonators, 677 dynamite sticks, 159 firearms, 3 tear gas cans, 46 typewriters, 2 tape recorders, 2 stencil machines and one addressograph.
8. Robert Cliche, the president of F.R.A.P., was eventually forced to abandon his post after the defeat of the party by Mayor Jean Drapeau's Civic Party.
9. The survey was carried out in March 1971 by two political scientists from Laval University. The fact that the survey was carried out five months after the events of October may affect its validity. On the other hand, and this is the position argued by the authors, a survey taken at the time of the events would have been even more invalid, since a high percentage of those interviewed would have undoubtedly refused to answer. See Michel Bellavance et Marcel Gilbert, *L'Opinion Publique et la Crise d'Octobre* (Montréal: Editions du Jour, 1971). Nevertheless, the extensive elaboration methods used by the authors provide us with a satisfactory degree of certainty.
10. For an overview of the role of *Le Devoir* during the October events, see Claude Ryan (ed.), *Le Devoir et la Crise d'Octobre 70*, (Montréal: Editions Leméac, 1971). On the rumour, see the article by Dominique Clift in the *Montreal Star* (October 29th, 1970) and Mr. Ryan's rejoinder in *Le Devoir* (October 30th, 1970).
11. Benjamin D. Singer, "Mass Media and Communication Processes in the Detroit Riot of 1967," *The Public Opinion Quarterly*, Vol. 34, Summer 1970.
12. A colloquium was held on November 7th and 8th, 1970, at Laval University, under the sponsorship of the Journalist Studies Programme and the Fédération Professionnelle des Journalistes du Québec; another one was held on the same day in Montreal and was organized by the Association of Journalists of the Quebec English Press.
13. B.R., "Une information totalitaire prise à son propre piège," in J. M. Piotte, (ed.), *Québec occupé* (Montréal: Editions Parti Pris, 1971), pp. 179-217; Claude-Jean Devirieux, *Manifeste pour la liberté de l'information* (Montréal: Editions du Jour, 1971); Claude Ryan (ed.), *Le Devoir et la Crise d'Octobre 70*, (Montréal: Editions Leméac, 1971).

The Media: Must We Serve as Tools for Terrorists?

RICHARD NIELSEN

Reprinted from the Toronto Star, *18 March 1971, by permission of the author.*

During the height of the FLQ crisis, at 10 p.m. on the Sunday following Pierre Laporte's abduction, I stood in the CBC newsroom and watched Premier Robert Bourassa declare on TV that the demands of the kidnappers would not be met. A murmur of approval and satisfaction at the Quebec premier's stand, which I am sure was echoed throughout the country, was the immediate reaction of almost everyone present.

Watching that scene and participating in it, I had the horrifying sense that the whole terrible business was simply a television show, the greatest yet devised, with TOTAL INVOLVEMENT, EMOTIONAL IDENTIFICATION, IMPACT and IMMEDIACY, all the things that in a normal week it's our task as television producers to attempt to contrive.

Match of Wit and Will

Could the kidnappers have succeeded—in a political sense—without television and radio? Could two small bands of desperadoes have raised themselves to a level where they were, in effect, bargaining as equals with the Prime Minister of Canada? Without us, would they even have tried? Would the Trudeau government have introduced the War Measures Act? Would Quebec Justice Minister Jerome Choquette have rejected ransom demands from Cross' kidnappers, and would the FLQ have impatiently and dramatically replied to this rejection with the kidnapping of Laporte unless like actors in an improvised play they had not felt that now the plot required some action from them? What pressure was exerted on the actors by that massive television audience, passive but intensely partisan, loyal to their political leaders but capable without doubt of an instantaneous withdrawal of that approval?

Had television and radio succeeded in converting the electorate into a mob demanding immediate satisfaction of its desires, creating a climate in which only one thing was really demanded of their leaders: that they do what the people—the mob—at that moment wanted done?

And were the terrorists clever enough to see that they could best destroy our institutions by forcing us to bypass them in favor of direct communication between the government and the governed via television?

On reflection I think that such a theory gives the terrorists too much credit. The terrorists were not that far-seeing but future terrorists may well count on just such a development. What the FLQ believed was that they too had a chance to appeal to a national audience, although they would have defined the nation and the audience in terms of Quebec.

In effect they had challenged the government to a match of wit and will, confident that television and radio would supply an audience. Just in case there was any doubt of such an audience being provided, they sent their messages to the disc jockey who appealed to the audience they most wanted to reach, and they demanded that the CBC French network carry their manifesto throughout Quebec.

It is impossible to say now precisely how the match between the FLQ and the government should be scored. Both have suffered deep wounds, but if those of the FLQ prove to be less than fatal, then their showing probably leaves them stronger than before they issued their challenge. Certainly the "great television audience" will in future take seriously any bout in which they are entered.

Audience Provided

In the weeks since the War Measures Act, like most broadcasters, I have resisted those outside and inside the industry who have advocated voluntary restraint or censorship. As any journalist knows, it is impossible to accept judgment from above, however benevolent, concerning what the public should be allowed to know, since the prime function of a journalist is to make such judgments for himself.

Having said this I nonetheless wonder whether television and radio journalists can do nothing but sit passively while we provide an audience for any group that wishes to involve our elected government in a confrontational drama. Maple Leaf Gardens and the O'Keefe Centre reserve the right to decide the events they will invite an audience to see. Is there not some such principle available to television and radio?

Newspapers do not as a general rule report suicides as such since it causes distress to relatives and friends of the deceased, and also because we have discovered that reporting suicides persuades others to do likewise. The press does not, as a rule, print articles about purely private relationships, however titillating. The courts place various restrictions on the freedom of the press which reports their activities. These are honorable precedents which have not compromised freedom of the press.

Might it not be possible for television and radio networks and private stations to agree that political acts which specifically threaten violence to governments should not be reported immediately?

TV Dramas

Most of the press (I hope) would not print a threat of assassination against a public figure if he or his family or even the police asked that the threat not be reported.

Why does the same restraint which applies to other threats of violence not apply in political kidnappings? Essentially because kidnapping is more than a *threat* of violence. It is in itself an *act of violence* which the press, television and radio feel compelled to report. But is a political kidnapping primarily an act of violence or is it a threat to commit a worse crime—murder—unless certain conditions are met? And, if it is a threat, should not the press, television and radio agree voluntarily now that in future they will not report or broadcast, for a specified period of time, anything except the simple fact of a kidnapping plus the identity of the victim?

The media should also restrict politicians or anyone else from communicating with the kidnappers through the media, whatever the circumstances, while such voluntary restrictions are in effect. They would, of course, report any debate in the Commons relating to such a kidnapping and reporters would continue to cover the story until it became possible to reveal all the relevant details.

The issue here is not one of press freedom. No one believes that the Canadian Manufacturers' Association or the Canadian Labour Congress should be able to exploit the media as they please to persuade or impress the public. Indeed it is the duty of the press to see that it isn't used in this way. The measures advocated here are designed to ensure that we are not, in future, used by terrorists.

There also should be some system which would enable a committee chosen by the working press to decide after a specified period of time whether in the public interest such a ban should continue or not.

The alternative, I fear, is many more dramas in which a handful of desperate men sit glued to their television screens watching the nation respond emotionally and none too wisely to their every move. There should be some way to deny them that and to safeguard our leaders from the cruel pressure of an electorate overstimulated from the effects of too much real life-and-death drama.

Information and Complaint Channels in a Canadian City

JOHN CLAXTON and GORDON McDOUGALL

Introduction

Two values central to Canadian society have a bearing on the role of communications. The first is the Canadian belief in democracy, in the sense of government by the people. C. Wright Mills places the role of communications in the democratic process in perspective by portraying two extremes, a public society and a mass society.

> The public and the mass may be most readily distinguished by their dominant modes of communication: in a community of publics, discussion is the ascendant means of communication, and the mass media, if they exist, simply enlarge and animate discussion, linking one *primary public* with the discussions of another. In a mass society, the dominant type of communication is the formal media, and the publics become mere *media markets:* all those exposed to the contents of given mass media.[1]

The use of a dichotomy of extremes such as this helps to focus attention on the importance of communication flows to the democratic system. Thus, to be consistent with democratic values, the communication system in Canada must facilitate discussion. Further, the system must enable elected representatives to tap this discussion so that they can learn the opinions and wishes of their constituents.

The second value bearing on the design of the communication system is the belief in the rights of the individual. Whether the individual concern is dissatisfaction with a government service, dissatisfaction with a commercial transaction, or simply the need for further in-

---

The impetus for this research study was a suggestion by Dr. B. D. Singer.

formation, there must be an adequate system of communication. That is, there must be a system to provide the individual with information about appropriate organizational receivers; the communications system must incorporate a flow *to* the individual, and a flow *from* the individual to the receiver.

It is evident that the systems available for a two-way flow of communications must be effective on two bases: they must facilitate the aggregation of individual opinions and interests to allow governments to head in the direction desired by the people, and they must ensure the protection of individual rights by providing channels for the communication of dissatisfaction.

Problems Associated with Communication Flows

To attempt to identify possible causes of restriction of the flow of communication it is useful to consider characteristics of the receiver (the organization), and of the individual sender. The organization, be it a government body or a commercial corporation, has by the nature of its hierarchical structure two intra-organizational characteristics that potentially restrict the flow of communication. First, there is generally a complex system within the organization required to link the person receiving the communication to the person capable of taking action. The record-keeping and paper flows associated with this system make the process of communication a time-consuming activity. Secondly, this flow within the organization is impersonal: the original enquiry or complaint becomes a series of pieces of paper or verbal messages that must be handled by the standard operating procedures of the system. The objective within the organization often becomes efficient processing of paper, rather than the effective solution of the senders' enquiries and problems.

A major inhibitor of communication flow associated with the sender is the possible lack of experience, knowledge, or ability regarding the processes for "sending" an enquiry or problem. The sender may be overwhelmed by questions like: Where should I take my problem? Whom should I speak to? What are my rights? This lack of knowledge may be compounded by the sender's view of the receiver, for given the large number of agencies potentially involved in a particular problem, the sender may be confused as to where to turn. It may require considerable time, energy, and patience to find out where he should take his problem. Further, the size of the receiver seems to take the balance of power out of the hands of the sender. Thus, the perceived complexity together with lack of knowledge may lead the sender to conclude that the expected results of his communication do not warrant the effort required.

Methods of Facilitating Two-Way Flows

A considerable array of channels has developed for facilitating communication flows between individuals and organizations. One channel that has been used since the beginning of the parliamentary system in Canada is that of elected government representatives. Both in theory and in fact in a democratic society these people serve as a major channel linking individuals and government bodies. A second channel of communication that has a long history of facilitating two-way flow is news publications. In particular, "Letters to the Editor" have allowed individuals to express their interests and concerns. Within the last decade radio call-in shows have been used as vehicles for public expression. More recently, newspapers have included "action-line" columns which allow individuals to seek assistance on problems of a more specific nature than appear in the "Letters to the Editor."

Another major communications channel available in some parts of Canada is provided by government-appointed ombudsmen. Rowat reviews the growth of this channel, concluding:

> The Ombudsman is an officer of Parliament who investigates complaints from citizens that they have been unfairly dealt with by government departments and who, if he finds a complaint is justified, seeks a remedy.[2]

The earliest appointment of this type was in Sweden in the eighteenth century. In Canada, Alberta and New Brunswick had ombudsmen by 1967. Most of the other provinces have been considering establishing this type of channel and there is also consideration being given to a federal ombudsman appointment.

Another category of channel available to facilitate two-way flow is that of special agencies, both government and private. To deal with consumer problems the Federal government established an agency (Box 99) in 1968 to which consumers can mail complaints or enquiries on consumer matters and be assured of quick action.[3] (From April 1968, to December 1969, a total of 9,800 letters had been received by this agency.) Another channel established for consumers with problems is the Consumers Association of Canada. In 1970 the association had 60,000 members and was conducting a drive to double its membership.[4] Its purpose has been to serve both as a means of redress for individual problems, and as a means of bringing to the attention of government the interests of a segment of the population.

Union organizations have also served as a method for communication of individual and group interests and problems. In addition many ad hoc agencies—for example, citizens' action committees and legal aid organizations—have been formed for communication and action in particular areas.

Finally, general information services form another category of two-way communication channel. The purpose of these services ranges from telling the sender where he should take his problem, to aiding in the solution of the problem itself. Several Canadian cities, including Calgary and Toronto, have established this type of service. The Federal Government in 1970 established an agency, Information Canada, which attempts to integrate Ottawa's scattered public information services. The agency's major task will be to give people information and assistance about various government programs in such fields as social security, citizenship and farm loans. Information

Canada established plans to open regional offices and to make greater use of broadcasting and neighborhood meetings in order to get its message across to the individual.[5]

Research into Two-Way Communication

Given an appreciation of the role of two-way communication in society, the possible problems associated with these flows, and the range of means available for two-way communication, the next step in understanding this area is to assess the nature of communications in present channels. The research study reported below attempts to do this by addressing, in part, certain issues raised by Dr. B. D. Singer.

> We must find out what recurrent, everyday coping problems people have, with which information channels can help them. . . . We should find out how they solve their problems and what information sources—mass media, interpersonal relationships, etcetera—they now use, and then attempt to provide channels to fit their needs. . . . By finding out what people need and want to know about coping, we shall be able to supply the updated roadmaps of our society which we all need.[6]

The present study describes a select number of complaint/information channels used by the citizens of London, Ontario. The channels—government representatives, mass media, and special agencies—were examined to determine the volume and nature of requests flowing through them during 1969.

Research Study

Three criteria were used to select the channels to be examined. First, for each of the channels studied the *initiation of communication* had to be in the hands of the individual. This criterion was established because the study's focus was on channels that allow the individual to obtain information, voice opinion, or take action on problems. The second criterion was that the availability of the channel be of *general knowledge*: this criterion attempted to ensure that the users of the channels came from all socio-economic sectors of the population. The final objective was to obtain information on a wide cross-section of communication topics; to attain this, the channels studied had to have the potential for *differences in usage.*

Using these criteria the following channels were selected for study:

1. three levels of government—the two London members of the federal parliament, the two London members of the provincial legislature, and the municipal office of the city clerk;
2. three media channels—the "open line" program of a London radio station, CFPL, the "Letters to the Editor" column in the London *Free Press*, and the "sound-off" column, an action-line column in the same newspaper.
3. two special agencies—the London City Police Department, and the London branch of the Consumers Association of Canada.

Four characteristics of each channel were studied. First, the topics handled by each communication channel were identified: examples of such topics were the morale of the youth of today, poor automobile warranties, family allowances. Secondly, data on the annual volume by topic in each channel was obtained. Thirdly, the channel procedures were noted, that is, the method used by the sender to contact the channel (telephone, letter, and so on), and the action taken upon receipt of the communication. (The expectation was that this type of data would help to explain both the users and the usage of the channels.) The final question asked was an open-ended request for "anything else pertinent to the flow of communication through the channel." This question was asked in an attempt to understand such aspects as the potential strengths and weaknesses of the channel, the apparent accomplishments gained through the channel, and the socio-economic characteristics of the users of the channel.

To collect the necessary data, elected members of the federal and provincial governments were contacted by means of a mailed questionnaire. The call-in program and "action-line" column were studied through a personal interview with the central figure involved in each case. The "Letters to the Editor" column was studied by content analysis of all letters appearing in the 1969 issues of the newspaper. Finally, the city clerk's office and the two special agencies were examined by personal interviews.

Findings

The city of London, Ontario had a population of 200,000 in 1969. During that year Londoners registered approximately 150,000 enquiries and complaints through the channels sampled. Of the "Letters to the Editor" received by the London *Free Press*, 856 were published.[7] The action-line columnist, who requests that people write to him (as opposed to phoning or personally visiting him) received approximately 5,000 letters in 1969. It was estimated that 33,000 calls were handled by the radio call-in show. The contacts with the two federal Members of Parliament numbered approximately 5,000, the two provincial Members received 7,000,[8] and the city clerk's office registered 12,000 letters. The two special agencies, the police department and the London branch of the Consumers Association of Canada, received 84,000 and 1,300 communications respectively.

Further detail on these communications is provided in Tables I through III. An examination of these tables reveals that the 150,000 communications fell into three categories: requests for information, complaints dealing with criminal and civil offences, and a wide range of "other complaints." One-quarter of the call-in program communications (8,250) dealt with requests for information such as time checks and sports scores. All of the communications with the police department (84,000) fell into the second category. The remaining 57,000 can be categorized as "other complaints."

The content analysis of the 1969 London *Free Press* "Letters to the Editor" is presented in Table I-A. The analysis was made by first identifying the central problem area involved in each letter, and then collapsing these into more general topic areas. Of the topic areas that emerged, only 25 per cent dealt with problems outside the local community. The prevalence of local issues may be related in part to London's spatial isolation and to the character of the newspaper. The community is served by major Toronto dailies, and it is possible that they serve as the channel for complaints dealing with provincial, national or international problems.

The second mass media channel, the radio call-in show, also shows a local orientation. The most noteworthy function of the call-in show is its use as a clearing-house for community information, ranging from the time checks and sport scores mentioned earlier, to requests that information about an upcoming church supper be put on the air. Finally, the number of communications through this channel, approximately 2,700 calls per month for a four-hour morning program, was extremely high. There are several possible reasons for this: the channel is well-known; contacting the channel is extremely simple; and response to an enquiry is immediate.

The action-line column, the final media channel studied, received approximately 400 letters per month. Most of these contacts dealt with a problem specific to the person writing the letter and most of the problems concerned economic transactions. A typical problem handled was that of an individual billed for merchandise which he had returned; in spite of his efforts to rectify the situation, the company involved continued billing him. The columnist judged that one-half of the people making use of this channel had tried unsuccessfully to deal with the problem on their own before turning to the action-line column. The other half did not feel capable of handling their own problem, and had contacted this channel without first attempting to solve the problem themselves.

The communications received by the four federal and provincial Members of Parliament were very similar to those received by the action-line column, in that 80 to 90 per cent of the 12,000 communications concerned personal-economic topics. The remaining 10 to 20 per cent dealt with more general problem areas.

The final government channel studied, the city clerk's office, received 12,000 letters in 1969. Again, the topics covered were problems of a personal nature. However, the problems were specific to matters under the jurisdiction of the city like streets, drainage, and garbage collection. In addition, the city clerk's office received many requests for assistance in determining the most appropriate channel for a particular problem.

The special agencies studied, the London City Police Department and the London branch of the Consumers Association of Canada, are different not only in the nature of the problems each deals with, but in their accessibility to the public. The police department is known to everyone and the telephone number is prominently displayed in the telephone directory. On the other hand, the Consumers Association of Canada is much less well-known and the only telephone number appearing in the London Telephone Directory in 1969 was the number of the Association's head office in Ottawa.

The Consumers Association of Canada and the "action-line" column deal with similar problems, but the newspaper column received 5,000 communications in 1969 while the CAC received 1,300. There may be a number of possible reasons for this discrepancy, but that of accessibility is no doubt operative: the "action-line" column, like the police department, is well known to the citizens of London as over 90 per cent of London households receive the London *Free Press*, while the CAC is not.

Discussion

Channel Functions

Observation of the communications channels studied shows five functions being served: these were to provide information, get action, provide assistance, bring pressure to bear, and influence public opinion.

The first function, provision of information, was being

filled by two channels: the radio call-in program and the city clerk's office. The nature of the information provided ranged from the relatively trivial to directions as to the appropriate channel for solution of a particular problem.

The second function, that of getting action, was served by channels that have direct control over a potential problem area. Of the channels sampled, the police department and the city clerk's office fall into this category. For example, the police department can locate a missing child, and the city clerk's office can start action to get a clogged sewer cleared.

Provision of assistance, particularly where the individual felt incapable of dealing with the problem on his own, was a major function of the federal and provincial Members of Parliament, and also of the action-line column. These channels took responsibility for seeing the problem through to a solution. This function is probably particularly important in instances where individuals with little education have to deal with large, complex organizations.

The fourth function was served when an individual's direct negotiations to solve the problem on his own had failed, and he then turned to one of the channels in an attempt to bring pressure to bear on the organization responsible for the problem. The federal and provincial Members of Parliament received many requests of this nature, as did the action-line column and the Consumers Association.

The final function served by the channels sampled was to provide an opportunity for the individual to influence public opinion. The two channels filling this function were the "Letters to the Editor" and the radio call-in program.

Channel Procedures

The second aspect of interest in comparing the channels of communication is the procedure required to contact the channel. The two major methods used were letter and telephone. As suggested earlier, the requirement that the communication be in writing probably presents a barrier, particularly to individuals with little education. Even for those capable of letter-writing, this form of communication requires considerably more effort than does a telephone call. Letter-writing is also inappropriate when there is a need for immediate response, as may be the case in requests to channels providing information.

A final factor that may make letter-writing seem a barrier is the perceived receptiveness of the channel. It is suspected that when the communications channel itself seems impersonal and complex, letter-writing would seem even more difficult than otherwise. On the other hand, when the channel is seen as personal and receptive, as was probably the case with the action-line column, the letter requirement would probably not provide as great a barrier.

Public Awareness of the Channel

A final comparison that aids in understanding the channels is that of differences among the channels in terms of public awareness. Although this aspect was not studied directly, other aspects suggested the importance of public awareness and familiarity. This contrast was noted earlier with regard to the police department and the Consumers Association. Similarly, the 15,000 requests for information received by the radio call-in program also support this suspicion. Finally, comparison of the action-line column with the Department of Consumer and Corporate Affairs complaint department, "Box 99," leads to a similar conclusion. Whereas the action-line column has continuous public exposure, the public awareness of "Box 99" appears to be much less general: during 1969, the third year for the action-line column, 5,000 communications were received from people in the city of London. On the other hand, 1969 was the second year for "Box 99," and with complaints coming from *all parts of Canada* a total of 6,683 were received.

Conclusions

Given the importance ascribed to two-way flows of communication in Canadian society, this study has attempted to aid in the understanding of a present set of communication channels. The discussion above considers three aspects of communication channels that would be important when developing further channels of complaint and enquiry. The first aspect considered was the *functions* which the channels filled; these functions were to provide information, get action, provide assistance, bring pressure to bear, and to facilitate public expression.

The second aspect, method of contact, was considered in terms of the function being filled. That is, if the function being filled is to provide assistance, the method required to contact the channel should be as simple as possible. Hence, the use of the telephone as opposed to letter-writing seems appropriate. Further, if the function is to provide information, the immediacy of the need may necessitate the use of the telephone.

The final aspect observed was differences in public awareness of the various channels. Since well-known channels receive greatest use, an important consideration in the development of future channels would be the early and extensive publication of their availability.

With these three aspects in mind the next step towards the understanding and improvement of communications channels is to assess the adequacies of present channels. That is, while this study attempts to determine the activities occurring in a limited sample of channels, a companion study to determine the strengths and weaknesses as seen by the potential users of the channels is required before a desirable model can be developed for future information and complaint channels.[9]

1. C. W. Mills, *The Power Elite* (New York: Oxford University Press, 1959), p. 304.
2. D. C. Rowat, *The Ombudsman* (Toronto: University of Toronto Press, 1968), p. 7.
3. "Box 99 for Consumers" in Department of Consumer and Corporate Affairs *Press Release*, 9 April 1968.
4. *Globe and Mail*, 23 September 1970, page 12.
5. *Globe and Mail*, 21 March 1970.

6. Benjamin D. Singer, "Access to Information: A Position Paper on Communication Channels and Social Change," Telecommunication Seminar, Canadian Department of Communication, Carleton University, May 16, 1970.
7. It was estimated that nine out of every ten letters received were published in the newspaper.
8. These figures were estimated by the elected Members, since accurate record was not kept.
9. For a further discussion outlining such research, see Singer, op. cit.

Table I-A MASS MEDIA CHANNELS

Letters To The Editor: Content analysis of 1969 issues of the London *Free Press.*

Topic Area	*Letters in 1969*	
	Number	*Per cent*
1. International	31	4
2. National	90	11
—Cost of living[1]		
—Federalism		
—CBC		
—Government/Economy		
3. Provincial	65	8
—Crime/Justice		
—Social Welfare		
—Ontario Health Insurance		
4. Municipal	249	29
—City council		
—Civic spirit		
—London Little Theatre		
—Police		
—London Free Press		
—Local radio stations		
—Education		
5. Minority Groups	102	12
—Indians		
—Negroes		
—Labour		
—Farmers		
—Women's Rights		
—Youth/Students/Hippies		

6. Religion/Morals	90	10
7. Animals	46	5
8. Pollution	18	2
9. Personal	72	8
10. Other	93	11
TOTAL	856	100

[1]The subtopics listed indicate major content areas.

Table I-B MASS MEDIA CHANNELS

Radio Call-in Show: "Open Line"[1]
Form of communication received by the channel: telephone calls
Volume of communication received: 2,700 calls per month[2]

Topic Area[3]	*Per cent of Calls*
1. Open line discussion of: —federal and provincial legislation —elections —war in VietNam —shoplifters —vagrancy/hippies —garbage collection —Humane Society —Ontario health insurance	54
2. Information —public service requests —requests for sport scores —time checks	25
3. Lost and Found	10
4. Crank calls screened out	11
TOTAL	100

[1]At the time of the study, "Open Line" was the call-in show on CFPL, London. According to Bureau of Broadcast measurement ratings it was the most popular of three such shows available in the London area.
[2]Based on analysis done by the radio station.
[3]Estimated by the hosts of the call-in show.

Table I-C MASS MEDIA CHANNELS

Newspaper Action-Line Column: "Sound-Off"[1]

Form of communication received by the channel: letter
Volume of communication received: 100 per week[2]

Topic Areas[2]

1. Problems with payment of insurance claims.
2. Landlord-tenant problems.
3. Dissatisfaction with volume billing, particularly book clubs, record clubs, etcetera.
4. Problems with automobile warranties.
5. Problems with government agencies: pensions, unemployment insurance, etcetera.

[1]At the time of the study "Sound-Off" was an action-line column appearing in the London *Free Press*.
[2]Estimated by the action-line columnist.

Table II-A GOVERNMENT CHANNELS

Federal Members of Parliament[1]

Form of communication received by the channel: telephone and letter
Volume of communication received: 2,000 per year per Member[2]

Topic Area[2]	*Per cent of Total*
1. Seeking assistance for personal-economic problems	90
—family allowance	
—old age security	
—unemployment insurance	
—veteran's allowance	
2. Other	10
—recognition of the Vatican	
—seal slaughter	
—Saturday mail delivery	

—amendments to criminal code
—tax reform
—Nigeria-Biafra

TOTAL	100

[1]The two Members of Parliament for London were contacted.
[2]Estimated by Members of Parliament.

Table II-B GOVERNMENT CHANNELS

Provincial Members of Parliament[1]
Form of communication received by the channel: telephone, letter and walk-in clinic[2]

Volume and Topic Areas[3]

1. Letters .... 10 per day per member
   —80 per cent personal problems
   —20 per cent other: laws, taxes, schools, medicine
2. Telephone .... 15 calls per day per member
   —mainly personal problems such as old age pensions, etc.
3. Clinic .... 15 calls per week
   —mainly personal

Municipal: City Clerk's Office
Form of communication received by the channel: letter
Total number of letters registered in 1969: 12,000

Topic Areas: Animals, weeds, streets, pollution, assessment, drainage.[4]

[1]The two provincial Members were contacted, but data was received from only one.
[2]One Member of Parliament was available for discussions with local constituents each Saturday morning at the London YMCA.
[3]Estimated by Member of Parliament.
[4]In addition to dealing with many of the problems directly, the city clerk's office redirected communications to the appropriate receiver.

Table III SPECIAL AGENCIES

London City Police Department

Form of communication received by the channel: telephone calls

Volume of communication received: 84,000 calls in 1969[1]

Topic Areas[1]

—property damage
—parking offences
—suspicious persons
—missing persons
—murder
—break and entry
—fraud

Consumers Association of Canada, London Branch

Form of communication received by the channel: telephone calls

Volume of communication received: 25 calls per week[2]

Topic Area

—primarily deal with dissatisfaction with purchases.

[1]Based on police records.
[2]Estimated by the London complaint chairman.

Citizens Communications in Canada

SANDRA GWYN

One of the most significant developments in Canadian communications in the 1970s has been the emergence of a nationwide movement towards citizens communications. Probably the best and certainly the easiest description of the movement defines citizens communications as being made up of people, as individuals or groups, using a broad range of communication techniques, especially film, videotape, cable television, and radio broadcasting, to communicate directly with other people, with institutions, or with governments.

Directly is the operative word. If citizens communications have a central tenet, it is that the traditional "gatekeepers" of communications flow—established media, such as mass-circulation newspapers and magazines or radio and television networks, and established media practitioners, such as journalists, editors, producers, and technicians—are bypassed. Instead, the average individual makes direct use of communication techniques for him or herself. Practical examples of citizens communications are:

—an Innuit village operating its own community radio station;

—a low-income tenants organization recording its own protest demonstration using a handheld videotape camera;

—a cable television program produced for, by, and about senior citizens;

—an anti-highrise community group making a video presentation to municipal officials, instead of preparing a written brief.

At its simplest level, the movement is the direct result of improved communications technology which has opened up a whole new range of communications options to the public at large. Ten years ago, the technology of television was so complex that only highly professional producers, writers, cameramen, and light and sound men could produce programs, and they had to be employed by large organizations. But the handheld video camera which appeared in 1968 is so easy to operate that almost anyone can learn to shoot a passable production in a matter of hours. These amateur productions can be distributed to the public over the local channels of cable television systems, whereas a decade ago the only systems of distribution were the closed-shop public and private networks. As a spinoff, the surge of interest in VTR and cable television has sparked a rediscovery of a range of other systems, among them film, radio broadcasting, radiotelephone networks, and 35 mm slides.

At a more complex level, the citizens communications movement can be seen as a direct expression of the nature of Canadian society in the 1970s. The technological pluralism that gave rise to the movement coincides with Canada's increasing social, cultural, and political pluralism. Communications have always been central to the Canadian mystique, from Harold Innis and Marshall McLuhan to the innovations of Expo and Labyrinth to becoming a world leader in cable television. As Neil Compton has written, "Fate seems to have destined this country to be a textbook example of the way in which a society and its culture can be shaped by the pressure and pull of communications media."[1] To some observers, the movement appears to be a marriage between "the medium is the message" concept and the National Film Board's proud tradition of social documentary. In fact, through its Challenge for Change/Société-Nouvelle programs established in the late sixties to experiment with media as agents of social change, the NFB has been the principal catalyst for citizens communications.

Community Development and Citizen Advocacy Through VTR and Film

The content of citizens communications is as varied as its

forms. Among other things, it includes community development, citizen advocacy, self expression, aesthetic exploration, and simple entertainment. These categories cannot be applied rigidly, for the aims, methods, and clientele of individual groups using media nearly always overlap.

The concepts of community development and citizen advocacy are the most important aspects of citizens communications and the ones on which considerable international attention has been focused. In this mode, social animators and group leaders use film and videotape cameras as tools for social change. Usually known as the "Fogo Process" after the island off the northeast coast of Newfoundland where it was first applied, the technique hinges on the discovery, made almost by chance, that under certain conditions the filming/taping/playback process can have profound effects on the human psyche. No formal evaluation of these effects has yet been undertaken, but an excellent theoretical explanation has been provided by Dr. Anthony Marcus, a psychiatrist at the University of British Columbia who has used VTR extensively in forensic therapy:

> Confronting himself on camera gradually helps a person develop an internal image of himself. External mirroring by verbal means often creates barriers, regardless of the leader's skill. Most individuals have difficulty communicating their emotional "hang-ups", but videotaping and the playback evoke a response on the emotional level. The simple device of reflecting an image magnifies the individual's self-image. The emotional dilemma induced by the gap between the image on the screen and the subjective feeling of the viewers, produces a crisis in which the person attempts to bring the two aspects into harmony, thus increasing his self-knowledge. He cannot remain aloof to himself and he is caught in the conflict between actual conduct and inner fearfulness.
>
> Videotaping pinpoints the failure of the individual to recognize his own problems and difficulties. The end result is that he confronts himself, remaining at the same time less defensive than when someone else confronts him. Video enables an individual to watch specifically for *himself*, a rever-

> sal of the normal group situation where it is the leader who is expected to act as catalyst most of the time. The camera becomes catalytic, eliminating the personal battle between leader and participant. As the group helps people to emerge as social beings, the videotape assists them to see themselves as others see them.[2]

This interpretation is well illustrated in practice in a report made by a field worker of the Extension Service of Memorial University of Newfoundland:

> The people in Deep Bay wanted to organize a local Improvement Committee, but no one was willing to stand up and speak. So they invited me to organize a five-night workshop on public speaking, and I brought along VTR equipment. The first night, only five people would stand up and say as much as, "I'm John Jones from Deep Bay." I played the tape back, and I think a lot of people were ashamed to see themselves sitting there, not saying anything. The reaction was, "If *he* can do it, *I* can." At the end of the third meeting, the last people got up and spoke. At the fifth session, we organized a mock meeting. The person who'd been the last to stand up and say his name was the one who offered to be chairman.[3]

Crucial to the Fogo Process is the fact that individuals, rather than outside animators, control the pace and direction of change. A first principle is that everyone interviewed has the right to edit his or her remarks before the tape or film is shown to anyone else. In practice the technique usually accelerates change, partly because it creates a sense of excitement and urgency, partly because it tends to neutralize inter- and intra-community hostilities.

The experiment on Fogo Island was launched in 1967 as a joint project of the newly-formed Challenge for Change unit of the National Film Board and the Extension Service of Memorial University of Newfoundland. Their aim was to explore whether and how the media, in this case 16 mm film, could be used to foster community development. Fogo Island was chosen because it represented most of the basic problems of rural Newfoundland, and, by extension, the problems of most small, isolated, rural communities. Lying ten miles off the northeast coast, Fogo is isolated from without. Fogo is also as seriously isolated *within* itself. Only four thousand people live on the island, but they live estranged from one another in ten sparse settlements. In every village each religious domination maintained its own one- or two-room school. Communications between communities were so poor that a child could grow up without visiting a village five miles away. The decline of the inshore fishery put 60 per cent of the fishermen on welfare. Only one community had local government; there were no active unions or co-operatives. A single future remained for the islanders: resettlement at the government's discretion.

The original mandate of the Memorial-Film Board team had been to make a film or series of films about the resettlement program. Although they intended to involve the islanders in choosing topics and locations, they expected to use a standard social documentary approach, centring filming and editing around specific issues. But as the project developed, this method changed radically. The team discovered that islanders were more open when short "vertical" films were made, each one the record of a single interview or occasion. Instead of being interwoven and intercut, these interviews were left virtually intact. As one team member later explained, "We discovered that if you intercut interviews on the basis of issues, what you nearly always get is one person who is all wrong, one person who is partly right, and a third person who is entirely right. He then becomes the 'smart guy' who puts the others down. This putting down can harm the individual within the community."[4]

The final result was twenty-eight short films totalling six hours. Each film centred around a personality or an event rather than an issue; each expressed an aspect of life on Fogo. "We let the co-operatives we had here before perish in our midst," said fisherman Andrew Brett. "We know we are not educated and we kept our tongues still. We should never do that." Of the prospect of resettlement, another fisherman said, "I've lived in towns and cities, but I don't want to move. I'd miss the sea."

Far more important than the actual content of the films, however, was the process of screening them. Group viewings were organized all over the island. Opposing factions within the communities were given the opportunity to examine each other's views without direct confrontation or hostility. The team was amazed to discover that people who would never have considered standing up and expressing their views at a public meeting were quite prepared to attend such a screening and watch themselves expressing precisely those views. By looking at each other and themselves, Fogo Islanders began to recognize their common problems. As important, they became conscious of their identity as Fogo Islanders, and they discovered that preserving the Fogo community mattered to nearly all of them.

Eventually, with the islanders' permission, the decision was taken to present this new consensus to politicians and civil servants by showing them the films. The impact was remarkable. As one film board official later explained, "We finally had fishermen talking to cabinet ministers. If you take fishermen to cabinet, they won't talk about the problems of their lives the way they will among other fishermen. But if you let government people look at films of fishermen talking together, the message comes through."[5] After the screenings, the comments of several ministers were recorded on videotape and played back on Fogo.

Without any formal evaluation it is difficult to determine exactly how much influence the filming process had on the subsequent development of Fogo Island. It is, however, evident that the cameras catalyzed a latent and inarticulated desire for change. At the same time, the filming-screening process opened new channels of communication between individuals, between communities, and between Fogo Islanders and decision-makers. The result of this improved communication has been visible change. Fogo boasts a new regional high school and the first successful fishing and shipbuilding co-operatives ever established in rural Newfoundland.

Although the Fogo experiment remains the most dramatic example of media used to effect social change, the technique has subsequently been applied with varying degrees of success in other parts of the country and in the United States. The Extension Service of Memorial University has developed a use of film and videotape that is almost certainly the most sophisticated and fully realized in the world. Audio-visual technology is an integral part of nearly all its social development projects in Newfoundland. Portable VTR units are standard equipment for each of the service's dozen fieldworkers, and they use them for everything from introducing themselves to a new community ("Come and see yourself on TV!" is an unfailing way to attract a crowd) to putting together Eskimo language news broadcasts for screening in the church halls of northern Labrador. Central to Extension's success is the fact that the media has not been treated as an entity in itself, but as one element of regular community development work. "We don't think of ourselves as media people, or experts in communications," the head of Extension's Social Development Branch explained. "Our main function is adult education; we help people exchange information and pass it along. VTR and film are practical and efficient means of handling information."[6] Another reason for success is that nearly all Extension's work with media has taken place in rural Newfoundland, a cohesive society where most people share a common culture and where, even now, outside influences remain relatively few.

Since 1967, the other partner in the Fogo experiment, The Challenge for Change Unit of the National Film Board, and its French counterpart, Société-Nouvelle, have taken an entirely different tack. Instead of developing a centralized approach, Challenge for Change/Société-Nouvelle have functioned more as "media midwives." Launched in the mid-sixties to encourage social change and community development through media techniques, Challenge for Change/Société-Nouvelle were put on a firm footing ($1.8

million annually) in 1970 on a five-year experimental basis that was to end April 1, 1975. Each of eight federal departments (Labour, Regional Economic Expansion, National Health and Welfare, Secretary of State, Communications, Manpower, Agriculture, Central Mortgage and Housing Corporation) contributes $100,000 annually to the programs. The balance has been supplied by the National Film Board.

From 1967 to 1972 Challenge for Change/Société-Nouvelle sponsored approximately twenty experimental film and VTR projects across the country, usually in cooperation with a local educational institution or citizens group. For example, in Rosedale, Alberta, a village in the Drumheller Valley where villagers, mostly retired coal miners, struggled along on low pensions without benefit of local government, sewers, water, or gas, it was discovered that VTR could be used effectively as a means of quickly organizing the community.

Unlike the Fogo experience where a new consensus was arrived at only after a long period of time, the Rosedale experiment took the form of a "video blitz" conducted with the Department of Continuing Education at the University of Calgary. A local group, working with a social animator, barnstormed the community with VTR equipment to pose a series of searching questions to everyone they encountered. Even more so than on Fogo, it was the process rather than the product that was important. The edited tapes were not shown to decision-makers outside the community; instead, they appeared to help the people who made them develop enough self-confidence to approach the decision-makers themselves.

Similarly, in an experiment sponsored jointly by Challenge for Change and the University of Saskatchewan in Moose Jaw, Saskatchewan, VTR helped restore a measure of identity to a community that appeared to have lost it. Here, the visible result has been the establishment of a stable community television organization.

The most imaginative variant on the Fogo technique has been developed in northeastern New Brunswick under the auspices of Société-Nouvelle. In this case, a film-maker/animator worked with the citizens of two small, depressed communities to make a feature film. "The purpose," the animator reported, "was not so much to do a patchup job on an existing social situation as to dig deeper to underlying values." He outlined the process:

> I just sat and talked and asked questions, and directed the conversation in some ways, always trying to get back to the same basic themes: the feeling of being impotent and the feeling that they could never take any initiative. They were humiliated by welfare assistance, they knew that even welfare was politicized. It always came back to these things. Sometimes I tried to get them onto themes that interested me, like, "Why the hell do you want to live here in all this misery?" They would say a few words but then they would go back to their own stories. So after a few weeks it was obvious to me that they had really built a story without knowing it, by telling me precise incidents.[7]

The final result was a fifty-minute film, *Le noce est pas finie.* Its theme is the manipulation of people by social and political forces they cannot control. Yet there is an inherent hope for something better. "I have lived all my life in fear," says one of the central characters in lines she improvised herself, "but I am growing old and I don't want to do that any more. We can't go back along the same paths. We must find new solutions." After screening throughout the region, Société-Nouvelle evaluated the effects of the film: In general, the people who recognized themselves in the film saw it as an expression of what they are: victims, sometimes innocent victims. But with reflection and discussion, they admitted their own complicity. "We have to change not only governments, but ourselves as well." The film, it seems, helped them look at responsibilities, priorities, and participation.

A second feature film, *Un soleil pas comme ailleurs,* was made in the same region the following year. In this case, socio-drama was carried one step further—the people acted out possible futures for the region, including the development of collective farms and co-operatives.

It is interesting to note that film, rather than the cheaper, quicker, and simpler technology of videotape, was used for both New Brunswick projects. The reason for this is that although VTR deals well with immediate issues and is a device for organizing groups, film often appears to work more successfully in situations that involve subtle cognitive or attitudinal changes. The immediacy of tape, its built-in instant-playback capability, can work against the slow process of consensus-building. On the other hand, film demands professionalism and film has a mystique. Community workers have found that this mystique can be an important element in the process of social change, for it creates a sense of excitement within a community and forces a planning process that clarifies issues. Also, the "visual briefs" that frequently result from media projects have more impact on decision-makers as a film presentation than as a trembling videotape on a tiny monitor. At Skyriver, Alaska, for example, a project for Alaskan Eskimos was developed on the model of Memorial University's Extension Service operations. The usual practice has been to use VTR to achieve consensus on an issue, and then to illustrate and define the consensus with a film presentation.

While a number of attempts have been made to adapt the Fogo technique for use in urban centres, only a few can be described as having been anything more than marginally successful. The reasons why are not difficult to find: in urban centres, where citizens are bombarded daily by the mass media, the impact of a carefully orchestrated film or VTR program is appreciably less than on, say, Fogo Island, where the filming/screening process can become a kind of community focal point. Also, in rural areas there are frequently entrenched taboos against face-to-face public debate which the cameras can help overcome by providing alternate means of communication.

However, the Fogo technique was successful at the Parallel Institute in Montreal. Founded in 1970, this organization provides technical and information services to citizens groups in a low-income district of the city and to the

Greater Montreal Anti-Poverty Co-ordinating Committee, which comprises sixteen welfare rights groups. Parallel uses VTR as an organizing tool, as a negotiating tool, as a recording secretary for meetings, and for training. One staff member has outlined Parallel's philosophy:

> Video helps to equalize the bargaining power of poor people when they confront welfare and government officials. The head of the welfare office, for instance, is going to be much more careful of what he says if there is all that shiny hardware along. Or the camera can be the place where officials direct their antagonism first. They're likely to say, "Get that camera out of here!" rather than, "Get those people out of here!"
>
> For once, the people have a means of controlling records of their own experiences. Tapes are also shown to people who are not yet involved in citizens groups to show them the confrontations of the groups. They get excited when they see other people taking on the welfare office and discover that they don't have to be afraid of the police coming and beating them up.[8]

It is important to recognize that the use of media to effect social change involves a number of dangers. The most obvious is that of raising expectations that cannot be fulfilled. Another is best described as the "media-freak syndrome." Communications hardware holds fatal fascination for some groups that become obsessed with form at the expense of content and with medium at the expense of message. At the same time as they strengthen personal identity, film and videotape also strengthen ego, and the goal of community development can be lost in a rush to make personal rather than collective statements. On Fogo Island five years after the original experiment, a serious problem developed in that some of the community leaders who emerged through the filming process proved to lack the organizational and managerial skills needed to keep the co-operative movement going over the long term. Only as a result of the strength and determination of the rank-and-file has the movement endured.

Crucial to the technique, therefore, is the skill and sensitivity of the animator. Probably the best explanation of his or her role was given by one of the participants at the 1972 Seminar on Film, Videotape, and Social Change:

> There are stages that are very important. I find it useful to remind myself that in terms of determining what choices or action a group might take, I want to be fully involved in making sure that people see what choices are open to them. In terms of what choices they *make*, that is entirely their business. As an organizer, as somebody working outside, I refuse to be involved in that decision.
>
> In terms of implementing that decision, of taking the action, I want again to be central to the strategy and tactics that they will use. It's very important to remember that the organizer—or the developer, or the social animator—has to be working through various choices and the implications of those choices. At the point of deciding what the action will be, the organizer has to be very careful he's not involved in that process. People must make the decision. The organizer moves in again to build the kind of competence, to make sure that the action, once decided upon by the people, is as effective as possible.[9]

CATV Programming

The rapid growth of cable television systems has catalyzed the citizens communications movement almost as much as videotape recording. Cable currently reaches into about one out of three Canadian households, and the number of subscribers is increasing at the rate of about 25 per cent a year. Thanks to the CRTC's ruling that any system with more than 3,000 subscribers must provide a channel for community programming, cable has also been established as an important distribution system for citizens communications. For many groups, the community cable channel is the cheapest and easiest means of gaining access to the media. At least one educational institution, Seneca College in Toronto, already offers a course in how to develop program material.

However, despite its potential, community cable programming has so far been something of a disappointment.

Two ambitious community projects which were spearheads for the entire movement—Project Intercom in Toronto, and Town Talk in Thunder Bay—collapsed before getting off the ground. Each fell victim to overdoses of rhetoric and a high degree of politicization among members, and each lacked broad-based community support.

One specific problem in cable programming is the uneasy relationship between the cable operator and the programming group. The cable operator frequently tends to look on community programming as a necessary evil, part of the price to be paid for a licence. Because he is liable for any actions of libel and slander under the terms of the Broadcasting Act, he frequently insists on full editorial control.

There are other problems, as well: many groups have discovered that producing effective program material requires an investment of time and energy that is out of proportion to the number of viewers they can hope to attract; moreover, cable programming may not really suit their purposes. Sitting alone in a living room watching a small screen can isolate viewers more than it brings them together. As several groups have discovered, tapes and films made by a community are often more effective when shown in church basements or village halls.

Finally, cable programming has yet to involve the broad social spectrum. "The notion that cable is Everyman's medium," concludes a study of programming undertaken in London, Ontario, "is at the least not justified by the data. Individuals who use the medium are generally middle-class professionals and individuals who have experience with other participatory channels, and often with other media."[10]

Even so, there are a few instances in which community cable programming has lived up to its advance notices. Almost always these are in areas which are poorly served by local media and which have a distinct degree of community consciousness. In metropolitan areas, community programming has to compete with the established and professional mass media. Also, metropolitan CATV systems frequently serve arbitrarily carved-up hunks of a city, rather than well-defined neighbourhoods.

Télévision Communautaire St. Félicien, in the Lac St. Jean area of Quebec, is the most dramatic case in point. Community television was launched here in 1970 as a joint project between Société-Nouvelle and the District School Commission. Three villages were involved within a ten-mile radius, each having a separate cable system. The experiment began with a five-day "media blitz" organized by animators provided by Société-Nouvelle. During this period, a total of forty people took an active part in producing three hours of programming nightly. Most recently, each system has produced about one or two hours nightly. The content ranges from regular coverage of local events and municipal council meetings (often with phone-in feedback) to news programs and documentaries.

In the beginning, most programming copied standard television formats, but gradually citizens began to adapt these to the realities of their own communities. As one of the project animators has explained:

> A girl who worked in a local bank offered to help write the local news program. It came out that she also wrote poetry. No one in Normandin knew that this girl was a poet. People thought that poets were quite bizarre. Then she read some of her poetry on the program, and people changed their minds about what a poet was. This led to a whole series about creativity, through which we were able to give a new value to the idea of the artist in a small community.

Another program concept developed was that of the group reading:

> We would transcribe a CBC broadcast on, say, agriculture, and play it for the group a couple of evenings later. Some would have seen it before, some not. In any case, seeing a broadcast passively in your living room is not the same as seeing it with a group of people. Afterward, the group would talk about the broadcast: What is that saying to us? We'd tape the discussion and play it over the community channel a few days later.

According to an evaluation of the project undertaken by

the Quebec Department of Education, about 20 per cent of the citizens in the area watch community television regularly. About 70 per cent watch "from time to time." As for direct participation, about 13 per cent of the people in the region have taken part in production: 31.4 per cent of these gave "novelty of experience" as their motive; 28.6 per cent were interested in getting experience in using the equipment; 14.2 per cent saw it as a way to meet people; the balance saw it either as a means of improving the community (8.6 per cent), a leisuretime activity (8.6 per cent) or as the first step in a TV career (8.6 per cent).

Another cable development pioneered in Quebec is that of "demand viewing." This was effected through the *Selectovision* project, organized in late 1972 by *Vidéographe*, a Montreal-based media resource and research centre, in co-operation with cable systems in Beloeil, Mont Laurier, and Pointe Gatineau. The administrators have outlined the project:

> Selectovision is in principle a simple idea. You use one channel for an animator and you free up at least one channel to broadcast tapes. Cable subscribers get a notice in the mail, announcing the experiment and containing a flyer with a list of tapes and a brief description of each. During the experiment, Selectovision broadcasts 10 to 12 hours a day, for 10 days.
>
> Behind the animator on the first channel is a large board. Subscribers phone in to the animator, and he writes their requests on the board. When it is finished, the animator checks the board to see which tape is most in demand—and that goes on the second channel. While the second tape is playing, people call in and give commentary on the first one. There might be quite a discussion. And of course, there are new requests coming in to be added to the scoreboard.

One result of this experiment was to give added weight to the argument that community programming is most effective in rural areas. For example, in Mont Laurier, a community 150 miles from Montreal, calls averaged about 372 daily. In Beloeil and Pointe Gatineau, suburbs of Montreal and Ottawa with cable populations about three times as great, calls averaged 320 to 342 respectively.

In urban centres, cable programming tends to be most successful when directed towards specific minority groups for whom the cable channel operates as a kind of closed-circuit information system, rather than directed at the community as a whole. Among the most notable examples are "Hellenic Mirror" produced for, by, and about the Greek community in Vancouver, and "Coming of Age" designed by the Ottawa Senior Citizens Council Broadcasting Committee as a "citywide tea social cum public platform for people over 65."

Community Radio

Recent interest in community radio has come about as a by-product of cable and VTR technology. Groups working with VTR and cable find themselves turning increasingly to radio. The reasons why are not difficult to find: radio is cheaper, easier, and more flexible.

In general, community radio involves a non-commercial, non-profit operation controlled by the community, usually by means of a group or board of directors representing different interests. As in the case of cable, programming can take virtually any form: documentaries, special interest programs for native and ethnic groups, drama productions, investigative community journalism, hot-line and disc-jockey shows.

But it is important to make a distinction between community radio in urban centres and in rural areas, particularly in northern and remote areas. In cities, community radio constitutes an alternative to existing broadcasting systems; in the hinterland it is usually the first and only system. The main development for community radio has been in the hinterland, particularly among native groups. Ten stations in Northern and mid-Canada currently hold community licences, the two most recent being at Baker Lake in the Keewatin and at Big Trout Lake in Ontario. Both these stations were established in 1973 expressly to provide a voice to native communities. In addition, a number of native communications groups, notably the Alberta Native Communications Society and the Indian News Media, produce programming regularly for broadcast over CBC and private stations.

In southern urban Canada, only one fully-fledged community station exists so far—Wired World in Kitchener-Waterloo, Ontario. The group behind this station coalesced round the local university station and, after a short and somewhat unsatisfactory detour into CATV production, began preparing weekly program packages for a local private radio station. In September 1973, Wired World received an FM licence to operate its own station and began programming in March 1974, eight hours a day. Much of this programming fills the gap created by the absence of a local CBC outlet in the area.

The growing number of other community radio groups get their message on the air through a variety of means: Neighbourhood Radio in Vancouver prepares program material regularly for CBC Vancouver; Teled Media in Halifax has prepared packages for a local commercial station. In 1973, Teled also sponsored a community contest, "Listen to the Sounds," in which people eighteen years or under were invited to submit their own programs. First prize went to a twelve-year-old girl for a series of man-in-the-street interviews on pollution.

Radio Centreville in Montreal, a group set up primarily to serve inner-city ethnic communities, broadcasts six hours daily, five days a week, on the audio channel of a local CATV system, and also via Radio McGill. At Espanola, Ontario, the CBC has experimented, on the whole successfully, with developing a community station round one of its low-power relay transmitters (LPRT) that are used to carry network programming to remote communities.

The real significance of all these groups is that they are the first of a new breed of radio stations that plan to serve cities, or sub-groups within cities, on the basis of programming made almost exclusively within those communities themselves. Just how viable these stations will prove to be in terms of audience response as well as finances is not known. However, this type of station has been successful in Britain where the BBC, long one of the most centralized broadcasting systems in the world, has developed over the past five years a network of local stations broadcasting mostly talk, such as phone-in programs, discussions, and educational material. There are at present twenty such stations and a typical example, Radio Sheffield, broadcasts six hours a day and attracts about 20 per cent of the local audience.

Community Media Resource Centres

A natural result of the interest in citizen communications has been the emergence of a number of community media resource centres designed to provide advice, expertise, and technical facilities to all groups that want to use the media. The most fully developed centres are Metro Media in Vancouver, Teled Media Services in Halifax, and Vidéographe in Montreal.

Metro Media was founded in 1971 through a merger of Intermedia, a co-operative artists workshop experimenting with media techniques, and the Inner City Service Project, a group that had been using VTR for community development purposes. Most of Metro Media's activity, in a city which is 80 per cent cabled, has been directed to helping various groups prepare program material for cablecast. The emphasis has been on programming for special interest and neighbourhood organizations. Another concern has been the preparation of educational tapes for organizations such as the Vancouver Day Care Centre Workers Training Program and for the People's Law School.

Although originally designed as a community programming production service, Teled Media has become increasingly oriented towards systems which are readily available, easy to use, and inexpensive—radio, 35 mm slides, posters, and newsletters. Interestingly, Teled has also developed a point system to measure the priorities of groups asking to use its facilities. Points are awarded according to the nature and size of the group involved, the amount of notice given, and the purpose for which equipment is requested. For example, a citizens action group, with more than twenty-four members, wishing to document their own protest march, and requesting equipment a week in advance, would get top priority. In the first year of operation about seventy-five individual groups borrowed Teled equipment or asked its advice more than 1000 times.

Despite their considerable achievements, by 1974 some doubt arose as to the longterm future of Teled and Metro Media. Neither organization had an assured base of funding. Each struggled to get by on an uncertain system of grants through Local Initiative and Opportunities for Youth Programs, research contracts with various federal and provincial agencies, and some local support. Further, as more and more community groups integrated media into their activities and purchased their own equipment, there appeared to be less need for resource centres.

Such constraints, however, do not apply to Vidéographe, a Montreal-based centre funded by the Quebec Government. Vidéographe is less concerned with community development and animation than with developing the full potential of a single medium, half-inch videotape for self expression. To achieve this objective, Vidéographe can draw on the best equipment bank of any media group in the country. A staff of seven operate out of a storefront centre in downtown Montreal with facilities which include highly-sophisticated editing equipment, half a dozen monitors, and a 115-seat theatre-in-the-round. The centre is open twenty-four hours a day; passersby are welcome to come in without charge to edit their own tapes, or to look at those in Vidéographe's library.

The facilities of Vidéographe are also available to groups and individuals who have a clear idea of what they would like to say via VTR and of the audience they want to reach. The staff considers requests; authors of approved projects get a production budget and technical assistance in producing tapes or "videogrammes." These videogrammes strike a rough balance between aesthetic exploration of media and socio-economic documentaries. All videogrammes are made available to a mailing list of over a thousand groups. Those interested in obtaining a particular production simply send in a blank tape which is dubbed and returned free of charge. Vidéographe has also concentrated applied research into editing videotape and has prepared a useful handbook on the subject, which is available to groups on request.

A number of Canadian educational institutions also function as resource centres for citizen communications. These include the Extension Service of Memorial University of Newfoundland, Xavier College in Sydney, Dawson College in Montreal, and Algonquin College in Ottawa. In northern New Brunswick, the College of Bathurst has been instrumental in developing Télé-Publik, a project through which programs with a community development orientation are aired over a local television station. In the West, the Extension Department of the University of Saskatchewan and the Division of Continuing Education and School of Social Welfare at the University of Calgary have each co-sponsored community media projects with Challenge for Change. In general, however, educational institutions have been surprisingly unreceptive to citizens communications. Groups using media frequently complain that although schools, community colleges, and universities have invested heavily in communications hardware, it is not fully used and is rarely shared with the community as a whole.

Outlook

By 1974 it seemed clear that the early pioneering days of citizens communications were over and that the movement had entered a second, less frenetic stage of consolidation and orderly development. The progress of a group like Wired World is a good symbol of the transition: a handful of eager university students running around with handheld VTR cameras developed into a broadly-based community group with enough financing and credibility to secure its own FM licence and to broadcast eight hours daily. It may be true that for every Wired World there were perhaps half a dozen groups that started out as hopefully but that over the long haul lacked the drive and stamina to endure. But this does not negate their value as social trailblazers.

For its part, by 1974 the Challenge for Change program has set aside its role as media midwife for that of earth mother nurturing a corps of full-time media counsellors in strategic locations across the country. Instead of the media blitz approach of the early seventies, these counsellors were emphasizing long-range projects. In Surrey, B.C., for example, one counsellor was using film and VTR to encourage people to participate in a community land-use project. It was a measure of the new mood that, instead of using rhetoric about "demystifying the media" and "process not product," he described the program as "a very conservative notion; getting people to depend on themselves rather than depending on remote governments to make all the decisions."

More than ever, money remained a major constraint because by 1974 the federal Opportunities for Youth and Local Initiatives Programs, which had made it possible for as many as two-thirds of all media groups to come into being, were being phased down. (A rough estimate is that about 90 per cent of all citizens communications activity is funded, directly or indirectly, out of public coffers. In 1973 a federal Task Force recommended a special funding program for citizens communications, but at the time of writing this appeared to be still some way away.)

Yet, money or no, there was little doubt that in one form or another, the citizens communications movement would survive. Though there are flaws in the record— the vast potential of cable television, for example, has yet to be successfully explored—these are far outweighed by the achievements, most notably, the establishment of an effective new technique for community development throughout the world. Most important of all, the citizens communications movement has proven that communications media, once the sole preserve of a professional élite can be used, to borrow Ivan Illich's phrase, as "tools of conviviality." Tools, in other words, "which give each person who uses them the greatest opportunity to enrich the environment with the fruits of his or her vision."

1. Neil Compton, "In Defence of Canadian Culture," in Norman Penlington (ed.), *On Canada, Essays in Honour of Frank Underhill* (Toronto: University of Toronto Press, 1971), p. 102.
2. Anthony Marcus, *Nothing Is My Number* (Toronto: General Publishing, 1971).
3. Sandra Gwyn, *Cinema as Catalyst*, Report of March 1972 Seminar on Film, Videotape, and Social Change (St. John's: Memorial University of Newfoundland, 1972), p. 10.
4. Ibid., p. 5.
5. Ibid.
6. Ibid., p. 9.
7. Ibid., p. 14.
8. Ibid., p. 17.
9. Ibid., p. 41.
10. Benjamin Singer, *Cablecast, An Analysis of Its Users and Their Attitudes* (Ottawa: Department of Communication, 1972).

Crisis Communication in Canada

T. Joseph Scanlon

> I knew exactly what had happened. It is hard to explain, but it just felt like the whole world had hit the house; it was terrific. I knew it was a bump and I thought of my husband in the mine...[1]

On October 23, 1958, the town of Springhill, Nova Scotia, was hit by a mine disaster, its second in just over two years.[2] The first sign came not in the form of a bulletin over radio or television or even by word of mouth. Instead, it came as an earth tremor or "bump", but that was enough for many in Springhill, especially those with relatives in the mine, to know that disaster had struck once again.[3]

Communications are always important to society for, in many ways, they are society. They are the means whereby the network of relationships that form society is established and maintained. Communications, however, have a special importance in times of crisis. They may be (1) the means of warning the community of impending disaster. They will certainly be (2) the way whereby the nature and extent of the crisis is explained. And they will be (3) essential to creating or recreating community organization following the impact of a disaster. In fact, communications are so important in the aftermath of disaster that the centres of communication may well be the centres of operational control as well.

Aside from its usefulness in understanding these stages of emergencies, the study of crisis communication is important for one other reason as well. During crises or disasters, most people become acutely aware of the information they receive. Information —reliable or not—becomes very important and very vivid to them. They will remember, sometimes for years, when, where, and how they received the first information of a crisis or disaster, though they may find it more difficult to recall exactly the content of that message. (Most people, for example, can still recall the circumstances of their first hearing of the news of the assassination of John Kennedy, though the details of that message may have faded.) This means that it is possible for researchers studying crisis communication to learn a great deal about communications in general because of the particularly vivid picture of reality available to them.

Disasters, man-made or natural, are no stranger to Canada. In 1974 alone, emergency conditions were created by blizzards in Newfoundland, a tornado in Windsor, floods in Ontario and all across the prairies. Past years have seen tornadoes in the prairies, hurricanes in Ontario, earthquakes in Quebec, and mine and fishing disasters in the Maritimes. Sometimes, real disaster is much closer than we care to admit: in 1963 an earthquake levelled forests near Trois Rivières, Quebec, and shifted permanently the route of the St. Maurice River. It could have meant devastation if it had hit any one of the five Canadian cities prone to earthquakes: Victoria, Vancouver, Ottawa, Montreal, or Quebec.[4]

The Warning System

Some crises or disasters are slow to build up and may well be preceded by a warning. Most are not. It should not be surprising, therefore, that we do not know too much about such warnings, especially from Canadian experience.[5] Perhaps the one Canadian crisis accompanied by a warning system was the Winnipeg flood of 1950 which lasted almost a month and saw the Red River slowly and steadily rise to peak of 30.3 feet above normal.[6] The slowness of this build-up allowed the community time to come to grips with the crisis. Members of the community could take part in the laborious process of filling sandbags and building dikes or in the administrative procedures necessary for planning large-scale evacuations.

Another crisis with some warning involved was the blast

from Hurricane Hazel in Toronto in 1954. There, a meteorologist, Fred Turnbull, issued a number of weather warnings, but these warnings were largely ignored.[7] The storm caught the city with unexpected ferocity because, despite the warning, no one in Toronto really believed that hurricanes could or would occur that far north. Yet there is evidence to show that the people should not have been so surprised. A study prepared by the Canada Department of Transport shows that during the fifty-year period from 1900 to 1949 there were twenty-five tropical storms passing over or close to Ontario and that "eight of these storms have produced weather of extraordinary severity as regards high winds and excessive precipitations." The authors conclude that the public in Ontario must be educated to expect the occurrence of hurricanes, however infrequently they may occur.[8]

Unfortunately there are two problems. First, such warnings may not be reliable. Sometimes the problem lies in the structure of the warning system. News reports about the tornado that struck Windsor on April 3, 1974, and killed eight persons, make it clear that there were problems in the warning system. According to one story, the tornado was sighted in Detroit, but by the time the information reached Windsor via Toronto, the tornado had already hit.[9] According to another story, there was some conflict between the local E.M.O. authorities and the Windsor weather office earlier the same day. The E.M.O. director for Windsor-Essex is reported as saying that he was criticized by the Windsor weather office for issuing a tornado watch the day the tornado struck. He said he did not reactivate the watch late that day because of the criticism.[10] There may also have been problems of semantics. The Dotto story says the terminology in reference to tornadoes used by the U.S. weather office is not used in Canada.

In 1973, advance warnings preceded the St. John River floods in New Brunswick but "the rain came twice as fast as the weather bureau had predicted . . . the flooding reached Fredericton several days before expected."[11]

Second, the public may respond to the warnings only to the extent of previous experience. According to one of the foremost scholars in this field, Russell Dynes:

> The meaning of the event and the potential threat to the community may be judged on the basis of recent memories of the population and those judgments may be inappropriate to new situations. In other words, people may base their actions on the worst experience they can remember.[12]

People only react to warnings to the extent they understand their meaning: a hurricane warning has little import to someone who has no experience of hurricanes. This explains why the people of Toronto ignored the warning of 1954 and why it seems likely that many of them, especially those hardest hit, would take precautions if such a hurricane warning were issued in Toronto again. It also explains why people in St. John's, Newfoundland, remained at home, cool and unperturbed for most part, when they were isolated by a blizzard in March 1974.[13] Many of these people had come from small communities where isolation is normal in winter and where the proper response—wait out the storm's fury—is well established as a pattern of behaviour.[14] Warning systems are, therefore, generally effective only if the population understands the nature of the threat. A population exposed to a new threat is unlikely to respond to any warning system, however adequate.

Strangely enough, by building up defences against disaster any feeling of natural caution that once existed may be eliminated. Kenneth Hewitt and Ian Burton point out in their book *The Hazardousness of a Place* that the flood control system on the Thames River in Southwestern Ontario has led to further building-up of the flood plain area:

> the engineer control works appear to create a powerful feeling of security . . . in the population . . . we have evidence from several past floods of the reluctance of people to listen to warnings if a structure has been built.[15]

Of course, those persons with experience may have just the opposite reaction. In his report on the Regina tornado,

Frank Anderson reports that one serviceman, James Templeton, had lived in Houston, Texas, during a tornado just a few months before a similar storm in Regina. He looked out the window and saw the funnel-like cloud approaching and yelled, "It's a cyclone." He and his roommate promptly followed the proper safety response: they went to the basement until the storm passed.[16]

Exactly the opposite occurred during the 1973 St. John River flood when, despite various warnings, the people of one area refused to evacuate. Rodney Kueneman reports that the people who were accustomed to some spring floods "did not think they would be in any greater difficulty than they normally were." So they stayed. That phenomenon—a level of expectation based on past experience—makes it easy to understand why.[17]

When Disaster Strikes

All of the preceding comments are somewhat speculative, especially insofar as they are based on Canadian experience. What happens when crisis or disaster actually strikes is much better known. First, information will flow very rapidly through the stricken community, often by word of mouth. Second, information about the crisis may induce over-response including convergence on the site of the disaster or the source of information. Third, communications systems will become extremely important to the community trying to cope with crises or disasters: the media may well change their role and their relative importance.[18]

These points show up even in non-academic studies. In their recent book on the 1914 Newfoundland sealing disaster, Cassie Brown and Harold Horwood tell what happened when the first real news of the disaster (253 men were lost) reached St. John's:

> business came to a stop, but sidewalks and streetcars were jammed with people all hurrying to the cable office on Water Street. The news had spread through the town by word of mouth: "Another Greenland disaster." The crowds grew until Water Street was impassable.[19]

This paper is concerned with crisis or disaster communication in relation to Canada, and that, at times, means that all one can do is cite limited Canadian data to support conclusions based on data collected elsewhere. In the case of diffusion of crisis information by word of mouth, however, this pattern is reversed. Most comprehensive research on interpersonal communication in crises has been done in Canada or by Canadian researchers. To date, the most complete tracing of "human communication chains" has been done by a team of researchers at Carleton University in Ottawa.[20]

The first important research in this area, done mainly by Canadians, occurred at the time of the Detroit riot in the summer of 1967 by a research team at the University of Western Ontario.[21] The research, based on interviews with persons arrested during the riot, showed just how critical interpersonal communication can be during a crisis. According to the data obtained by the research team, nearly three-quarters of those arrested had learned of the riot either through direct personal experience (27 per cent), through direct personal communication (39 per cent) or by phone (9 per cent). Only one-quarter had learned by radio (17 per cent) or television (9 per cent).[22]

This data on the importance of interpersonal communication at times of crisis is supported by other Canadian research. A study done in Kingston, Ontario, after the finding of kidnapped British diplomat James Cross (during the October crisis of 1970) showed one-third (34 per cent) had first heard the news by word of mouth.[23] A study in North Bay, Ontario, following a shoot-out in the downtown area which included the murder of a policeman, showed almost half (49 per cent) first heard by word of mouth.[24] Even in the case of the death of a Governor General—when it was generally known that the person in question (Georges Vanier) was old and not well—one-quarter (24 per cent) learned first by word of mouth.[25] In fact, the only study that contradicts the importance of word-of-mouth as a critical vehicle of first news about a crisis is one done in the Ottawa-Hull area following the murder of Pierre Laporte.

There, 80 per cent heard first from the media. That 80 per cent figure is suspect, however, because only 55 per cent of those in the sample were interviewed.[26] Some other studies suggest that those who are most mobile and active are not only hardest to reach for interviews but that they are also much more likely to have heard by word of mouth.[27] To put it another way: the same people who are at home listening to radio and/or television are most likely to hear the news directly from radio and/or TV and to be at home when an interviewer calls.

Human Communication Chains

The importance of word-of-mouth as a first source of information is not, however, a new finding.[28] What *is* new is Canadian research into just how those word-of-mouth channels operate. This work—done by a research team at Carleton University—is giving us access to a completely new body of knowledge about the nature of human communications.[29]

What the Carleton researchers have done is to set up a stand-by research team ready to move into a community in the wake of a crisis or disaster.[30] The team then, first of all, inquires of a sample of persons in the community how they first heard the news of the event. (This follows the normal pattern of studies of diffusion of news—studies looking at how people hear news.)[31] Then, in every case where the person in the sample heard from someone else, the researchers attempt to (and usually do) track down that source and that source's source until the original source—either a medium such as radio or television, or a participant or eyewitness—is located. The original Carleton study, in Kingston, shows that some of these human communication chains followed seven stages from person to person.[32] In North Bay, one chain was followed through ten successive links.[33] (In other words, the research team located and talked to ten different people, each of whom had passed the news along to someone else who had not yet heard it. The first was, of course, a person who was an eyewitness to the event; the tenth was a person who did not hear about the event until thirty-six hours after it happened and who, by chance, had shown up in the sample.)

The research is still in pioneer form but it is already giving some fresh insights into the nature of human communication. It suggests, first of all, that most human communication—even under crisis conditions—follows normal socio-economic patterns. Persons talk to persons like themselves, i.e., persons who belong to the same family, the same occupation, or the same social and/or religious group. The majority of the contacts in all of the chains are between persons who live together in family units, between people who work together, or between people who customarily spend their leisure time together.

But there are breaks in these normal patterns, and it appears that the nature of the breaks can be identified. People break the normal socio-economic barriers when they are close to an event in terms of time and/or distance. The participant, the eyewitness, the rescue worker, all of these are likely to talk to persons near them, even persons with whom they would not normally converse. Equally important, individuals who hear the news very quickly are likely to pass it on to anyone nearby. (It is a commonplace to expect individuals to rush around telling other people about a news event, but these same individuals are not likely to run down a corridor shouting, "Hey, guess what happened yesterday!")

People also break the normal socio-economic barriers when they are in service positions where the nature of their work forces them to have relationships with people of different social and economic classes. Thus, sales personnel, waiters, cab drivers, bus drivers, police, and firemen pass on information; for example, an explanation is required as to why a bus is late or a road blocked.

The third break also occurs in a relatively normal way. It happens when a person belongs to more than one socio-economic group. Someone who hears something at work will pass it on to those at home or at church or at the club. If the informant's working and family environments cover more than one social and/or economic class, then normal barriers are broken.

This third area of leakage is the most important by some standards. For what the existence of such multi-group membership means is that information communicated officially, let's say from the police department to a transportation agency, will spill out not only to those with whom the police have informal relationships (their families and friends, etc.) but also to those with whom the transportation people have informal relationships (their families and friends, etc.). Any one official communication may be the stimulus not to just one but to a whole series of unofficial communications.

But the most interesting break, and the one still being explored, occurs when the passage of information takes place accidentally, frequently because it is overheard. The Carleton research suggests that when important information is moving across a community at high speed, there is a great deal of overhearing involved. Secretaries overhear their bosses talking. Waiters overhear customers talking. Nurses overhear patients talking. None of these communications is intended for the recipient. They are not only heard, but also passed on, and the originator of the message is not aware that he or she has inspired the message flow.

The Importance of Radio

Research has established the crucial importance of person-to-person oral communication; however, radio emerges as the mass medium people turn to first in an emergency. In a cross-Canada survey done for the Special Senate Committee on Mass Media, respondents were asked, "Which of the following media would you tune to in an emergency news crisis?" Three out of four times, the answer was "radio" ranging from a low of 67 per cent in Newfoundland, to a high of 85 per cent in Saskatchewan.[34] Studies of crisis communication testify to the significance of this response. The Detroit riot data showed radio to be twice as important as television.[35] The Kingston study showed radio informed about one and a half times as many as were informed by television.[36] The North Bay study showed radio as the most important mass medium, although this study suggested it is more important in the morning hours, with television assuming relatively more importance in the evening.[37] However, the Newfoundland data contradicted this finding. In St. John's radio was the most important medium for *first information* about a declaration of a state of emergency whether that news was heard in the evening or in the morning.[38] Despite the growth of television, radio is clearly the most important *electronic* medium for first information in time of crisis, although word-of-mouth may be most important of all. This is fairly easy to explain: radio is much more available away from home. It is relatively easy for many persons to carry on other duties with radio as a background noise. Radio can also be used in a car without causing a major distraction to the driver.[39]

Communications and Recovery

Communications are, however, not only important in conveying just the initial information of the crisis. Their importance continues as the community attempts to recover. In the first disaster study ever published, *Catastrophe and Social Change*, a study of the Halifax explosion of 1917, Samuel Prince wrote:

> The vital place of communications in society was recognized at once. It is a major influence in association and upon it in disaster depends the immediacy as well as the adequacy of relief.[40]

One of the persistent problems of disaster relief is that when a request is made for some kind of assistance—whether it is for people or blankets or cars—the response may be far greater than the demand.[41] Where a handful of people are needed, hundreds may show up. Where a few blankets are needed, truckloads may arrive. This phenomenon shows up both in serious academic studies and in the less formal descriptions of disaster written by journalists.

In his book, *Great Canadian Disasters*, Frank Rasky quotes a conversation between dike workers who had asked for more help and more food and the CBC reporter who had had their appeal broadcast:

> "Lots of dike men?"
> "Mister, we got enough men here to drink the flood."
> "Oh? And how about sandwiches?"
> "We've been filling sandbags with 'em for two hours—and we still got three tons left."[42]

Thus, while all of the responses to these requests for help were well intentioned, the fact that they were not controllable created problems. (It is obvious that one cannot put out a mass media call for just three doctors or just ten blankets.) Similar problems were revealed in Springhill where Beach and Lucas report that "all but one of the miners interviewed went to the mine within a few minutes of the impact."[43] They also showed up in Singer's study of the London area blizzard:

> The radio announcer found it necessary to request that no further calls be made for the purpose of billeting . . . The same problem arose when the supply of manpower exceeded the need.[44]

The only Canadian evidence of convergence causing real problems is reported in a very brief report on the Sarnia tornado in 1953:

> Work was hampered at first by pedestrian spectators. These were brought under control within two or three hours . . . . The riot act was read. Anticipating an invasion of vehicle-born sightseers over the weekend, plans were made to exclude the entry of vehicles to the city on Saturday and Sunday.[45]

Singer's study also suggests one final conclusion of crisis or disaster research and that is that the centre of communication tends to assume decision-making power:

> The centrality of the radio announcer is understandable when it is remembered that he was in possession of most of the new information and therefore in a good position to direct or recommend action. This vantage point was recognized by the public who sought the announcer's counsel and the announcer himself who did not hesitate to recommend a course of action.[46]

Something similar happened during the St. John's blizzard as hot-line show radio personnel attempted to aid those in need of help; but in St. John's the mayor, Dorothy Wyatt, had her own widely-publicized phone lines available and she answered a good many calls directly.[47]

The media similarly assumed very different and important functions during the October crisis of 1970 when the terrorist FLQ (Front de Libération du Québec) used two radio stations in Montreal, CKAC and CKLM, to communicate its messages about the kidnapped Cross and Laporte to the public and the authorities. The terrorists would simply telephone the switchboard operator at one of these stations, notify her where a communique could be found and rely on the station to pick it up, broadcast its contents, and communicate them to other media and the authorities. The director of public affairs for CKLM, one of the people who received FLQ communiques, commented later:

> It is important for someone studying the crisis to realize the important role the media had to play all of a sudden during the crisis when we were a part of everything, especially myself and one or two other broadcasters.
>
> We were the mediators between the FLQ and the government. That's far beyond the normal responsibilities of the news media.[48]

In summary then, communications systems can play a critical role in crises. They are involved in warning and in acquainting a community with the nature of a crisis. They affect the response patterns. They may assume a certain amount of authority as the centre of information. And their functions, which are relatively easy to perceive under such stress conditions, may tell us a good deal about non-crisis communications. Because crisis communications are fast and urgent they can be identified and studied in a way the more leisurely casual communications patterns can not.

All of the studies mentioned, of course, have practical value in terms of dealing with future crises or disasters. By identifying the failures of past warning systems we can build better ones for the future. We are now very much aware, for example that a community literally turns off its communications systems during the night-time hours. By examining those persons left out of communications systems at various times, for example, the very old or the very young, we can develop ways of overcoming these limitations. By coming to understand convergence or over-response we can work out ways to control such phenomena. By finding the nature and source of rumor we can devise methods to limit spread of rumor in future events.

1. Woman quoted in H.D. Beach and R.A. Lucas (eds.), *Individual and Group Behavior in a Coal Mine Disaster* (Washington: National Academy of Sciences, National Research Council, 1960), p. 16.
2. The first disaster, in November 1956, killed thirty-nine. The second one, November 1958, took seventy-five lives. Frank Rasky, *Great Canadian Disasters* (Toronto: Longman, 1961), pp. 118-19.
3. The Beach-Lucas study suggests those with relatives in the mine could more readily identify the bump as a mine disaster. Beach and Lucas, *Coal Mine Disaster,* p. 17.
4. There are a number of sources for Canadian disaster material; one of the best is Kenneth Hewitt and Ian Burton, *The Hazardousness of a Place* (Toronto: University of Toronto Press, 1971). Another is A.B. Lowe and G.A. McKay, *The Tornadoes of Western Canada* (Ottawa: Canada Department of Transport, 1962). Finally, there is Rasky, *Great Canadian Disasters.*
5. There is, however, a literature on the subject. It is discussed at some length in Russell R. Dynes, *Organized Behavior in Disaster* (Lexington, Mass: D.C. Heath, 1973). See particularly chapter 3.
6. Rasky, *Great Canadian Disasters*, p. 186.
7. Ibid., p. 72.
8. A.H. Mason, M.K. Thomas, and D.W. Boyd, "The October 15-16, 1954 Storm, 'Hurricane Hazel' in Ontario." Meteorological Branch, Canada Department of Transport Circular-2606, TEC 210, reprinted June 8, 1967.
9. Lydia Dotto, "Better Reporting of Tornadoes Sought," *The Globe and Mail*, May 30, 1974, p. 5.
10. Mike McAteer, "E.M.O. Chief Says Weathermen Criticized His Tornado Alert," *Windsor Star*, May 29, 1974, p. 3.

11. Rodney Kueneman, "The 1973 St. John River Flood Response" (Ottawa: Canada E.M.O. 73/193, 1973), p. 9.
12. Dynes, *Organized Behavior in Disaster*, p. 74.
13. Unpublished study by Carleton University crisis research team, School of Journalism, Carleton University, Ottawa, March 1974. Hereafter referred to as the "St. John's-Wyatt Study."
14. Ibid. Literature on this subject makes clear this is proper behaviour. See Allan P. Bristow, *Police Disaster Operations* (Springfield: Charles C. Thomas, 1972), pp. 96-98.
15. Hewitt and Burton, *The Hazardousness of a Place*, p. 40.
16. Frank W. Anderson, *Regina's Terrible Tornado* (Frontier Book No. 9), p. 3.
17. Kueneman, "St. John River Flood Response," p. 9.
18. See Benjamin D. Singer, *The Social Functions of Radio in a Community Emergency* (Toronto: Copp Clark, 1972); and Gerald Steven Alperstein, "Some Reactions by the Montreal News Media to the October 1970, Canadian Crisis." M.A. thesis, Syracuse, 1972.
19. Cassie Brown and Harold Horwood, *Death on the Ice* (Toronto: Doubleday Canada, 1974), p. 235.
20. There are now two Carleton studies: T. Joseph Scanlon, "Not Two Steps But One and One-Half" (Ottawa: Carleton University, 1971); and T. Joseph Scanlon, "The North Bay/Slater Study" (Ottawa: Carleton University, 1974).
21. Benjamin D. Singer, Richard N. Osborn, and James A. Gerchwenden, *Black Rioters* (Lexington, Mass.: Heath Lexington Books, 1970).
22. Ibid., p. 44.
23. Scanlon, "Not Two Steps But One and One-Half," p. 6.
24. Scanlon, "The North Bay/Slater Study," unpublished data.
25. Asghar Fathi, "Problems in Developing Indices of News Values," *Journalism Quarterly*, Autumn 1973, p. 498.
26. Dennis P. Forcese, Hugh McRoberts, Stephen Richer, and John DeVries, Paper presented at the annual meeting of the Canadian Sociology and Anthropology Association, St. John's, Newfoundland, June 1971, p. 4.
27. This was a conclusion of the "St. John's-Wyatt Study."
28. There are many studies in this area. The most useful are summed up in Bradley S. Greenberg, "Diffusion of News About the Kennedy Assassination," and Stephen P. Spitzer and Nancy S. Spitzer, "Diffusion of News of Kennedy and Oswald Deaths," in Bradley S. Greenberg and Edwin Parker (eds.), *The Kennedy Assassination and the American Public* (Stanford: Stanford University Press, 1965), pp. 89-98 and 99-111.
29. The methodology is described in T. Joseph Scanlon, "News Flow About Release of Kidnapped Diplomat Researched by J-Students," *Journalism Quarterly*, vol. 28, no. 1 (Spring 1971), pp. 35-38.
30. Ibid.
31. See note 28.
32. Scanlon, "Not Two Steps But One and One-Half."
33. Scanlon, "The North Bay/Slater Study."
34. "Good, Bad or Simply Inevitable," *Report of the Special Senate Committee on Mass Media*, vol. 3 (Ottawa: Queens's Printer, 1970), p. 43.
35. Singer, Osborn, and Gerchwenden, *Black Rioters*, p. 44.
36. Scanlon, "Not Two Steps But One and One-Half", p. 6.

37. Scanlon, "The North Bay/Slater Study," unpublished data.
38. "The St. John's-Wyatt Study."
39. Scanlon, "Not Two Steps But One and One-Half," p. 9. A significant proportion heard the news first on a car radio.
40. Samuel H. Prince, *Catastrophe and Social Change* (New York: Columbia University, 1920), p. 62.
41. Allen H. Barton, *Communities in Disaster* (New York: Doubleday, 1970), pp. 186-87.
42. Rasky, *Great Canadian Disasters*, p. 184.
43. Beach and Lucas, *Coal Mine Disaster*, p. 18.
44. Singer, *Social Functions of Radio in a Community Emergency*, p. 24.
45. E.E. Massey, *Observations on The Sarnia Tornado of 21 May 1953* (Ottawa: Defence Research Board, 1953), p. 4.
46. Singer, *Social Functions of Radio in a Community Emergency*, pp. 37-38.
47. "The St. John's-Wyatt Study."
48. Alperstein, "Reactions by the Montreal News Media to the October 1970, Canadian Crisis," pp. 24-25.

Canadian Communications: A Resource Guide

VICTOR G. PADDY AND VINCENT F. SACCO

Introduction

The importance of communications technology to Canadian society has often been underestimated in the past. Unique Canadian conditions, such as the large geographical area, the dispersed population, the concern for national unity, and the burgeoning sense of national consciousness, create a social milieu in which the media of communication play a vital role. In Canada, as in other industrialized countries, the understanding of communication structures and processes is an essential prelude to the formation of suitable public policy and the direction of national development.

As Canada's social and political structures grow more complex, and as the amount of knowledge and information multiplies, it is increasingly important that Canadian social scientists understand the workings and effects of Canadian communication media. It is imperative, therefore, that Canadian social science students be encouraged to develop active theoretical and empirical interests in both the social and technological aspects of communication. Yet, such encouragement is not always apparent. In fact, the novice communication student in Canada is confronted with a number of obstacles which may dissuade him from developing research interests in mass communications. Until recently, for instance, there did not even exist a basic textbook or reader in Canadian communications, and presently there exist few readily available bibliographies of Canadian writings and research on the media.

Even the material which exists can very often not be systematically located and the student may find that he has to search intensively to locate information basic to an understanding of communications in Canada.[1] The student is no doubt very often perplexed and frustrated in his search for relevant behavioural literature and must turn to journalistic sources in order to attempt to satisfy research requirements. The end results of such conditions may be the student's disenchantment with mass communications as an area of research and he may focus his attention instead on those areas that he perceives as being more fruitful.

The present paper is an attempt to remedy this situation somewhat by providing the reader with information necessary to a systematic understanding of communications in Canada. The material contained herein is based on the authors' conceptions of the needs of the undergraduate communications student and is intended to serve as a research tool as well as a basic information guide.

The paper is divided into three major sections. The first part is a discussion of Canadian university courses and programs dealing with communications and the mass media. In the second part the reader is provided with an overview of the various federal and provincial governmental bodies involved in media regulation and the formation of media policy. The final section of this paper is a compilation of various types of bibliographical sources, including a list of Royal Commission and government task force reports, a list of journals which frequently feature Canadian media-related material, a bibliography of mass communication bibliographies, and a select bibliography of readily available works dealing with communications in Canada.

Communications and Mass Media: The University Scene

In an article appearing in the January 1972 issue of the *American Journal of Sociology*, Herbert Gans explained why American sociologists have been showing relatively little research interest in the mass media of the United States. According to Gans, there are numerous reasons which account for this "drastic famine which shows no signs of abating." Chief among these reasons are the difficulty and costliness of mass communication studies:

> The methods which must be used for these studies are often unusually complicated, they do not lend themselves to small projects that can be done by a lone researcher with a heavy teaching load and the funds for larger studies are in short supply.[2]

But, Gans contends, financial and methodological considerations alone cannot explain the dearth of mass media research in the United States. There are other reasons which explain why relatively few sociologists write scholarly essays on the media and why even fewer take part in or conduct smaller, less complicated, less costly empirical studies.

One reason has to do with the disciplinary structure of sociology. The study of mass media has often been lumped with the study of public opinion, propaganda, collective behaviour, and even the sociology of leisure rather than existing as an independent field of inquiry. Another reason has to do with sociology's conception of time and timelessness. Since much media-related behaviour is transitory and faddish in nature, it is very often extremely difficult (if not impossible) to mobilize a research project in time to study such behaviour.

Gans also states that American sociological disinterest in mass communications can partially be explained in terms of the sociologists' personal and professional ambivalence towards the media:

> Many sociologists—like educators generally—are hostile towards them [the mass media] partly because they are often successful competitors for the student's time and interests. Also, they cater largely to an audience of lower status and sociologists are often not inclined to study groups of lower status unless they are defined as social problems. . . . Moreover, if only because mass media content is aimed at a lower status audience sociologists often do not watch television or keep up with the other media in the first place, and thus can not know what there is to be researched. . . . In some instances, however, just the opposite is true, sociologists are so deeply immersed in the media that they are not sufficiently detached to develop research curiosity. I suspect

that this is particularly true of informational content and of the news media generally.[3]

Although Gans has concerned himself with American sociology and its failure to develop a lasting and consistent research interest in the mass media, his comments are equally applicable to the Canadian scene. A survey taken by the Canadian Sociology and Anthropology Association in 1973, for instance, revealed that relatively few sociologists were interested in the study of communications (mass or otherwise) or in the related area of public opinion.[4] With respect to teaching and research, there exist in Canada few sociology departments that list communications as a major area of concentration. McGill, Calgary, York, Manitoba, Western Ontario, and Montreal are the possible exceptions. Several other sociology departments offer graduate and undergraduate communication courses on an irregular basis, yet have no specific interest in this area.

Although the study and teaching of the social aspects of communications media have usually been associated with sociology, they are by no means the exclusive domain of that discipline. Media-related studies can prove to be a fruitful area for psychologists, political scientists, historians, and other social scientists. Yet, as with sociology, our research revealed relatively little interest existing in other social science departments save the political science departments at Carleton and Guelph and the psychology departments at Brock and Montreal.

Thus, within Canadian universities the traditional social sciences have largely neglected the social and behavioural aspects of modern communications and its technology, a situation that has also been noted by at least one government report.[5] There are several reasons for this situation in Canada. The relatively late development of the social sciences in Canada is one factor, abetted by the fact that large numbers of Canadian social scientists received their graduate training at foreign universities, which has meant that many areas of Canadian social reality have remained unexplored. In addition, the French-English language problem has worked to impede the development of a cumulative body of knowledge about aspects of Canadian society, the mass media being no exception. It should also be noted that it is only within recent decades that government and private funding agencies have been interested in providing grants for social science research.[6] There are in Canada, however, approximately a dozen universities offering either interdisciplinary programs in communications or separate programs in communication studies. Each of these programs is briefly described below.[7]

Carleton University

The Journalism Department at Carleton University offers a four-year course leading to a Bachelor of Journalism degree with Honours as well as a one-year post B.A. program leading to the same degree. The aim of the program is not to train technicians but to give students the ability to investigate, interpret, and communicate in any of the mass media. Courses are designed to give students both professional skills and an understanding of how media function in order that they can adapt to the various areas of modern journalism. In the academic year which began in 1974, the Journalism Department initiated a program in graduate studies leading to the degree Master of Journalism.

University of Guelph

Students interested in communications may choose this as an area of concentration at the undergraduate level. At present, communications is not available as a major. The objective of communication courses is to provide the student with an understanding of some aspects of the human communication process. The program is interdisciplinary in nature, with courses being offered by the following departments: Consumer Studies, Drama, Extension Education, and Political Studies.

Concordia University (Formerly Loyola and Sir George Williams University)

There is a Department of Communication Arts at Concordia. The purpose of the overall program is to allow the student to develop his or her creative, critical, and intellectual potential in the context of a media-oriented society. Related studies in the humanities, sciences, and social sciences are an integral part of the program. The primary concern of the program is to investigate "media man" and "media world," to understand more fully the role of media in society, to examine critically the goals of society as projected in media, and to assess realistically the responsibilities of media vis-à-vis that society. The curriculum is designed:

1. for students who intend to continue graduate studies in communications;
2. for future writers, critics, communication arts consultants, directors, and performers;
3. for future teachers in the field of radio, television, film, and theatre;
4. for students who plan a career in the areas of publicity, promotion, advertising, and public relations.

The department offers a B.A. degree and a post B.A. diploma program.

McGill University
Communication studies at McGill provide an interdisciplinary program including courses and seminars in the departments of Sociology, Anthropology, Psychology, Linguistics, Political Science, English, Film, and Management. The choice of seminars and upper level courses depends on the candidate's interests. These may fall into either the macro or micro areas of the field, emphasizing interpersonal or intergroup (mass communications) perspectives. Interpersonal communication studies focus on linguistic, symbolic, and socio-psychological questions while mass communications may deal with the social, political, or cultural aspects of media development, functioning, and effects. Both areas of interest are predicated on an understanding of communications theories which explain the processes involved in sending, receiving, and understanding messages. McGill offers an M.A. in communications and an ad hoc Ph.D. in English (communications).

At the time of writing there exists the strong possibility that in the near future McGill will be offering a Ph.D. in communications.

University of Montreal
The communications section at the University of Montreal is associated with the Psychology Department and offers courses in communication studies at the B.A. and M.A. levels. The orientation of the department is, of course, psychological, with an emphasis on experimental social science.

Ryerson Polytechnical Institute
Ryerson has a journalism program and a radio and television arts program, both of which lead to the degree Bachelor of Applied Arts. Although both programs are profession-oriented, they stress the need for studying communications and mass media in a wider social science context.

Saint Paul University and University of Ottawa
These two universities jointly offer communications studies through the Institute of Social Communications. The program of studies offered is essentially interdisciplinary and is worked out in close co-operation between the two universities and their faculties. The Institute offers a one-year diploma of University Studies in social communication, a three-year Bachelor of Arts with concentration in social communications, and a four-year Bachelor of Arts with specialization in social communications. The four-year Bachelor of Arts degree is presented in three clearly defined perspectives; a humanistic perspective, a scientific perspective, and a productive perspective.

Simon Fraser University
The Department of Communication Studies at Simon Fraser is an interdisciplinary teaching and research centre that works in close co-operation with several other departments in the university. The department provides programs in the communications media (social uses and effects of

TV, film, and radio), and communications theory and behaviour (research and study in the areas of intrapersonal, interpersonal, and group communications). At the undergraduate level, students may either enrol in an honours in communication studies or in a general degree program with a major in communication studies. The Department of Communication Studies also offers a graduate program leading to an M.A. in communication studies. The emphasis of graduate instruction in this department falls into two major areas:

1. the study of communications media and social change i.e., the relationship between the forms, methods, and contents of such media and social change;
2. the study of communications behaviour, including individual, interpersonal, and small group communication.

University of Waterloo

The University of Waterloo offers an interdisciplinary communication studies program at the undergraduate level. Those enrolled in general degree programs at the university may select communication studies as a major area of study. Students enrolled in honours programs may elect communication studies as a minor area of study. In each case, a total of five communication course credits must be taken to qualify for the appropriate degree recognition.

The communication studies program consists of a set of introductory core courses and three theme areas. The core segment provides a distinct focus while at the same time it contributes to an interdependent set of studies. The three theme areas are: mass media systems, communications systems design, and communication and environmental studies.

The University of Western Ontario

The Journalism Department at the University of Western Ontario offers a four-year course leading to a Bachelor of Arts degree in Journalism, as well as a Master of Arts degree in Journalism which replaces the former diploma program. The department also plans to phase out gradually its undergraduate program. As noted elsewhere, the Sociology Department offers a Master of Arts degree with communications as specialization, as well.

The University of Windsor

One of the most comprehensive communication courses in Canada is offered by the Department of Communication Arts at the University of Windsor. The department, which is associated with the faculty of social sciences, offers a general degree with a major in communication arts as well as an honours degree with a major in communication arts. Courses and seminars range from such theoretical concerns as broadcasting study and communications policy to such pragmatic interests as film-making and radio and television production. Although the Department of Communication Arts currently offers courses of study only at the undergraduate level, there is the possibility that the department will be offering a program of graduate studies in the near future.

Communications and Mass Media: The Government Scene

This section of the paper will briefly overview the topic of mass communications as it relates to the governmental sectors of Canadian society. First, an attempt is made to acquaint the reader with the Canadian Radio-Television Commission and the Department of Communications, the two main bodies responsible for research implementation and policy co-ordination at the federal level. The second part of this section is an analysis of federal-provincial relations regarding communications in Canada. The authors will review the existing policies of each province noting where the conflict with present federal policy lies.

The *Canadian Radio-Television Commission (CRTC)*[8] came into existence as a result of the Broadcast Act of 1968. The Act provides the Commission with the authority to regulate, supervise, and license all Canadian broadcasting, both public and private.

The policy recommendations of the Commission are implemented by the eight CRTC branches that are concerned with the pragmatics of planning, development, and broadcast programming as well as licensing, legal and technical considerations. In addition to overall policy development, a vital function of the CRTC is the holding of public hearings in which the Commission considers broadcasting applications, proposed regulations, and other matters of public interest and contention.

A partial list of CRTC publications is included in the bibliographical part of this paper.

Communications Canada came into being as the Department of Communications in April 1969. The department has the responsibility of helping to ensure than an expanding variety of telecommunications services are available to Canadians. To that end, it undertakes and sponsors much of the relevant research conducted in Canada. It also promotes a wide range of studies designed to provide policy-makers with an appreciation of the social, cultural, and economic consequences of the adoption and implementation of new communications technology. A significant amount of the department's research program has been devoted to the study of satellite technology, largely because satellites appear to be the most economical and efficient means of extending communication services to the far Canadian North and other relatively isolated areas.

Research reports and publications generated by the department in conjunction with other federal departments, or as a result of research contracts with Canadian universities, include *Instant World, Branching Out, Privacy and Computers, Proposals for a Communications Policy for Canada,* and *Computers/Communications Policy.*

In early 1974, Communications Canada began publishing on a quarterly basis a Canadian communications journal entitled *In Search: The Canadian Communications Quarterly*. More information about this journal and the Communications Canada publications already mentioned is included in the bibliographical section of this paper.[9]

The Provinces

At a conference of provincial premiers in August 1972, tentative guidelines were set down with respect to the regulatory and policy-making role to be played by Canadian provincial governments. Foremost was the premiers' recognition of the need to organize provincial bodies responsible for the orderly development of communications. Accordingly, those provinces lacking a minister responsible for communications took immediate steps to rectify the situation. Further, the premiers acknowledged the importance of communications in the social and economic development of the provinces and expressed reservations with regard to federal policy and jurisdiction in the area of communications control and regulation. Following this conference, three interprovincial communications conferences were held in an attempt to develop some consensus regarding provincial priorities and strategies.

Once this groundwork had been laid, provincial representatives met with representatives of the federal government in late 1973 for the first (and to date only) federal-provincial communications conference. At this conference, the federal and provincial positions were debated and their opposing views with respect to communications regulation and control became readily apparent. Federal Communications Minister Gerard Pelletier insisted that federal jurisdiction in the communications field was essential in order to ensure national unity.

The various provincial views, although divergent, were basically in accord with the position put forth by the Ontario representative Gordon Carton. Carton argued that communications, as an industry, is so vital to the economic and social well-being of the province that the provincial government must play an extremely active role.

The present federal-provincial imbroglio is perhaps best viewed historically. The British North America Act of 1867, which delineated federal and provincial constitutional powers, obviously made no mention of broadcasting. When broadcasting began to develop in Canada, the federal government assumed jurisdiction, arguing that broadcasting was similar in nature to interprovincial trade and therefore a federal matter. Today, the question of who has jurisdiction in the communications field is the prime obstacle which prevents the formation of a comprehensive national communications policy. As will become obvious, however, this is not the only bone of contention. The remainder of this section will be taken up with an attempt to outline the state of communications within each province, noting wherever possible, each province's point of divergence from the federal communications policy.

Alberta In Alberta, the main telecommunications carrier, the Alberta Government Telephones, is a crown corporation. Recent federal initiatives have caused some concern among provincial policy-makers anxious to maintain sole ownership and regulatory control of Alberta Government Telephones.

Further, it should be noted that the Alberta government also believes that some provincial input into the regulation of cable television is necessary.

British Columbia British Columbia's Minister of Transport and Communications, Robert Strachan, has expressed some dissatisfaction with the present federal communications service. He has contended that provincial jurisdiction over the British Columbia Telephone Company and over cable systems in the province is necessary to provide improved communication services in British Columbia, particularly in the rural and northern areas of the province. Strachan has also criticized the CBC's centralization and its irrelevance to much of the British Columbian way of life. Finally, Strachan has suggested the formation of a national commission representing the eleven governments, to take over the majority of the communications policy and planning functions for Canada.

Manitoba Since 1908, the Manitoba Telephone System has been a crown corporation of the province. Recent federal government policies and working papers which would alter the nature of the Manitoba Telephone System have caused some consternation within the Manitoba goverment. It is in this area that opposition to federal communications initiatives exists.

In May 1974, the Government of Manitoba issued a comprehensive discussion paper on cable television entitled *Broadcasting and Cable Television: A Manitoba Perspective.* This paper, the first of a series of studies on all aspects of telecommunications in Manitoba, reasserts that province's concern for the integrity of its telephone system, maintaining that just as broadcasting and cable television cannot be considered in isolation from each other, neither can either of them be considered in isolation from the vital role played by the Manitoba Telephone System.

New Brunswick The Province of New Brunswick has indicated that broadcasting and cable television coverage in the province are inadequate, and that improvements by the federal government are necessary.

Unlike Quebec, Ontario, or British Columbia, New Brunswick has appeared to be satisfied with continued federal control in communications. However, the province considers it essential that an improved consultative process between federal and provincial governments be established to ensure fair consideration of both federal and provincial views in the generation and implementation of broadcasting policies.

Newfoundland Newfoundland's Department of Transportation and Communications has not, as of this writing, articulated any firm positions or objectives in the communications field. A recent Newfoundland position paper on communications, however, suggests that the provincial role will be one of policy co-ordination as opposed to detailed program administration.

The position paper, rather than disputing federal jurisdiction in communications, points to federal failings in providing Newfoundland with acceptable broadcast reception. Further, although the Newfoundland government supports

CBC's plan to establish French-language radio and television in the province, it is that government's belief that these goals have taken precedence over the provision of adequate English broadcasting throughout the province.

Northwest Territories Although the Northwest Territories' Department of Information co-operates with Communications Canada on certain projects and provides recommendations to that federal body regarding the planning of communications facilities, the department itself has produced little research material of a sociological or technological nature in the area of mass communications. The main concern is with developing effective internal communications programs and with improving the dissemination and two-way flow of information within the Territories. To this end, the Department of Information has concentrated on developing and expanding radio broadcasts and newspaper circulation in both English and native languages, placing emphasis, wherever possible, on local organization and participation.

Nova Scotia Basically, the Government of Nova Scotia has supported New Brunswick's policy, accepting continued federal jurisdiction in the area of communications, with the qualification that a meaningful federal-provincial consultative process ensue.

However, the province has contended that three complex issues remain. Firstly, the issue of selecting communication priorities must remain in the hands of the provinces. Secondly, the Nova Scotian government believes that decentralization with regard to communications technology and research fundings is vital to the development of communications in the Maritime provinces. Finally, the Province of Nova Scotia believes that any federal regulatory agency must be structured to take into account provincial planning and priorities.

Ontario Ontario's Ministry of Transportation and Communications was established in 1971, with the Communications Branch given the mandate to investigate all matters related to forging an Ontario telecommunications policy.

A major result of this mandate has been the publication of *Communications in Ontario* (1973). This report details the perceptions of a cross-section of Ontario residents regarding the impact of communications technology on their daily lives, and is the first in a projected series of similar studies. Other research undertaken by the ministry ranges from communications law and federal-provincial jurisdictional matters to the socio-economic effects of telephone rate increases for the Ontario resident.

At the Federal-Provincial Conference of Ministers of Communications (November 1973), Ontario's major concern was with cable. The argument made was that cable was local in nature, not interprovincial, and should therefore fall under provincial jurisdiction. In addition, Ontario argued that the existing federal regulatory system concerned with the regulation of telecommunications carriers, broadcasters, and cable distributors, was insensitive to provincial needs and required a major overhaul.

Prince Edward Island The Province of Prince Edward Island has not had a Department of Communications, and until recently communications problems were dealt with on an ad hoc basis. However, reacting to federal and other provincial initiatives, as well as to internal changes, the Government of Prince Edward Island in July of 1973, appointed the Minister of Industry and Commerce responsible for communications.

Since then, with the assistance of The Council of Maritime Premiers, Prince Edward Island has taken a more active role in communication concerns. A work group has been established to define and implement specific policy directions in computer technology. Moreover, the department has been studying the feasibility of establishing an education network through the use of cable television.

Quebec Quebec's Department of Communications, established in 1969, is the oldest and most active provincial department in Canada. In 1971, Jean-Paul L'Allier, the Minister of Communications for Quebec, published a policy statement entitled *Toward A Quebec Communications Policy* outlining Quebec's need and reasons for establishing its own overall communications policy. In 1973 L'Allier issued a second major statement, *Quebec Master of Its Own Communications Policy.* In it L'Allier emphasized the province's responsibility to formulate a communications policy for Quebec, inextricably linked with Quebec's fundamental way of life.

In the federal-provincial sphere, Quebec has not merely staked out a verbal jurisdictional claim to various communications matters, as have Ontario and British Columbia. For instance, in December 1972, the province passed a law giving its Public Service Board jurisdiction over what could be all telecommunications. In September of 1973, Quebec published regulations that all cable companies within the province were ordered to obey. Although not substantially different from federal regulations as applied through the CRTC, these require all cable and broadcasting outlets to be owned and controlled by Quebec residents by 1976.

The Federal Minister of Communications, Gerard Pelletier, has warned L'Allier that the federal government considers Quebec's actions on regulatory cable companies illegal, but has not, as yet, taken steps to defend its federal jurisdiction.

Finally, "cultural sovereignty," a campaign slogan used by the Quebec liberals in the recent provincial election, appears to be key phrase in Quebec's communications policies and priorities.

Saskatchewan At the Federal-Provincial Communications Conference in November of 1973, Saskatchewan's Minister for Telephones, John Brockelbank, expressed dissatisfaction with federal broadcasting service. He also emphasized that Saskatchewan must maintain its ability to develop telecommunication services in order to ensure their availability to all residents of the Province of Saskatchewan.

It is interesting to note here that in all three Prairie Provinces, the main or only telephone company is a crown corporation. These provinces argue that their telephone company should remain the only common carrier to own and rent out the hardware used for cable television.

The Yukon Territory The Government of the Yukon Territory has occasionally been involved in communications research projects of a minor nature, generally related to its immediate operating needs. Currently, in association with Communications Canada, the territory is involved in a comprehensive examination of communications requirements for federal and territorial government agencies in the territory.

Bibliographical Sources

Select Bibliography

Following is a select bibliography of books, articles, and published reports dealing with various aspects of communications and the mass media in Canada. In selecting material for this bibliography, the authors were concerned that each item fulfill two requirements: (1) that it be easily accessible, and (2) that it help provide some understanding of communications and the media in Canada. (Whether the items were generated by Canadian writers or researchers was considered to be of less importance.) Because of the scarcity of published material, the authors occasionally chose to be more inclusive rather than exclusive. This bibliography, however does not claim to be comprehensive. Rather, it is intended to serve as a basic bibliography for the student and the interested researcher.

The bibliography is categorized under a number of subheadings to facilitate usage. The categories are not mutually exclusive and a number of the items would fit just as well into other categories.

Broadcasting in Canada

Allard, T.J. "Canadian Private Broadcasting." *Gazette*, vol. 15, no. 2 (1969), pp. 145-49.

Dizard, Wilson P. *Television: A World View*. Syracuse: Syracuse University Press, 1966.

Glynn, R. "The Canadian System." In *Television Impact on American Culture*. Edited by W. Elliot. East Lansing, Michigan: Michigan State University Press, 1956.

Gordon, Ken. "Community Control of CATV." *In Search*, Spring 1974, pp. 18-21.

Information Services, CBC. *CBC: A Brief History and Background*. Ottawa: Information Services, CBC Head Office, September 1970.

Jamieson, Don. "A National Broadcasting Policy." *Canadian Communications*, vol. 2 (1962), pp. 11-18.

Johansen, Peter W. "Television Parliament: What the Commons Report Left Out." *Journal of Canadian Studies*, vol. 8, no. 4 (November 1973), pp. 39-51.

Lavole, Elzear. "L'Evolution de la Radio au Canada Français avant 1940." *Recherches Sociographiques*, vol. 12, no. 1 (January-April 1971), pp. 17-49.

McCormack, Thelma. "Canada's Royal Commission on Broadcasting." *Public Opinion Quarterly*, vol. 23 (1959), pp. 92-100.

Peers, F.W. *The Politics of Canadian Broadcasting*. Toronto: University of Toronto Press, 1967.

Prang, M. "The Origin of Public Broadcasting in Canada." *Canadian Historical Review*, vol. 46 (1965), pp. 4-31, 131-41.

Scanlon, T. Joseph. "Colour T.V.: New Language?" *Journalism Quarterly*, Summer 1967, pp. 225-30.

Shea, Albert. *Broadcasting The Canadian Way*. Montreal: Harvest House, 1963.

Singer, Benjamin D., and Green, Lyndsay. *The Social Functions of Radio in a Community Emergency*. Toronto: Copp Clark, 1972.

Smith, John H. "The Canadian Broadcasting Corporation." *Gazette*, vol. 15, no. 2 (1969), pp. 139-43.

Spry, Graham. "The Canadian Broadcasting Corporation: 1936-61." *Canadian Communications*, vol. 2 (1961), pp. 13-26.

———. "The Decline and Fall of Canadian Broadcasting." *Queens Quarterly*, vol. 34, no. 1 (Spring 1970), pp. 92-100.

Toogood, Alexander F. *Canadian Broadcasting in Transition*. Ottawa: Canadian Association of Broadcasters, 1969.

______. "The Canadian Broadcasting System: Search for a Definition." *Journalism Quarterly*, vol. 48, no. 2 (Summer 1971), pp. 331-38.

Vidmar, Neil, and Rokeach, Milton. "Archie Bunker's Bigotry: A Study in Selective Perception and Exposure." *Journal of Communications*, vol. 24, no. 1 (Winter 1974), pp. 36-47.

Weir, E.A. *The Struggle for National Broadcasting in Canada*. Toronto: McClelland and Stewart, 1965.

Culture, Canadian Identity, and the Media

Beattie, Earle. "In Canada's Centennial Year: U.S. Mass Media Influence Probed." *Journalism Quarterly*, vol. 44, no. 4 (Winter 1967), pp. 667-72.

Beveridge, James. "Culture and Media in Canada." *The American Review of Canadian Studies*, vol. 3, no. 1 (Spring 1973), pp. 135-45.

Comer, Henry. "American T.V.: What Have You Done to Us." In *Broadcasting and the Public Interest*. Edited by J.H. Pennybacker and W.W. Braden. New York: Random House, 1969.

Compton, Neil. "Television and Canadian Culture." *Commentary*, vol. 38, no. 5 (November 1964), pp. 75-79.

Eggleston, W. "Canadian Magazines and the O'Leary Report." *Gazette,* vol. 7 (1961), pp. 275-82.

Hart, Jim A. "The Flow of News Between the U.S. and Canada." *Journalism Quarterly*, vol. 40 (1963), pp. 70-74.

James, Clifford Rodney. *The National Film Board of Canada: Its Task of Communication*. Columbus, Ohio: Ohio State University Press, 1968.

Litvak, Isaiah, and Maule, Christopher. *Cultural Sovereignty: The Time and Reader's Digest Case in Canada*. New York: Praeger, 1974.

McCormack, Thelma. "Writers and the Mass Media." In *Canada: A Sociological Profile*. Edited by W.E. Mann. Toronto: Copp Clark, 1968.

Maistre, Gilbert. "L'Influence de la Radio et de la Télévision Américaines au Canada." *Recherches Sociographiques*, vol. 12, no. 1 (January-April 1971), pp. 51-75.

Mousseau, Monique. "Consommation des Mass Media: Biculturalisme des Mass Media ou Bilinguisme des Consommateurs." *Canadian Review of Sociology and Anthropology*, vol. 9, no. 4 (November 1972), pp. 325-46.

Peers, Frank. "The Nationalist Dilemma in Canadian Broadcasting." In *Nationalism in Canada*. Edited by Peter Russell. Toronto: McGraw-Hill, 1966.

______. "Oh Say Can You See?" In *Close the 49th Parallel Etc.: The Americanization of Canada*. Edited by Ian Lumsden. Toronto: University of Toronto Press, 1970.

Rotstein, A., and Lax, G. (eds.). *Getting It Back: A Program for Canadian Independence*. Toronto: Clarke Irwin, 1974.

Scanlon, T. Joseph. "Canada Sees the World Through U.S. Eyes: One Case Study in Cultural Domination." *Canadian Forum*, September 1974, pp. 34-39.

Scheer, Chris J., and Eiler, Sam W. "A Comparison of Canadian and American Network Television News." *Journal of Broadcasting*, vol. 16 (1972), pp. 159-64.

Schwartz, Mildred. *Public Opinion and Canadian Identity*. Toronto: Fitzhenry and Whiteside, 1967.

Singer, Benjamin D. "American Invasion of the Mass Media in Canada. " In *Critical Issues in Canadian Society*. Edited by Craig Boydell, Carl Grindstaff, and Paul Whitehead. Toronto: Holt, Rinehart and Winston, 1971.

Smythe, D.W. "Culture and Communications." In *The U.S. and Us*. Edited by Gordon McCaffery. Toronto: Canadian Institute on Public Affairs, 1968.

Education and the Media

Abbey, David S. *Now See Hear! Applying Communications to Teaching Profiles in Practical Education #9.*

Toronto: Ontario Institute for Studies in Education, 1973.

Connachie, T.D. *Television for Education and Industry.* Vancouver: Mitchell Press, 1969.

Elkin, Frederick. "Family Life, Education and the Mass Media." In *The Canadian Family.* Edited by K. Ishwaran. Toronto: Holt, Rinehart and Winston, 1971.

Lambert, Richard. *School Broadcasting in Canada.* Toronto: University of Toronto Press, 1963.

Rosen, Earl, and Whelpdale, E. (eds.). *Educational Television Across Canada: The Development and State of E.T.V., 1968.* Toronto: Metropolitan Educational Television Association of Toronto, 1969.

General

Beattie, Earle. "Canadian Mass Media: Development and Economic Structure." *Gazette*, vol. 15, no. 2 (1969), pp. 125-37.

———. "Mass Media." In *Canadian Annual Review.* Edited by J. Saywell. Toronto: University of Toronto Press, 1971.

Black, Edwin R. "Canadian Public Policy and the Mass Media." *Canadian Journal of Economics,* vol. 1 (1968), pp. 368-79.

Braithwaite, Max. *Servant or Master: A Casebook of the Mass Media.* Toronto: Book Society of Canada, 1968.

Buttram, Keith; Cooper, Harriet; Matlin, Evelyn; and Mallock, Kati. *Basic Issues in Canadian Mass Communication.* 13 booklets. Montreal: McGill University Bookstore, 1974.

Clement, Wallace. *The Canadian Corporate Elite.* Toronto: McClelland and Stewart, 1975.

Cloritier, Jean. *La Communication Audio-scripto-visuelle à l'heure des self-media; ou, l'ère d'Emérée.* Montreal: Les Presses de l'Université de Montréal, 1973.

Compton, Neil. "The Mass Media." In *Social Purpose for Canada.* Edited by Michael Oliver. Toronto: University of Toronto Press, 1961.

Fischer, H., and Merrill, J. (eds.). *International Communication*. New York: Hastings House, 1970.

Gordon, Donald R. *The New Literacy*. Toronto: University of Toronto Press, 1971.

Institute for Motivational Research Inc. *The Motivational Research Study of Newspapers, Magazines, Television and Radio in 4 Canadian Communities*. 5 vols. Croton-On-Hudson, New York: 1963.

Irving, John. *Mass Media in Canada*. Toronto: Ryerson Press, 1962.

Kesterton, Wilfred, and Moir, John S. "Communications." In *The Canadians 1867-1967*. Edited by J. Careless and R.C. Brown. Toronto: Macmillan, 1967.

Languirand, Jacques. *De McLuhan à Pythagore*. Montreal: R. Ferren, 1972.

McCormack, Thelma. "Social Theory and the Mass Media." *Canadian Journal of Economics and Political Science*, vol. 27 (1961), pp. 479-89.

______. "Social Changes in Mass Media." *Canadian Journal of Sociology and Anthropology*, vol. 1 (1964), pp. 49-61.

______. "Innocent Eye on Mass Society." In *Society and Mass Media*. Edited by Alan Wells. Palo Alto, Calif.: National Press Books, 1972.

Minifie, James. "Mass Media and Their Control." In *Canadian Society: Pluralism, Change and Conflict*. Edited by Richard J. Ossenburg. Toronto: Prentice-Hall, 1971.

Porter, John. *The Vertical Mosaic*. Toronto: University of Toronto Press, 1965.

Repath, Austin. *Mass Media and You*. Toronto: Longman, 1966.

Rockman, Arnold. "Communications, Culture, Change, Canada." In *Social and Cultural Change in Canada*, vol. 2. Edited by W.E. Mann. Toronto: Copp Clark, 1970.

Scanlon, T. Joseph. "After Keith Davey - What?" *Nieman Reports*, vol. 25, no. 1 (March 1971), pp. 3-6.

Singer, Benjamin D. (ed.). *Communications in Canadian Society*. 2nd rev. ed. Toronto: Copp Clark, 1975.

Watson, Patrick. *Conspirators in Silence*. Toronto: McClelland and Stewart, 1967.

Journalism

Adam, Stuart. *A Reader in Canadian Journalism and Communication*. Toronto: Prentice-Hall, 1975.

Bambrick, Kenneth. "Summary of Survey Results: Canadian Broadcast News Staffs, 1968-1970." *Journalism Quarterly*, vol. 48 (1971), pp. 757-60.

Carrol, Jack. *The Death of the Toronto Telegram and Other Newspaper Stories*. Toronto: Simon and Schuster, 1971.

Editors of *Queens Quarterly. How Can Canadian Universities Best Benefit the Profession of Journalism as a Means of Molding and Elevating Public Opinion*. Toronto: Copp Clark, 1903.

Gordon, D.R. *Language, Logic and the Media*. Toronto: Holt, Rinehart and Winston, 1966.

Keate, Stuart. "How Good Are the Newspapers of Canada?" *Nieman Reports*, September 1966, pp. 28-31.

Lapassade, Georges. "Québec: Analyse d'un Journal Contestaire." *L'Homme et la Société*, vol. 16 (April-June 1970), pp. 71-94.

Last Post. "An Anatomy of the Time, Canada Lobby and How it Controls What is Published." In *Canada: A Sociological Profile*. Edited by W.E. Mann. 2nd rev. ed. Toronto: Copp Clark, 1971.

McDayter, Walt (ed.). *A Media Mosaic*. Toronto: Holt, Rinehart and Winston, 1971.

Macdonald, Dick (ed.). *The Media Game*. Montreal: Content Publishing Co., 1972.

Price, Warren. *The Literature of Journalism*. Minneapolis: University of Minnesota Press, 1960.

Prince, Vincent. "La Presse Canadienne-Française." *Gazette*, vol. 15, no. 2 (1969), pp. 93-103.

Purcell, Giles. "The Canadian Press." *Gazette*, vol. 15, no. 2 (1969), pp. 151-58.

Sullivan, Barbara. "The Underground Press in Canada." In

Canada: A Sociological Profile. Edited by W.E. Mann. 2nd rev. ed. Toronto: Copp Clark, 1971.

Wilson, C. Edward. "Why Canadian Newsmen Leave Their Papers." *Journalism Quarterly*, vol. 43 (1966), pp. 769-72.

———. "News Staff Hiring Practices of Canadian Dailies." *Journalism Quarterly*, vol. 48 (1971), pp. 755-57.

Journalism Histories

Bruce, Charles. *News and the Southams.* Toronto: Macmillan, 1968.

Cook, Ramsay. *The Politics of John W. Dafoe and the Free Press.* Toronto: University of Toronto Press, 1963.

Elliot, Dobbins L. "The Canadian Labour Press from 1867: Chronological Annotated Directory." *Canadian Journal of Economics and Political Science*, vol. 14 (1948), pp. 220-45.

Falardeau, Jean-Charles. "La Génération de la Relève." *Recherches Sociographiques*, vol. 6, no. 2 (May-June 1965), pp. 123-33.

Hamlin, Jean, and Beaulieu, André "A Perçu du Journalisme Québécois d'Expression Française." *Recherches Sociographiques*, vol. 7, no. 3 (September-December 1966), pp. 305-48.

Haworth, Eric. *Imprint of a Nation.* Toronto: Baxter Publishing Co., 1969.

Hudson, Robert V. "John Wesley Dafoe: Canada's Liberal Voice." *Journalism Quarterly,* vol. 47, no. 1 (Spring 1970), pp. 151-53.

Kesterton, W.H. *A History of Journalism in Canada.* Toronto: McClelland and Stewart, 1967.

Nichols, Mark Edgar. *The Story of the Canadian Press.* Toronto: Ryerson Press, 1948.

Pelletier, Jean-Guy. "La Presse Canadienne-Française et La Guerre des Boers." *Recherches Sociographiques*, vol. 4, no. 3 (September-December 1963), pp. 337-49.

Valois, Jocelyne. "La Presse Feminine et le Rôle Social de la Femme." *Recherches Sociographiques*, vol. 8, no. 3 (September-December 1967), pp. 351-76.

Legislation and the Media in Canada

Atkey, Ronald G. "The Law of the Press in Canada (1)." *Gazette*, vol. 15, no. 2 (1969), pp. 105-24.

———. "The Law of the Press in Canada (2)." *Gazette*, vol. 15, no. 3 (1969), pp. 185-200.

Babe, Robert E. "Public and Private Regulation of Cable Television: A Case Study of Technological Change and Relative Power." *Canadian Public Administration*, Summer 1974, pp. 187-225.

Grant, Peter. "The Regulation of Program Content in Canadian Television: An Introduction." *Canadian Public Administration*, vol. 2 (1968), pp. 322-91.

———. *Broadcasting and Cabletelevision Regulatory Handbook*. Toronto: Law Society of Upper Canada, 1973.

———. *Canadian Broadcasting Law and Administrative Policy*. Toronto: CCN Canadian Ltd., 1975.

Hull, W.H. "Control of Broadcasting: The Canadian and Australian Experiences." *Canadian Journal of Economics and Political Science*, vol. 28, no. 1 (February 1962), pp. 114-26.

Johansen, Peter W. "The Canadian Radio-Television Committee and the Canadianization of Broadcasting." *Federal Communications Bar Journal*, vol. 26, no. 2 (1973), pp. 183-208.

———. "The C.R.T.C. and Canadian Content Regulation." *Journal of Broadcasting*, vol. 17 (Fall 1973), pp. 465-73.

Mallen, Bruce. *Report on Legislation, Acts, Regulations and Controls of the Federal and Provincial Government which Affect the Mass Media in Canada*. Montreal: Sir George William University, 1969.

Malone, William Robert. "Broadcast Regulation in Canada: A Legislative History." Mimeographed. Cambridge, Mass., 1962.

Miller, Robert E. "The C.R.T.C.: Guardian of the Canadian Identity." *Journal of Broadcasting,* vol. 17 (Spring 1973), pp. 189-97.

Richardson, G.W. "Survey of Canadian Broadcasting Legislation." *Canadian Bar Review*, vol. 15 (1937), pp. 93-98.

Marketing and Advertising

Banting, Peter M. *Marketing in Canada*. Toronto: McGraw-Hill Ryerson, 1973.

Elkin, Frederick. *Rebels and Colleagues: Advertising and Social Change in Canada*. Montreal: McGill-Queen's University Press, 1973.

———. "A Study of Advertisements in Montreal Newspapers." *Canadian Communications*, vol. 1, no. 1 (Spring 1961), pp. 15-22, 30.

———. "Advertising in French Canada and Deviations in the Context of a Changing Society." In *Explorations in Social Change*. Edited by G. Zollschan and W. Hirsch. New York: Houghton Mifflin, 1964.

———. "Advertising Themes and Quiet Revolutions: Dilemmas in French Canada." *American Journal of Sociology*, vol. 75, no. 1 (July 1969), pp. 112-22.

Firestone, O.J. *Broadcasting Advertising in Canada, Past and Future Growth*. Ottawa: University of Ottawa Press, 1966.

———. *The Economic Implications of Advertising*. Toronto: Methuen Publications, 1967.

Mahatoo, W.H. (ed.). *Marketing Research in Canada*. Toronto: Thomas Nelson, 1968.

Mallen, Bruce, and Litvak, Isaiah. *Marketing: Canada*. Toronto: McGraw-Hill, 1968.

Media Determinants and their Critics

Carey, James W. "Harold Adams Innis and Marshall McLuhan." *Antioch Review*, vol. 27, no. 1 (Spring 1967), pp. 5-39.

Carpenter, Edward, and McLuhan, Marshall (eds.). *Explorations in Communications*. Boston: Beacon Press, 1960.

Creighton, Donald. *Harold Adams Innis: Portrait of a Scholar*. Toronto: University of Toronto Press, 1957.

Crosby, Harry H. *The McLuhan Explosion: A Casebook on Marshall McLuhan and Understanding Media*. New York: American Book Co., 1968.

Duffy, Dennis. *Marshall McLuhan*. Toronto: McClelland and Stewart, 1969.

Innis, Harold. *Empire and Communication.* Oxford: Clarendon Press, 1950.

_______. *The Bias of Communication* Toronto: University of Toronto Press, 1951.

_______. *Changing Concept of Time.* Toronto: University of Toronto Press, 1952.

McLuhan, Marshall. *Understanding Media.* New York: McGraw-Hill, 1964.

_______. *Culture Is Our Business.* Toronto: McGraw-Hill, 1970.

Rockman, Arnold. "McLuhanism: The Natural History of An Intellectual Fashion." In *Canada: A Sociological Profile.* Edited by W.E. Mann. 2nd rev. ed. Toronto: Copp Clark, 1971.

Theall, Donald. *The Medium is the Rear View Mirror.* Montreal: McGill-Queen's University Press, 1971.

Miscellaneous

Carney, T.S. *Content Analysis: A Technique for Systematic Inference from Communications.* Winnipeg: University of Manitoba Press, 1972.

Holsti, Ole, R. *Content Analysis for the Social Sciences and Humanities.* Toronto: Addison-Wesley, 1969.

Morton, Osmond. "Democracy and the Mass Media." *The Canadian Forum*, July 1969, pp. 83-85.

Singer, B.D. *Feedback and Society.* Lexington, Mass.: D.C. Heath, 1973.

_______. "Mass Feedback and Coping." *In Search*, Spring 1974, pp. 10-13.

Tate, E., Hawrush, E., and Clark, S. "Communication Variables in Jury Selection." *Journal of Communications*, vol. 24, no. 3 (Summer 1974), pp. 130-39.

Taylor, James R. "Information Overload - The Human Perspective." *In Search*, Spring 1974, pp. 14-17.

_______. *Man in the North.* 3 vols. Montreal: Arctic Institute of North America, 1971-72.

Weston, J.R., and Kristen, C. *Teleconferencing: A Comparison of Attitudes, Uncertainty, and Interpersonal Atmos-*

pheres in Mediated and Face-to-Face Group Interaction. Ottawa: Department of Communications, 1974.

Politics and the Media

Best, Micheal. "Interlocking Ownership: Press, Radio, T.V." In *Politics Canada*. Edited by Paul Fox. Toronto: McGraw-Hill, 1966.

Black, J.B., and Blanchette, A.E. "Influence of the Mass Media on the Conduct of Foreign Policy." *International Perspectives,* July-August 1974, pp. 42-45.

Eayers, J. "Foreign Policy and Broadcasting in Canada: Problems of Liaison and Control." *Canadian Public Administration,* vol. 3 (1960), pp. 107-17.

Ferguson, George Victor. *Press and Party in Canada*. Toronto: Ryerson Press, 1955.

Gordon, D.R. *The News and Foreign Policy*. Toronto: Baxter Publishing Co., 1964.

Johansen, Peter W. "Election Campaigns and the Mass Media." *The Quarterly of Canadian Studies*, Winter 1972, pp. 199-210.

Knowles, A.F. "Notes on Canadian Mass Media Policy." *Canadian Public Administration*, vol. 10 (1967), pp. 223-33.

Lemieux, Vincent. "Le Jeu de la Communication Politique." *Canadian Journal of Political Science*, vol. 3, no. 3 (September 1970), pp. 359-75.

McPhail, Thomas; Woelfel, Joseph; Woelfel, John; and Gillham, James. "Political Radicalization as a Communication Process." *Communication Research*, vol. 1, no. 3 (July 1974), pp. 243-61.

Paldo, Kristian. "Does Advertising Influence Votes? An Analysis of the 1966 and 1970 Quebec Elections." *Canadian Journal of Political Science*, vol. 6, no. 4 (December 1973), pp. 638-55.

Qualter, T.A. "Politics and Broadcasting: Case Studies of Political Interference in National Broadcasting Systems." *Canadian Journal of Economics*, vol. 28 (1962), pp. 225-34.

Scanlon, T. Joseph. "Canada and the United States: Similarities in Campaign Coverage and Problems." *Nieman Reports*, vol. 28, no. 4 (Winter 1973), pp. 12-17.

Scarrow, H.A. "Communication of Election Appeals in Canada." *Journalism Quarterly*, vol. 36 (1959), pp. 219-20.

Telecommunications

Chapman, J. "Why is Canada So Interested?" *In Search*, Spring 1974, pp. 4-8.

English, Edward H. (ed.). *Telecommunications for Canada: An Interface of Business and Government*. Toronto: Methuen, 1974.

Thirteenth Report by the International Telecommunications Union on Telecommunications and the Peaceful Uses of Outer Space. Booklet Number 15. Geneva: International Telecommunications Union, 1974.

Bibliography of Bibliographies

This section lists a number of bibliographies dealing with the topics of communications and the mass media. Unfortunately, several of the items listed have only limited access. It should also be noted that many of these bibliographies have a decided American or international emphasis, rather than a specifically Canadian one. They are included, however, because of their broader theoretical and empirical utility.

General

Blum, E. *Basic Books in the Mass Media*. Urbana: University of Illinois Press, 1972.

CRTC. *Bibliography: Some Canadian Writings on the Mass Media*. Ottawa: Information Canada, 1974.

De Bonville, Jean. *Ouvrages de Référence Utiles dans l'Etude des Mass Media et la Pratique de l'Information*. Quebec: Bibliothèque de l'Université Laval, 1973.

Gordon, D. "The Media." In *Read Canadian*. Edited by R. Fulford, D. Godfrey, and A. Rotstein. Toronto: James, Lewis and Samuel, 1972.

Hansen, D., and Parsons, J. *Mass Communication: A Research Bibliography*. Santa Barbara: The Glendessary Press, 1968.

Staff of the Centre for Communication Research. *A Bibliography of Literature Used in Communication Theory Courses*. Austin: University of Texas at Austin, 1973.

Versailles, A. *Communications Bibliographie*. Montreal: La Conseil de Développement Social du Montréal Métropolitain.

International

Mowlana, H. *International Communication: A Selected Bibliography*. Dubusque, Iowa: Kendall/Hunt Publishing Co., 1971.

Smith, B, and Smith, C. *International Communication and Political Opinion: A Guide to the Literature*. Princeton, N.J.: Princeton University Press, 1956.

Journalistic

Kesterton, W.H. "Source Materials for a History of Canadian Journalism." *Canadian Communications,* vol. 2 (1960), pp. 18-28.

Lunn, A.J. "Bibliography of the History of the Canadian Press." *Canadian Historical Review,* vol. 12 (1941), pp. 116-433.

McCoy, R. *Freedom of the Press: An annotated Bibliography*. Carbondale and Edwardsville: Southern Illinois University Press, 1968.

Price, W., and Pickett, C. *An Annotated Journalism Bibliography 1958-1968*. Minneapolis: University of Minnesota Press, 1970

Woodsworth, A. *The Alternate Press in Canada (A Checklist)* . Toronto: University of Toronto Press, 1972.

Miscellaneous

Barber, J. *A Bibliography of the Works of Edmund S. Carpenter*. Ottawa: available at CRTC library.

Goldberg, Tony. "A Selective Bibliography of the Writings of and about Marshall McLuhan." *Journal of Broadcasting,* Winter 1967-68, pp. 179-82.

Grant, Peter. *Communications and Public Policy in Canada: A Comprehensive Annotated Bibliography of Sources for Canadian Lawyers and Economists.* Toronto: University of Toronto Press, 1975.

Satellite Communications Bibliography. Ottawa: available at CRTC library.

Radio and Televison

Barber, J., and Thomson, P. *Pay Televison Bibliography.* Ottawa: available at CRTC library, 1972.

______. *Political Broadcasting Bibliography.* Ottawa: available at CRTC library, 1973.

Barcus, F.E. "A Bibliography of Studies of Radio and Television Program Content 1928-1958." *Journal of Broadcasting* , vol. 4, no. 4 (1961), pp. 355-69.

Broadcasting Bibliography. Pamphlet MSS. Ottawa: available at CRTC library.

The Effects of Television on Children, A Short Bibliography. Ottawa: Secretary of State Library, 1973.

Sparks, K. *Bibliography of Doctoral Dissertations in Television and Radio.* Syracuse: The School of Journalism Newhouse Communications Centre, 1970.

A Select List of Canadian Radio-Television Commission Publications

A Non-Commercial Alternative in Children's Programming: The OECA Example. Ottawa: CRTC, 1973.

A Proposal for an FM Radio Policy in the Private Sector, Ottawa: CRTC, 1973.

A Short Chronology of Communications in Canada 1846-1930: Internal Report, Research Branch. CRTC, November 1973.

Canadian Broadcasting "A Single System": Policy Statement on Cable Television. Ottawa: CRTC, July 1971.

Dore, Margaret. *Final Report on Children's Television.* Montreal: CRTC, 1972.

Local Programming on Cable Television. CRTC, Summer 1972.

Pulyk, Marcia. *Women in Advertising: A Collection of Selected Articles.* Ottawa: CRTC, 1974.

A Chronological List of Federal Royal Commissions and Other Investigative Reports into Mass Communications in Canada

Report of The Royal Commission on Radio Broadcasting. Ottawa: Printer to the King's Most Excellent Majesty, 1929.

Report of The Royal Commission on National Development in the Arts, Letters, and Sciences, 1949-1951. Ottawa: Printer to the King's Most Excellent Majesty, 1951.

Report of The Royal Commission on Broadcasting. 2 vols. Ottawa: Queen's Printer, 1957.

Report of The Royal Commission on Publications. Ottawa: Queen's Printer, 1961.

Report of The Committee on Broadcasting, 1965. Ottawa: Queen's Printer, 1965.

White Paper on Broadcasting, 1966. Ottawa: Queen's Printer, 1966.

Report of The Special Committee on Hate Propaganda in Canada. Ottawa: Queen's Printer, 1966.

Report of The Royal Commission on Bilingualism and Biculturalism: Book 1, The Official Languages. Ottawa: Queen's Printer, 1967.

A Domestic Satellite Communications System for Canada. Ottawa: Queen's Printer, 1968.

To Know and Be Known: Report of the Task Force on Government Information. 2 vols. Ottawa: Information Canada, 1969.

Report of The Royal Commission on Bilingualism and Biculturalism: Book 4, The Cultural Contribution of The Other Ethnic Groups. Ottawa: Queen's Printer, 1970.

Report of The Special Senate Committee on Mass Media. 3 vols. (The Davey Committee) Vol. 1, *The Uncertain Mirror*. Ottawa: Queen's Printer, 1970. Vol. 2, *Words, Music, and Dollars*. Ottawa: Queen's Printer, 1970. Vol. 3, *Good, Bad or Simply Inevitable*. Ottawa: Queen's Printer, 1970.

Instant World: A Report on Telecommunications Policy in Canada. Ottawa: Information Canada, 1971.

Branching Out: Report of The Canadian Computer/Communications Task Force. 2 vols. Ottawa: Information Canada, 1972.

Privacy and Computers: A Task Force Report. Ottawa: Information Canada, 1972.

Computer/Communications Policy: A Position Statement by The Government of Canada. Ottawa: Information Canada, 1973.

Proposals for a Communications Policy for Canada: A Position Paper of The Government of Canada. Ottawa: Information Canada, 1973.

Canadian Media Journals

Access: Challenge for Change/Société Nouvelle, published three or four times a year by The National Film Board of Canada.

Broadcaster, a monthly published by R.G. Lewis and Co. Ltd., Toronto.

Canadian Communications Law Review, published by the Faculty of Law at The University of Toronto.

Content, published monthly by Content Publishing Ltd., Montreal.

In Search/En Quête, a bilingual Canadian Communications Quarterly published by the Information Services of The Department of Communications (Communications Canada).

Other Canadian journals and magazines which periodically feature Canadian media related articles include the following:

The Canadian Forum, a bi-monthly publication of the Canadian Forum Ltd., Toronto.

Macleans Magazine, published by Maclean-Hunter Limited, Toronto.

Media Probe, an irregularly published magazine of critical comment on mass media and communications published by Media Probe, Toronto.

Queen's Quarterly, published for the Quarterly Committee of Queen's University by McGill-Queen's University Press, Montreal.

Recherches Sociographiques, a French language journal published by The Department of Sociology and Anthropology at The University of Laval, Montreal, Quebec.

Saturday Night, a monthly magazine published by Second Century Canada Publications Inc., Toronto.

International journals (generally American) which occasionally feature Canadian media articles include the following:

Gazette, an international journal published in Amsterdam.

Journal of Broadcasting, published quarterly by The Association for Professional Broadcasting, Philadelphia.

Journal of Communication, published quarterly by the Annenberg School Press, Radnor, Pennsylvania, in cooperation with the International Communication Association.

Journalism Quarterly, published by the Association for Education in Journalism.

Nieman Reports, a quarterly published by the Nieman Foundation.

Public Opinion Quarterly, published by the American Association for Public Opinion Research.

Telecommunication Journal, the monthly magazine of the International Telecommunication Union, the United Nations specialized agency for telecommunications.

Canadian Communications Research Information Centre

The Canadian Communications Research Information Centre, an agency of the Canada Council and UNESCO, was recently established in Ottawa, under the directorship of Jocelyn R. Mauerhoff.

The centre functions as a communication clearing house, providing Canadian media researchers and others interested in various aspects of mass communications, with information, contacts, and other forms of assistance generally associated with co-ordination facility.

Although the centre has minimized its role as a communication library, it does collect material not readily available through trade or government publishers, and it began publication of a newsletter late in 1974.

1. Government reports, for instance, by their very nature are often not well known or easily accessible.
2. Herbert Gans, "A Comment: Famine in Mass Media Research," *American Journal of Sociology*, vol. 77 (January 1972), p. 698.
3. Ibid., p. 700.
4. Desmond M. Conner and James E. Curtis, *Sociology and Anthropology in Canada* (Montreal: Canadian Sociology and Anthropology Society, September 1970).
5. Royal Commission on Bilingualism and Biculturalism, *Book 1: The Official Languages* (Ottawa: Queen's Printer, 1967), p. 195.
6. For a discussion of some of these developments, particularly the funding of social science research, see Fred Schindeler and C. Michael Lanphier, "Social Science Research and Participatory Democracy in Canada," in W.E. Mann (ed.), *Social and Cultural Change in Canada*, vol. 2 (Toronto: Copp Clark, 1970), pp. 64-87.
7. These descriptions are based on personal correspondence received from university representatives and on calendars and other promotional materials published by the universities mentioned.
8. As this paper is being written, a Bill is before the House of Commons that would eliminate the CRTC and replace it with a Canadian Radio-Television Telecommunications Commission (CRTTC).
9. For a more comprehensive listing of Communications Canada publications see *Reports and Studies Published by the Department of Communications of Canada* (Ottawa: Information Services, Communications Canada, 1974).

On the Authors

WILFRED H. KESTERTON is a Professor of Journalism at Carleton University. He is the author of *A History of Journalism in Canada*, and a co-editor of *A Century of Reporting; un Siècle de Reportage.*

ROBERT F. LATHAM is presently directing the Environment Study in the Long Range Planning Department of Bell Canada in Montreal.

W. BRIAN STEWART works for the CBC as Assistant to the Vice-President of Corporate Affairs.

ANDREW D. CAMERON is a sociologist with the Secretary of State, Ottawa. He also lectures at the Institute of Social Communications, Saint Paul University, Ottawa.

JOHN A. HANNIGAN, a native of Ottawa, is completing his Ph.D in Sociology at the Disaster Research Center of Ohio State University.

ALLAN E. GOTLIEB is the author of *Disarmament and International Law, Canadian Treaty-Making*, and *Human Rights, Federalism and Minorities.* He is a former Deputy Minister of Communications Canada.

RICHARD J. GWYN is a political journalist and the author of *The Shape of Scandal* and *Smallwood, The Unlikely Revolutionary.* He formerly served as Director of the Socio-Economic Planning Branch of Communications Canada.

JOHN ALAN LEE is Associate Professor of Sociology at the University of Toronto.

JOHN PORTER is Professor of Sociology at Carleton University and author of *The Vertical Mosaic* and *Canadian Social Structure: A Statistical Profile.*

T.C. SEACREST comes from a four-generation newspaper family and has maintained his interest in the press in his research into the relationship between press coverage of crime and public attitudes towards crime.

SENATOR KEITH DAVEY proposed and then chaired the Special Senate Committee on Mass Media whose controversial report appeared in 1970.

HARRY J. BOYLE is a playwright, humourist, essayist, and novelist. Since 1968 he has been Vice-Chairman of the Canadian Radio-Television Commission.

TERENCE QUALTER is Professor of Political Science at Waterloo University.

ALVIN TOFFLER has achieved worldwide fame as author of *Future Shock*. He is also the author of several other books and communications consultant to major coporations and educational institutes.

FRANK W. PEERS is a Professor of Political Economy at the University of Toronto and author of *The Politics of Canadian Broadcasting, 1920-1951.*

FREDERICK ELKIN is Professor of Sociology at York University. His publications include *Child and Society*, *Family in Canada* and *Rebels and Colleagues: Advertising and Social Change in French Canada.*

GARTH S. JOWETT is an Associate Professor in the Department of Communication Studies, University of Windsor. He has recently completed a book, *The Democratic Art: A Social History of Movie-Going in America.*

BARRY R. HEMMINGS has recently completed a report for the Department of Communications on the use of communication tools by community groups in Ontario.

MILDRED SCHWARTZ is Professor of Sociology, University of Illinois (Chicago Circle). She is the author of a number of studies on public opinion.

BENJAMIN D. SINGER is Professor of Sociology, University of Western Ontario. He has written books and scholarly articles on riots, communication, and coping.

THELMA McCORMACK is Professor of Sociology, York University. She is completing a book on social theory and the mass media of communication.

MAXWELL COHEN is Macdonald Professor of Law at McGill University. From 1964 to 1969 he was Dean of the Faculty of Law at McGill University. He served as Chairman of the Minister of Justice Special Committee on Hate Propaganda in Canada.

DANIEL LATOUCHE teaches Political Science at the Université du Québec à Montréal and at McGill University's Centre for French-Canadian Studies.

RICHARD NIELSEN is an executive producer with the CBC.

JOHN CLAXTON is Assistant Professor in the Faculty of Business, University of British Columbia.

GORDON McDOUGALL is Assistant Professor in the Faculty of Business, University of Windsor.

SANDRA GWYN is a freelance writer and editorial consultant based in Ottawa.

T. JOSEPH SCANLON is Associate Professor of Journalism at Carleton University.

VICTOR PADDY received an M.A. in Sociology from the University of Western Ontario.

VINCENT SACCO teaches Sociology at the University of Western Ontario.

Index

1 2 3 4 5 #131211 79 78 77 76 75